THE NATURE OF
SOUTHWESTERN COLORADO

The Nature of Southwestern COLORADO

Recognizing Human Legacies *and* Restoring Natural Places

Deborah D. Paulson & William L. Baker

University Press of Colorado

To my parents, Alice and Ken,
for showing me the beauty of nature. DEB

To Karl Urban and Bob Frenkel
for showing me the trail. BILL

Published by the University Press of Colorado
5589 Arapahoe Avenue, Suite 206C
Boulder, Colorado 80303

 The University Press of Colorado is a proud member of
the Association of American University Presses.

The University Press of Colorado is a cooperative publishing enterprise supported, in
part, by Adams State College, Colorado State University, Fort Lewis College, Mesa State
College, Metropolitan State College of Denver, University of Colorado, University of
Northern Colorado, and Western State College of Colorado.

∞ The paper used in this publication meets the minimum requirements of the American
National Standard for Information Sciences—Permanence of Paper for Printed Library
Materials. ANSI Z39.48-1992

Library of Congress Cataloging-in-Publication Data

Paulson, Deborah D.
  The nature of southwestern Colorado : recognizing human legacies and restoring natural
places / Deborah D. Paulson and William L. Baker.
    p. cm.
  Includes bibliographical references and index.
  ISBN-13: 978-0-87081-848-6 (cloth : alk. paper)
  ISBN-10: 0-87081-848-1 (cloth : alk. paper)
  ISBN-13: 978-0-87081-849-3 (pbk. : alk. paper)
  ISBN-10: 0-87081-849-X (pbk. : alk. paper) 1. Biotic communities—Colorado. 2.
Nature—Effect of human beings on—Colorado. I. Baker, William L. (William Lawrence)
II. Title.
  QH105.C6P38 2006
  333.95′1609788—dc22

                                                              2006019466

Design by Daniel Pratt

15   14   13   12   11   10   09   08   07   06   10   9   8   7   6   5   4   3   2   1

This publication was supported in part by the Charles Redd Center for Western Studies.

Contents

Like many in our highly industrialized society, we are drawn to natural places, and southwestern Colorado has long been a favorite place of escape from our hectic urban work lives. Noted geographer Yi Fu Tuan has written that modern people escape *to* nature because, in their ignorance of it, nature seems simple, perfect, and without problems.[1] Nature has filled the need for escape through the ages and will continue to do so, but nature provides more than just escape. Eventually, we realized that we wanted a deeper connection to the nature of southwestern Colorado, and we joined ongoing efforts to understand,

Preface

protect, and restore the natural world there. This book is an invitation for others to join these efforts.

Located at the interface of the semiarid canyon and mesa country of the Colorado Plateau and the southern Rocky Mountains in the Four Corners area (see Map 0.1), southwestern Colorado is naturally diverse. Also juxtaposed are two cultures—an Old West grazing, mining, farming, and timbering culture and a New West tourism and recreation culture. Increasingly, these cultures are mixing and transforming as money, power, and politics flow across the interface—leading to collaborations, initiatives, and watershed groups that are beginning to forge new relationships between people and land.

Southwestern Colorado may be a favorite place for a new relationship to emerge, and that possibility is one of the inspirations for this book. While its population is increasing rapidly, the region is far from major urban centers and has a much smaller population, so there is still time to rethink how development might proceed. What happens here is of national interest, given the area's many tourist destinations, including prominent national parks and monuments (Mesa Verde, Black Canyon, Canyons of the Ancients, Colorado National Monument), large wilderness areas (e.g., Weminuche), and other attractions (e.g., the Durango-Silverton Railroad, Telluride music festivals). Nature figures prominently in these attractions and is the inspiration for efforts to redefine the role of people in this place.

Southwestern Colorado remains more natural than many other places, but it, too, has been changed by people, especially over the last 100 years. A major part of this book is about human legacies on the land, persistent alterations in the physical or biological environment left behind from a land use. Examples are an abandoned mine shaft, a non-native invasive species, and a landscape transformed by logging. Some land-use changes are essential for people (e.g., conversion to agriculture), but our concern is with legacies that have significantly reduced, or created problematic relationships with, the natural world. Such legacies provide opportunity and motivation for restoration, by which we mean moving an ecosystem toward or within its historical range of variability (see Box—Range of Natural Variability, pp. 161–162).

We need to clarify what we mean by "nature" and "natural" because nature has become complicated, at least within academic circles, in recent years. We use the term in its traditional meaning, as expressed by Yi Fu Tuan: "Nature is what remains or what can recuperate over time when all humans and their works are removed."[2] Thus, a place is more or less natural according to the level of human presence and ma-

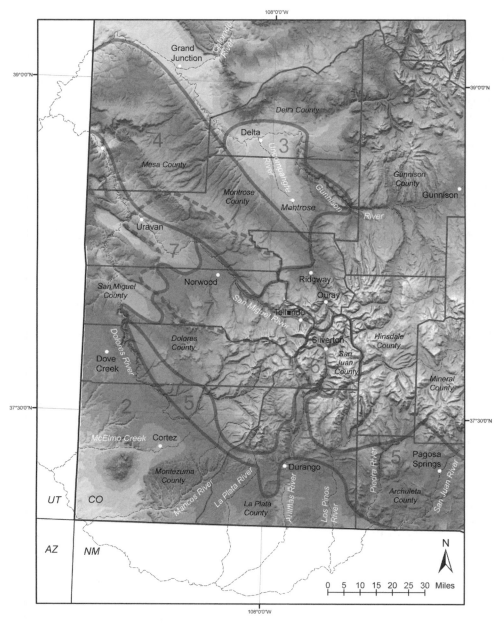

Map 0.1. *The regions covered in this book are indicated by broad lines enclosing large numbers, which correspond with each chapter number: 2 = Desert Plateau, 3 = Uncompahgre Valley, 4 = Uncompahgre Plateau, 5 = Ponderosa Pine, 6 = Upper Animas. The San Miguel River watershed (7) overlaps areas covered in Chapters 2 and 4 and so is shown by a broad dotted line. Also shown are counties, major towns, and rivers.*

nipulation of natural processes. Humans have modified even global processes, such as the climate, and no place remains completely untouched. But many places are little impacted or have few lasting legacies and thus could be restored to a more natural state. This distinction between humans and nature is useful to retain because humans have often reduced the diversity of life that has evolved here; what is natural and what is a result of human manipulation must be sorted out if natural diversity is to be restored. Recognizing human legacies is thus a key theme of this book.

A culture needs to value the existence of a nature separate from humans to recognize and protect it, but at another level people are clearly a part of nature. Aldo Leopold's land ethic requires that humans do their best to coexist with the rest of nature as one "plain member."[3] We embrace this ethic. Another helpful concept is Gary Nabhan's "cultures of habitat," referring to the cultures of Native Americans and other groups who lived in a place for generations. They developed an intimate knowledge of the natural world that enabled them to successfully inhabit places over time, an understanding most people today lack.[4] In this book we hope to make a small contribution toward building cultural knowledge of the natural world. Unlike Nabhan and other ethnoecologists, we have not specialized in the knowledge and ecology of Native American cultures of habitat. But, while of great value, that knowledge is not all that is needed today. In much of the American West, the human population is now many times that of former Native American populations and could not subsist using the lifeways of Native Americans or early settlers.

New types of connections to places are needed—connections that will help resist or reshape the modern forces that alienate people from nature. A new culture of habitat would enable people to know places in ways that will help them visit and reside in southwestern Colorado without diminishing the vibrant natural beauty and diversity that still exist there. It would give people, including those living in towns and cities, opportunities to engage the natural world in meaningful ways. This would involve not only recognizing human legacies but also forging new collective visions about how to live with and within the natural world.

Thus, this book reports on innovative projects and approaches that, at their best, involve people of diverse backgrounds in finding new ways of thinking about and interacting with a particular place. Of course, the global economic system strongly influences options, even in southwestern Colorado, but it is our hope that innovation can also arise from the local—that people still have some choices, which include maintaining and restoring nature.

As a society we may know as much cr more (though not the same things) about the natural world as the Native Americans did, but this knowledge is held in fragmented chunks by experts and specialists. People as a whole, not experts, must craft the visions appropriate for our time. If people are to help weave a more beautiful fabric in a place, they must recognize and appreciate the many colors and intricacies of the land they inhabit. By sharing what we have learned thus far in that endeavor, we hope to give the reader new eyes with which to view the nature of this place—eyes that see beyord the spectacular scenery or the value of the resources to recognize the diversity of life around them and the ways human actions influence that life.

ORGANIZATION OF THE BOOK

We begin with a review of what is known about Native American influences on the environment of southwestern Colorado. Then, six places in southwestern Colorado (see Map 0.1), encompassing much of the region's natural diversity, are explored. These places were chosen primarily to highlight the region's major ecosystems, but they are often also delimited by a cohesive human story or history. Major ecosystems addressed include low-elevation grasslands, sagebrush, and pinyon-juniper woodlands (Chapters 2, 4) and the semi-desert shrublands of the Uncompahgre Valley (Chapter 3). Above these low-elevation ecosystems, the montane zone's mixed mountain shrublands (Chapter 3) and ponderosa pine forests (Chapter 5) are also covered. Subalpine grasslands and forests are a focus of Chapter 6. Riparian ecosystems are included in these chapters. In Chapter 7 we look at the interrelations of these ecosystems in the San Miguel River watershed, which extends from the alpine to the desert.

The region's major ecosystems provide the organization, but our attention is focused on the biotic communities of these ecosystems. An ecosystem comprises the biotic community, its physical environment, and the interactions between the two (e.g., nutrient cycles, energy flows). Plant and animal communities are the biotic component of ecosystems. Our focus is on the ecology of plant communities (vegetation), including the key trees, shrubs, grasses, and flowers (or "forbs"), as vegetation is the foundation of local ecologies. We also consider some of the animal members of these biotic communities. Unlike the equally important soil communities of bacteria and fungi, the plant and animal world is visible and easier for nonspecialists to study.

In each of these six chapters, major past and current human influences on the ecology of the place are highlighted. We examine current attempts by various groups of people to restore places and we describe some of their successes, as well as ecological and cultural challenges they are facing. We describe important natural features and introduce the detective game of deciphering past and current human legacies. We point out the legacies wherever we can recognize them. In the final chapter we reflect on what can be learned from experiences of both Native Americans and early Euro-American groups, as well as the last century of legacies, including the new ones of today. And, finally, we try to understand what is needed for a land ethic and contemporary culture of habitat to flourish in southwestern Colorado. Many groups are working to preserve and restore that region's natural world. We think they are on to something.

HELPFUL TOOLS AND GUIDES TO ACCOMPANY THIS BOOK

This book is not a field guide, although we try to help the reader identify some key plants. Some of the books and field guides listed here may be good complements. For identifying birds, we use National Geographic's *Field Guide to the Birds of North America*,[5] National Audubon Society's *The Sibley Guide to Birds*,[6] and Kenn Kaufman's *Focus Guide to the Birds of North America*.[7] The *Colorado Breeding Bird Atlas*, edited by Hugh Kingery, has very specific location maps and a wealth of natural history information.[8] *Birds of Western Colorado Plateau and Mesa Country* has specific information on birds in a major part of our study area.[9] *Amphibians and Reptiles in Colorado* by Geoffrey Hammerson[10] and *Mammals of Colorado* by James Fitzgerald, Carron Meaney, and David Armstrong are the best sources of information on those groups.[11]

If only one plant book can be obtained, a guide to weeds may be best. *Troublesome Weeds of the Rocky Mountains*, published by the Colorado Weed Management Association, has color pictures and is available free of charge at most county weed offices.[12] *Weeds of the West* by Tom Whitson and colleagues covers a wider range and has excellent photographs.[13]

Because there are so many different plants, no comprehensive general guides with pictures are available, so we generally try to show a picture or describe key plants. Plant guides use different common names for a particular plant—there are no standard names, and many plants do not have common names. However, the online PLANTS database[14] has a complete list of common names, which we used. This database also has range maps and some pictures of plants. Where we give formal Latin names, we used *Colorado Flora: Western Slope* by William A. Weber and Ronald C. Wittmann as our authority.[15] This is a botanical key with only a few pictures, but it is the only guide that is complete for the area covered by this book. G. K. Guennel's two-volume *Guide to Colorado Wildflowers* has paintings of many of the showier plants.[16] *Handbook of Rocky Mountain Plants* by Ruth Ashton Nelson has descriptions of many of the plants, along with some pictures, but is not complete for the area.[17] *Flora of the San Juans* by Susan Komarek covers the mountain area and has some drawings of plants.[18] To learn botanical terms, we suggest *How to Identify Plants* by H. D. Harrington and L. W. Durrell.[19] Taking a field trip with the Colorado Native Plant Society may be useful. There are Southwestern and Plateau chapters with field trip schedules.[20] To understand the region's geology and physical setting, good sources are *The Western San Juan Mountains: Their Geology, Ecology, and Human History* by Rob Blair[21] and *Roadside Geology of Colorado* by Halka Chronic and Felicie Williams.[22]

DEBORAH PAULSON AND WILLIAM BAKER
LARAMIE, JUNE 2005

NOTES

1. Tuan, *Escapism*.
2. Ibid., 20.
3. Leopold, *Sand County Almanac*.
4. Nabhan, *Cultures of Habitat*.
5. National Geographic Society, *Birds of North America*.
6. Sibley, *Sibley Guide to Birds*.
7. Kaufman, *Focus Guide to Birds*.
8. Kingery, *Colorado Breeding Bird Atlas*.
9. Righter et al., *Birds of Western Colorado*.
10. Hammerson, *Amphibians and Reptiles*.
11. Fitzgerald, Meaney, and Armstrong, *Mammals of Colorado*.
12. Colorado Weed Management Association, *Troublesome Weeds*. The association is on the Web at: http://www.cwma.org/.
13. Whitson et al., *Weeds of the West*.
14. See Web site: http://plants.usda.gov.
15. Weber and Wittmann, *Colorado Flora: Western Slope*.
16. Guennel, *Colorado Wildflowers*, Vols. 1 and 2.
17. Nelson, *Rocky Mountain Plants*.
18. Komarek, *Flora of the San Juans*.
19. Harrington and Durrell, *How to Identify Plants*.
20. See Web site: http://www.conps.org.
21. Blair, *Western San Juan Mountains*.
22. Chronic and Williams, *Roadside Geology of Colorado*.

Acknowledgments

We would like to acknowledge and thank the Association of American Geographers for financial support from the Anne U. White Fund. The University of Wyoming (UW) granted Paulson a year's sabbatical leave for this book project. The American Studies program at UW provided much-appreciated office space and support during the sabbatical year, and the Department of Geography provided material support throughout the project. Thanks to the Charles Redd Center for support for the cost of including color photographs in the book.

Thanks also to Dawn Marano for seeing promise in the book and assisting us through an early setback in the project. Sandy Crooms, Laura Furney, Daniel Pratt, and Darrin Pratt skillfully guided us through the publishing process, and Cheryl Carnahan did a wonderful job of copyediting. Detailed comments of two anonymous reviewers were very thoughtful and helpful.

This book would not have been possible without the help of many people who generously gave their time for interviews and provided us with data, maps, or documents. We especially want to thank the following people, to whom we turned numerous times for advice and help: Bob Ball, Fred Blackburn, Peter Butler, Amanda Clements, Mallory Dimmit, Jim Ferguson, Jim Garner, Daniella Howell, Peggy Lyon, Maggie McCaffrey, Harley Metz, Jeff Redders, Rick Sherman, Bill Simon, Leslie Stewart, Dean Stindt, Mark Varien, Scott Wait, Bruce Watkins, Bob Welch, and Pat Willits. None of these people is responsible for the conclusions we draw in this book.

Many others provided essential help on a specific topic, often giving several hours of their time: Karen Adams, Tony Apa, Ron Arant, Joe Ashor, Victoria Atkins, Steve Baker, Nancy Berry, Ann Bond, Jim Boyd, Dave Bradford, Robert Bratlinger, Clait Braun, Karla Brown, Debbie Burch, Steve Buskirk, Carolyn Byrd, Mary Chapman, Sonja Chavez de Baca, Marilyn Colyer, Rod Cook, Wayne Cooley, Dave Crawford, Bill Day, Bob Dressel, Karen Eisenhart, J. Todd Ellison, James Ferriday, Nathan Fey, Bill Fisher, Nancy Fishering, Penny Frazier, Richard Gibbons, Steve Glazer, Art Goodtimes, Howard Greager, Craig Grother, Rebecca Hammond, Carla Harper, Dave Harper, Art Hayes, Kathy Hayes, Karen Henderson, Tony Hoag, Jim Howell, LouAnn Jacobson, Matt Janowiak, Mike Jensen, Clyde Johnson, Sarah Johnson, Laura Johnson-Boudreaux, Jeff Jones, Adam Keller, Ron Lambeth, Doug Lard, Robbie Baird LaValley, Janet Linthecum, Kelly Liston, Linda Luther, Ed Marston, Lew Matis, Kevin McKelvey, Steve Monsen, Brad Morrison, Brian Muller, Dennis Murphy, Kathy Nickell, Stephanie Odell, Sara Oyler-McCance, Mark Pearson, Larry Perino, Camille Price, Tim Reader, Floyd Reed, Mike Rozycki, Walt Rule, Josh Sale, Charlie Scheltz, Dave Schneck, Pam Schnurr, Ann Shepardson, Bruce Short, Marie Templeton, Tara Thomas, Mac and Sandy Thompson, Gary Thrash, Karen Tucker, Mark Tucker, Rowdy Wood, Li Yin, Jessica Young, Paul Zaenger, and Pam Zoline.

Many of these people read drafts of small parts of the book in which they were involved, but we would also like to thank the following people for their comments on early drafts of entire chapters: Jocelyn Baker, Susanna Goodin, Jeanne Holland, Alison and Matt Holloran, Lissa Howe, Kathy Jensen, Bob Kelly, Frieda Knobloch, MaryLou Larson, Dawn Marano, Linda Miller, Amanda Rees, Doug Shinneman, Sarah Strauss, and Mark Varien.

Many others helped in smaller but still important ways: Ivan Archer, Clair Baldwin, Brad Banulis, Abigail Baron, Phyllis Becker, Ron Bell, Eric Bergman, B. J. Boucher, Eric Brennemann, Paul Camel, Marc Catlin, Myron Chase, Chris Closter, Margie Connolly, Dave Dallison, Greg Dudgeon, Laura Duncan, Mary Etzkorn, Colleen Fair, Debbie Felker, Mike Ferland, Katie Fite, Bruce Fowler, Lance Fretwell, Scott Gillihan, Len Goyke, Dora Griffith, Jamie Hall, Adell Heneghan, Barb Horn, Wayne Hubert, Michael Japhet, Steve Kandell, Ron Klatt, Linda Knipp, Paul Krabacher, Tammy Larson, Laura Lewis, Jorge Maldanado, Dan Manier, Carl McAlister, Rob Molacek, Bernice Musser, Kristen Philbrook, John Porter, Robin Sell, Jamie Seller-Baker, Jan Sennhenn, Tanya Shenk, Susan Spackman, Richard Speegle, Cliff Stewart, Paul Swain, Dan Tallman, Shelly Theroux, Gerald Thygerson, David Wells, Winston Wetlauter, Jim Wetzel, and Penny Wu.

To all these people and those we have forgotten to mention, our deepest gratitude.

THE NATURE OF
SOUTHWESTERN COLORADO

Native Americans in Southwestern Colorado

Before Euro-Americans began to transform the landscapes of southwestern Colorado, Native Americans had long been living in and interacting with its natural ecosystems. Few still believe Native Americans lived in perfect balance with their environment, essentially as a part of wild nature. Humans are more innovative and powerful than any other species. Although Native Americans almost certainly had a far less separate and controlling attitude toward wild nature than Euro-Americans did,[1] their subsistence practices sometimes led to long-lived, sustainable communities and sometimes to degradation of their environment.[2]

Recognizing this variety of impacts, scholars have studied how and where different groups of Native Americans shaped the landscapes of North America over a span of 10,000 years or more. Some scholars argue that Native Americans, through burning and hunting in particular, had profound influences virtually everywhere in the Americas.[3] Others, however, suggest that some places were transformed but others were not.[4] Careful study is needed of Native Americans' influence in specific places. In this chapter we review what is known today about the influence of Native Americans on the natural communities of southwestern Colorado and attempt to draw out lessons from their practices and experiences.

PEOPLING OF THE AMERICAS STILL DEBATED

Archaeologists do not agree on the date of human arrival in North America. For many years the earliest radiocarbon dates of human-related sites and artifacts in the Western Hemisphere, south of the Bering Land Bridge, were only a little over 11,000 years before present (B.P.). This is when Clovis points, a style of projectile point found widely in North America but not in the Old World, first appear in the archaeological record. A similar but distinctive point style of the same age—the Goshen point— has been found widely in Montana, Wyoming, and northern Colorado. Clovis and Goshen points appear in a number of widespread locations rather suddenly in the archaeological record, suggesting a relatively rapid spread of the people who used these tools.[5] The large size of these points and their association with large mammals, especially mammoth, suggest a specialization in big-game hunting.

Today, the idea that the Clovis (and Goshen) people were the first inhabitants of North America is being challenged. Popular magazines and Web sites sometimes give the impression—with artists' colorful renditions of prehistoric life 15,000 years or more ago—that pre-Clovis cultures of the Americas are now widely known and accepted. In fact, these renditions are based on scanty evidence, usually a few stone artifacts and some possibly butchered animal remains in questionable context. The few proposed pre-Clovis sites in North America are not accepted by all archaeologists.[6]

The only widely accepted evidence of pre-Clovis humans in the Americas to date comes from the Monte Verde site in southern Chile.[7] This carefully excavated site is dated at 12,500 B.P. and is far south of the Bering Land Bridge where people probably first entered the New World. Some archaeologists question the validity of the Monte Verde evidence,[8] but a number of Clovis-age sites are known from southern

South America.[9] The sudden appearance of people across two continents is difficult to explain. One theory postulates that the earliest people in the Americas spread first along the coasts.[10]

When and where people first arrived and how they spread across North America are still in question and a matter of active research.[11] However, given the paucity of pre-Clovis evidence, it is probably safe to assume that the first people in the North American interior, numerous enough to have had an environmental impact, appeared about 11,000 years ago (see Table 1.1). In Colorado, Clovis points are still the earliest known human artifacts.[12]

EARLY HUNTERS AND GATHERERS AND PLEISTOCENE MEGAFAUNA

The impact of early big-game hunters on the large animals of North America also remains under debate. Many large mammals present in the Pleistocene became extinct about 12,000 to 10,000 B.P., the time of widespread appearance of human hunters.[13] Clovis and Goshen points disappear and are replaced in the archaeological record by another widespread style of point, the Folsom point, around 10,900 B.P., after the disappearance of the mammoths and most other Pleistocene megafauna. Folsom points (10,900–10,200 B.P.) are associated with a large, now-extinct species of bison (*Bison antiquus*) (see Table 1.1).[14]

A popular theory today is that early-arriving hunters, meeting inexperienced prey, drove the large Pleistocene mammals (e.g., mammoth, mastodon, camel, horse, tapir, ground sloth) to extinction.[15] A similar megafaunal extinction wave may have happened after humans arrived in Australia about 50,000 years ago.[16]

Others, however, are not convinced that early big-game hunting actually led to or hastened the extinction of Pleistocene megafauna. Evidence of actual Clovis-age megafaunal kills has only been found for mammoths and mastodons,[17] and even mammoths are associated with Clovis artifacts at only about a dozen sites, mainly on the Great Plains.[18] If Paleoindians caused the demise of over thirty species of megafauna, why haven't more actual kill sites for these species been located? New dating techniques indicate also that, except for mastodons and mammoths, the megafauna disappeared before the widespread appearance of Clovis artifacts.[19] Only fifteen of the thirty-five species that became extinct at the end of the Pleistocene are known to have persisted beyond 12,000 B.P. when Clovis hunters first appeared.[20]

Another possible, many think probable, cause of the Pleistocene extinctions is the warming followed by a rapid episode of cooling (the

Table 1.1. Native American chronology in southwestern Colorado up to historical Utes.[1]

Years Before Present[2]	Group(s) in Southwestern Colorado	Comments
PALEOINDIAN		
11,300–10,900	Clovis complex Goshen complex Folsom complex	Hunters of Pleistocene megafauna; wide-ranging across North America; uncommon in southwestern Colorado
10,900–10,200		Strongly associated with *Bison antiquus* kills; relatively few points found in southwestern Colorado
10,000–7,500	Foothills/Mountain complex	Mountains of Montana, Wyoming, and Colorado; hunted deer, elk, bighorns, and smaller mammals and also foraged
ARCHAIC		
8,400–2,000	Uncompahgre complex/ Mountain Tradition	Long-lived flexible subsistence strategy based on broad resource base, hunting and gathering; at times included year-round living at elevations over 7,000 feet and substantive pit or basin houses
AGRICULTURAL or FORMATIVE		
2,500–700	Ancestral Puebloans (Anasazi)	South and southwest of San Juan Mountains; committed to maize production; at times lived in dense population clusters
	Fremont and Gateway	Scattered sites along lower Dolores and San Miguel drainages; smaller groups, less sedentary, less dependent on agriculture than Ancestral Puebloans
	Aspen tradition	High variability in subsistence strategies among nonhorticultural groups in response to possible climate and population stress
PROTOHISTORIC and HISTORIC		
900?–present	Ute	Numic-speaking, hunting-and-gathering people who probably entered Colorado from Great Basin; Colorado Utes obtained horses as early as 1640
600?–400	Navajo	Athapascan-speaking; sacred sites in La Plata Mountains but probably had moved to northern New Mexico by mid-1600s.

1. Pitblado, "Peak to Peak in Paleoindian Time"; Reed and Metcalf, *Colorado Prehistory.*
2. Radiocarbon years are not perfectly correlated to calendar years; calendar years were increasingly longer than radiocarbon years between 3,500 and 18,000 years ago. At the time of the Clovis and Folsom groups, 2,000 years should be added to obtain the date in calendar years (Robert Kelly, University of Wyoming, pers. comm., March 4, 2002). We use radiocarbon years because most of the literature still has uncorrected dates. Overlap occurs between categories because the boundaries between eras are often not sharp, and the longest estimated range for each era is used. Question marks indicate uncertain dates.

Younger Dryas) at the end of the Pleistocene.[21] The warming may also have been associated with a 400- to 500-year drought.[22] It is also possible that the combination of climate-related stress and a new predator (humans) pushed some species beyond their ability to adapt.

Regardless of whether Paleoindians were a major cause of megafaunal extinctions, preindustrial people were clearly capable of causing extinctions. When arriving in a new place with an unfamiliar ecosystem, humans typically apply technologies they know, often with initial negative impacts on some of the species and ecosystem processes in their new homes. Many species extinctions occurred on Pacific islands, for example, shortly after the first settlers arrived.[23]

The question for those who would restore ecosystems today is how far back in time is the best model for restoration. Some argue that the human-driven extinction of Pleistocene grazers left the grasslands and savannahs that evolved with them empty and in need of grazers. Others have gone so far as to advocate the "restoration" of elephants from Asia.[24] Some grazing advocates also argue that plants in arid ecosystems evolved with grazers and benefit from cattle, if they are managed to mimic large predator-driven native herds (see Box—Holistic Management, pp. 6–8).

Regardless of whether humans drove megafauna to extinction in southwestern Colorado, the climate and vegetation of the Four Corners region have changed significantly since that time.[25] Plant and animal communities at the end of the Pleistocene were unlike those found today and included species' juxtapositions that no longer occur, with spruce growing close to desert plants on the Colorado Plateau.[26] Large herbivores evolved in the Great Basin before the Pleistocene, but the environment then, and more so during the Pleistocene, was cooler and had vegetation more typical of higher elevations today.[27] New ecosystems appeared fairly rapidly at the end of the Pleistocene.[28] Only after the glaciers retreated did pinyon-juniper, sagebrush, and ponderosa pine ecosystems develop in the region.[29]

Southwestern Colorado may also be somewhat unusual, as no records exist of Pleistocene megafauna from southwestern Colorado south and west of the Gunnison Basin.[30] Pleistocene mammoth and bison remains are not uncommon west of the Colorado River in Utah and in northern Arizona, but except for one mammoth find, they are missing from the record east of the Colorado River in Utah.[31] Clovis and Folsom artifacts are also scarce in southwestern Colorado relative to neighboring regions, suggesting this region was not used heavily by early hunters.[32] Bonnie Pitblado, an archaeologist who has specialized in the Paleoindian occupation of southwestern Colorado, reports only five known Clovis and two known Folsom artifacts from the corner of Colorado bounded by the Colorado River and the San Juan Mountains.[33] Folsom points have been much more commonly found nearby, in places such as the San Luis Valley.[34] Lack of evidence of megafauna and sparse early big-game hunters in southwestern Colorado could be a result of insufficient searching for evidence[35] or could be characteristic of the region. As discussed under "Subsistence Practices of the Utes," even the modern bison (*Bison bison*) was likely rare in southwestern Colorado. If this area lacks a history of grazing by modern bison or other large, herd herbivores, the implications for grazing management today are significant (see Box—Holistic Management, pp. 6–8).

NATIVE AMERICANS IN POST-PLEISTOCENE SOUTHWESTERN COLORADO

Native American occupation of southwestern Colorado began to increase about 9,500 years ago. Except for a period of significant agricultural development in the lower elevations of the region from about

BOX—HOLISTIC MANAGEMENT

Holistic Management (HM) is "a process of goal setting, decision making and monitoring which integrates social, ecological and economic factors"[1] for managing rangelands. HM also offers the prospect that more cattle can be grazed while land health is improved; practitioners even suggest that HM can help end rangeland conflicts.[2] However, rangeland science suggests that basic HM grazing principles are not supported, and simpler grazing strategies (e.g., reduced stocking) work as well or better to maintain rangeland health.[3]

A fundamental aim of HM is to mimic the behavior of large herds of native grazing animals.[4] This usually means moving livestock together to get a short-duration, high-intensity herd effect (often called short-duration grazing), which HM considers necessary to (1) disturb and compact soil, producing a good seed bed for plant regeneration; and (2) trample standing dead plant material onto the soil surface, which increases photosynthesis by allowing sunlight to reach the base of grass plants and helps protect the soil from erosion and rapid moisture loss through evaporation.[5] Grazing and animal impact are considered by HM to be essential to maintain efficient nutrient cycling—without grazing, plants may become "over-rested" with too much standing dead leaf material, leading to declining rangeland health.[6] In HM the timing, intensity, and frequency of grazing are adjusted to mimic herd behavior, which includes sufficient recovery time after grazing.[7] Monitoring is used to evaluate and adjust grazing.

However, southwestern Colorado likely lacks a history of herds of large grazing animals since the end of the Pleistocene, if ever. After the Pleistocene, increasing aridity limited larger herbivores, and the region has since been characterized by small-bodied herbivores (pronghorn, bighorn sheep, deer) that can move long distances to find water and appropriate forage.[8] Mature pronghorn, bighorn sheep, and deer typically weigh < 200 pounds, much less than mature cattle (800–1,200 pounds). Mature bull elk can approach the weight of mature cattle, but it is unlikely they existed in numbers that rival today's cattle herds.

In the Great Plains, where herds of large herbivores have long been present, adaptations to grazing and ecosystem processes linked to these herbivores are common, but such adaptations are generally absent in the more arid portions of the West.[9] Some cool-season grasses in arid parts of the region lack physiological adaptations to grazing by large herbivores.[10] Biological soil crusts, which provide the primary source of nitrogen for these ecosystems, disappear with grazing by large herbivores (see Box—Biological Soil Crusts, pp. 150–152). Even if some large herbivores are artificially missing from these ecosystems today as a result of human-caused extinctions, reintroducing them now would likely alter the region's current ecology (e.g., destroy biological soil crusts), given the long history without herds of large grazers.

If an evolutionary basis for grazing large herbivores is absent, could a method of grazing them be created that minimizes damage to the region's ecology using the HM process of observation, monitoring, adaptation, and planning?[11] Some thoughtful HM practitioners are experimenting with longer rest periods to allow more recovery after cattle grazing.[12] Perhaps people willing to closely observe nature—whether ranchers, environmentalists, or scientists—will eventually converge on an ecologically based management process for livestock grazing in this region.

A "new ranch" movement has arisen, based on HM, that more closely marries science and rancher observation,[13] but its chosen indicators of land health focus on rapid cycling of nutrients and retention of water and soil to produce a good cover of grass important to herbivores, particularly domestic livestock. Common indicators include close spacing between perennial plants, little bare ground, actively photosynthesizing plants with little standing litter, abundant litter on the soil, good infiltration of water into soil, and little soil erosion.[14]

While some of these indicators of land health are likely to have universal acclaim (e.g., little soil erosion), others, such as rapid nutrient cycling and little bare ground, are based on an assumed history of herds of large herbivores and may be inappropriate in this semiarid region. Other important indicators are not included, and some may conflict with those listed here. For example, while biologically diverse communities are a goal of HM, distinctions are not made between native and non-native plants, which could allow loss of native plants not adapted to livestock grazing. Also, in sagebrush and pinyon-juniper ecosystems, a diverse assemblage of cyanobacteria, lichens, and mosses covering the spaces between native plants is a key indicator of land health, given its importance to nitrogen cycling and its vulnerability to loss with livestock grazing (see Box—Biological Soil Crusts, pp. 150–152).

If HM is to succeed as part of a meaningful new ranch movement,[15] a variety of interests must be brought together. HM has provided ranchers with new understanding of the importance of biological diversity, soils, hydrology, and nutrient cycles and new tools to plan, monitor, and adapt their operations. However, HM's credibility for maintaining rangeland health in the West is weak, as its theoretical foundation is an unsupported evolutionary history of large grazing animals. At least where HM is used on public lands, contrary scientific evidence and competing values and indicators for rangeland health must be addressed and used to create a transparent and verifiable management process that has credibility in the scientific community. There is no reason practitioners of HM, scientists, environmentalists, and the interested public cannot together create as good a vision as is possible for grazing semiarid lands, built around a common interest in land health.

NOTES

1. Stinner, Stinner, and Martsolf, "Biodiversity as an Organizing Principle," 199.
2. Dagget, *Beyond Rangeland Conflict*; Sayre, *New Ranch Handbook*.
3. Pieper and Heitschmidt, "Is Short-Duration Grazing the Answer?" Holechek et al., "Short-Duration Grazing."
4. Savory, *Holistic Management*; Sayre, *New Ranch Handbook*.
5. Savory, *Holistic Management*.
6. Ibid.
7. Ibid.; Sayre, *New Ranch Handbook*.
8. Young, Evans, and Tueller, "Great Basin Plant Communities"; Patou and Tueller, "Evolutionary Implications for Grazing Management"; Vavra and McInnis, "Grazing in the Great Basin."
9. Mack and Thompson, "Evolution in Steppe"; Patou and Tueller, "Evolutionary Implications for Grazing Management"; Vavra and McInnis, "Grazing in the Great Basin."
10. Mack and Thompson, "Evolution in Steppe."
11. Savory, *Holistic Management*.
12. Howell, "Grazing in Nature's Image—Part 2."
13. Sayre, *New Ranch Handbook*.
14. Ibid.
15. Ibid.

1000 B.C. to A.D. 1300, the groups that used Colorado were hunters and gatherers.[36] In the mountains of Colorado and Wyoming, a unique late Paleoindian strategy called the Foothills/Mountain complex developed (see Table 1.1). Unlike the contemporaneous big-game specialists of the Great Plains, these late Paleoindians were probably hunters and gatherers who used a more diverse subsistence strategy based on a wide variety of animals, ranging from bighorn sheep and deer to rodents, reptiles, and fish, as well as some plants.[37] Although late Paleoindian presence is well established in the region, relatively few points from this period have been found in southwestern Colorado.[38] This suggests that populations were small, and groups probably moved over long distances, with territories extending outside southwestern Colorado.[39]

An even more diverse subsistence strategy is thought to have been typical of the Archaic period, which lasted 6,000 to 7,000 years.[40] Southwestern Colorado has, by some measures, the highest diversity of vegetation types in the United States[41] because of the great elevational range and geologic complexity. Yet compared with other regions, foraging resources were less abundant, requiring substantial seasonal movements up and down in elevation.[42] At high elevations archaeological evidence is still scarce, but significant evidence indicates repeated use of high-elevation game drives and small base camps.[43] Some long-term house sites are known from midelevation Archaic sites just north of the San Juan Mountains, but evidence of similar structures is lacking in the southern San Juan Mountains.[44]

Some researchers suggest that the mountains of Colorado were home to groups of people whose lifeways changed relatively little from the start of the Archaic until the arrival of the Utes.[45] Even the Utes did not usher in clear changes in subsistence practices. William Buckles, who studied the archaeological record of Utes and their predecessors on the Uncompahgre Plateau, could not separate Ute sites from the hunting-gathering strategy he called the Uncompahgre Complex.[46] This complex may have included several cultural groups from at least middle Archaic times (about 3500 B.C.) up to and including the historical Utes. As Steve Cassells points out, "The explanation for this extraordinary longevity must lie in their early striking of an optimal balance with the arid environment."[47]

More recent analyses suggest that the long Archaic period was not entirely stable and that groups shifted settlement patterns and subsistence practices as they adapted to climatic changes and, possibly, population increases.[48] Throughout the Archaic, however, the same species of animals provided the subsistence base, indicating they were never overexploited to the point of extirpation from the region. The Archaic period ends around 500 B.C. to A.D. 1 in southwestern Colorado,[49] over-lapping with the appearance of maize and the development of agriculture in the Four Corners region beginning about 1000 B.C.[50]

AGRICULTURAL GROUPS OF SOUTHWESTERN COLORADO

Within Colorado, only in the southwest did strongly agricultural populations flourish. The Ancestral Puebloans who lived in the southwestern corner of Colorado were part of the larger Pueblo world that once spread across the Four Corners region (see Map 1.1). Often referred to as the Northern San Juan or Mesa Verde Anasazi, these pueblo-dwelling people lived around the northern tributaries of the San Juan River, reaching their northern limit near the towns of Dove Creek, Colorado, and Monticello, Utah. East to west, they extended from near Pagosa Springs to the Colorado River. Dense populations of Ancestral Puebloans lived during various periods on Mesa Verde and in the San Juan River Basin and the McElmo-Montezuma Valley area.[51]

North of Dove Creek, agricultural sites are known along lower-elevation rivers, particularly the Dolores and San Miguel, but are much less common and show similarities to both the Ancestral Puebloan and Fremont cultures.[52] The highly variable Fremont culture is known primarily from north and west of the Colorado River in Utah and northwestern Colorado.[53] Alan Reed suggests that the area south and west of the Uncompahgre Plateau was the home of a distinctive cultural complex, which he named the Gateway tradition.[54] The Gateway tradition (400 B.C.–A.D. 1200) is characterized by limited reliance on corn production, lack of locally produced pottery, and simple, small-scale housing.[55] Populations were probably never dense and remained relatively mobile and dependent on hunting.[56]

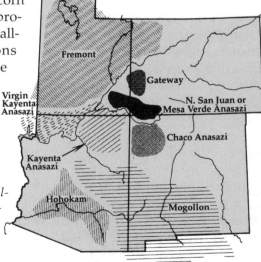

Map 1.1. *Distribution of agricultural groups of the American Southwest. Reprinted from figure 8-6 in Cassells (1997), with permission of author.*

The rise and collapse of agriculture in southwestern Colorado was not an entirely linear process (see Table 1.2). The earliest known sites of maize found in southwestern Colorado are from above Durango and from the Cottonwood Cave site on the Uncompahgre Plateau, both consisting of a small cluster of houses dated about 300–200 B.C.[57] Agricultural groups were sparse for the next 800–900 years. Lack of storage facilities and selection of sites at higher elevations suggest that foraging continued to be an important source of food or at least a buffer against crop failures.[58] After A.D. 500, Ancestral Puebloans became more settled and highly dependent on maize production, but settlement patterns fluctuated. Populations grew, declined, and grew again before they finally peaked and collapsed around A.D. 1300.[59] By the A.D. 1200s, a peak population of 13,000–30,000 Ancestral Puebloans had converted large areas in far southwestern Colorado to agricultural fields.[60]

Evidence of agriculture groups disappears rather suddenly throughout southwestern Colorado around A.D. 1300; the nature and cause of the exodus remain a much-discussed mystery. From A.D. 1300 until the takeover of the territory by Anglo-Americans in the second half of the 1800s, the hunting-and-gathering Utes were the main cultural group in southwestern (and all of western) Colorado. Thus, a relatively short period of agriculture punctuated the very long-standing lifeway of hunting and gathering. How did the agriculturalists use and shape the landscape of southwestern Colorado? Why did they leave?

Ancient Farming Landscapes

The hunting-and-gathering people who moved widely from low to high elevations utilizing a diversity of plant and animal resources left little evidence of how they may have altered natural communities.[61] The ancient Puebloan farmers, in contrast, left multistory buildings that capture the imagination and still define the place centuries after their departure (see Plate 1).

Corn production (and to a lesser extent beans and squash) eventually supported a Puebloan population in a part of southwestern Colorado that at its peak may have exceeded the current population of the same area. The sheltered cliff dwellings of Mesa Verde and the many canyons of the Colorado Plateau shape the image of the Puebloans, but those dwellings represent only the final phase, lasting less than a century. The real story is on the mesas and uplands, where the Ancestral Puebloans lived and farmed for several centuries. While some buildings remain visible, many of the upland houses and settlements are

Table 1.2. Overview of prehistoric agriculture in Ancestral Puebloan region of southwestern Colorado.[1]

Date	Subsistence Practices	Population
Basketmaker II ~300 B.C.–A.D. 500	Oldest known maize in Colorado about 300 B.C. Maize probably provided bulk of calories, but hunting and foraging still important Pit houses and rock shelters, near springs or other permanent water Year-round occupation of sites uncertain	Relatively few known sites, indicating low population densities Population concentrations in Animas, western Montezuma-McElmo drainage, and drainages now under Navajo Reservoir
Basketmaker III A.D. 500–750	Small, dispersed hamlets, mostly of 1–2 households Probably year-round occupation of sites with good agricultural land near springs and pinyon-juniper woodlands Sites shifted frequently (10–15 years) Wild meat in diet declined; increased reliance on corn, beans, squash, and wild weedy species Food storage facilities larger, more substantial	Population declined A.D. 375–575, followed by rapid increase, suggesting migration a factor Possibly 2,000–3,000 people by A.D. 725 Concentrated in Mancos–Mesa Verde and Montezuma-McElmo drainages
Pueblo I A.D. 750–900	Villages of 50 to 500, as well as dispersed single-family sites on good agricultural uplands Populations aggregated in villages and then dispersed, possibly in search of new lands Large villages disappeared (migration?) with population decline late in period Dependence on and storage of maize increased	Population rose and then dropped sharply, probably influenced by migration in response to drought Population estimates: A.D. 800 = 6,000, A.D. 860 = 10,000, A.D. 920 = 2,500 Occupation of region at peak widespread but spotty; concentrations in Dolores and Mancos–Mesa Verde drainages until decline beginning A.D. 880
Pueblo II A.D. 900–1150	Period began with small, widely dispersed residential sites Chacoan influences appeared around A.D. 1080, including great houses, some social differentiation, and some long-distance trade	Population increased through this period Estimates range from 8,900 at beginning of period[2] to 24,300 by end of period[3] Concentrated in Mesa Verde–Mancos and

Period		
Pueblo III A.D. 1150–1300	With Chacoan influence, some communities (e.g., Lowry) consisted of community centers associated with small, scattered settlements on deep-soiled uplands	Montezuma-McElmo drainages; Chimney Rock flourished in Piedra drainage
	Further agricultural intensification evidenced by use of check dams, terraces, and small reservoirs to control water	Drought in mid-1100s coincided with end of Chaco in New Mexico and increased violence and cannibalism in southwestern Colorado
	Populations moved to aggregated villages, the largest with 500 or more people	Period began with drought
	Villages located near springs in or near canyon heads; cliff dwellings common	Population stable or declining until A.D. 1200, then population peak in early to mid-1200s
	Long-distance trade decreased	Population estimates range from 13,000[4] to 30,000[5]
	Water-control structures increased, but most corn still produced with relatively low-intensity dryland or runoff techniques	Concentrated in Montezuma-McElmo and Mancos–Mesa Verde drainages and to lesser extent in Ute Mountain
	Wild plant and animal resources possibly locally depleted; rabbits main game, access to deer possibly socially restricted; wild turkeys raised intensively as meat source	Rapid and complete depopulation of region by agricultural groups by 1290–1300; cause(s) still debated

1. Lipe, Varien, and Wilshusen, *Colorado Prehistory*; Varien et al., "Southwestern Colorado Settlement Patterns."
2. Duff and Wilshusen, "Prehistoric Population Dynamics."
3. Lipe and Varien, "Pueblo III."
4. Wilshusen, "Estimating Population in the Central Mesa Verde Region."
5. Mahoney, Adler, and Kendrick, "Changing Scale and Configuration of Mesa Verde Communities."

today mounds of rubble covered by sage and pinyon-juniper or were removed when the land was plowed by Euro-American farmers.

The earliest farmers in the region (Basketmaker II, see Table 1.2) were widely scattered and few in number, with most sites known from the Animas drainage, the Cedar Mesa area of southeastern Utah, and the area where Navajo Reservoir now stands.[62] Evidence suggests that during the early agricultural period, hunting and foraging, as well as corn production, were important.[63] After A.D. 600, households occupied sites year-round, and maize (corn), beans, and squash—as well as weedy species such as pigweed, goosefoot, and sunflower (see Table 1.3)— came to dominate the diet, with corn by far the most important single

Table 1.3. Plants used by Puebloans in Sand Canyon and their prevalence in upper Sand Canyon today. Use by Puebloans is based on macrobotanical evidence from the Sand Canyon project.[1] Estimates of prevalence (D = dominant, C = common but not dominant, U = uncommon) are based on visits in 2001 and 2002. Minor occurrences of plants are omitted.[2]

	Sand Canyon Project	Upper Sand Canyon
TREES		
Twoneedle pinyon (*Pinus edulis*)	X	D
Utah juniper (*Sabina osteosperma*)	X	D
SHRUBS		
Alderleaf mountain mahogany (*Cercocarpus montanus*)	X	C
Antelope bitterbrush (*Purshia tridentata*)	X	D
Big sagebrush (*Seriphidium tridentatum*)	X	C
Cliff fendlerbush (*Fendlera rupicola*)	X	U
Fourwing saltbush (*Atriplex canescens*)	—	U
Gambel oak (*Quercus gambelii*)	X	C
Greasewood (*Sarcobatus vermiculatus*)	X	U
Mormon tea (*Ephedra viridis*)	X	U
Rabbitbrush (*Chrysothamnus* sp.)	X	U
Singleleaf ash (*Fraxinus anomala*)	X	U
Skunkbush sumac (*Rhus aromatica* subsp. *trilobata*)	X	—
Stansbury cliffrose (*Purshia stansburiana*)	X	C
Utah serviceberry (*Amelanchier utahensis*)	X	C
FORBS		
Cheno-Ams (*Chenopodium* or *Amaranthus*)	X	—
Coyote tobacco (*Nicotiana attenuata*)	X	—
Goosefoot (*Chenopodium* sp.)	X	—
Groundcherry (*Physalis* sp.)	X	—
Kingcup cactus (*Echinocereus triglochidiatus*)	X	U
Pigweed (*Amaranthus* sp.)	X	—
Plantain (*Plantago* sp.)	X	—

continued on next page

Table 1.3—*continued*

	Sand Canyon Project	Upper Sand Canyon
Pricklypear *(Opuntia* sp.)	X	C
Purslane *(Portulaca* sp.)	X	—
Ribseed sandmat *(Chamaesyce glyptosperma)*	X	—
Spiderflower (*Cleome* sp.)	X	—
Sunflower *(Helianthus* sp.)	X	U
Tansymustard *(Descurainia* sp.)	X	U
Whitestem blazingstar *(Acrolasia albicaulis)*	X	—
Winged pigweed *(Cycloloma atriplicifolium)*	X	—
Yucca *(Yucca* sp.)	X	C
GRAMINOIDS		
Indian ricegrass *(Achnatherum hymenoides)*	X	C
Sedge *(Cyperaceae* sp.)	X	—

1. Adams, "Macrobotanical Remains"; Adams and Bowyer, "Sustainable Landscape."
2. Common names are from the PLANTS online database, http://plants.usda.gov. Latin names are from Weber and Wittmann, *Colorado Flora.*

food.[64] Hunting and foraging continued, but people became more reliant on agriculture as populations increased.[65]

Puebloan-style communities did not appear in Colorado until about A.D. 750. Populations of farmers in Colorado fluctuated and shifted over time (see Table 1.2). The first dense populations were in the Dolores River Valley, downstream from present-day Dolores. The largest populations, near the end of the Puebloan presence, were concentrated on deep and fertile loess soils of the Great Sage Plain, a triangular area bounded by McElmo Creek on the south, Montezuma Creek on the west, and the Dolores River to the northeast (see Map 1.2). The Mesa Verde region of the Mancos River drainage also supported dense populations. Outside these areas, population densities in Colorado were much lower except for relatively brief periods in localized areas, such as the Chimney Rock area of the Piedra drainage.[66]

The Pueblo region of the northern San Juan is the most intensively studied pre-Hispanic setting in Colorado. Yet many aspects of Puebloan subsistence and social organization remain uncertain.[67] The Puebloans' primarily dryland agricultural practices required a rather extensive land base, estimated at nine acres of land in production for an average household of seven people on the fertile Great Sage Plain.[68] As climatic conditions fluctuated, affecting precipitation and the length of the growing season, communities responded by moving within the region to favored areas. For example, during the dry A.D. 800s the Dolores River Valley,

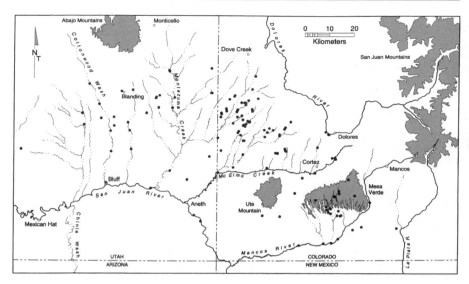

Map 1.2. *Distribution of community centers, dating between* A.D. *1050 and 1290. Reprinted from Varien and Wilshusen (2002), figure 1.3. Courtesy, Crow Canyon Archaeological Center, Cortez, Colorado.*

near the present town of Dolores, supported high populations, while nearby lower-elevation areas on the Great Sage Plain were sparsely populated.[69] Later, climate changes favored the Great Sage Plain, and populations rose there while the Dolores Valley was left almost empty.[70]

Did peak populations of 13,000–30,000 people in the northern San Juan area[71] stretch the limits of production and begin to degrade the resource base? Populations rose and fell twice during the agricultural period in southwestern Colorado, first during the Pueblo I period and again during the last phase, the Pueblo III period.[72] Was the exodus from the region a case of environmental collapse, similar to that postulated by Jared Diamond in his book *Collapse* to have ended the great Chaco Canyon Puebloan society in northern New Mexico?[73] After deforestation of the Chaco Canyon area, building timbers were transported from mountains forty-five miles away.[74] This response to forest depletion required a complex, hierarchical, and interdependent social system that eventually ended when drought stressed the system.[75]

Evidence of resource degradation from major archaeological projects in southwestern Colorado is equivocal. In advance of the McPhee Dam project, intensive archaeological studies were conducted on the Dolores River Valley where Pueblo I populations expanded from A.D. 600 until the late 800s, then rapidly became depopulated (see Table 1.2).[76] Juniper, the preferred building material, was apparently depleted in the local area during that time; and large areas of sagebrush, pinyon-juniper woodland, and, to a lesser extent, Gambel oak woodlands were cleared for crop production.[77] Woodland depletion around population concentrations may have been a factor in the frequent movement of early Pueblo communities of the Dolores River Valley.[78]

Populations of wild animals and their distribution were affected by changes in the vegetation and by the direct impacts of people. Sage-grouse (*Centrocercus* spp.) lost some of the sagebrush habitat on which they strongly depend, and winter habitat and traditional migration routes of mule deer were settled by humans.[79] The desert cottontail (*Sylvilagus audubonii*) increased relative to the mountain cottontail (*Sylvilagus nuttallii*), possibly in response to agricultural clearing.[80] It is not obvious that changes such as these could explain the complete human depopulation of the area, however.

Researchers from Crow Canyon Archaeological Center have intensively studied the settlement and land-use patterns of the Ancestral Puebloans on the Great Sage Plain and Mesa Verde region; much of this research is summarized in *Seeking the Center Place*.[81] The Great Sage Plain was home to an estimated 10,000 people during the late Pueblo III period, the vast majority of southwestern Colorado's population at that time.[82] Mark Varien and his colleagues have documented the location of the 130 known community centers in the region (see Map 1.2), giving a picture of the portions of the landscape that were used intensively and more extensively over the last three centuries of Puebloan agriculture.[83] Community centers shifted over time, but during the last seventy-five years of occupation (A.D. 1225–1300), when populations were probably at their peak, much of the population was in large community centers, mostly clustered in the area between McElmo and Montezuma creeks (see Map 1.3).

Varien and his colleagues estimate that communities may have competed for the best agricultural land, even to the point of violent conflict, but that only a quarter to a half of the land within about a mile and a half of community centers would have been under production at any one time.[84] By this time the eastern portion of the Great Sage Plain had fewer pockets of population. Thus, a large proportion of the landscape was available for other resources, such as firewood and wild plants.[85]

Other Crow Canyon archaeologists have learned much about the status of food and fuel resources from the excavation of Sand Canyon Pueblo, a 400-room community center that was occupied throughout the 1200s until the Puebloans left southwestern Colorado. Study of the plant materials found in cooking and refuse sites at the pueblo and

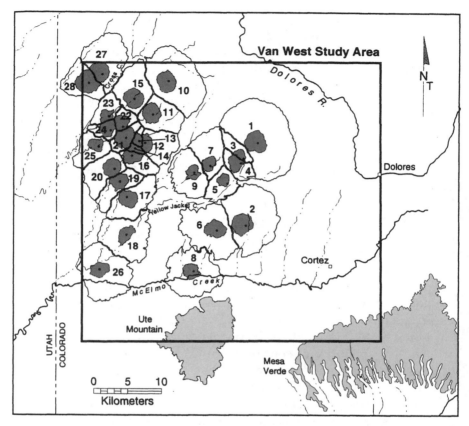

Map 1.3. *Community catchments in the Van West study area,* A.D. *1225 to 1290. The locations of the community centers are represented by dots, the hatched polygon is the two-km catchment, and the open polygon is the seven-km catchment. Reprinted from Varien, Van West, and Patterson (2000), figure 4. Courtesy, Crow Canyon Archaeological Center, Cortez, Colorado.*

surrounding associated sites shows that (1) pinyon-juniper woodlands around this large community center were adequate to provide fuel wood and probably building timbers until the Puebloans left, (2) people were preparing and selecting foods in ways that indicate starvation was not prevalent, and (3) the plants and fuels the people used did not change significantly over the last 100 years of occupation.[86] All of these findings suggest a landscape that was not severely degraded.

The extent to which game and other animal populations were impacted in the region is difficult to determine. Deer and other big game decreased in the diet as population increased, indicating that big game was depleted near settlements.[87] Eventually, even jackrabbits and cottontails declined, while turkeys, raised as domesticated animals by the Ancestral Puebloans, became the most important protein source.[88] The most significant decline in deer and predators (judged from bones) occurred in the A.D. 1200s, when the population was large and concentrated in and near community centers. Yet while big game was depleted locally around Sand Canyon, for example, people apparently did not hunt in nearby areas, such as in Dolores Canyon or on Sleeping Ute Mountain, where human populations were low and big game was more plentiful.[89] Possibly, as populations grew, intercommunity conflict or warfare restricted travel away from communities,[90] or people simply became more agricultural and less interested in the wildlands surrounding them.[91] In either case, the lack of travel would have limited the impacts of these large populations outside their agricultural areas.

There is no widespread agreement about what caused the sudden departure from Sand Canyon and the rest of southwestern Colorado just before A.D. 1300. While the evidence from the Great Sage Plain suggests that environmental degradation was not severe, some archaeologists working there note, "It is also likely ., . . that the claimed land accessible to . . . these . . . communities was somewhat depleted of soil nutrients, local game, and potential fuel wood after more than 700 years of human presence."[92] A strong drought from A.D. 1276 to 1299 and possibly cooler temperatures and more unpredictable rainfall in the 1200s likely contributed to subsistence stress.[93] By the mid- to late 1200s, skeletal evidence from nearby Mesa Verde indicates a low-quality diet and nutritional stress, especially for women and children.[94] The dominance of aggregated and cliff-side dwellings and clear evidence of massacres indicate that the Puebloans experienced widespread warfare during their last century in Colorado, probably among themselves.[95]

The rapid exodus of the Ancestral Puebloans from southwestern Colorado—under circumstances of warfare likely precipitated by competition for resources—could certainly be viewed as a collapse of the economic and social system. Yet some archaeologists and anthropologists are reluctant to view it this way. For example, after documenting the vulnerability of the dense, highly integrated population—dependent on favorable environmental conditions—to even moderate changes in those conditions, Jeffrey Dean and Carla Van West conclude, "Puebloan emigration . . . at the end of the thirteenth century should not, however, be viewed as failure. Rather, the movement of people to areas where they could survive was but another adaptive step in the continuing evolution of Puebloan societies."[96] Some evidence indicates that the Ancestral Puebloans were attracted by new, nonhierarchical religious and social organizations that were developing to the south, where the

Rio Grande Pueblos and Hopis live today,[97] so pull factors may indeed have played a role.

To view the Ancestral Puebloan exodus from southwestern Colorado as adaptation rather than failure, however, misses a lesson. As human economies become more intensive and specialized to meet growing human demands, they are much less able to adapt, without great human suffering, to changing circumstances outside their control.[98] What is notable in this story is that a moderately overtaxed but not highly degraded environment probably played a key role in ending Puebloan agriculture in Colorado.

Are Ancestral Puebloan Legacies Evident in Current Plant and Animal Communities?

Clearly, the Puebloans highly modified the environment of southwestern Colorado while they lived there, and their buildings still dot the landscape 800 years after their departure (see Plate 1). But did the Puebloans more permanently alter the plant and animal communities of the area they inhabited? Some think cultivated Puebloan fields have left a legacy in present plant distributions.[99] For example, fourwing saltbush, greasewood, and rabbitbrush (see Table 1.3) might indicate good agricultural soils formerly cultivated by Puebloans.[100] However, these plants also occur today in areas never cultivated and are common outside the Puebloan region, so the association with Puebloans is weak and unreliable.

Meredith Matthews suggests that the Puebloans were probably intercropping about seven native forbs and short shrubs (pigweed, tansymustard, other mustards, purslane, groundcherry, Cheno-Ams, and goosefoot—see Table 1.3) among rows of maize.[101] These native plants are pioneers, plants found early in plant succession after disturbance. They were encouraged by farmers but likely not domesticated. They were probably used as greens early in their growth and for seeds later on. Although these plants cannot be identified to species from the archaeological remains, it is likely they are the same as, or closely related to, present species. None of these native pioneer plants seems particularly abundant today.

Alteration of the physical environment by Puebloan buildings, water-storage structures, and other physical features had more lasting effects, but generally only in small, scattered areas. Abandoned habitations may create piles of rock, while flat rocks used as check dams on ephemeral streams may still remain in place (see Figure 1.1), trapping sediment and altering patterns of runoff, sedimentation, and plant habitats.[102]

Figure 1.1. *A remnant Puebloan check dam at Hovenweep National Monument.*

Early researchers identified a suite of plants supposedly indicating former habitation sites and other physical structures, but there are two explanations for this suite. Richard Yarnell suggested that "the distribution of certain species appears to have been brought about wholly or in part by the aboriginal occupants,"[103] suggesting these species were introduced. However, Arthur Clark argued that the flora on former sites may differ from the surrounding flora simply because rock piles and other remains of Puebloan sites favor certain native plants.[104] Moreover, it is not clear that there really is a distinctive flora of former habitation sites. On Cajon Mesa on the Colorado-Utah border, which now contains Hovenweep National Monument, a recent reevaluation suggests that only one plant, pale desert-thorn (also called pale wolf-berry) (see Plate 2), fairly consistently distinguishes former Puebloan sites.[105] Pale desert-thorn remains the most tantalizing of the possible Puebloan introductions.

The Puebloans also used native plants for many purposes, including food, fiber, medicine, and ceremonies. Analysis of preserved pieces of plants in hearths, fire pits, refuse areas, and middens typically identifies a suite of several dozen plants that were commonly used. The Dolores Archaeological Project found that the most used wild-food plants were the seeds of pinyon and juniper and the fruits of yucca, pricklypear (see Plate 3), and skunkbush sumac (see Plate 4).[106] At Sand Canyon (see Table 1.3) the most frequently encountered noncultivated food plants were pricklypear, Cheno-Ams, groundcherry, and purslane, the last three associated with agricultural fields.[107] Common fuel sources were twoneedle pinyon, Utah juniper, corn cobs, and alderleaf mountain mahogany.[108] Yucca leaves provided fiber for a variety of uses (see Figure 1.2). Thus, the heavily used wild plants were "weedy" species in agricultural fields or common trees and shrubs, and most remain common in the area today.

During their occupation the Ancestral Puebloans altered animal and plant populations in the area of settlements. However, even during peak occupation, the area significantly altered was small relative to the ranges of most species. All the animals the Puebloans are known to have hunted had recolonized the area by the time of Euro-American settlement and probably well before that time, although there are some unpublished records of bison associated with early Pueblo times but not later.[109] No plant extinctions are known, but if agriculture caused extinction of a rare plant, that could be missed in the archaeological record.

It appears that after the Puebloans left the region around A.D. 1300, plant succession proceeded to restore agricultural fields to native plant communities. On Mesa Verde, cultivated fields have become woodlands now several centuries old.[110] Significant, permanent alteration of natural plant communities as a result of the Puebloan presence appears remarkably absent. It is difficult to imagine a similar recovery of the landscape from the much briefer period of Euro-American occupation, especially

Figure 1.2. *Ancestral Puebloans used the leaves of Lanana yucca* (Yucca baccata) *for many purposes.*

in light of introductions of several aggressive non-native plants (see Boxes—Cheatgrass, pp. 61–63; Smooth Brome, pp. 281–282; Crested Wheatgrass, pp. 85–86).

POST-PUEBLOAN NATIVE AMERICANS IN SOUTHWESTERN COLORADO

Less is known about the people who used the region from A.D. 1300 to the mid-1700s when official explorers began to keep written records of contact. It is not known when the first Utes arrived in the area south and west of the San Juans, but by the time the first Europeans explored the area, Utes were the sole inhabitants, and it is possible they had arrived before the Puebloans left.[111] Their early presence is difficult to distinguish in the archaeological record from the hunting-and-gathering Archaic groups.[112]

The Utes are related to other Numic-speaking peoples of the Great Basin, including the Paiutes and Shoshoni[113] Assemblages of ceramic shards and tools associated with the ancestral Utes can be found in western Colorado dating after A.D. 1100, possibly indicating the time of ancestral Ute immigration from the West.[114] It is not known whether they arrived slowly in small family groups—which integrated with the Gateway, Fremont, or others—or came rapidly, replacing other groups.[115] The oral history of the Utes themselves gives no other home than their historical territory in Utah and Colorado.[116]

The Navajo also have associations in southwestern Colorado. The Navajo are Athapascan-speaking people, as are the Apaches and the Bloods of Canada.[117] Language and archaeological evidence suggest that the Navajo or their ancestors migrated to the Southwest relatively recently, within the last 500 to 1,000 years.[118] The earliest archaeological evidence of distinctively Navajo presence in the Southwest is a hogan from Navajo Reservoir in northern New Mexico that dates to A.D. 1541.[119] The Navajo's oral tradition gives the La Plata Range in the San Juan Mountains as their place of origin,[120] suggesting their first home in the Southwest was in Colorado. By the mid-1600s they had moved to northern New Mexico and were growing corn and other crops on the floodplains there.[121] By the 1700s most Navajo had moved farther south and west in response to hostilities with Spaniards and Utes.[122] Most relevant to the story, then, is how the Utes made their living and how that affected the natural communities of southwestern Colorado.

The Utes of Southwestern Colorado

The Colorado Utes were undergoing major changes in subsistence practices, territories, and social organization when the first Euro-American explorers arrived in their territory. By the early 1600s, well before Euro-Americans began settling the eastern seaboard in large numbers, some Utes were trading meat and skins for knives and horses at Spanish outposts in New Mexico.[123] The acquisition of the horse beginning around A.D. 1650, more than previous technological changes (e.g., bow and arrow), had a major impact on long-standing subsistence strategies.[124] Most groups of Colorado Utes began to travel to the Great Plains for bison. Although they never took on the large-group organization of the Plains Indians, the Ute groups that adopted the horse began to develop some of their traits. The mounted Utes became more powerful and wealthier than the unmounted Utes of Utah, both in the eyes of explorers who met them[125] and among the Utes themselves.[126] Buffalo-skin tepees replaced brush-covered wickiups,[127] and raiding other tribes, especially for horses and slaves, became common.[128] Loosely organized small-family groups became organized into larger bands, at least for bison hunts, and chiefs became more powerful.[129]

When Euro-American explorers first came to Colorado, there were six bands of Utes in Colorado and five in Utah.[130] Three bands—the

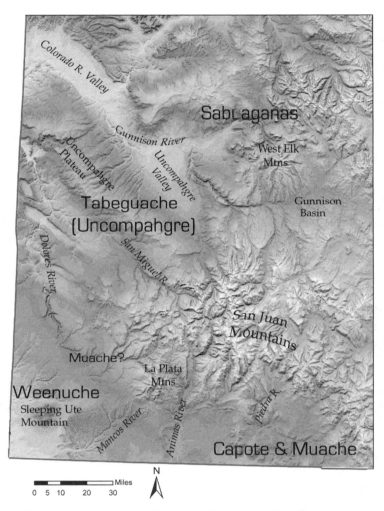

Map 1.4. *Ute Indian bands in southwestern Colorado at the time of Euro-American contact, based on Stewart (1952), Jefferson, Delaney, and Thompson (1972), Petersen (1977), Callaway, Janetsky, and Stewart (1986), Delaney (1989), Sánchez (1997), and Simmons (2000).*

Weenuche, Tabeguache, and Capote—were in southwestern Colorado (see Map 1.4). The Sabuaganas, or Elk Mountain Utes, were encountered just northeast of our study area in 1776 by the early Spanish explorers Fathers Dominguez and Escalante.[13] The horse apparently led to changes in the territories of Ute bands between the times of early and later explorers. The first recorded encounter with Spanish explorers was the expedition of Juan Maria Antonio Rivera in 1765. Rivera reported Muache along the Dolores River west of the La Plata Mountains,[132] but by the 1800s the Muache were either in southern Colorado and northern New Mexico[133] or east of the San Luis Valley.[134] The Capote were mainly in the San Luis Valley and northern New Mexico[135] but also used the area south of the San Juan Mountains as far west as the Animas River.[136]

The Tabeguache and Weenuche (sometimes Weeminuche) Utes occupied most of our study area at the time Euro-American exploration took place. The Weenuche, although they adopted the horse early, did not range to the east in search of bison as did the other Colorado Utes.[137] They traded with the Spaniards, the Navajo, and the bison-hunting Utes but remained relatively isolated, continuing their annual circuits between winter camps in the lower valleys of the La Plata, Mancos, and Animas rivers and the mountain meadows of the La Platas and the Mount Wilson area in midsummer.[138] The Weenuche territory extended into southeastern Utah, and early ethnographies suggest they relied heavily on this area.[139] The Tabeguache were centered on the Uncompahgre Plateau. They did travel far for bison, onto the Great Plains of eastern Colorado and perhaps beyond.[140]

Subsistence Practices of the Utes

Contrasting the hunting-and-gathering Utes with the Ancestral Puebloan and Gateway cultures, William Buckles noted, "It appears that the Numic speakers and other nomads have long had cultures which were not specilized [sic] for limited resources or environments but utilized almost all resources. They perpetuated while other groups who became specialized for limited environments failed."[141]

The picture of the Utes that emerges is one of highly mobile, hunting-and-gathering groups of related families that used a wide diversity of plant and animal food. Well-worn trails through the mountains, recognized and used by early explorers and settlers, attest to the Utes' wide-ranging circuits of travel for subsistence and trade.[142] The Tabeguache gathered during winter in the relatively warm Uncompahgre Valley.[143] They also gathered for bison hunts and rendezvous with neighboring Utes in the summer.[144]

The Utes' mobile lifestyle left relatively little material evidence on the landscape.[145] Sites discovered since 1990 suggest that Colorado Utes depended heavily on big game.[146] Ethnographic research on historical Utes also suggests that Colorado Utes had a greater variety of big game available than the Utes of Utah did.[147] Rabbits and fish were much less important to the Colorado Utes than to most Utah Utes.[148] Big game, as

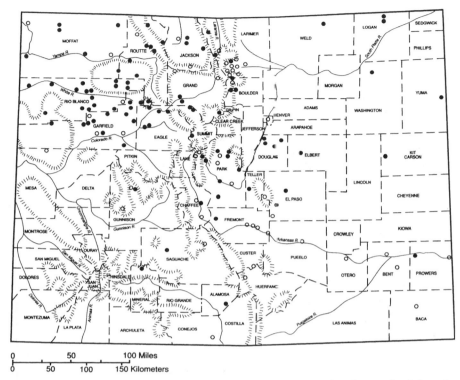

0   50   100 Miles
0   50   100   150 Kilometers

Map 1.5. *Recent distribution of bison* (Bison bison) *in Colorado, emphasizing the area west of the Great Plains. Solid circles are specimens, open circles are literature citations. Reprinted from figure 1 in Meaney and Van Vuren (1993), with permission of the Denver Museum of Nature and Science.*

well as smaller mammals, grouse, and some fish, were eaten by all Utes,[149] but Colorado Utes did not eat some foods eaten by Utah Utes, including grasshoppers and lizards.[150] Thus, Utes had broad diets that varied depending on the resource base and cultural preferences.

Surprisingly, bison were probably not an important food source for the Utes of southwestern Colorado before the horse because bison were rare in southwestern Colorado. Very little archaeological or historical evidence exists of bison in southwestern Colorado south of the Colorado River from the San Juan Mountains west.[151] This apparent absence is an anomaly, since bison occurred at all elevations across the northern half of Colorado into northeastern Utah into historic times and at times were present in moderate numbers in the mountain parks (see Map 1.5).[152] Modern bison were also found in the San Luis Valley and Gunnison Basin but less than in the Great Plains. Bison were found across sagebrush and grasslands from western Wyoming to the Columbia Basin and into northern California, although more sporadically than on the Great Plains.[153] Modern bison were also present at scattered locations in New Mexico and Arizona[154] but were likely rare west of the Rio Grande and are not recorded in most of Utah and Nevada.[155]

By the 1850s bison had been exterminated west of the Rockies,[156] where patchy grasslands may have kept herds small and isolated. Small herds would have been more susceptible to extinction because of severe weather and other natural hazards, as well as human hunting, especially after use of the horse was adopted.[157] Some have speculated that bison were extirpated from the Uncompahgre Plateau by Native American hunting,[158] but we could find only two records of bison bones at archaeological sites in southwestern Colorado—a house site in Paradox Valley dating to the agricultural period[159] and a bison scapula from a Ute site in the Glade Park area near Grand Junction.[160]

Recent examination of archaeological Ute sites across western Colorado shows that deer were the most common large game animal in southwestern Colorado, whereas bison and pronghorn were more common in northwestern Colorado.[161] At two Ute sites in western Montrose and San Miguel counties—each with approximately 3,000 bones—bighorn sheep, deer, and cottontail were identified but no bison.[162] At least three early news articles refer to bison in southwestern Colorado, and the Ute Mountain Ute report bison in the region.[163] However, the scarcity of records of bison in southwestern Colorado strongly suggests bison were never common there, which has implications for livestock grazing in the region (see Box—Holistic Management, pp. 6–8).

Plants also varied in importance in Ute diets. The Weenuche, who inhabited the arid Colorado Plateau, had less access to game and relied more on plants than did the Tabeguache, whose territory was more mountainous.[164] Of plants used by Utes, *Chenopodium* and *Amaranthus* ("Cheno-Ams") are most commonly found in archaeological sites,[165] but a variety of fruiting shrubs as well as leaves, roots, and fruits of forbs were also used (see Table 1.4).[166] Few of the root crops available to more northern Utes were found in southwestern Colorado, and only five were common (see Table 1.4). Utes are known to have stripped aspen and ponderosa pine for the inner bark, and some scarred trees still bear witness to this use.[167] The seeds of certain grasses, such as Indian ricegrass, were also gathered and processed, and wild tobacco was harvested.[168] Ethnographies identify pinyon nuts and acorns of Gambel oak as favorite Ute foods;[169] both have a high caloric content.[170] The Weenuche recognized family ownership of specific plots of pinyon trees, suggesting the importance of this resource (see Figure 1.3).[171]

Figure 1.3. *A Native American woman extracting pinyon nuts from cones. Courtesy, Nevada Historical Society, Reno.*

Ute Legacies

Although the subsistence practices of the Colorado Utes are broadly known, little is recorded or understood about the extent to which their hunting and gathering altered the region's flora and fauna. The Ute's "wickiups" were conical structures, built of brush and about three to twenty feet in diameter (see Figure 1.4), that served a variety of functions.[172] Because of their ephemeral nature, relatively few Ute habitation sites have been found, and the long-term impact of these houses on the ecosystem was almost certainly negligible.

The Utes likely underwent significant ecological change after the mid-1600s as horses and guns were adopted and opportunities for trade expanded. Recent studies of Great Plains Indians and bison suggest that horse-mounted Indians' increased efficiency in hunting for trade and the impacts of their large herds of horses on the vegetation may already have been leading toward the bison's slow demise even before Europeans began to slaughter the herds.[173]

Table 1.4. Plants native to southwestern Colorado known to have been used by Indians as food.[1]

TREES—NUTS OR OTHER FRUITS
  Rocky Mountain juniper (*Sabina scopulorum*)
  Twoneedle pinyon (*Pinus edulis*)
  Utah juniper (*Sabina osteosperma*)

SHRUBS—FRUITS
  Black chokecherry (*Padus virginiana* subsp. *melanocarpa*)
  Currant (*Ribes* spp.)
  Elderberry (*Sambucus* spp.)
  Grayleaf red raspberry (*Rubus idaeus* subsp. *melanolasius*)
  Silver buffaloberry (*Shepherdia argentea*)
  Skunkbush sumac (*Rhus aromatica* subsp. *trilobata*)
  Utah serviceberry (*Amelanchier utahensis*)

FORBS AND FERNS—ROOTS
  Hairy brackenfern (*Pteridium aquilinum* subsp. *lanuginosum*)
  Onion (*Allium* spp.)
  Rocky Mountain pond-lily (*Nuphar lutea* subsp. *polysepala*)
  Sego lily (*Calochortus nuttallii*)
  Springparsley (*Cymopterus* spp.)

FORBS—LEAVES
  Cheno-Ams (*Chenopodium* family or *Amaranthus*)
  Coyote tobacco (*Nicotiana attenuata*)
  Mint family (*Lamiaceae*)
  Mustard family (*Brassicaceae*)
  Pricklypear (*Opuntia* spp.)

FORBS—SEEDS AND FRUITS
  Cattail (*Typha* spp.)
  Cheno-Ams (*Chenopodium* family or *Amaranthus*)
  Common sunflower (*Helianthus annuus*)
  Pricklypear (*Opuntia* spp.)
  Rocky Mountain beeplant (*Cleome serrulata*)

GRASSES—SEEDS
  Indian ricegrass (*Achnatherum hymenoides*)

1. Callaway, Janetski, and Stewart, "Ute"; Reed, "TransColorado Natural Gas Pipeline"; Greubel, "Closer Look at Ute Subsistence." Common names are from the PLANTS online database, http://plants.usda.gov. Latin names are from Weber and Wittmann, *Colorado Flora*.

The horse's influence for the Tabeguache Utes, on the other hand, may have decreased pressure on game in their territory around the Uncompahgre Valley because some of their hunting shifted to the plains bison.[174] Early Anglo-American explorers described the Tabeguache territory as having ample forage and abundant game.[175] This description of a July 1853 gathering of Utes in the Uncompahgre Valley, observed by the E. F. Beale expedition, illustrates the affluence of the Tabeguache and their visiting neighbors at that time:

Figure 1.4. *Uintah Ute wickiup (ca. A.D. 1874) by J W. Powell and A. H. Thompson. Courtesy, Denver Public Library, Western History Collection, Denver, Colorado.*

We saw on the hillsides and river bottoms, a vast number of gayly-colored lodges, and numerous bands of Indians arriving from the northward. Upon approaching, we were received by a number of the oldest men, who invited us to ascend a low, but steep hill, where most of the chiefs were seated. From this point we had a view of an animated and interesting scene. On every side fresh bands of Indians were pouring in, and the women were kept busy in erecting lodges. . . . Horses harnessed to lodge poles, on which were packed their various property, and in many cases their children, were arriving, and large bands of loose horses and mules were being driven to the river side to drink or to pasture. Some of the young men were galloping around on their high-mettled horses, and others, stretched lazily on the grass. . . . All the males, from the old man to the stripling of four years, were armed with bows and arrows, and most of the men had serviceable rifles.[176]

At the time of this rendezvous the Tabeguache were still self-sufficient, though their subsistence practices were changing. On this same trip, Beale visited a Ute village in a mountain valley just east of present-day Montrose. The Utes had corn and a large herd of tame goats, so trade was obviously influencing subsistence.[177] Beale also reported that deer, antelope, and elk were still plentiful in the mountain valleys but that bison had become more difficult to obtain on the plains.[178] Within ten years of this visit, however, reports of food shortages and scarcity of game among the Tabeguache and other Utes were common.[179]

The Weenuche had a long history of trading hides, furs, and meat with the Jicarilla Apache and Pueblos and later with the Spaniards and Americans.[180] The Weenuche, although they probably numbered only about 1,000,[181] may also have impacted game and fur-bearing animal populations, especially as hunting for trade grew in importance. Little is known about this period of game decline, but with rifles, horses, and the motivation to hunt for trade, the Utes may have contributed to the depletion of their own game resources.

Countering the impact of guns and horses, however, was the Utes' population decline after contact. Estimates in the mid-1800s vary, but most indicate that the Tabeguache, Weenuche, Muache, and Capote together constituted fewer than 4,000 people.[182] The Utes suffered disease outbreaks in 1861–1862 and 1883 and earlier, so populations were likely reduced from former levels.[183] Julian Stewart estimated that the population of all Utes, including those in Utah, never exceeded 10,000, however.[184]

With the 1873 Brunot Treaty and later agreements, the "Southern Utes" (Muache, Capote, and Weenuche) were forced onto a narrow strip of land along the Colorado–New Mexico border, an area similar to today's Southern Ute and Ute Mountain Ute reservations. In 1881 the Tabeguache Utes, along with the White River Utes of northern Colorado, were forced onto the Uintah Reservation in Utah.[185] By the end of the century the Southern Ute population had declined to under 1,000,[186] and in 1930 the total Ute population on Colorado and Utah reservations was less than 2,000,[187] probably near its nadir. Even if this represented only a tenth of the Ute population at contact, considering their large territory, overall population densities were never high.

Some argue that Native Americans played a major role in limiting populations of ungulates,[188] but if indeed Ute populations were never high, they and hunter-gatherers before them probably did not greatly alter their natural environment. Though their hunting may have influenced game populations, all the plants and animals they are known to have used persisted into Euro-American times (see Table 1.4). As vulnerable as the now-rare Gunnison sage-grouse and sharp-tailed grouse would have been to Native Americans' hunting on leks in the spring, Euro-Americans arriving in southwestern Colorado found populations large enough to hunt. The top carnivores, wolves and grizzlies, were present, although the Utes had long had horses and guns.

Another way the Utes and other groups before them could have profoundly influenced the natural landscape and native ecosystems was with the use of fire. The degree to which Indians burned acres of land becomes a significant question when we seek to restore landscapes to more natural conditions. Did Indians increase fire frequency over a large enough area for a long enough period of time that natural communities from the time of contact were a product of Indian burning? If so, then intentional burning might be considered necessary today to restore an area, using pre-Euro-American conditions as a guide. On the other hand, if burning by Indians was uncommon, intentional burning today could lead to unprecedented disturbance and deleterious changes in natural communities, including reduced biological diversity.

A recent review of evidence of burning by Indians in the Rocky Mountains shows that most of the evidence cited by previous researchers comes from early accounts of Euro-American scientists and settlers that are unreliable.[189] Early Euro-Americans did not understand the extent to which fires are naturally ignited by lightning, leading them to attribute all fires to either Indians or early settlers. It has been speculated, for example, that the large Lime Creek fire of 1879, which still shapes ecosystems on the west side of the Animas River drainage north of Durango, may have been started by Utes angry at white intrusions. In a careful study, however, local historian Allen Nossaman found no evidence to support that supposition.[190]

Early accounts suggest that lightning was responsible for 1 percent or less of fires in the Rockies, but this must be seriously in error since the percentage of lightning-ignited fires today, when there are many more people, typically exceeds 50 percent.[191] Indians likely ignited some fires, as they had logical reasons to do so, and there are a few reliable accounts of them actually setting fires. However, evidence that Indians significantly altered the natural fire frequency in the Rocky Mountains is limited to low-elevation valleys and travel routes in parts of the northern Rockies, although other areas have received limited study.[192]

The Uncompahgre Plateau was the favorite hunting territory of the Tabeguache Utes, and local people often say the Utes burned the plateau regularly to increase forage for game and, later, horses. However, pinyon nuts, available only from mature pinyon-juniper woodlands, were likely an important staple for the Utes and other peoples of the Uncompahgre Complex.[193] It seems unlikely that Indians would intentionally burn mature pinyon-juniper woodlands on the plateau on a large scale, given the value of the pinyon-nut resource.

There is no firm basis for the idea that Indians significantly altered natural vegetation by setting fires throughout southwestern Colorado. A more likely hypothesis, and it is only that, is that the fire regime of southwestern Colorado, and the Rockies in general, was relatively unaltered by Indians' ignitions outside camping areas and travel corridors.[194]

CONCLUDING THOUGHTS

Native Americans had a long but hard-to-decipher role in shaping the landscapes of North America before Euro-Americans arrived. We probably will never know just how or to what extent Native Americans altered the natural communities of southwestern Colorado, but as a whole, wild nature was certainly much less altered under Native American tenure than it is today. Many of the lands the earliest Euro-Americans explored had probably experienced significant Native American population declines as a result of diseases brought by Euro-Americans.[195] Even though populations were likely higher and had greater impacts prior to the introduction of diseases, the natural world remained intact enough to rebound within decades to the point that most Native American imprints were difficult to see when Euro-Americans arrived.

Were humans to disappear from the same region today, it seems unlikely that the signs of more recent occupation would so quickly become obscure. In one century of trying to make a living on the land, modern societies have left a legacy of impoverished nature that will long be visible to any who follow, as we document in the following chapters. Looking over what is known of Native American presence in southwestern Colorado, the best guide for restoration is still the natural world as it existed with the Utes.

NOTES

1. Deloria, "American Indians and Wilderness."
2. Diamond, *Third Chimpanzee*; Krech, *Ecological Indian*; Flores, *Natural West.*
3. Martin, "Pleistocene Overkill"; Pyne, *Fire in America*; Kay, "Are Ecosystems Structured Top-Down."
4. Vale, *Fire, Native Peoples.*
5. Cassells, *Archaeology of Colorado.*
6. Fiedel, "Peopling of the New World"; Roosevelt, "Who's on First"; Lynch, "Commentary"; Kelly, "Maybe We Do Know."
7. Dillehay, *Monte Verde*; Meltzer et al., "Pleistocene Antiquity of Monte Verde."
8. Fiedel, "Response to Dillehay"; Lynch, "Commentary."
9. Kelly, "Maybe We Do Know."
10. Dixon, *Bones, Boats, and Bison.*
11. Borrero, "Prehistoric Exploration of Fuego/Patagonia"; Dixon, *Bones, Boats, and Bison*; Dillehay, *Settlement of the Americas.*
12. Cassells, *Archaeology of Colorado.*
13. Fiedel, "Peopling of the New World."
14. Cassells, *Archaeology of Colorado*; Dixon, *Bones, Boats, and Bison.*
15. Martin and Klein, *Quaternary Extinctions*; Alroy, "Multispecies Overkill Simulation."
16. Roberts et al., "New Ages for Continent-Wide Extinction."
17. Fiedel, "Peopling of the New World"; Grayson and Meltzer, "Clovis Hunting and Large Mammal Extinction."
18. Dixon, *Bones, Boats, and Bison.*
19. Elias, "Quaternary Paleobiology Update."
20. Grayson and Meltzer, "Clovis Hunting and Large Mammal Extinction."
21. Guthrie, "Late Pleistocene Faunal Revolution"; Grayson, *Desert's Past.*
22. Haynes, "Clovis-Folsom Geochronology."
23. Steadman, "Prehistoric Extinctions of Pacific Island Birds."
24. Martin and Burney, "Bring Back the Elephants!"
25. Adams and Petersen, "Environment."
26. Graham, "Evolution of New Ecosystems"; FAUNMAP Working Group, "Spatial Response of Mammals."
27. Vavra and McInnis, "Grazing in the Great Basin"; Betancourt, "Late Quaternary Biogeography"; Grayson, *Desert's Past.*
28. Graham, "Evolution of New Ecosystems."
29. Betancourt, "Late Quaternary Biogeography"; Nowak et al., "30,000 Year Record of Vegetation Dynamics."
30. Russ Graham, FAUNMAP coordinator, Denver, Colorado, pers. comm., May 15, 2002.

31. Agenbroad and Hesse, "Megafauna, Paleoindians, Petroglyphs and Pictographs."
32. Lipe, Varien, and Wilshusen, *Colorado Prehistory*; Pitblado, "Late Paleoindian Occupation"; Anderson and Faught, "Paleoindian Artefact Distributions."
33. Pitblado, "Peak to Peak in Paleoindian Time."
34. Ibid.
35. Pitblado, "Late Paleoindian Occupation"; Russ Graham, FAUNMAP coordinator, Denver, Colorado, pers. comm., May 15, 2002.
36. Lipe, Varien, and Wilshusen, *Colorado Prehistory*; Reed and Metcalf, *Colorado Prehistory*.
37. Lipe and Pitblado, "Paleoindian and Archaic Periods"; Pitblado, "Paleoindian Presence in Southwest Colorado"; Pitblado, "Peak to Peak in Paleoindian Time."
38. Anderson and Faught, "Paleoindian Artefact Distributions."
39. Pitblado, "Late Paleoindian Occupation"; Lipe and Pitblado, "Paleoindian and Archaic Periods."
40. Lipe and Pitblado, "Paleoindian and Archaic Periods."
41. Wickham et al., "Diversity of Ecological Communities."
42. Black, "Archaic Continuity in the Colorado Rockies"; Adams and Petersen, "Environment."
43. Cassells, *Archaeology of Colorado*.
44. Lipe and Pitblado, "Paleoindian and Archaic Periods"; Reed and Metcalf, *Colorado Prehisory*.
45. Black, "Archaic Continuity in the Colorado Rockies."
46. Buckles, "Uncompahgre Complex."
47. Cassells, *Archaeology of Colorado*, 115.
48. Reed and Metcalf, *Colorado Prehistory*.
49. Lipe and Pitblado, "Paleoindian and Archaic Periods"; ibid.
50. Lipe and Pitblado, "Paleoindian and Archaic Periods."
51. Lipe, "Basketmaker II."
52. McMahon, "Paradox Valley."
53. Madsen and Simms, "Fremont Complex."
54. Reed, "Gateway Tradition."
55. Ibid.
56. Crane, "Cultural Adaptation"; ibid.
57. Lipe, "Basketmaker II."
58. Ibid.
59. Lipe, Varien, and Wilshusen, *Colorado Prehistory*.
60. Lipe and Varien, "Pueblo III (A.D. 1150–1300)."
61. Gleichman and Gleichman, "Lower Sand Canyon Survey."
62. Lipe, "Basketmaker II."
63. Ibid.
64. Wilshusen, "Basketmaker III."
65. Lipe, "Concluding Comments."

66. Varien et al., "Southwestern Colorado Settlement Patterns"; Mahoney, Adler, and Kendrick, "Scale and Configuration of Mesa Verde Communities."
67. Varien and Wilshusen, *Seeking the Center Place.*
68. Varien, Van West, and Patterson, "Competition, Cooperation, and Conflict."
69. Petersen and Matthews, "Man's Impact on the Landscape"; Schlanger, "Patterns of Population Movement."
70. Schlanger, "Patterns of Population Movement."
71. Wilshusen, "Estimating Population in the Central Mesa Verde Region"; Mahoney, Adler, and Kendrick, "Scale and Configuration of Mesa Verde Communities."
72. Wilshusen, "Estimating Population in the Central Mesa Verde Region."
73. Diamond, *Collapse.*
74. English et al., "Source of Architectural Timber at Chaco Canyon."
75. Diamond, *Collapse.*
76. Wilshusen, "Estimating Population in the Central Mesa Verde Region."
77. Petersen and Matthews, "Man's Impact on the Landscape."
78. Kohler and Matthews, "Long-Term Anasazi Land Use and Forest Reduction."
79. Petersen and Matthews, "Man's Impact on the Landscape."
80. Ibid.
81. Varien and Wilshusen, *Seeking the Center Place.*
82. Wilshusen, "Estimating Population in the Central Mesa Verde Region."
83. Varien, Van West, and Patterson, "Competition, Cooperation, and Conflict."
84. Ibid.
85. Ibid.
86. Adams, "Macrobotanical Remains"; Adams and Bowyer, "Sustainable Landscape."
87. Lipe, "Concluding Comments"; Kohler, "Final 400 Years of Prehispanic Agricultural Society"; Driver, "Faunal Variation and Change."
88. Lipe, "Concluding Comments."
89. Driver, "Faunal Variation and Change."
90. Lipe, "Concluding Comments."
91. Driver, "Faunal Variation and Change."
92. Van West and Dean, "Environmental Characteristics Mesa Verde Region," 38.
93. Ibid.
94. Kohler, "Final 400 Years of Prehispanic Agricultural Society."
95. Kuckelman, "Thirteenth-Century Warfare in the Central Mesa Verde Region."
96. Dean and Van West, "Environment-Behavior Relationships in Southwestern Colorado," 98.
97. Lipe, "Depopulation of the Northern San Juan"; Varien et al., "Southwestern Colorado Settlement Patterns."
98. Diamond, *Collapse.*
99. E.g., Weir, "Palynology, Flora and Vegetation of Hovenweep"; Winter and Litzinger, "Floral Indicators of Farm Fields."
100. Weir, "Palynology, Flora and Vegetation of Hovenweep."

101. Matthews, "Agricultural Intensification and Multiple Cropping Practices."
102. Adams, "Anthropogenic Ecology."
103. Yarnell, "Implications of Distinctive Flora on Pueblo Ruins," 669.
104. Clark, "Vegetation on Archaeological Sites."
105. Litzinger and Winter, "Vegetation on Archaeological Sites of Cajon Mesa."
106. Matthews, "Dolores Archaeological Program Macrobotanical Data Base."
107. Bowyer and Adams, "Sand Canyon Archaeobotanical Report."
108. Ibid.
109. Fred Blackburn, environmental historian, Cortez, pers. comm., May 22, 2002.
110. Wyckoff, "Secondary Forest Succession"; Floyd, Romme, and Hanna, "Fire History and Vegetation Pattern."
111. Reed, "Numic Occupation of Western Colorado."
112. Buckles, "Uncompahgre Complex."
113. Rhode and Madsen, "Where Are We?"
114. Reed, "Numic Occupation of Western Colorado."
115. Rhode and Madsen, "Where Are We?"
116. Simmons, *Ute Indians of Utah, Colorado, and New Mexico.*
117. Cassells, *Archaeology of Colorado.*
118. Wilshusen and Towner, "Post-Puebloan Occupation."
119. Ibid.
120. Ibid.
121. Ibid.
122. Cassells, *Archaeology of Colorado*; ibid.
123. Opler, "Southern Ute of Colorado"; Hafen, "Historical Summary of Ute Indians."
124. Opler, "Southern Ute of Colorado"; Callaway, Janetski, and Stewart, "Ute"; Delaney, *Ute Mountain Utes.*
125. Warner, *Dominguez-Escalante Journal.*
126. Smith, *Ethnography of Northern Utes,* 26, 33.
127. Smith, "Cultural Differences and Similarities."
128. Hafen, "Historical Summary of Ute Indians."
129. Jefferson, Delaney, and Thompson, *Southern Utes*; Smith, "Cultural Differences and Similarities"; Malouf and Findlay, "Euro-American Impact."
130. Callaway, Janetski, and Stewart, "Ute."
131. Petersen, "Tabehuache and Elk Mountain Utes."
132. Sánchez, *Explorers, Traders, and Slavers*; Carson, *Across the Northern Frontier*; Simmons, *Ute Indians of Utah, Colorado, and New Mexico.*
133. Jefferson, Delaney, and Thompson, *Southern Utes.*
134. Callaway, Janetski, and Stewart, "Ute"; Simmons, *Ute Indians of Utah, Colorado, and New Mexico.*
135. Jefferson, Delaney, and Thompson, *Southern Utes.*
136. Delaney, *Ute Mountain Utes.*
137. Ibid.
138. Ute Mountain Ute Tribe, *Early Days of the Ute Mountain Ute*; ibid.
139. Stewart, *Culture Element Distributions*; Callaway, Janetski, and Stewart, "Ute."

140. Opler, "Southern Ute of Colorado"; Jefferson, Delaney, and Thompson, *Southern Utes*; Smith, "Cultural Differences and Similarities"; Petersen, "Tabehuache and Elk Mountain Utes."

141. Buckles, "Uncompahgre Complex," 1165.

142. Petersen, "Tabehuache and Elk Mountain Utes"; Simmons, *Ute Indians of Utah, Colorado, and New Mexico.*

143. Callaway, Janetski, and Stewart, "Ute"; Crum, *People of the Red Earth.*

144. Callaway, Janetski, and Stewart, "Ute"; Petersen, "Tabehuache and Elk Mountain Utes."

145. Callaway, Janetski, and Stewart, "Ute"; Wilshusen and Towner, "Post-Puebloan Occupation."

146. Greubel, "Closer Look at Ute Subsistence."

147. Smith, *Ethnography of the Northern Utes*; Callaway, Janetski, and Stewart, "Ute."

148. Smith, "Cultural Differences and Similarities."

149. Ibid.

150. Stewart, *Culture Element Distributions*; ibid.

151. Hayward, Beck, and Tanner, "Zoology of the Upper Colorado River Basin"; Roe, *North American Buffalo*; McDonald, *North American Bison*; Fitzgerald, Meaney, and Armstrong, *Mammals of Colorado.*

152. Fryxell, "Former Range of Bison"; Meaney and Van Vuren, "Recent Distribution of Bison in Colorado."

153. Butler, "Bison Hunting in the Desert West."

154. Truett, "Bison and Elk in the American Southwest."

155. Roe, *North American Buffalo.*

156. Ibid.

157. Van Vuren, "Bison West of the Rocky Mountains."

158. Meaney and Van Vuren, "Recent Distribution of Bison in Colorado."

159. Kasper, "Animal Resource Utilization."

160. Conner, Davenport, and Piontkowski, "Archaeological Investigations."

161. Greubel, "Closer Look at Ute Subsistence."

162. Ibid.

163. Fred Blackburn, environmental historian, Cortez, pers. comm., May 6, 2003.

164. Callaway, Janetski, and Stewart, "Ute"; Greubel, "Closer Look at Ute Subsistence."

165. Reed, "TransColorado Natural Gas Pipeline."

166. Callaway, Janetski, and Stewart, "Ute."

167. Martorano, "Culturally Peeled Trees and Ute Indians."

168. Callaway, Janetski, and Stewart, "Ute."

169. Stewart, *Culture Element Distributions.*

170. Reed and Metcalf, *Colorado Prehistory.*

171. Stewart, *Culture Element Distributions.*

172. Reed and Metcalf, *Colorado Prehistory.*

173. West, E., *Contested Plains*; Flores, *Natural West.*

174. Petersen, "Tabehuache and Elk Mountain Utes."

175. Heap, *Central Route to the Pacific*.
176. Ibid., 194.
177. Ibid.
178. Ibid.
179. Petersen, "Tabehuache and Elk Mountain Utes."
180. Ute Mountain Ute Tribe, *Early Days of the Ute Mountain Ute Tribe*; Delaney, *Ute Mountain Utes*.
181. Jefferson, Delaney, and Thompson, *Southern Utes*; Delaney, *Ute Mountain Utes*.
182. Stewart, *Ute Indians*; Delaney, *Ute Mountain Utes*.
183. Thornton, *American Indian Holocaust*.
184. Stewart, *Ute Indians*; Delaney, *Ute Mountain Utes*.
185. Simmons, *Ute Indians of Utah, Colorado, and New Mexico*.
186. Reed, *Southern Ute Indians of Early Colorado*.
187. Stewart, *Ute Indians*.
188. Kay, "Aboriginal Overkill."
189. Baker, "Indians and Fire in the Rocky Mountains."
190. Nossaman, *Many More Mountains, Vol. 2*.
191. Baker, "Indians and Fire in the Rocky Mountains."
192. Ibid.
193. Buckles, "Uncompahgre Complex."
194. Baker, "Indians and Fire in the Rocky Mountains."
195. Thornton, *American Indian Holocaust*.

The country lying between the Mancos and Dolores is generally dry and sterile, yet is everywhere covered with fragments of broken pottery, showing its former occupation by a considerable number of inhabitants; it is now utterly deserted. Near the mountains it is pretty well timbered; farther west, trees become more scattered and smaller, the pines confined to narrow valleys, the uplands dotted with groves of piñon and cedar [juniper], with wide intervals covered with sage-bushes and soap-plant, *Yucca angustifolia*.
—Newberry 1876[1]

CHAPTER TWO

Desert Plateau Country

It can take a while to sink in. These harsh, dry canyons and mesas on the eastern edge of the Colorado Plateau are now some of the country's most remote, least inhabited places. The arid silence is enveloping, while the hundred-mile vistas in the light of day give a sense of isolation, perhaps insulation, from the modern world And in many ways one has left the modern world. For here an ancient world still dominates the landscape—grown over by the natural world but not paved over or drowned out by modern life.

When it does sink in, that these are old fields and abandoned towns that once housed hundreds of people, the land becomes even more captivating, altering one's sense of the place and of time (see Plate 1). Although the Puebloan people who lived here walked south over 700 years ago, the sites have never been abandoned spiritually:

> Tewa beliefs dictate that *Teji* or ruins remain *P'okwin* [sacred] and the only acceptable behaviors are offerings of prayer meal along with prayers. The Tewa word *P'owaha*, through mythic time and space, brings the present and the past into a singular continuum of space and time. . . . [T]he process of archaeology is painful to observe from the Tewa perspective because archaeologists do not comprehend space, time, and Being of Puebloans. Space joins time in Tewa knowing and being. From this basis arises the perception that *any* Pueblo dwelling once occupied by *Towa* or Pueblo peoples as a category continues to be a spiritual habitation.[2]

The sense of time and space brought to bear on places in this chapter will differ considerably from the Tewas' sense of their ancestral homeland, our focus being on the natural world that has reclaimed the land. It is good to remember, however, that the descendants of the ancestral Puebloans have not abandoned these sites.[3]

Probably not coincidentally, croplands today are concentrated on the deep red soils of the Great Sage Plain between Dove Creek and Cortez, where most of Colorado's Puebloans once farmed. Disappointment, Gypsum, Dry Creek, Paradox, and the lower Dolores and San Miguel valleys (see Map 2.1), which were marginal areas of pre-Euro-American agriculture, today support mainly grazing and hay production.

These desert valleys and canyons are semiarid environments of high solar radiation and heat, with little more precipitation than Phoenix, Arizona.[4] Rocks vary from the soft, erodible, saline Mancos shale slopes of Mesa Verde and the Easter egg–colored shales of the uranium-bearing Morrison Formation, which form slopes in the San Miguel and Dolores canyons, to the harder, more resistant Dakota sandstone mesa tops. Low precipitation and high temperatures enhance geologic variation, leading to some striking side-by-side vegetation differences[5] and some endemic plants (plants restricted to an area, often even a particular rock type). Precipitation comes about equally in spring storms, peaking in March and April, with the "North American Monsoon" from about July 1 to mid-September.[6]

The most prominent plant communities are sagebrush, often in flatter settings with deeper soils, and pinyon-juniper woodlands on more sloping, rockier settings with shallow soils. The general term *sagebrush* (*Artemisia* to many, *Seriphidium* to some) hides subtle variation in the landscape, as there is a sagebrush species for most major environmental settings. About twenty species and subspecies occur in the West from southern British Columbia to northern Mexico.[7] The area covered by this chapter (see Map 2.1) contains five main species. Deep soils in riparian and other moist settings have basin big sagebrush, which can reach ten feet tall (see Figure 2.1). Adjacent shallower soils and broad uplands often have Wyoming big sagebrush. typically only two to three feet tall (see Figure 2.2). Calcareous rocks and other bedrock exposures have black sagebrush, which is dark in color and often only a foot tall.

It retains its flower stalks over winter. Little sagebrush ("low sagebrush" to some) may be just as short, but it is grayish green, has a rounded top, does not keep its flower stalks over the winter, and is often found on soils with a buried impermeable layer.[8] Bigelow sagebrush (*Artemisia bigelovii*) has an open inflorescence and is scattered on rocky canyon slopes. Sharp boundaries between soils may lead to sharp boundaries between sagebrush species (see Figure 2.3).

Pinyon-juniper woodlands extend across the semiarid, intermountain West from eastern Oregon to western Texas. Utah juniper and Colorado pinyon dominate in southwestern Colorado, with occasional Rocky Mountain juniper at high elevations. This is the mix of species throughout western Colorado and eastern Utah.[9] In both sagebrush and pinyon-juniper, a few spring flowers may appear in mid-March, and the spring blooming peak can be over in June. A second wave of green-up and flowering often occurs after the monsoon starts, and some familiar members of the sunflower (Composite) family (e.g.,

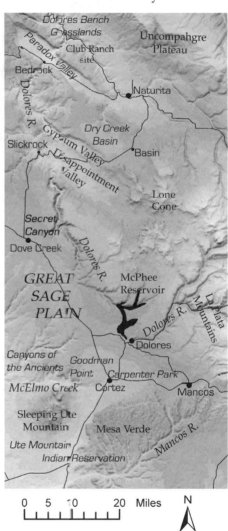

Map 2.1. *Map of desert valleys and canyons covered in this chapter.*

Figure 2.1. *Basin big sagebrush* (Seriphidium tridentatum*) at Goodman Point.*

yellow rabbitbrush) may flower into early fall. During the exceptional drought of 2002, many flowering plants did not come up, or, if they did, they did not flower and much of the landscape remained brown all summer, with the late-season composites done flowering in July.

In this chapter we examine the accounts of explorers and early settlers to decipher how the landscape farmed by the Ancestral Puebloans looked at the time of Euro-American settlement. We look at how the Puebloan landscape is and is not being protected by its new designation as a national monument. We also describe the advent of open-range grazing and how subsequent overgrazing transformed the grasslands, sagebrush, and pinyon-juniper ecosystems of this area. We highlight the challenges of trying to restore these ecosystems, which still provide winter and spring forage to a much reduced livestock industry. The expansion of Euro-American farming and a period of mineral exploration during the uranium boom have also transformed the landscape. Featured in this place are the modern decline of the Gunnison sage-grouse, the beginnings of an effort to restore the sagebrush ecosystem, and the need to find new ways to live on these semiarid lands if their natural diversity is to persist.

Figure 2.2. *Wyoming big sagebrush* (Seriphidium wyomingensis) *in Paradox Valley.*

Figure 2.3. *In Dry Creek Basin a sharp boundary separates shallow, rocky soils supporting little (low) sagebrush* (Seriphidium arbusculum) *or black sagebrush* (Seriphidium novum) *on the left from deeper, less rocky soils supporting Wyoming big sagebrush on the right.*

LEGACY OF PAST HUMAN USES

Early Euro-American Impressions of the Vegetation and Wildlife

Don Juan Maria Antonio de Rivera was the first Euro-American visitor to write an official report of his exploration of the region where Colorado's Ancestral Puebloans had lived. Unfortunately, on his 1765 exploration of what was then a frontier of Spanish New Mexico, he recorded little about the vegetation or wildlife.[10] The Dominguez-Escalante expedition, eleven years later (1776), generally followed Rivera's route and reported "the pasturages continued in great abundance" near the present town of Mancos, followed by a "sagebrush stretch of little pasturage" on the Great Sage Plain between the Mancos and Dolores rivers.[11]

Following the same general route across southwestern Colorado, the Old Spanish Trail became a well-worn trade route connecting Santa Fe and Los Angeles from 1830 to 1850.[12] People traveled this route to trade, not to linger or settle, and by horse rather than wagons, so few traces of the trail remain.[13] Trappers entered the streams of the southern San Juan Mountains in the 1820s and 1830s but were a minor presence, and none is known to have recorded observations.[14]

By the mid-1800s the U.S. government began to send official expeditions, which produced detailed reports. The first in the area was Macomb's 1859 "Exploring Expedition," recorded by J. S. Newberry, quoted in the epigraph at the start of this chapter.[15] During July, when Macomb's expedition followed the Old Spanish Trail across southwestern Colorado, rains were frequent, but forage was still sparse once they left the southern base of the La Plata Mountains: "hence in a northwesterly direction for about one hundred and twenty miles, over gloomy barrens, covered chiefly with *Artemesiae* [sagebrush], but affording scanty pasturage in some of the small valleys."[16]

The Hayden surveys of 1875 and 1876 also reported limited grazing lands in this region, largely because of the lack of water. Henry Gannett described the grazing potential during the 1876 survey: "Mesa Verde, on which there is much good grass, has practically no water on its surface. . . . The Great Sage Plain contains a little grass among the sage and piñon pine, but water is so extremely scarce that this can never be utilized."[17] Similarly, George Chittenden, topographer on the 1875 expedition, wrote of the Montezuma-McElmo region: "[S]uch uncertain and limited and inaccessible [water] supplies amount to very little watering in a country, and leave it really a broken, ragged desert, supporting no animal life but reptiles and only a stunted growth of vegetation."[18] For an 1877 engineering survey, E. H. Ruffner wrote of the area south and west of the Dolores River: "[P]iñon, sage and cacti, soap-plant [yucca] here and there, with tufts of bunch-grass, alone vary the monotony and rescue it from being wholly a barren desert with its burning alkaline soil."[19]

The uplands along the lower Dolores River to the north were similar, according to Gannett:

> The plateaus . . . on the drainages of the San Miguel and Dolores Rivers, contain little land suitable for grazing; sage and piñon pine being the principal productions and water being extremely scarce. Exception to this must be made in favor of the country for 20 miles north and west of the San Juan Mountains. As far from the mountains as the supply of water in little streams extends the grass is good, interspersed with groves of timber. Saucer and Gypsum Valleys contain some gramma grass with sage, and might do for a winter range for stock.[20]

Most of the canyons were dry except for brief periods of runoff. Describing the canyons of the Great Sage Plain feeding into McElmo and Montezuma creeks, William Henry Jackson wrote:

> Their summits and sides are usually clothed with a growth of scrubby piñon and juniper trees, increasing in density and size as we approach the divide on the north, while the valleys below sustain dense masses of sage-brush and greasewood, that, in some places, attain a height of 10 to 12 feet. Vigorous, fresh-looking cottonwoods line the main channels, and are as deceptive to the thirsty traveler as a mirage. One may travel for miles in the parched bed of the wash at their feet . . . and not be able to find a drop of water anywhere in their vicinity.[21]

In contrast to the early explorers, some local history paints an image of a land of bountiful native grass. For example, describing early Montezuma County, based on interviews with early Euro-American settlers, Ira Freeman wrote: "It seems a little strange to think of this whole country as being covered with grass, but it was. There was always a little sage brush in the grass, but the grass was the dominant growth and held the sage brush in check. '[22] Freeman also reported on his interview with early Dolores cowboy George McNefee: "George says he knew every road and trail. . . . At first the grass grew in billowing waves above the stinted sage. Then . . . the sage took over and there was much less grass. The shortgrass in the white sage held its own better than the bluestem, so that there was always considerable winter feed . . . but the rolling land, where the soil was rich and deep, became a sea of purple sage."[23]

The grasses in billowing waves were likely needle and thread, Indian ricegrass, and muttongrass (see Figure 2.4). These cool-season native bunchgrasses were a dominant part of the vegetation west of the Rockies, where bison and other large animals that graze in large herds may never have been abundant[24] (see also Chapter 1). Another of the taller grasses, bluestem, or western wheatgrass (see Box—Rhizomes Versus Bunchgrasses, pp. 116–117), is found on moister soils with abundant clay. The sage is likely a mix of basin (see Figure 2.1) and Wyoming (see Figure 2.2) big sagebrushes, and the white sage is winterfat (see Plate 5a). The short grasses of this region are blue grama and James' galleta (see Plate 6).

How might these contrasting perspectives of early explorers and settlers on the original abundance of sagebrush and grass be reconciled? One explanation is that sagebrush naturally varied from place to place in the abundance of grass, and differing observations may simply reflect this spatial variation. The Mancos Valley upstream of Mesa Verde and the Big Bend region of the Dolores River, now inundated by McPhee Reservoir, stood out to explorers. Ruffner called the Big Bend of the Dolores River "an oasis in the dry desert region surrounding it,"[25] and of the Mancos River he wrote: "The valley of the Mancos is very attractive. To the traveler from the west, after a passage of the deserts, the barren, arid wastes that intervene between running water, it seems doubly so, a sort of garden region, with its groves of lofty spruce and cottonwood and willows bordering the clear and sparkling stream with well-grassed banks."[26]

A second explanation is that early settlers may remember the better years rather than year-to-year variations. Scientific studies document that forage abundance varies dramatically from year to year throughout sagebrush country.[27] Another explanation is that sagebrush was, in places at least, large and dense, obscuring the understory grasses. Referring to the Montezuma Valley west of Mesa Verde in 1877, Ruffner wrote about "its immense sage-brush, almost rendering it impassable."[28] Bunchgrasses may occur beneath tall, dense big sagebrush, even though at a distance the landscape appears dominated by sagebrush. Finally, explorers' views were likely influenced by their memories of moist, productive grasslands in the eastern United States; the sagebrush plain and uplands were probably not as sterile as portrayed by some early easterners.

Bunchgrasses were probably much more abundant in the past in sagebrush and pinyon-juniper woodlands but not as uniformly lush as some local history implies. Perhaps in the good years, when the grass was up, sagebrush country appeared to be covered with grass. In the

Figure 2.4. *Three common cool-season bunchgrasses: (a) needle and thread grass (Hesperostipa comata), (b) Indian ricegrass (Achnatherum hymenoides), and (c) muttongrass (Poa fendleriana).*

drought years the bunchgrasses may not have been so visible. A few small areas, such as Goodman Point and Carpenter Park (described later in this chapter), have escaped livestock grazing for decades. Such places provide more clues about natural communities of the Great Sage Plain.

Open-Range Grazing

Uninspiring reports by early explorers of the Great Sage Plain did not stop cattlemen or settlers looking for new land. The Weenuche and Navajo brought the first livestock into the region.[29] During the 1700s and 1800s the Navajo established large flocks of sheep and goats in their territory south of the San Juan River. By 1833 some Navajo were allowed to use the Weenuche territory north to Sleeping Ute and the La Plata Mountains.[30] While continuing to trade mainly weapons and the fruits of hunting, the Weenuches had their own flocks of sheep and, to a lesser extent, goats.[31] The Utes were the first to herd cattle in the area that became Montezuma County when they agreed to herd shorthorn cattle brought in by two cattlemen in the early 1870s rather than let in the cattlemen themselves.[32]

Euro-American settlement was at first concentrated near mining towns and supply centers, such as Durango, but by the late 1870s large cattle herds were being moved into the plateau and canyon country of the Weenuche, who had been restricted to a narrow strip of land along the New Mexico border.[33] Cattle ranching expanded rapidly in the lower Dolores and San Miguel region after the expulsion of the Tabeguache Utes from their territory in 1881.[34] Settlers moved first to the few oases and rapidly found ways to utilize the more hostile uplands. By the time E. H. Ruffner surveyed the area in 1877, there were twenty-seven ranches in the Mancos Valley, most very small but one with 1,500 head of cattle.[35]

Huge cattle herds soon dominated the region. By 1880 the Mancos and Dolores River valleys were home to at least five "large" herds of cattle.[36] The Great Sage Plain from the Mancos River to Cross Canyon at the Utah line had a herd of 5,000 head as early as 1879, and by 1884 that herd had grown to 12,000.[37] The Southern Utes continued to try to use their former territory for hunting and grazing, and violent encounters between Indians and settlers and squatters continued for over a decade.[38] In 1895 the Weenuche refused to join the Capote and Muache Utes in accepting division of their land into 160-acre private allotments and opening the reservation to homesteading. The separate Ute Mountain Ute Reservation was created for the Weenuche, who continued to hold their land in common and graze sheep and cattle on it.[39]

To the north, the famous Club Ranch (San Miguel Cattle Company) was started on the lower San Miguel River in 1881, with investment money from R. W. Johnson of the famous Johnson and Johnson Surgical Supply Company.[40] Various accounts put their herd at 2,500 to 3,500 cattle after the turn of the twentieth century,[41] though it may have been larger earlier. In 1883 James Galloway brought 1,200 head of cattle into Paradox Valley, and other herds followed.[42] By 1890 nearly 30,000 cattle grazed in the region served by the railroad shipping point at Placerville on the San Miguel River,[43] making Placerville one of the largest cattle shipping points in the world.[44]

Operators large and small used the open range and tended to follow the same routes between summer and winter ranges. Paradox Valley, Dry Creek Basin, and Gypsum Valley were the winter range for herds that summered in the higher country around Lone Cone.[45] Cattle similarly moved between winter ranges in McElmo Canyon, Montezuma Valley, and eastern Utah and summer range in the higher country east and north of Dolores.[46] As more cattlemen moved to the region throughout the 1880s, the range became crowded. This first wave of ranchers depended almost entirely on public land, and as homesteaders claimed the valleys, the large herds could not be sustained.[47]

Senator George E. West described moving his cattle three times in the 1870s and 1880s, first from Mancos Valley to Montezuma Valley, then to Dove Creek, and finally to land leased from the state in Archuleta County.[48] In each case the range became overstocked, and he and other cattlemen moved out. Also, the severe drought years of 1879–1880 led to large losses of cattle and sheep in Colorado.[49] The winters of 1880–1881 and 1885–1886 were severe in Colorado,[50] and the winter of 1889–1890 led to major stock losses throughout the West.[51] As West told it, "In the year 1889 the craze to get out of the cattle business was as great as it had been to get in."[52]

End of Open-Range Grazing

Large cattle speculators in southwestern Colorado lasted less than two decades, but settlers continued to use public-domain lands as open range, and overgrazing soon resumed.[53] Between 1908 and 1914, when cattle markets were weak, large numbers of sheep were brought in to graze the same public lands. The sheep industry flourished in the area for several decades, peaking at about 130,000 head in Montezuma and San Miguel counties in 1929.[54]

In the 1890s the government began withdrawing land that had been open to homesteading, thus establishing reserves of public lands. In the first years of the 1900s these lands came under the jurisdiction of the newly established U.S. Forest Service, which implemented grazing permits and quotas. Livestock numbers remained high, however, especially during World War I, when ranchers increased herds to supply the war.[55] Homesteading increased on the Great Sage Plain in the 1920s,[56] decreasing the open winter range available to cattlemen. Nonreserved public lands continued as open range until the Taylor Act of 1934 established grazing committees that later were the basis for the Bureau of Land Management.[57]

David Lavender, who died in 2003 at age ninety-three, recounted his time on the Club Ranch when his father-in-law owned it in the 1920s and 1930s. In *One Man's West*, Lavender paints a vivid picture of the overgrazing of Paradox Valley (see Map 2.1),[58] an important winter range for the Club Ranch and other herds. Paul Camel, who worked for Lavender until the ranch was sold to a uranium company, estimated that Lavender wintered 1,000 head in Paradox Valley on land leased from the Galloway ranch.[59]

Lavender described the shortage of feed he faced each year in Paradox and the impacts on the winter range: "The dreary month of April rolled around. . . . In April there was no hay. Last summer's crop had been devoured. . . . Cattle bawled hungrily on the feed lots."[60] During these lean months they shipped in "cotton cake" (pressed cottonseed) to sustain the cows, but it was not enough:

> For bulk the animals had to eat brush. Up on the ditchbank we
> could see willow stubs, as big around as our thumbs, which they
> had gnawed like beavers, trying to fill the hollow places in their
> stomachs. It hadn't been enough for some of them. A couple of dead
> ones lay near by. . . . [N]othing remained but inedible saltbush, shiny
> green greasewood, drab sage, and spreading acres of canaigre
> [tanner's dock, or wild rhubarb, *Rumex hymenosepalus*], a low, broad-
> leafed, obscene-looking plant. . . . [W]hen snow softened their
> spines, tumbleweed served as a fodder of sorts and kept many a cow
> from starving.[61]

The cycle of heavy grazing from fall through spring was not limited to Paradox Valley but occurred on low-elevation lands throughout the region. Robert Bement, who worked for the Soil Conservation Service in Dolores, Dove Creek, and Mancos, remembers the sagebrush ranges of his childhood near Bayfield in the 1930s and later in the Mancos–Dove Creek area of the late 1940s as "in terrible shape," with "only sagebrush, cheatgrass brome [cheatgrass], and lupine."[62]

Each rancher may well have known the range was deteriorating, but there was little point in reducing his or her use since other ranchers would simply increase theirs. The profit from overuse goes to the overuser while the cost of overuse is shared by the whole group of users, a case of "The Tragedy of the Commons," outlined in a famous essay by Garrett Hardin.[63] When natural resources are fully open and accessible, Hardin argued, they tend to be overused. In some places local groups of users together have created common-property management schemes that protect the resource.[64] But in the open-range days people had barely settled into towns, life was difficult, and a frontier mentality toward natural resources prevailed, as did competition for grass. Norwood author Howard Greager stated it simply: "[T]hey just didn't figure it out early enough."[65]

Return of Agriculture to the Great Sage Plain

All sagebrush land is not alike, so although large areas were impacted primarily by grazing, better land was converted to crop agriculture. Big sagebrush is an indicator of deep, fertile soils, and early entrepreneurs strove to bring water to the same big sagebrush areas the Ancestral Puebloans had once farmed in present-day Montezuma and Dolores counties. Although the area's economy was built primarily on mining and timber,[66] agriculture also developed early.

The first ditch from the Dolores River reached the Great Sage Plain in 1889, but settlement was initially limited because the region had poor transportation to markets.[67] As the railroad arrived, irrigation and homesteading expanded, and around 1920 the population began to increase.[68] By 1959 over 50,000 acres were irrigated in Montezuma County.[69] Between 1911 and 1960 much of the Great Sage Plain not reached by irrigation was cleared for dryland farming.[70] Wheat and dry beans were the major nonhay crops, with corn on relatively little land.[71] Today, very little natural vegetation remains on the Great Sage Plain, and sagebrush in particular has been replaced by croplands (see Plate 7).

By the 1950s farmers envisioned a large dam project to ensure a more dependable supply of water.[72] After surviving President Carter's "hit list" of un-economic dam projects, the Dolores Water Project (McPhee Dam) was built in the early 1980s, with the first water used in 1987.[73] This project also provided water to the Ute Mountain Ute Tribe, including irrigation water to develop farm and ranch enterprises under the 1988 Colorado Ute Water Rights Settlement Act.[74]

Although irrigated agriculture expanded toward Dove Creek and more land was cleared after the Dolores Project was completed, harvested cropland has actually decreased since 1978 in Montezuma and Dolores counties.[75] Agriculture has also become less diverse. Hay crops, mostly alfalfa, have always constituted the largest portion of cropland in Montezuma County, and hay crops grew in importance while the number of acres in dry beans and wheat declined sharply from 1982 to 1997.[76] In 1997 hay accounted for 74 percent of harvested cropland in Montezuma County.[77] Some of this hay supports the county's 30,000 cows and calves and 2,000 horses,[78] but approximately 80 percent is sold outside the county to dairies, horse stables, and Native American reservations in the Southwest.[79]

The Radium, Vanadium, and Uranium Booms

While agriculture was expanding in Montezuma and Dolores counties, the northern region of the plateau and canyon country was experiencing cycles of boom-and-bust mining. Soon after the boom of open-range grazing ended, a new resource was discovered in the early 1900s, and waves of unrestrained extraction began. The new resource was carnotite, a uranium- and vanadium-bearing rock found along the Uravan mineral belt, extending in an arc from Gateway to just south of Slickrock (see Map 2.2). Thousands of prospectors once combed the now empty-seeming landscape of the Colorado Plateau, setting up mining camps of tents, trailers, and tar-paper shacks.[80] In southwestern Colorado hundreds of miles of roads were bulldozed into remote country in the area from the Uncompahgre Plateau almost to Dove Creek to encourage prospecting.[81] Slickrock and Paradox Valley each had mills to process the ore. The last mill at Uravan closed in 1984. The history of uranium mining is discussed in more detail in Chapter 7.

Uranium is not exhausted in the area, however. Writing in 1981 before the Uravan mill closed, geologist William Chenoweth described the area's potential: "The known reserves and the favorable geology for undiscovered potential resources are expected to result in the Uravan area being a source of uranium and vanadium ore for many years to come."[82] With recent U.S. energy policy again promoting nuclear energy, uranium doubled in price from 2003 to 2004, and uranium companies have renewed mining in the Uravan mineral belt.[83]

WHAT IS HAPPENING NOW?

One could view the human presence in far southwestern Colorado today as similar to that of the Ancestral Puebloans. Cultivation of the Great Sage Plain and valleys to the south of the Dolores River, if financially uncertain in today's commodity markets, is extensive and unlikely to disappear. The agriculture is very different, of course. Irrigated

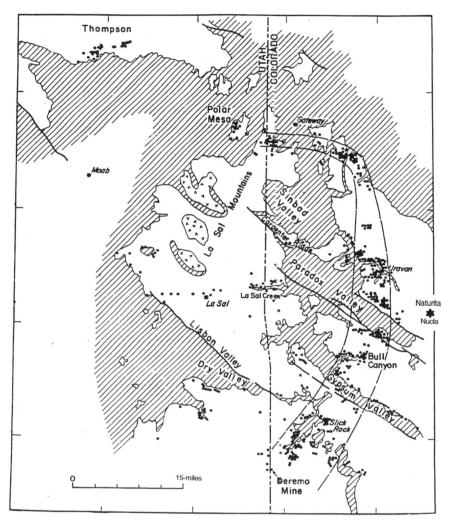

Map 2.2. *Location of uranium-vanadium deposits in the Morrison Formation in south-western Colorado and southeastern Utah. Reprinted from Chenoweth (1981), p. 165. Courtesy, New Mexico Geological Society, Socorro.*

hay and alfalfa for feeding cattle and horses, rather than food crops for people, now dominate the landscape. Fields are larger, farming house-holds fewer, and populations clustered in larger towns than existed even at the height of the Puebloan period. But the same general area is the hub of agricultural activity.

The dry valleys and mesas from north of Dove Creek to the San Miguel River, after an initial homesteading burst, once again support only small pockets of crop agriculture. This part of the region has very few residents, and they use public and private lands primarily for live-stock production. A few years ago it appeared that the roads and scars of uranium mining would continue to slowly disappear, but they are being reopened and expanded in a new burst of exploration and ex-traction, mostly for oil and natural gas (see Box—Coal-bed Methane and Natural Gas, pp. 90–92). The ranching community remains depen-dent on the now-depleted winter range. The newest use of land, rural subdivision, reaches even into this harsh region, and recreational pres-sures are growing.

Pressures on the natural world have not slackened, only shifted, but this time there is more resistance to unrestrained exploitation. More people are visiting and living in the region for its amenities—spectacu-lar vistas, remote country for recreation, archaeological resources, and quiet, natural places. Many people are working to protect and restore the cultural and natural values of this place.

Canyons of the Ancients National Monument

In June 2000 President Clinton proclaimed 164,000 acres of Bureau of Land Management (BLM) land in western Montezuma County as the Canyons of the Ancients National Monument (see Map 2.3).[84] The area contains the highest density of archaeological sites in the nation—at least 20,000 known sites, mostly Ancestral Puebloan (Anasazi).[85] The business community mostly quietly favored formal recognition of this area to boost visitation, but an anti-monument group vocally resisted. The Clinton administration began discussing greater protection for the area, and Senator Ben Nighthorse Campbell proposed a National Con-servation Area to stem the monument designation. Campbell's effort was halted by the anti-monument group, which wanted no special des-ignation at all, so the Clinton administration created a national monu-ment. The Mountain States Legal Foundation challenged the monument designation in federal court but lost.[86]

Management of the land within the monument was not strongly changed by its new designation. Grazing continued under general BLM guidelines.[87] The proclamation creating the monument, however, pre-vents gravel pits, removal of landscaping rock, and hard-rock mining (including uranium). An eleven-member citizen advisory committee—representing local governments, grazing interests, mining, cultural re-sources, the Ute Mountain Ute Tribe, the Santa Clara Pueblo, and the public at large—was appointed in 2003 to help BLM develop the monu-ment plan. The committee made recommendations on guidelines for

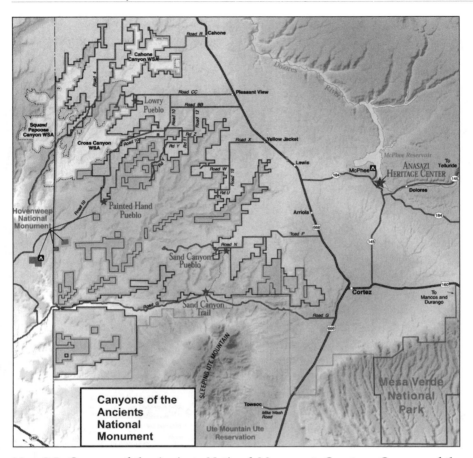

Map 2.3. *Canyons of the Ancients National Monument. Courtesy, Canyons of the Ancients National Monument, Cortez, Colorado.*

balancing resource use (from energy development to recreation) with cultural and natural resource protection.

The balancing act is tough. The monument includes McElmo Dome, which contains the largest developed natural carbon dioxide deposit in the world.[88] Carbon dioxide fizzes soft drinks and is used in dry ice, but most of the McElmo Dome carbon dioxide is pumped up from 8,000 feet below the surface and travels in a pipeline 500 miles to near Lubbock in western Texas, where it is used to enhance pumping from depleted oil wells. In 2002 there were forty-four carbon dioxide wells in five groups on the monument.[89] Eighty-five percent of the monument was already leased for oil and gas when the monument was created, but the monument is closed to further leasing, except in special cases.[90]

In 2002 a proposed major seismic project to map oil reserves, some of which are outside the area already leased, was challenged by local environmental groups. A settlement kept seismic work away from archaeological sites and minimized impacts to other resources,[91] but seven oil wells were proposed as a result of the survey. With the current national emphasis on oil and gas, more exploration and development are expected.[92]

Perhaps the biggest impact of the monument designation will be increased public interest in the area and its resources. Greater public scrutiny of how the land is managed could lead to improved practices in grazing and oil and gas development. On the other hand, increased visitation is placing pressure on resources. User-created bike, horse, and foot trails have already proliferated in popular lower Sand and Rock Creek canyons. Because these are unplanned trails, they may be crossing sensitive vegetation and cultural resources.[93] The Advisory Committee has recommended increasing the number of access points to the monument to disperse people.[94] One problem with increased access is the increased potential for vandalism and looting of cultural sites, which likely has already occurred. Such pressure requires increased law enforcement and criminal investigation, but so far BLM has not received funding to meet this need.[95]

The monument's goal is to protect the resources from both intentional and unintentional damage without excessive signs and facilities that would alter the area's remote and undeveloped character.[96] The monument offers visitors a sense of mystery and discovery not available in national parks such as Mesa Verde. Still, monument staff must reach and educate many new visitors about user impacts and the illegality and damage of collecting artifacts or otherwise altering sites. The Anasazi Heritage Center near Dolores is the entryway to Canyons of the Ancients, where essential information about the monument is provided.

Challenges of Grazing Semiarid Lands of the Colorado Plateau

That the natural communities of the Colorado Plateau were degraded by cattle and sheep is generally agreed.[97] Virginia Simmons, describing the Ute perspective, says that many plants the Southern Utes needed for food, medicine, baskets, and tools were depleted by early livestock grazing.[98] Effects of livestock grazing vary with season of use, intensity, length and repetition of grazing, and the characteristics of the pre-grazing community; but preferred forage species have declined relative to less palatable plants across much of the West (see Box—

Increasers and Decreasers, pp. 205–206).[9c] Canyons and mesas of the Colorado Plateau are winter range, grazed heavily year after year during the critical spring growing season. An understanding of changes in plant communities brought about by livestock grazing is essential for effective restoration efforts. Changes in communities can be deciphered from historical accounts, experiments, relicts (see Box—Remnants and Relicts, pp. 183–184), and long-term observations.[100]

Paradox lost? Cheatgrass invasion of Paradox Valley. Early photographs that illustrate the landscape in the late 1800s to early 1900s can be especially helpful in understanding vegetation change. Museums in small towns often have photographs of landscapes among the usual pictures of notable residents and horses and buggies along Main Street. At the Rimrocker Historical Society's museum in Naturita we found a photograph from 1897 looking west down Paradox Valley (see Figure 2.5). It was exciting to relocate the original photo point.

The vegetation of Paradox Valley has been highly altered over the last 100 years. The small shrub in the 1897 photograph is likely winterfat (see Plate 5a), and the grasses are probably blue grama and James' galleta (see Plate 6). These species are now present in only small amounts in the grassland in this area. Historical accounts support this interpretation of the natural vegetation here. L. G Denison and L. A. York, describing the winter range for early cattle herds in their book *Telluride: Tales of Two Early Pioneers,* say, "The nutritious grasses are the gramma and white sage."[101] White sage is a common name for winterfat, a shrub known to be desirable to livestock and susceptible to overgrazing.[102] The 1897 photograph shows a range still dominated by native plants but heavily utilized by livestock.

In 1999 the view was dominated by cheatgrass, a non-native annual grass that began transforming western grasslands and shrublands in the first half of the twentieth century. Cheatgrass now dominates most of the flats from the east end of Paradox Valley to near the Dolores River. Sagebrush, a few annuals, and an occasional native perennial grass occur in the cheatgrass. On the low rounded hills in the upper left quarter of our 1999 picture, broom snakeweed (see Plate 5b), a small, poisonous native shrub that increases under grazing,[103] is dominant. When we visited Paradox Valley during the exceptionally dry year of 2002, cheatgrass was barely visible at this site, but native species were also sparse. Cheatgrass is known to fluctuate dramatically in abundance and is especially common during wetter years—its seeds lie dormant in the soil waiting for the next rains (see Box—Cheatgrass, pp. 61–63).

Figure 2.5. *A view of eastern Paradox Valley looking west toward the La Sal Mountains, Utah, in (a)* A.D. *1897 and (b)* A.D. *1999. (a) Courtesy, Rimrocker Historical Museum of Western Montrose County, Naturita, Colorado.*

Cheatgrass began to spread across the West between 1900 and 1930. The excerpts by David Lavender in *One Man's West*, discussed in the "Open-Range Grazing" section, indicate that extreme overgrazing in Paradox Valley continued at least until the 1930s when Lavender was ranching. Overgrazing disturbed the soil and weakened native plants, creating ideal conditions for the invasion and spread of cheatgrass.

Howard Greager, a local rancher and author of *The Hell That Was Paradox*, remembered the old-timers in his youth talking of tall grasses here. Greager told us that according to the elders, "Originally in East Paradox, you couldn't see a horse laying down. It was that way everywhere. You could graze the desert all year long."[104] Greager said the grass was western wheatgrass (see Box—Rhizomes Versus Bunchgrasses, pp. 116–117), but when he himself first visited the Paradox Valley in 1936, cheatgrass was already common. As early as 1897, the photo suggests it would have been impossible to hide "a horse lying down" in the grass.

Years of overgrazing resulted in the loss of an abundant forage base and the natural ecosystem in Paradox Valley. Almost certainly lost along with the western wheatgrass were the other cool-season grasses typical of the Colorado Plateau (Indian ricegrass, needle and thread, muttongrass; see Figure 2.4). Even the warm-season grasses (blue grama and James' galleta; see Plate 6), which initiate growth later in the summer

BOX—CHEATGRASS

Today the honey-colored hills that flank the northwestern mountains derive their hue not from the rich and useful bunchgrass and wheatgrass which once covered them, but from the inferior cheat which has replaced these native grasses. The motorist who exclaims about the flowing contours that lead his eye upward to far summits is unaware of this substitution. It does not occur to him that hills, too, cover ruined complexions with ecological face powder.

—Aldo Leopold, *A Sand County Almanac*[1]

A walk through dried cheatgrass (see box figure) in early summer will fill one's socks, as the prickly awns of cheatgrass seeds engage any clothing as a dispersal agent. Cheat, aptly named, is one of the worst invasive plants of the West, eventually dominating most overgrazed land or abandoned cropland at lower elevations but also entering natural, undisturbed vegetation.[3] Once established, cheatgrass can outcompete native plants as well as increase fires and soil erosion.[4] A winter annual that greens up and dries early, it depletes spring soil moisture, leaving native perennials susceptible to drought. After abandonment, croplands in Idaho stayed cheatgrass-dominated for decades, but after fifty years a native grass dominated some areas protected from livestock use, offering hope.[5] However, with more than 25 million acres of the Great Basin in Nevada and Utah dominated by cheatgrass, the problem is daunting.[6]

Cheatgrass was first documented in the West in southern British Columbia in 1889 and was found in the foothills of the Rockies in eastern Colorado by 1897.[7] Scientists using genetic markers have evidence of a half dozen separate introductions into the West from different sources in Europe and Asia linked to people immigrating from those areas,[8] the grass perhaps arriving in grain shipments or with imported sheep.[9] Cheatgrass rarely dominates grasslands in its native range—perhaps it is held in check by natural insects and diseases or nutrient limitations.[10]

After introduction, cheatgrass expanded between about 1900 and 1915,[11] spreading primarily along railroad lines.[12] Cheatgrass became a contaminant of winter wheat fields, which expanded after 1915. Winter wheat is planted in fall, also a perfect planting time for cheatgrass.[13] Cheat germinates, then overwinters as a seedling, before growing and flowering in spring.[14] By about 1930, cheatgrass had expanded from initial introduction sites to cover much of its present range in the West.[15] As Aldo Leopold observed, "[T]he spread was so rapid as to escape recording; one simply woke up one fine spring to find the range dominated by a new weed."[16]

The most frightening trait of cheatgrass in the western United States is its tendency to produce abundant fine, dry fuel that leads to immense fires (1.7 million acres mostly in northern Nevada in 1999)[17] that then encourage more cheatgrass, which leads to more fires.[18] This vicious cheatgrass-fire cycle perpetuates and allows the expansion of cheatgrass and the destruction of sagebrush and other ecosystems in the West. W. D. Billings sounded the alarm in 1990 when he said, "[M]ore apparent is the threat [of cheatgrass] to large, integrated, and operational ecosystems that could disappear once and for all. This is true for the sagebrush biome and has now become

Cheatgrass, or downy brome (Anisantha tectorum).

common in the pinyon-juniper zone at higher elevations," adding that
"a number of native plant and animal species are at risk of being
eliminated locally and even regionally."[19] The BLM's report, *The Great
Basin: Healing the Land*, contains this epitaph: "[A] large part of the Great
Basin lies on the brink of ecological collapse."[20]

Emergency efforts are under way.[21] Most promising in the short term
is "greenstripping" cheatgrass expanses with plants that stay green all
summer, allowing fires to be contained.[22] In the long term, cheatgrass
must be reduced to allow reestablishment of native plants, yet a method
to achieve this has not yet appeared. Fortunately, in much of southwestern Colorado only a few areas have unbroken expanses of cheatgrass
vulnerable to these large fires, but further expansion of cheatgrass
remains a major threat. Cheatgrass is a terrible symptom of a failure to
establish a land ethic,[23] but the massive efforts under way to restore
cheatgrass-damaged landscapes indicate society's willingness to work
out the details of such an ethic.

NOTES

1. Leopold, *A Sand County Almanac*, 165.
2. Hull and Pechanec, "Cheatgrass—a Challenge."
3. Svejcar and Tausch, "Anaho Island, Nevada"; Belnap and Phillips, "Soil Biota in Ungrazed Grassland."
4. Young and Allen, "Cheatgrass and Range Science."
5. Hironaka and Tisdale, "Secondary Succession in Annual Vegetation."
6. U.S. Department of the Interior, Bureau of Land Management, *Great Basin: Healing the Land*.
7. Mack, "Invasion of *Bromus tectorum*."
8. Novak and Mack, "Tracing Plant Introduction and Spread."
9. Kostivkovsky and Young, "Invasive Exotic Rangeland Weeds."
10. Ibid.
11. Mack, "Invasion of *Bromus tectorum*."
12. Ibid.
13. Ibid.
14. Klemmedson and Smith, "Cheatgrass (*Bromus tectorum* L.)."
15. Mack, "Invasion of *Bromus tectorum*."
16. Leopold, *Sand County Almanac*, 165.
17. U.S. Department of the Interior, Bureau of Land Management, *Great Basin: Healing the Land*.
18. Billings, "*Bromus tectorum*, a Biotic Cause of Ecosystem Impoverishment"; Whisenant, "Changing Fire Frequencies."
19. Billings, "*Bromus tectorum*, a Biotic Cause of Ecosystem Impoverishment," 320.
20. U.S. Department of the Interior, Bureau of Land Management, *Great Basin: Healing the Land*, 1.
21. U.S. Department of the Interior, Bureau of Land Management, *Great Basin: Healing the Land*.
22. Harrison et al., "Forage Kochia Helps Fight Range Fires."
23. Leopold, *Sand County Almanac*.

and also are more grazing-resistant, have been largely replaced by cheatgrass in Paradox Valley.

A large portion of East Paradox is owned and managed by BLM, an agency that has struggled for more than sixty years with the legacy of cheatgrass. The area has been managed as a "common allotment," at times having as many as twenty-three operators. An original range survey was done in 1944, then updated in 1958 when a 56 percent reduction in livestock use and elimination of spring grazing were recommended. In 1966 these recommendations were implemented. Then, after a court decision in 1976, livestock grazing was restricted to about 700 cows on 10,000 acres of valley land for two winter months, January and February.[105] In 1995 an assessment of changes in Paradox Valley since 1975 was completed by Amanda Clements, BLM ecologist in Montrose. She concluded that "twenty years later, conditions appear to have worsened in terms of soil protection, biodiversity, forage production, and plant community stability." Interestingly, the change to winter grazing in 1976 is now viewed as insufficient: "While winter grazing has been regarded as the least vulnerable time to graze, Paradox Valley may present an exception to that rule. This area is low and warm enough that greenup often seems to start around February."[106]

Dean Stindt, BLM range conservationist in Norwood, tried using grazing to eradicate cheatgrass in East Paradox for four to five years in the late 1990s but gave up on that approach, as it was difficult to manage cattle effectively or to be successful with planting perennial grasses.[107] Land managers are uncertain about how to proceed. There are worries about wind erosion if the area is plowed, about unintended impacts if herbicide is used to kill the cheatgrass, and about the problem of limited success with establishing native perennials in the wake of cheatgrass removal.

Paradox Valley illustrates how complete the transformation of the vegetation can be under the influence of livestock grazing when an aggressive non-native plant is present. Unfortunately, this transformation to cheatgrass is expanding in the lower elevations of southwestern Colorado. Cheatgrass may be one of the most serious current threats to the integrity of these ecosystems.

Dolores bench grasslands. Fortunately, not all grasslands of the Colorado Plateau region of southwestern Colorado have been transformed as completely as those at East Paradox. State Highway 141 downstream from Uravan runs across the lower benches of the Dolores River Canyon. Although this area was also part of the Club Ranch winter range, here the grasslands retain a large component of native grasses. How-

Figure 2.6. *Geologic strata of southwest-*
ern Colorado's canyon country based on
Chronic and Williams (2002).

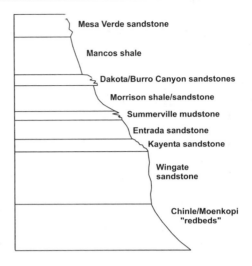

Mesa Verde sandstone

Mancos shale

Dakota/Burro Canyon sandstones

Morrison shale/sandstone

Summerville mudstone

Entrada sandstone

Kayenta sandstone

Wingate
sandstone

Chinle/Moenkopi
"redbeds"

ever, these grasslands remain
under threat from livestock
grazing. Despite frequent claims
to the contrary, livestock management in this region has not
changed sufficiently from the
practices that created the degraded natural communities that
now typify the Colorado Plateau.
The landscape of the Dolores
River Canyon and uplands is
shaped by the arrangement of the major geologic strata (see Figure
2.6). Some strata (e.g., Wingate) typically form cliffs or slopes, while
others (e.g., Dakota) form benches or mesa tops. The bench at the top
of the Kayenta sandstone, below the white and red, smooth, sloping
Entrada sandstone, has scattered patches of grassland, although many
benches are also covered by pinyon-juniper woodland (see Plate 8).
Grassland patches are likely on places with deeper soils, while woodlands are found on somewhat rockier sites. Grass can often outcompete
trees where soils are finer in texture.

The grassland community on these benches appears throughout
the Colorado Plateau in southwestern Colorado and southeastern Utah
in isolated patches on mesa tops, benches, and other flat settings,[108]
although the composition varies somewhat from place to place. The
natural composition of these grasslands can be reconstructed based on
"relicts" that have likely never been grazed by domestic livestock (see
Box—Remnants and Relicts, pp. 183–184). Some relict grasslands were
found in the early 1980s on isolated mesas and benches above the
Dolores River in the canyons south of Bedrock. BLM staffer Jim Ratzloff
reached these sites by helicopter. On these ungrazed relicts, the bulk
of the vegetation is usually two or more of the three major cool-season
bunchgrasses, typically needle and thread and Indian ricegrass (see
Figure 2.4a, b). Blue grama and James' galleta (see Plate 6), along with
a medley of forbs, are also present (see Table 2.1). Cheatgrass has
reached some of these relicts but is a minor component.

On the grassland benches of the lower Dolores River Canyon, three
of the native cool-season grasses are still common; but often during

Table 2.1. Common plants of the Dolores bench grasslands compared with two relict sites along the Dolores River.[1] Abbreviations: D = dominant, X = present but not dominant.

	Bench Grassland	Relict 1	Relict 2
SHRUBS			
Broom snakeweed (*Gutierrezia sarothrae*)	D	—	—
Fourwing saltbush (*Atriplex canescens*)	X	X	—
Winterfat (*Krascheninnikovia lanata*)	—	X	X
Wyoming big sagebrush (not in Weber and Wittmann 2001)	X	—	
GRASSES			
Blue grama (*Chondrosum gracile*)	X	X	X
Fendler's threeawn (*Artistida purpurea*)	X	—	—
Indian ricegrass (*Achnatherum hymenoides*)	X	—	D
James' galleta (*Hilaria jamesii*)	D	D	D
Needle and thread (*Hesperostipa comata*)	D	D	D
New Mexico feathergrass (*Hesperostipa neomexicana*)	D	—	—
Sand dropseed (*Sporobolus cryptandrus*)	D	—	—
Squirreltail (*Elymus elymoides*)	—	X	X
FORBS			
Fineleaf hymenopappus (*Hymenopappus filifolius* var. *cinereus*)	X	X	—
Plains pricklypear (*Opuntia polyacantha*)	X	X	—
Rose heath (*Chaetopappa ericoides*)	X	—	—
Rosy gilia (*Gilia sinuata*)	—	X	—
Scarlet globemallow (*Sphaeralcea coccinea*)	X	—	X
Tulip pricklypear (*Opuntia phaeacantha*)	X	—	—
Whipple's fishhook cactus (*Sclerocactus whipplei*)	X	X	—
Woolly plantain (*Plantago patagonica*)	D	X	—
NON-NATIVES			
Annual wheatgrass (*Eremopyrum triticeum*)	X	—	—
Cheatgrass (*Anisantha tectorum*)	D	X	—
Common pepperweed (*Lepidium densiflorum*)	D	—	—
Redstem stork's bill (*Erodium cicutarium*)	D	—	—

1. Common names are from the PLANTS online database, http://plants.usda.gov. Latin names are from Weber and Wittmann, *Colorado Flora*.

spring, when the needle and thread and Indian ricegrass should be two feet high and in seed, only short mounds of grass remain (see Plate 9). Repeated spring grazing has resulted in weakened grass plants that are often just little circular rings of grass, missing a live center (see Figure 2.7). Cool-season grasses and forbs grow in the spring using stored carbohydrates built up during previous growing seasons. Without periods of rest during their growing season, which allow them to rebuild those reserves and set seed, they eventually die. This is why range scientists recommend fall rather than spring grazing in these ecosystems,[109] although fall may be another critical growth period for cool-season grasses.[110]

Figure 2.7. *A native bunchgrass at the Dolores bench grasslands site, illustrating the dead center that can result from overgrazing by livestock.*

The native grasses on the benches would almost certainly recover with better grazing management. A short distance downstream from the confluence with the San Miguel River, a two-track road winds its way down the canyon rim through a sparse pinyon-juniper woodland. These rock ledges once sheltered the cabin of John Christian (see Figure 2.8), a Danish carpenter who worked for the Club Ranch. Christian built his cabin using timbers from the abandoned hanging flume built along the canyon wall in the late 1800s. The area around the cabin was almost certainly heavily grazed by Christian's stock, but today the native cool-season grasses are large and bushy and have some of the dead remains of previous years' growth at their bases. They also have many flowering stems and tend to have live centers, in contrast to bunchgrasses on the bench. While cattle can reach these slopes, they apparently concentrate on the bench tops. The health and dominance of native cool-season grasses on the site of Christian's former homestead suggest that native grasses can recover from overgrazing. The bench top, however, continues to be negatively impacted by current grazing practices. During the extreme drought year of 2002, for example, bench grasslands along this reach of the Dolores River were grazed heavily during spring, leaving virtually no aboveground green plant parts (see Plate 9).

This area is part of the large Mesa Creek BLM allotment, leased by a ranch that operates over the same general area the Club Ranch used. Allotment records show that the problem exists not just on the bench grasslands. In April 2002 a BLM biologist wrote to the range conservationist on this allotment complaining about a nearby riparian area that had been severely overgrazed: "Livestock use in this portion of the creek and the associated terraces is unconscionable. It is an insult to those members of the American public who own these lands."[111]

Figure 2.8. *John Christian cabin at the Dolores bench grasslands site in (a) the early days (date unknown) and (b)* A.D. *2001. (a) Courtesy, Rimrocker Historical Museum of Western Montrose County, Naturita, Colorado.*

In 1993 a Coordinated Resource Management Plan (CRMP), developed between the rancher and BLM with some public involvement, was adopted for the allotment.[112] The allotment is to be managed using Holistic Management principles (see Box—Holistic Management, pp. 6–8). According to the CRMP, allotment management would include allowing plants to fully recover from grazing before regrazing, along with frequent monitoring and biannual planning. Our observations and allotment records suggest that the plan has not been well implemented and that plants continue to be regrazed without adequate recovery. The biannual planning sessions have not been ongoing. Monitoring studies of the Mesa Creek allotment in 1996 and 1997 showed increases in broom snakeweed (see Plate 5b) and declines in perennial grass cover in several pastures.[113] In spite of these findings, the ranch's herd size was recently increased.

The Dolores bench grasslands belie the common claim that degraded plant communities are a legacy of past grazing rather than a result of current management. Unlike Paradox Valley, the degradation of the Dolores bench grasslands is ongoing. Cool-season grasses still dominate large patches 20–50 feet in diameter, and, if managed well, these grasses might someday regain ground. However, the site may lose remaining cool-season grasses if current management practices continue because cheatgrass is common and is ready to replace depleted native species.

Of pinyons, junipers, and grass: Lessons from Sand and Moccasin canyons. Grasslands are the exception rather than the rule on the Colorado Plateau. Much of the winter range of southwestern Colorado is pinyon-juniper woodland or sagebrush. Ranchers and federal land management agencies responded to the loss of desirable forage species in both pinyon-juniper woodland and sagebrush by eradicating trees and shrubs thought to be holding back desired grasses and forbs. In the 1950s control of sagebrush using chemicals (2,4-D) or mechanical means, such as mowing, was popular. A similar technique, chaining, was used in pinyon-juniper woodland (see Chapter 4). These were aggressive programs whose goal was clear—"eradication of sagebrush"[114] and "eradication of pinyon-juniper woodland."[115] Today, the biological value of these woodlands and shrublands is more widely recognized, but hostility toward native trees and shrubs persists.

Very few patches of pinyon-juniper woodland in southwestern Colorado have escaped long-term, ongoing livestock grazing, but some pockets that have escaped suggest that the trees themselves are not the cause of forage scarcity. Sand and Moccasin canyons, both now in Canyons of the Ancients National Monument, provide a telling contrast. Once a thriving Puebloan community center (see Plate 10), upper Sand Canyon appears never to have been heavily grazed by livestock. More likely, based on the remains of a homestead there, it has had a long period of rest. Upper Sand Canyon is part of an active allotment, but it lacks water and is effectively isolated by a steep section 1½ miles from the canyon top, so livestock rarely use it. Nearby Moccasin Canyon remains actively grazed. Sand Canyon shows that native cool-season bunchgrasses and other native plants can flourish beneath pinyons and junipers in the canyon country without livestock grazing. Moccasin Canyon, in contrast, has lost much of its bunchgrass.

In the woodland at the head of Sand Canyon, near the main ruin, the native cool-season bunchgrasses, Indian ricegrass and muttongrass (see Figure 2.4b, c), are abundant among the trees (see Figure 2.9). These two grasses are difficult to distinguish unless they have seed stalks. When they do, ricegrass has an open inflorescence and muttongrass has a narrow seed stalk. The abundance of native bunchgrass in flat pinyon-juniper woodlands is unusual in southwestern Colorado because most flat sites are heavily grazed.

The canyon itself provides enough variation in slope, soils, and aspect to support distinctive plant communities. The south-facing slopes of the upper canyon are dry and boulder-strewn with sandstone rocks and outcrops, but even so, bunchgrass remains prominent, although not as dense as on the flats. Muttongrass is the dominant bunchgrass throughout the canyon's slopes, with only scattered Indian ricegrass and other grasses also present. On the northerly slope are abundant Gambel oak, Utah serviceberry, and other shrubs that are absent or less common on the south-facing slopes. A little farther down the canyon the dry, southeast-facing slopes support abundant muttongrass along with a favorite deer browse, antelope bitterbrush shrubs (see Plate 11).

The muttongrass in upper Sand Canyon is often found in the shade of trees or shrubs, which has meaning for land management. A common idea was that pinyon-juniper woodlands have become denser as a result of livestock grazing, fire suppression, and climatic change.[116] Increased trees were thought to shade and outcompete grass, effectively desertifying the landscape, turning it into a kind of moonscape of woody vegetation and nothing else.[117] Graphs were constructed showing that as trees became thicker, grass declined.[118]

Upper Sand Canyon solidly challenges the relevance of that idea in this area, as not only is there abundant bunchgrass in a mature woodland, but there appears to be more grass under trees than in openings.

Figure 2.9. *Native bunchgrasses (especially muttongrass and Indian ricegrass) beneath trees of the pinyon-juniper woodland near the entrance to upper Sand Canyon.*

Restriction of bunchgrass to the shade of trees seems to increase toward lower, drier elevations along the trail. Not everyone believed trees were desertifying the landscape—some studies found that trees

Figure 2.10. *Near absence of native grasses and forbs in a chained pinyon-juniper woodland near the head of Moccasin Canyon.*

may actually favor grass by offering protective shade,[119] as appears to be the case here. But these voices were drowned out in the rush to chain pinyon-juniper woodlands to increase forage depleted by cattle grazing. Sites such as upper Sand Canyon show how vegetation responds without heavy grazing and are essential to an understanding of these ecosystems.

The head of Moccasin Canyon is a relatively flat area of chained woodland, comparable in setting to the head of Sand Canyon. This chained woodland is heavily grazed by livestock and has little bunchgrass (see Figure 2.10), although some native shrubs remain. Instead of bunchgrasses and a diversity of forbs, the chained site contains large openings with bare ground and crested wheatgrass (see Box—Crested Wheatgrass, pp. 85–86), which was planted after chaining. A nearby pipeline is dominated by green rabbitbrush, a native shrub favored by disturbance.

The slopes of Moccasin Canyon have not been chained, but they lack the abundant muttongrass and antelope bitterbrush that dominate the pinyon-juniper woodland at Sand Canyon. It is not easy to tell when the loss occurred, but it appears to have been some time ago. A few bunchgrasses and antelope bitterbrush can still be found, but not as abundantly as at Sand Canyon. Active and past livestock grazing has created a more open woodland, where grass is sparse and the woodland floor lacks litter. Fortunately, some beautiful plants are resistant to grazing and continue to grace these canyons in the spring (see Plate 12), but the understory is bare relative to that at Sand Canyon. So much of the canyon country is like Moccasin that it is difficult to believe Moccasin might have once been like Sand Canyon. Yet these two canyons are close to each other and are physically very similar, differing mainly in their history of livestock use.

Would it be possible to restore bunchgrass cover and natural diversity to Moccasin Canyon? The more shaded slopes that still have some bunchgrass might recover within a few decades with better livestock management. Sagebrush communities that still contain some native bunchgrasses can recover with a few decades of rest.[120] But the drier, southerly-facing slopes that seem to lack grass might require a longer period to recover or even some reseeding of native plants that have been lost. Upper Sand Canyon might serve as a model for restoration.

Once restored, could cattle grazing continue without again decreasing the diversity and abundance of grasses and forbs? That might be possible, but we know of no example at the present time where native bunchgrasses and other native plants have been sustained in this kind of canyon environment under present methods and intensities of livestock grazing. Even upper Sand Canyon, with its intact bunchgrass understory and diversity of native plants, offers little annual forage production, and it is prone to very reduced forage during severe droughts. During the drought of 2002, muttongrass grew little and was dried by mid-May. Yet cattle were not taken off grazing allotments, such as Moccasin, until late May, allowing cool-season plants no chance to recover after grazing that year. Many other plants did not come up or withered without flowering. Forage production was a small fraction of that in a moist year.

The blame for the poor condition of semiarid rangelands in the West cannot be placed on drought but on failing to learn to live with it. A major problem here and throughout the Colorado Plateau is that the livestock industry depends too heavily on arid, low-elevation sites for winter and spring forage. A large percentage of grasses and forbs of these communities grows and blooms in the spring, when winter moisture is still available—the characteristic that makes winter range so valuable to ranchers. By spring a typical ranch operation has run out of hay and needs to get livestock off the hayfields to begin irrigating. So the cool-season grasses and forbs of low-elevation grasslands, sagebrush, and pinyon-juniper woodlands have been, and commonly continue to be, grazed every year during their peak growing season.

It has been difficult to manage livestock grazing in a way that supports both ranches and native plant and animal communities across the intermountain West.[121] Economically viable ranches that maintain native, semiarid ecosystems might be possible, but they will require a new culture of innovation and respect for this difficult environment and its natural communities (see Box—Twenty-first-Century Grazing, pp. 74–75). Ranches and public grazing allotments will need more acreage per cow so that pastures can be rested regularly, particularly in the spring. Herd sizes will need to be adjusted more quickly in response to drought years.[122] Innovative approaches, such as grass banks (areas reserved for grazing only in dry years), can help maintain a base herd through a drought but will likely require leaving some allotments "open"—that is, not leased.

The needed changes, if livestock grazing is to be a productive part of a restored West, are probably nothing short of revolutionary. Society at large will benefit most from the changes, but the burden of change

BOX—TWENTY-FIRST-CENTURY GRAZING

Some "new environmentalists" are staking out what they call a "radical center" that makes room for public-land grazing while promoting good land stewardship (e.g., *Ranching West of the 100th Meridian*).[1] This is an important goal, but this radical center may have underestimated the challenges of grazing arid western rangelands in ways that maintain their natural integrity. The costs to the West's natural communities from

past and current livestock grazing are well documented in the allotment files of any agency office and are clear to those with some ecological knowledge who visit public rangelands today. These costs and the subsidies upon which the ranching industry has depended are also described by Deb Donahue in *The Western Range Revisited*.[2] The needed changes will not come about by declaring a radical center that celebrates present western ranching as sustainable.[3]

A substantive revolution based around a new relationship among ecology, economy, and society is required. A key part of that revolution must come from within the ranching community itself. Western ranching culture has always been centered on animals—horses, cows, or sheep. But innovative approaches to ranching are shifting the focus

Jim, Savanna, and Daniela Howell on their ranch east of Montrose, Colorado.

toward plant communities and the ecology of the natural ecosystems upon which ranching depends.

Jim and Daniela Howell (see box figure), who live east of Montrose, Colorado, are among those leaders who have made the shift. When talking about ranching with the Howells, the topic is likely to be plants. While walking their land, Jim is looking at the spacing of plants, learning their names, and wondering if he has left enough plant litter to protect the soil. As practitioners and teachers of Holistic Management (see Box—Holistic Management, pp. 6–8), the Howells manage plant communities on their ranch to meet multiple goals, such as raising beef cattle for profit, providing wildlife habitat for its own sake and for their outfitting business, producing clean water and a diverse biotic community that includes predators, and restoring the productivity of the land. Each year Jim and Daniela lay out a detailed grazing plan and regularly measure to see if their land and plants are responding over time as they expected, and they adjust accordingly.

Most important is the Howells' view that managing the land is a constant learning process. The Howells recognize natural ecosystems as complex and dynamic systems that exist at timescales that require several human generations to appreciate. Jim points out that livestock grazing in the West is only a little over 100 years old, and ranchers have yet to adapt to the special challenges of grazing low-productivity arid ecosystems, where plants sometimes require more than a year to recover after grazing.[4] As Jim has written, "When dealing with the land, we always have to assume our decisions are wrong, and then monitor for the first signs that we're veering off-track."[5] Such openness to learning is key to restoration of arid, degraded landscapes under livestock grazing.

Another part of the revolution will involve forging a common vision of healthy rangelands through sincere discussions and learning about natural communities and the role of herbivores within them. Ranchers' and naturalists' visions of healthy plants and ecosystems can be quite different (see Box—Holistic Management, pp. 6–8). To begin to resolve these differences and achieve twenty-first-century landscapes that are truly restored, an atmosphere is needed in which all ideas can be brought forward and assessed in light of evidence. Until a common vision arises, it should be expected at least that grazing on public lands will be monitored and adjusted based on a broad suite of ecologically based indicators of land health, including native biodiversity.

NOTES

1. Knight, Gilgert, and Marston, eds., *Ranching West of the 100th Meridian*.
2. Donahue, *Western Range Revisited*.
3. Knight, Gilgert, and Marston, eds., *Ranching West of the 100th Meridian*, xiii.
4. Howell, "Grazing in Nature's Image—Part 2."
5. Howell, "Measuring the Desert," 14.

would fall on ranchers. If people want more than livestock production from these lands on which ranching families have built their homes and communities, society will likely need to help ranchers financially to make the shift. Cattle managed in a way that would sustain the full diversity of the natural world would go a long way toward ending "range wars" in the West. A knowledgeable and engaged public could provide the impetus and support for change.

Restoring Sagebrush Ecosystems and the Gunnison Sage-Grouse

Like the pinyon-juniper woodlands, the sagebrush communities that characterize the lower elevations of the West have been slow in gaining appreciation. In the past, sagebrush was seen as undesirable, and there was little concern as sagebrush communities were widely altered and replaced throughout the West.[123] Even some scientists have been influenced by the negative perception of sagebrush. As recently as 1988, weed scientists approached sagebrush as a weed problem: "Of over 47 million ha of rangeland in Wyoming, 20.9 million ha are *infested* with big sagebrush. In 11 western states, *Artemisia* species *infest* 122 million ha"[124] (emphasis added). This perception was supported by studies of areas where livestock grazing had weakened and removed bunchgrasses, facilitating invasion of some grasslands by sagebrush,[125] and observations that livestock grazing commonly decreased native bunchgrasses inside sagebrush communities.[126] However, while grasslands have been invaded by sagebrush in some areas, historical research suggests that much of the intermountain West was dominated by sagebrush before Euro-American settlement.[127]

Early management was focused on eradicating sagebrush to increase grass for livestock.[128] Thousands of acres of sagebrush were sprayed with 2,4-D before research began showing the adverse effects of this chemical on native forbs and other shrubs.[129] The development and expanded use of new chemicals, such as Tebuthiuron (Spike), in the 1970s and 1980s[130] did not necessarily change management goals but simply led managers to use a more selective chemical. After sagebrush had been killed, the land was often planted with a single species of non-native grass, crested wheatgrass (see Box—Crested Wheatgrass, pp. 85–86), greatly reducing the natural diversity.[131] Sadly, crested wheatgrass may be able to persist indefinitely.[132]

Sagebrush remnants: Goodman Point and Carpenter Park. Two small areas of sagebrush in Montezuma County escaped decades of heavy grazing, and today these remnants (see Box—Remnants and Relicts, pp.

183–184) serve as testaments to the biological diversity and productivity of natural sagebrush communities. Goodman Point is the easternmost outlier of Hovenweep National Monument (see Map 2.1). It was once home to large populations of Puebloans. Although this small area (about 143 acres) was withdrawn from homesteading in 1889 and never settled, the surrounding area was settled by over seventy families,[133] some of whom used a spring at the site as a water source.[134]

The site was probably fenced shortly after it became a unit of Hovenweep National Monument in 1951 and 1952, and since that time only a stray cow or two have grazed the area.[135] The sagebrush there is on the deep loess soils that are so desirable for dryland farming. The site has both basin big sagebrush (see Figure 2.1) on deeper soils, especially in draws, and Wyoming big sagebrush (see Figure 2.2). Most notable is that beneath this sagebrush (see Plate 13) is abundant native bunchgrass, especially Indian ricegrass, needle and thread, and muttongrass (see Figure 2.4). The flora also includes a diversity of forbs (see Table 2.2). Plate 13 was taken during the drought year of 2002, yet grass is abundant among the mature sage. This small remnant is very important, as it is the only relatively ungrazed patch of big sagebrush on deep soils currently known in southwestern Colorado.

Carpenter Park on the north edge of Cortez (see Map 2.1) is another area not heavily grazed for decades, probably because of its location on the edge of town.[136] The area was a party and dumping place until 1996, when, after several years of effort, Cortez residents Fred Blackburn and Victoria Atkins succeeded in convincing the city to formally protect the area as a city park. Blackburn and Atkins recognized this site as a significant and rare example of how the Great Sage Plain probably appeared at the time of Euro-American settlement.[137] The park has been used as a "living classroom" by Cortez high school teacher Mike Ferland, who frequently takes students in his field biology class to this and another local natural area.[138]

Carpenter Park is hilly and much rockier than Goodman Point. Here, black sage, rather than basin big sage, coexists with the widespread Wyoming big sage. Marilyn Colyer, a botanist at Mesa Verde National Park, surveyed Carpenter Park for plants in 1993 and found fifteen species of native grass, forty-eight species of native forbs, and fourteen species of shrubs in addition to sagebrush—a very diverse community.[139] The area is not pristine—Colyer found twenty-eight species of non-native plants, including some noxious ones. Yet Carpenter Park gives a rare glimpse of the plant community that evolved here.

Clearly, mature sagebrush can contain abundant bunchgrass and forbs, supporting the idea that it is livestock grazing, not maturing

Table 2.2. Common plants of Goodman Point and Carpenter Park sagebrush communities.[1]

	Goodman Point[2]	Carpenter Park
TREES		
Twoneedle pinyon (*Pinus edulis*)	X	—
Utah juniper (*Sabina osteosperma*)	X	—
SHRUBS		
Basin big sagebrush (*Seriphidium tridentatum*)	X	—
Black sagebrush (*Seriphidium novum*)	—	X
Broom snakeweed (*Gutierrezia sarothrae*)	X	—
Bud sagebrush (*Picrothamnus desertorum*)	—	X
Fourwing saltbush (*Atriplex canescens*)	—	X
Skunkbush sumac (*Rhus aromatica* subsp. *trilobata*)	—	X
Spineless horsebrush (*Tetradymia canescens*)	—	X
Wyoming big sagebrush (not in Weber and Wittmann 2001)	X	X
Yellow rabbitbrush (*Chrysothamnus viscidiflorus*)	—	X
FORBS		
Bastard toadflax (*Comandra umbellata*)	X	X
Flaxleaf plainsmustard (*Schoenocrambe linifolia*)	X	—
Foothill deathcamas (*Toxicoscordion paniculatum*)	X	—
Kingcup cactus (*Echinocereus triglochidiatus*)	—	X
Plains pricklypear (*Opuntia polyacantha*)	X	X
Sand lupine (*Lupinus ammophilus*)	X	—
Scarlet globemallow (*Sphaeralcea coccinea* subsp. *dissecta*)	X	—
Sego lily (*Calochortus nuttallii*)	X	—
Toadflax penstemon (*Penstemon linarioides*)	X	—
Western stoneseed (*Lithospermum ruderale*)	X	—
GRAMINOIDS		
Blue grama (*Chondrosum gracile*)	—	X
Indian ricegrass (*Achnatherum hymenoides*)	X	X
James' galleta (*Hilaria jamesii*)	—	X
Muttongrass (*Poa fendleriana*)	X	—
Needle and thread (*Hesperostipa comata*)	X	X
Prairie junegrass (*Koeleria macrantha*)	X	—
Purple threeawn (*Aristida purpurea*)	—	X
Squirreltail (*Elymus elymoides*)	X	—
NON-NATIVES		
Cheatgrass (*Anisantha tectorum*)	X	X
Smooth brome (*Bromopsis inermis*)	X	—
Yellow sweetclover (*Melilotus officinale*)	X	—

1. Common names are from the PLANTS online database, http://plants.usda.gov. Latin names are from Weber and Wittmann, *Colorado Flora*.

2. Species list for Goodman Point was provided by Charlie Schelz, biologist, National Park Service, Moab, Utah.

sagebrush, that is the cause of a depauperate sagebrush flora. In a recent review of evidence from across the West, Bruce Welch and Craig Criddle exposed as false the idea that sagebrush is naturally sparse or that it suppresses grass and forb production.[140] Unfortunately, long-

Figure 2.11. *Gunnison sage-grouse* (Centrocercus minimus), *displaying male. Courtesy, Louis Swift.*

held beliefs are hard to replace, and such false assumptions continue to misguide sagebrush management.

The plight of the Gunnison sage-grouse. Today, there is a legacy of overgrazing, sagebrush control, and non-native plants, but society may be entering an era of sagebrush restoration[141] as the value of these plants for wildlife is more widely recognized. Sage thrashers, Brewer's sparrows, and sage sparrows are some of the most conspicuous birds that rely heavily on sagebrush during the breeding season,[142] and mule deer depend on sagebrush for winter forage. Sagebrush also supports a remarkable diversity of fungi and insects.[143] However, it is concern for the Gunnison sage-grouse, a bird some have called the spotted owl of the desert,[144] that is now fueling restoration efforts.

When settlers first arrived in southwestern Colorado they found Gunnison sage-grouse (see Figure 2.11) in most sizable areas of sagebrush.[145] In the 1890s "prairie chickens," as sage-grouse were called in the area, were served along with other wild game in restaurants in Durango and Montezuma County.[146] The Gunnison sage-grouse once was found over a wide geographic area from southwestern Kansas to southeastern Utah, with its main historical range in Colorado around the San Juan Mountains.[147] This grouse is now recognized as a species distinct from the larger greater sage-grouse that occurs more widely across the northern plains, northern steppe. and Great Basin (see Map 2.4).[148]

The only sizable population of Gunnison sage-grouse today is in Colorado's Gunnison Basin, where the population was estimated at fewer than 3,000 birds in 2004.[149] There are six other much smaller, isolated populations in Colorado, ranging from 10 to 245 birds (see Map 2.5). The greater sage-grouse, though still much more numerous than the Gunnison, has also been reduced to a fraction of its historical numbers.[150] As one reporter summarized, "Perhaps no other native species is so widely distributed and so widely imperiled."[151]

Map 2.4. *(a) Historical range of sage-grouse, and (b) current range of greater sage-grouse and the Gunnison sage-grouse (the southwestern Colorado piece). Courtesy, Sara J. Oyler-McCance.*

The major threat to both Gunnison and greater sage-grouse is permanent loss and fragmentation of sagebrush, as well as more reversible degradation of sagebrush communities.[152] Between the 1950s and 1993 the extent of sagebrush communities in southwestern Colorado declined by 20 percent.[153] Spraying with 2,4-D in the 1960s and 1970s, for example, likely led to losses of Gunnison sage-grouse (and sharp-tailed grouse) in the Glade area north of Dolores, where retired Dolores-area game warden Bill Fisher recalled both species as once common.[154]

Beginning in the 1990s, local conservation plans were developed for each Gunnison sage-grouse population by state and federal agencies and local land users. The smaller populations may contain essential genetic diversity for the continued viability of the Gunnison sage-grouse as a whole.[155] The conservation plans proposed voluntary actions to help these subpopulations,[156] but while the plans were being developed and subsequently, grouse populations in southwestern Colorado continued to decline. In December 2000 the U.S. Fish and Wildlife Service (USFWS) designated the Gunnison sage-grouse as a "candidate" species for listing under the Endangered Species Act.[157]

On the brink: The Dove Creek sage-grouse population. The smallest population of the Gunnison sage-grouse, the Dove Creek population, is in serious trouble. Male sage-grouse (see Figure 2.11) congregate during the spring mating season on a few display grounds called leks. Based on counts at leks, the population in 1998 was estimated to be 81–135 adult birds, down from about twice that many as recently as 1994.[158] In 2004 the estimated population was only 10 birds.[159] One of the main

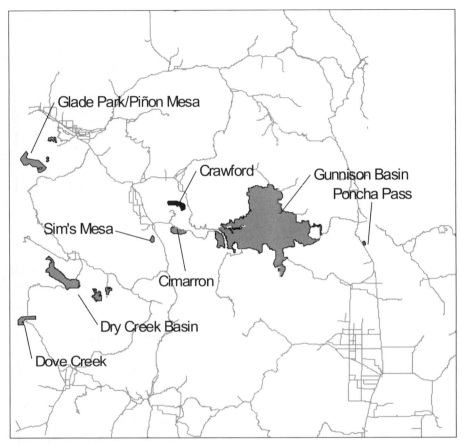

Map 2.5. *Current populations of Gunnison sage-grouse. Courtesy, Sara J. Oyler-McCance.*

problems for the Dove Creek population has been loss of its sagebrush habitat to agriculture. Ironically, 26,000 acres of its former habitat have now been rested from agriculture under the federal Conservation Reserve Program (CRP) because that land is highly erodible and has marginal value as cropland.[160] Most of the CRP land was planted to smooth brome (see Box—Smooth Brome, pp. 281–282), which forms a dense monoculture unsuitable to the grouse. Wildlife managers are encouraging landowners to plant sage and other native species on CRP land, but few landowners are willing to return farmland to sage, and CRP land could eventually be returned to cropland.[161]

Listing under the Endangered Species Act is almost always contentious. After designation of the grouse as a candidate species, Colorado

Division of Wildlife (CDOW) researchers were denied access to some private lands in the Dove Creek area to study or count the grouse.[162] Landowners were concerned that eventual listing of the grouse could restrict land use, which indeed it could. Yet without the threat of listing, it is unlikely that local conservation plans would have been developed at all.

A major loss for the Dove Creek sage-grouse came in 1996 with the sale of the 2,880-acre Rogers Ranch, one of the largest remaining areas of occupied habitat for that sage-grouse population. The little remaining unplowed sagebrush in the Dove Creek area is highly fragmented or, like the Rogers Ranch, is located at higher elevations on the margins of the best habitat. At this higher elevation, Gambel oak and mixed mountain shrubs combine with sagebrush, an unusual habitat for sage-grouse. However, sage-grouse had been using this area for nesting and, most important, for winter habitat.

This large ranch, about five miles northeast of Dove Creek, sold for $735,000,[163] inexpensive relative to other purchases for conservation. The local game warden nominated the land for conservation purchase or easement, but the sale took place before those interested in the sage-grouse learned of it.[164] The subdivision of the ranch into seventy lots of thirty-five-plus acres for the Secret Canyon development set in motion the loss of this important sage-grouse habitat. Roads now fragment the former ranch land, and although few houses had been built by 2002, all lots were sold. Some owners have cleared their sagebrush, but even if sage is not cleared, sage-grouse usually do not persist within a half-mile of dwellings.[165] Although the local game warden suggested ways to mitigate impacts on sage-grouse and other wildlife—clustering houses and restricting dogs, for example—such restrictions were not required by law or implemented by the developer (see Box—Land-Use Legislation and Government Policy, pp. 295–296).

The story of Dove Creek's sage-grouse is a tragedy in two acts representing two eras. The loss was set in motion by the Old West—large-scale replacement of the sagebrush ecosystem by agriculture—and completed by the New West—creation of subdivisions without planning. Looking back, the moments the tragedy could have been averted, as in all classical tragedies, are clearer now, and the outcome does not seem to have been inevitable. Long ago, land marginal for agriculture—land taxpayers now pay farmers not to plow as part of the Conservation Reserve Program—could have been left unplowed so the grouse were not left with inadequate habitat. A public agency could have purchased the Rogers Ranch at the time of sale or found a conservation buyer. Or the developer might have chosen to subdivide another place without grouse or, at least, planned the development to minimize adverse effects on grouse. None of these things happened, so today the last hope is (1) that the people with land in the subdivision take an interest in the grouse and do what they can to minimize disturbance to its habitat and (2) that other sagebrush nearby is restored in time to prevent loss of this important population.

The challenge of restoring degraded sagebrush: Dry Creek Basin. Fortunately, not all the Gunnison sage-grouse populations have lost sagebrush habitat to the extent the Dove Creek population has. For the San Miguel Basin population of the Gunnison sage-grouse, the challenge is to restore much more widespread but degraded sagebrush habitat while limiting future loss: the degradation and fragmentation of intact habitat by oil and gas and residential development. After the Gunnison Basin, the San Miguel Basin population (see Map 2.5, where this population is labeled Dry Creek Basin) was the largest remaining Gunnison sage-grouse population in 2004, estimated at 245 birds.[166]

Dry Creek Basin is the lowest-elevation portion of the San Miguel Basin sage-grouse habitat. It provides critical winter habitat for birds that nest at higher elevations in the San Miguel Basin. With three known leks, Dry Creek Basin also had its own breeding population until 2004 or 2005, when breeding birds disappeared from the leks.[167] Although they are degraded, the sagebrush communities provide winter cover, winter food, and the largest area of sagebrush habitat occupied by Gunnison sage-grouse outside the Gunnison Basin.[168]

Rural subdivision is reducing important breeding habitat of the San Miguel Basin population at higher elevations, but Dry Creek Basin is hot and dry in summer and very sparsely populated. It is the kind of place writer Debra Donahue argued is too dry to sustain livestock grazing,[169] but it was once the winter range for huge herds of sheep and cattle and remains important winter range for livestock, deer, and elk. Today, a high diversity of sagebrush and salt-desert shrubs remains, but sagebrush communities have lost most cool-season bunchgrasses and forbs, and bare ground dominates the spaces between the sagebrush (see Plate 14). Large sections of land, especially private land, have been cleared of sage for crops and to increase forage for livestock, fragmenting formerly more continuous stands of sagebrush (see Plate 15).

Because of its heavy use by wildlife and past heavy use by livestock, many observers believe the basin was once highly productive. In 1991 the Bureau of Land Management and CDOW, which manage large areas of public land in Dry Creek Basin, and the Natural Resource

Figure 2.12. *An area of Dry Creek Basin plowed in 1961 and seeded to crested wheat-grass, then disked and seeded with native grasses in 1997.*

Conservation Service and Conservation Districts, which work with private landowners, formed a working group. The vision that united the group was restoration of abundant forage. By 1994 the group had developed a CRMP for the basin.[170] The main goal of the CRMP was to improve the water quality of the San Miguel River by reducing bare ground, and thus sediment and salt runoff, from the uplands while also meeting the needs of livestock, big game, and Gunnison sage-grouse.

Restoration was focused on reducing sagebrush, under the belief that old, dense sagebrush was suppressing grasses and forbs. In 1996 and 1997 three large sagebrush treatments were conducted on the far west end of Dry Creek Basin, funded by two cost-share grants for water-quality improvement from the Environmental Protection Agency totaling over $250,000. One large treatment was an attempt to improve an area where the BLM had plowed Wyoming big sagebrush and seeded crested wheatgrass (see Box—Crested Wheatgrass, pp. 85–86) in 1961.[171] By the 1990s sagebrush had reestablished on the site, but there was little grass or forb cover under the sage,[172] so 550 acres were disked in large strips (see Figure 2.12) and drill seeded with forbs and native grasses. Project planners were surprised when what grew after this treatment was crested wheatgrass, with few seeded native grasses or forbs surviving. This suggests it will be difficult to restore the thousands of acres on which crested wheatgrass has been planted in Dry Creek Basin.

Another 700 acres of Wyoming big sagebrush were treated with the herbicide Tebuthiuron (commonly called Spike). The intent was to "thin" the sage, but over a large area the kill was almost 100 percent. Spike has been the most popular and also the most controversial method of removing sagebrush in the basin in recent years. Long known to be

BOX—CRESTED WHEATGRASS

There is a growing body of knowledge that suggests that crested wheatgrass alters the environment in many undesirable ways. . . . [T]he continued conversion of native prairie and planting of crested wheatgrass or other exotic species seems ill advised.[1]

Anything with "wheat" in its name sounds healthy, but this particular wheatgrass (see box figure) is a threat to native communities and biological diversity throughout the Great Plains and the West.[2] This grass (or grasses—as many as eight species are called crested wheatgrass) was imported from the windy, dry steppes of central Asia in 1897 by an agricultural scientist from South Dakota. Beginning in the 1930s, it was widely planted on overgrazed land and abandoned cropland.[3] The grass now occupies about 26 million acres in North America.[4]

Crested wheatgrass is resistant to cold, drought, and grazing,[5] but it also decreases nitrogen and alters soil, often preventing reestablishment of native plants and leading to a long-lasting monoculture.[6] In some cases it also spreads into surrounding native wheatgrass communities and native prairies, where it can outcompete and diminish native species.[7] In the West, crested wheatgrass has replaced large areas of sagebrush, leading to significant declines in native plants, birds, mammals, and reptiles.[8]

Crested wheatgrass (Agropyron desertorum).

Millions of acres of crested wheatgrass are the legacy of two failures. First was the overgrazing and failed cultivation of arid lands that led to extreme erosion and the Dust Bowl. Second was the use of a tough, competitive non-native grass as a quick fix rather than rethinking land uses with the goal of perpetuating diverse native ecosystems. Today, some efforts are under way in southwestern Colorado to remove crested wheatgrass from sites where it was planted, but the grass is preventing restoration of native plants in degraded sagebrush and pinyon-juniper ecosystems.[9]

NOTES

1. Lesica and DeLuca, "Effects of Crested Wheatgrass," 409.
2. Ibid.
3. Rogler and Lorenz, "Crested Wheatgrass—Early History."
4. Lesica and DeLuca, "Effects of Crested Wheatgrass."
5. Rogler and Lorenz, "Crested Wheatgrass—Early History."
6. Lesica and DeLuca, "Effects of Crested Wheatgrass."
7. Pyke, "Demography of Introduced and Native Grasses"; Heidinga and Wilson, "Impacts of an Invading Alien Grass."
8. Reynolds and Trost, "Response of Native Vertebrate Populations to Crested Wheatgrass."
9. For example, the Spring Creek/Dry Creek project on the Uncompahgre Plateau includes removal of crested wheatgrass from some areas as a project goal.

a delayed-response herbicide with unpredictable kill rates, depending on soil type and moisture,[173] Spike appears to react strongly in the soils of Dry Creek Basin. Sagebrush recovery after applying Spike has been "very low, or non-existent" in the basin.[174] Spike has been popular among private landowners in the basin because it is relatively cheap and effective.[175] Adjacent to the 700-acre Spike treatment, 365 acres of sagebrush were brush beat (mowed to ground level) at about the same time.

Thus, all together, 1,600 acres of mature sagebrush were removed. The most controversial part of these treatments was their potential impact on the Gunnison sage-grouse. In a letter to the BLM following the treatments, Clait Braun, then CDOW Avian Research Program manager and a grouse advocate, stated:[176]

[T]he brush beating, disking, and tebuthiuron treatments of BLM (and private) lands are all negative to the Gunnison sage grouse in the short term as all treatments are too large. Brush beating and disking should be in strips with untreated strips twice the width of treated strips. Narrow strips are better than wide strips. Use of tebuthiuron in the San Miguel Basin should be discontinued on

public lands as it is too effective in killing sagebrush. Positive
responses of sage grouse to tebuthiuron treatments have not been
demonstrated anywhere in the range of the sage grouse.

All studies of the effects of herbicide treatments leaving less than 5
percent sagebrush canopy cover show major declines in sage-grouse
breeding populations.[177] The CRMP defended this treatment as reasonable because the area was thought to be potential but unoccupied habitat for grouse, and it was hoped the treatments would eventually produce younger, more productive sagebrush habitat.[178]

It is difficult to judge to what extent the treatments were a success.
Although the project was supposed to include monitoring, the only
systematic assessment of the success of these treatments by the CRMP
group was monitoring of the vegetation on the brush-beat treatment
area in 1997 and 1999. That limited monitoring and our observations in
2002–2005 indicate that warm-season grasses (blue grama and James'
galleta; see Plate 6) did increase on some of the brush-beat area compared with nearby untreated areas. Increases in the taller cool-season
grasses that provide cover for grouse, especially squirreltail, occurred
in some areas but not others. Unfortunately, the 1999 monitoring also
indicated a fairly large increase in cheatgrass, and by 2005 cheatgrass
had extensively invaded parts of the Spiked and some of the brush-
beat treatment areas. Cheatgrass and the native, but weedy, broom
snakeweed (see Plate 5b) are weeds of concern in the basin. More extensive, continued monitoring could have helped managers understand
the conditions under which cheatgrass becomes a problem in the basin.

Shortly following these and other sagebrush treatments on private
land, the region experienced a deep drought from 2000 to 2003, and a
major die-off of sagebrush occurred over a broad region from the Uncompahgre Plateau to the Great Sage Plain, with Dry Creek Basin at the
center. By early 2004 a quantitative field study found about 26 percent
of Wyoming big sagebrush was dead and 69 percent was defoliated.[179]
With average to good rainfall in 2004 and 2005, much of the remaining
sage appeared to be recovering, but the sagebrush across the basin
had been effectively thinned by the drought. Native grasses and forbs
had not yet expanded onto the extensive bare ground under the sage,
however.

So the question of how to restore highly degraded, low-elevation
sagebrush ecosystems remains. Art Hayes, a BLM biologist with extensive experience with sagebrush restoration in the Gunnison Basin, believes both climate and grazing after treatment affect success.[180] The
1996 and 1997 treatments were rested from grazing for two years, but
much more time may be required for forage species to recover. Scientific

studies have found that where native bunchgrasses and forbs have been depleted, recovery may require much longer periods of rest from livestock grazing (e.g., twenty-five to fifty years).[181]

There are lessons for restoration here. First, large areas of an ecosystem should not be transformed to meet a narrow goal because there will likely be unintended consequences. Though the sagebrush at the west end of Dry Creek Basin was potential habitat for the Gunnison sage-grouse, grouse were not a high priority of the CRMP at the time.[182] The CRMP was focused instead on reducing erosion. In attempting to do this quickly, large treatments went ahead without, in our opinion, adequate concern for the sage-grouse and other sagebrush-dependent species. Large-scale actions under high uncertainty about results easily become costly, large-scale failures.

Second, large-scale events, such as the 2002–2003 sage die-off, show the need for a long-term, landscape-level view. If the sagebrush die-off is natural rather than induced by human-caused global climate change, it may be that sagebrush expands and contracts over long time frames. Sage-grouse have persisted through past fluctuations, perhaps by moving into what was previously unoccupied sagebrush. When lands are managed on the premise that only currently occupied habitat needs protection, animals that function at the landscape scale may have no place to move to as the landscape changes.[183] Over the long term, there may be no such thing as marginal sagebrush habitat for sage-grouse in this area.

Finally, this case illustrates the need for true adaptive management—a concept much invoked but rarely implemented.[184] In adaptive management, actions are designed to test assumptions and learn from surprises encountered. Subsequent management is then adjusted to incorporate what has been learned.[185] Much could have been learned about the response of vegetation in Dry Creek Basin to the variety of treatments. In fact, learning was a stated goal of the CRMP: "[M]uch experimentation and adaptation will occur."[186] But monitoring took place on only one of the treatment types and did not continue.

Without long-term commitment to monitoring and learning, adaptive management is an empty slogan. In our experience observing multi-stakeholder groups, participants tend to be pragmatic, hands-on people, and enthusiasm for systematic observation and inclusive discussion of results wanes quickly after the on-the-ground work is done. The limited success of efforts to restore the land through sagebrush treatments and the sudden sage die-off suggest that these ecosystems are still not understood. Recognizing this, the most recent treatment on CDOW land included a baseline survey, and small tests have been conducted to compare different treatment approaches. The challenge will be finding time and money for the needed experiments and monitoring, as most of the agencies' funding is still dedicated to directing "habitat improvement."

Loss of candidate status for Gunnison sage-grouse. In April 2005 the CDOW released a rangewide conservation plan for the Gunnison sage-grouse.[187] The plan was strongly criticized by grouse advocates in local working groups for underestimating the threat of extinction and for lack of strong plans to protect and restore habitat.[188] The conservation plan did, however, describe the precarious status of the species: "Gunnison sage-grouse occupy a small fraction of their historical range, having been extirpated by habitat conversion from much of their presumed historical distribution. . . . Potential threats to Gunnison sage-grouse are varied but numerous. Low genetic diversity, genetic drift from small population sizes, habitat issues (loss, degradation, and fragmentation from a variety of causes), the interaction of these with predator communities, and impacts of drought are the most significant threats facing Gunnison sage-grouse."[189]

Thus, it surprised most and troubled many when, in April 2006, the USFWS announced that the Gunnison sage-grouse did not warrant protection under the Endangered Species Act (ESA), citing a single unpublished paper[190] based on what many biologists consider flawed data.[191] As of this writing, several groups have issued an "intent to sue" over this decision.[192] With the USFWS decision, the grouse lost its status as a candidate species.

Even though it provided no regulatory teeth, candidate status was the basis for several successful efforts to protect sage-grouse habitat. Gas companies had begun expanding into sagebrush habitat of the San Miguel Basin in 2004 (see Box—Coal-Bed Methane and Natural Gas, pp. 90–92).[193] The BLM's only stipulation on leased public land was that drilling not occur within a quarter mile of an active lek. Most BLM lands in Dry Creek Basin had already been leased for oil and gas, but several unleased parcels in grouse habitat were withdrawn from auction in 2005 when members of the San Miguel Basin Gunnison Sage-Grouse Working Group and San Miguel County officials objected, based on the bird's candidate status. Similarly, San Miguel County's Open Space program and CDOW were able to prioritize the purchase of several conservation easements restricting development of grouse habitat, based on the bird's candidate status. Candidate status was not enough to protect the sage-grouse, however, as new drilling, housing, and roads continued to degrade and fragment its habitat.

BOX—COAL-BED METHANE AND NATURAL GAS

Natural gas development is booming throughout the West because it is a cleaner-burning fuel than coal, and government subsidies and gas prices have increased, encouraging more exploration and development. Conventional natural gas (mostly methane) is found deep in sedimentary rocks, but coal-bed methane (CBM) is found in shallower wells that are cheaper to drill.[1] In the southwest, CBM is concentrated on about 106,000 acres in the northern San Juan Basin of northwestern New Mexico and southern La Plata and Archuleta counties in Colorado.[2] CBM production in the San Juan Basin began in 1988 but boomed in the 1990s. With 3,000–4,000 CBM wells[3] and 20,000–25,000 conventional gas wells, the San Juan Basin produced about 80 percent of U.S. CBM gas and about 4 percent of total U.S. natural gas in A.D. 2000, but proposed CBM development in Wyoming may eventually dwarf these amounts.[4]

Wells have nearly saturated accessible lands at the currently allowed density. Industry wants to increase well density and expand development, in some cases into roadless areas on public lands. About 1,550 new CBM wells are expected within the San Juan Basin in about ten to twenty years,[5] along with about 10,000 new conventional gas wells.[6] Gas drilling is also increasing elsewhere in southwestern Colorado, including Dry Creek Basin.

Surface impacts of gas development are both direct and indirect, but total impact depends mainly on the density of wells and roads. CBM well densities were 1 per 320 acres until 1992, which increased to 1 per 160 acres in 2000 for nearly all areas and could increase even further.[7] Direct impacts include a new road, a 1- to 2-acre drilling site, and, after drilling, a smaller production area, as well as compressors, power lines, and pipelines. About 5 acres are directly affected per well.[8] Pipelines may follow existing roads, but they increase road width and not all are reseeded, so weeds are a concern. Unfenced open pits containing toxic chemicals, when not filled in and reseeded as required, are hazards to wildlife.[9]

Directly impacted areas are significant but small compared with areas altered by proximity to wells, roads, and compressor sites. A 2002 study quantified the total area affected by conventional gas development (1,000+ wells) in 166 square miles (about 106,000 acres) of the Big Piney–LaBarge field in southwestern Wyoming.[10] Here, well density is 5–6 per square mile on average, not much denser than in the San Juan Basin. About 4 percent of the Big Piney–LaBarge field is directly impacted by infrastructure (roads, well pads), but 97 percent of the area lies within 0.25 mile of infrastructure. Between 52 and 73 percent of the area is within 100 meters of a road. Road density in the area exceeds 8 miles per square mile,[11] more than three times as high as road density on any national forest in the region.[12]

Disturbance of wildlife by noise, traffic, fragmentation, increased hunting, and harassment extends some distance from roads and other infrastructure. Gas drilling near Pinedale, Wyoming, decreased reproduction of sage-grouse and use by sagebrush obligate songbirds (e.g., Brewer's sparrow, sage sparrow), birds that are declining in the West.[13] Successful sage-grouse reproduction occurred an average of 0.70 mile from a road, while unsuccessful females nested an average of 0.17 mile from a road, demonstrating that the impact of roads extends into the bordering habitat.[14] Large natural gas compressors (up to 10,000 hp at a site), which pressurize gas for movement in pipelines, increase noise sufficiently to affect sage-grouse at distances of 0.3 mile.[15] Sage-grouse are also vulnerable to predatory birds that perch on overhead power lines.[16]

Gas development also negatively affects surface landowners, who cannot legally prevent development of valid subsurface rights. In La Plata County, wells cannot generally be placed within 400 feet of a residence and the county requires some visual mitigation, but property values are decreased up to 22 percent by the presence of a well on the property.[17] Ranchers have complained that gas access roads are rutted and prone to weeds and leaks from chemical pits and that companies are not taking care of the land.[18] Explosive levels of methane have been found seeping into houses, forcing energy companies to purchase them, and there is concern for possible contamination or depletion of domestic water wells.[19]

By using legal tools and applying public pressure, citizens can modify and even significantly reduce the impacts of natural gas development.[20] The Western Governors Association has produced guidelines for "Best Management Practices" (BMPs) for CBM development[21] that could minimize environmental impacts and address concerns of surface landowners. The BMPs are a positive step, but they are voluntary and weakly worded (e.g., "whenever practical"). Some efforts are under way to legislate mandatory practices. Wyoming recently required negotiations between mineral and surface owners before a final permit to drill is awarded. The Colorado legislature has considered a similar bill.[22]

The HD Mountains, east of Bayfield, are a test case for responsible CBM development. Public lands in the area are already leased, and BLM is producing an environmental impact statement that will direct the way leases are developed. The HDs contain a roadless area, rare old-growth ponderosa pine forest, and potential habitat for Mexican spotted owls. Public opposition to road development and CBM wells within the HDs is formidable, including unanimous opposition by county commissions in the two affected counties; town councils in Durango, Bayfield, and Agnacio; and the BLM's Southwest Resource Advisory Council.[23] Pressure has mounted for BLM to allow only directional drilling from outside the HDs.[24]

Of course, gas development has considerable economic value. Half or more of La Plata County's property tax revenues come from energy developments.[25] BP America is the largest operator in the basin and the second-largest oil and gas company in the world, but some CBM development is local. The Southern Ute Indian Reservation southeast of Durango has developed both conventional and CBM wells. Tribal net worth grew from $39 million in 1989 to $1.2 billion in 2002,[26] allowing the tribe to substantially improve its living conditions and gain more control over its future. But a spokesman for the Southern Ute Grassroots Organization told the *Denver Post:* "[T]he pumps and compressors, they're like a cancer. There will be portions of our land that will be so contaminated that they'll be unusable for future generations."[27]

NOTES

1. Bryner, *Coalbed Methane Development.*
2. U.S. Department of the Interior (USDI), Bureau of Land Management, and U.S. Department of Agriculture (USDA), Forest Service, *Coal Bed Methane in the Northern San Juan Basin.*
3. Bryner, *Coalbed Methane Development.*
4. Schober, "Conservation Easements Contain Pitfalls."
5. USDI Bureau of Land Management and USDA Forest Service, *Coal Bed Methane in the Northern San Juan Basin.*
6. Bryner, *Coalbed Methane Development;* Schober, "County Gas Well Permits."
7. Greenhill, "Ranchers to Industry: Shape Up."
8. Clarren, "Colliding Forces."
9. Schober, "County Gas Well Permits."
10. Weller et al., *Fragmenting Our Lands.*
11. Ibid.
12. Baker and Knight, "Roads and Forest Fragmentation."
13. Ingelfinger, "Effects of Natural Gas on Sagebrush Passerines"; Braun et al., "Effects of Alteration of Sagebrush on Avifauna."
14. Lyon, "Potential Effects of Natural Gas on Sage-Grouse"; Lyon and Anderson, "Potential Gas Development Impacts on Sage Grouse."
15. U.S. Department of the Interior, Bureau of Land Management, *Draft Environmental Impact Statement for Powder River Basin Oil and Gas,* chapter 4, 270.
16. Braun, Oedekoven, and Aldridge, "Oil and Gas in Western North America."
17. Greenhill, "Gas-Well Spacing May Fall to 80 Acres."
18. Greenhill, "Ranchers to Industry: Shape Up."
19. USDI Bureau of Land Management and USDA Forest Service, *Coal Bed Methane in the Northern San Juan Basin.*
20. Darin and Stills, *Citizen's Guide to Oil and Gas Decisions.*
21. Western Governors Association, *Coal Bed Methane Best Management Practices.*
22. D'Ambrosio, "Bill Proposed to Force Talks Before Drilling."
23. Pearson, "Public Comments: Don't Drill the HDs."
24. D'Ambrosio, "County Compiles Criticism on HDs."
25. Adam Keller, county planner, Durango, Colorado, pers. comm., July 13, 2001.
26. Bryner, *Coalbed Methane Development.*
27. Cited in Greene, "Drilling Tests Utes' Values," 9A.

Had the Gunnison sage-grouse been granted protection as a threatened or endangered species, stricter restrictions on oil and gas (and other) development, including stipulations of no surface occupancy in occupied or potential habitat, might have been possible. Local working groups have indicated an intent to continue their efforts, but without either candidate status or protection under the ESA, the Gunnison sage-grouse's future hangs precariously and ultimately on the voluntary actions of oil and gas companies, real estate developers, and landowners to protect its sagebrush habitat.

CONCLUDING THOUGHTS

The desert plateaus and canyons of the Colorado Plateau have significant legacies from livestock and mining and remain under stress. Now there is talk of restoration, and some places suggest that possibility. But highly degraded sites may require difficult and expensive replanting of native species and many decades of rest to achieve success. There is impatience with the slow pace of recovery and restoration. People have tried to force nature to adapt to their needs, but this has generally failed. If restoration is to succeed, people will need to more systematically ask questions and monitor responses of the land. Nature has provided strong messages about the elements that must be heard for a culture of habitat and a land ethic to develop: these semiarid lands have low capacity for livestock grazing, are prone to severe drought, and recover very slowly from any disturbance. It is time to begin the work of shaping land uses to match the severe, semiarid reality of this country.

NOTES

1. Newberry, *Report of the Exploring Expedition from Santa Fe*, 86. He is describing the "Great Sage Plain" on his 1859 trip.
2. Tito Naranjo in Varien et al., "Native American Issues and Perspectives," 403.
3. It is legal to enter most ruins on BLM lands, but as more people explore the region, negative impacts are growing. Even careful walking on ruins is likely to disturb the site in some way. Although we will not point out any particular ruins in this chapter, visitors may make their own discoveries of the structural remains of Ancestral Puebloans' long tenure in this part of Colorado. We encourage visitors to reflect on their presence here by observing ruins from a distance, out of respect for both Puebloan spirituality and the value of sites to archaeologists who have only begun to uncover and study the ruins. Each professional excavation produces ob-

jects and other data that are carefully curated for subsequent research and education. Excavation is inevitably destructive, however, so unexcavated sites are valuable storehouses of information awaiting the time, resources, and new technologies to study them.

4. Keen, "Weather and Climate."
5. Spencer and Romme, "Ecological Patterns."
6. Keen, "Weather and Climate"; Adams and Comrie, "North American Monsoon."
7. McArthur, "Sagebrush Systematics and Evolution."
8. Tisdale and Hironaka, *Sagebrush-Grass Region*.
9. West, "Distribution, Composition, and Classification of Woodlands."
10. Sánchez, *Explorers, Traders, and Slavers*; Carson, *Across the Northern Frontier*.
11. Warner, *Dominguez-Escalante Journal*, 13.
12. Heap, *Central Route to the Pacific*.
13. Ibid.
14. Nossaman, *Many More Mountains, Vol. 1*.
15. Newberry, *Report of the Exploring Expedition from Santa Fe*.
16. Ibid., 5.
17. Gannett, "Report on Arable and Pasture Lands of Colorado," 346.
18. Chittenden, "Report of George B. Chittenden," 361.
19. Ruffner, *Annual Report upon Explorations and Surveys*, 1782.
20. Gannett, "Report on Arable and Pasture Lands of Colorado," 345.
21. Jackson, "Report on the Ancient Ruins," 412.
22. Freeman, *History of Montezuma County*, 111.
23. Ibid., 112.
24. Mack and Thompson, "Evolution in Steppe with Few Large, Hooved Mammals."
25. Ruffner, *Annual Report upon Explorations and Surveys*, 1781.
26. Ibid., 1780.
27. Passey, Hugie, and Williams, "Herbage Production and Composition Fluctuations"; Davis, Tueller, and Bruner, "Estimating Forage Production from Shrub Ring Widths."
28. Ruffner, *Annual Report upon Explorations and Surveys*, 1780.
29. Delaney, *Ute Mountain Utes*.
30. Ibid.
31. Ibid.; Simmons, *Ute Indians of Utah, Colorado, and New Mexico*.
32. O'Rourke, *Frontier in Transition*.
33. Ibid.; Simmons, *Ute Indians of Utah, Colorado, and New Mexico*.
34. Rockwell, *Uncompahgre Country*.
35. Ruffner, *Annual Report upon Explorations and Surveys*.
36. Freeman, *History of Montezuma County*.
37. O'Rourke, *Frontier in Transition*.
38. McPherson, "Canyons, Cows, and Conflict"; Simmons, *Ute Indians of Utah, Colorado, and New Mexico*.
39. Wyckoff, *Creating Colorado*.
40. Rockwell, *Uncompahgre Country*.

41. Ibid.; unidentified newspaper account, Rimrock Historical Museum, Naturita, Colorado; Paul Camel, Nucla, Colorado, pers. comm., May 20, 1999.
42. O'Rourke, *Frontier in Transition.*
43. Ibid.
44. Rockwell, *Uncompahgre Country.*
45. Denison and York, *Telluride: Tales of Two Early Pioneers.*
46. West, "Oldest Range Man"; Freeman, *History of Montezuma County.*
47. Freeman, *History of Montezuma County*; O'Rourke, *Frontier in Transition.*
48. West, "Oldest Range Man."
49. Gordon, "Report on Cattle, Sheep, and Swine."
50. Ibid.; Cook and Redente, "Development of the Ranching Industry in Colorado."
51. Young and Sparks, *Cattle in the Cold Desert.*
52. West, "Oldest Range Man," 122.
53. O'Rourke, *Frontier in Transition.*
54. Ibid.; U.S. Department of Commerce, Bureau of the Census, *Agriculture, 1930.*
55. O'Rourke, *Frontier in Transition.*
56. Freeman, *History of Montezuma County.*
57. O'Rourke, *Frontier in Transition.*
58. Lavender, *One Man's West.*
59. Paul Camel, Nucla, Colorado, pers. comm , May 20, 1999.
60. Lavender, *One Man's West*, 102–103.
61. Ibid., 103–105.
62. Bement, "Colorado Rangelands," 209.
63. Hardin, "Tragedy of the Commons."
64. Baden and Noonan, *Managing the Commons.*
65. Howard Greager, Norwood, Colorado, pers. comm., October 9, 2001.
66. Magnan and Seidl, "Economic Base of Montezuma County."
67. Freeman, *History of Montezuma County.*
68. Connolly, "Goodman Point Historic Land-Use Study."
69. Freeman, *History of Montezuma County*; U.S. Department of Commerce, Bureau of the Census, *U.S. Census of Agriculture: 1959.*
70. U.S. Department of Commerce, Bureau of the Census, *U.S. Census of Agriculture: 1959.*
71. Ibid.
72. John Porter, general manager, Dolores Water Conservancy District, pers. comm., April 15, 2002; Connolly, "Goodman Point Historic Land-Use Study."
73. John Porter, general manager, Dolores Water Conservancy District, pers. comm., April 15, 2002.
74. See Web site: http://utemountainute.com/ farm_and_ranch.htm.
75. U.S. Department of Commerce, Bureau of the Census, *1978 Census of Agriculture*; U.S. Department of Commerce, Bureau of the Census, *1982 Census of Agriculture*; U.S. Department of Commerce, Bureau of the Census, *1987*

Census of Agriculture; U.S. Department of Commerce, Bureau of the Census, *1992 Census of Agriculture*; U.S. Department of Agriculture, Statistical Service, *1997 Census of Agriculture*.

76. U.S. Department of Commerce, Bureau of the Census, *1982 Census of Agriculture*; U.S. Department of Agriculture, Statistical Service, *1997 Census of Agriculture*.
77. U.S. Department of Agriculture, Statistical Service, *1997 Census of Agriculture*.
78. Ibid.
79. Jan Sennhenn, Cooperative Extension director, Montezuma County, pers. comm., July 5, 2005.
80. Athearn, "Last Great Mining Boom"; Athearn, "Cleaning up the Uranium Country."
81. Ringholz, *Uranium Frenzy*; Athearn, "Cleaning up the Uranium Country."
82. Chenoweth, "Uranium-Vanadium Deposits of the Uravan Mineral Belt," 170.
83. Dion, "Uranium Mining Resurfaces Near Naturita."
84. Clinton, "Establishment of the Canyons of the Ancients National Monument."
85. Canyons of the Ancients, Overview (brochure), Anasazi Heritage Center, Dolores, Colorado.
86. Binstock, "Archaeopolitics."
87. LouAnn Jacobson, director, Anasazi Heritage Center, Cortez, Colorado, pers. comm., March 28, 2002.
88. Stevens, Pearce, and Rigg, *Natural Analogs for Geologic Storage of CO_2*.
89. Ibid.
90. LouAnn Jacobson, director, Anasazi Heritage Center, Cortez, Colorado, pers. comm., March 28, 2002; Clinton, "Establishment of the Canyons of the Ancients National Monument."
91. Banda, "Seismic Drilling at Monument."
92. Clark, "Oil Wells on the Horizon for Canyons of the Ancients."
93. Peggy Wu, recreation planner, Dolores, Colorado, BLM and Forest Service, pers. comm., May 28, 2002.
94. Grazier, "Panel's Plan Would Expand Canyon's Access."
95. Rodebaugh, "Need Cited for Protection of Canyons."
96. Victoria Atkins, archaeologist, Anasazi Heritage Center, Dolores, Colorado, pers. comm., May 21, 2002.
97. Freeman, *History of Montezuma County*; O'Rourke, *Frontier in Transition*; Bement, "Colorado Rangelands."
98. Simmons, *Ute Indians of Utah, Colorado, and New Mexico*.
99. Wallace, *Western Range*; Young, "Changes in Plant Communities in the Great Basin"; Young, Evans, and Tueller, "Great Basin Plant Communities—Pristine and Grazed"; Miller, Svejcar, and West, "Implications of Livestock Grazing."
100. E.g., Wallace, *Western Range*; Young, "Changes in Plant Communities in the Great Basin"; Young, Evans, and Tueller, "Great Basin Plant Communities—Pristine and Grazed"; Miller, Svejcar, and West, "Implications of

Livestock Grazing"; Hanson and Stoddart, "Effect of Grazing upon Bunch Wheat Grass"; Ellison, "Influence of Grazing."

101. Denison and York, *Telluride: Tales of Two Early Pioneers*, 84.
102. Rasmussen and Brotherson, "Response of Winterfat to Release from Grazing."
103. Cole, Henderson, and Shafer, "Holocene Vegetation and Grazing Impacts at Capitol Reef"; McDaniel and Ross, "Snakeweed: Poisonous Properties."
104. Howard Greager, Norwood, Colorado, pers. comm., October 9, 2001.
105. Agency file, East Paradox Common Allotment No. 7101, BLM, Montrose, Colorado.
106. Paradox Valley Trend and Vegetation Assessment, BLM, Montrose, Colorado, 1995.
107. Dean Stindt, BLM range conservationist, Norwood, pers. comm., October 9, 2001.
108. Kleiner and Harper, "Environment and Community in Grasslands of Canyonlands."
109. Bork, West, and Walker, "Cover Components on Long-Term Seasonal Sheep Grazing Treatments."
110. Howell, "Cool Season Grasses"; Dean Stindt, BLM range conservationist, Norwood, pers. comm., October 9, 2001.
111. Jim Ferguson, BLM biologist, Montrose, letter dated April 24, 2002, to Dean Stindt, range conservationist, Mesa Creek allotment file, BLM, Montrose, Colorado.
112. Mesa Creek allotment file, Uncompahgre Basin Resource Area, BLM, Montrose, Colorado.
113. Mesa Creek Monitoring Studies, 1996, 1997, Mesa Creek allotment file, BLM, Montrose, Colorado.
114. Hull, "Eradication of Big Sagebrush."
115. Lanner, "Eradication of Pinyon-Juniper Woodland."
116. West and Young, "Intermountain Valleys and Lower Mountain Slopes."
117. E.g., Arnold, Jameson, and Reid, *Pinyon-Juniper Type of Arizona*.
118. Pieper, "Overstory-Understory Relations in Pinyon-Juniper Woodlands."
119. Clary and Morrison, "Large Alligator Junipers Benefit Early-Spring Forage"; Schott and Pieper, "Influence of Canopy Characteristics on Understory Grasses."
120. Anderson and Inouye, "Landscape-Scale Changes in Plant Species."
121. Young and Sparks, *Cattle in the Cold Desert*.
122. Thurow and Taylor, "Viewpoint: The Role of Drought in Range Management."
123. Hull, "Eradication of Big Sagebrush"; Vale, "Sagebrush Conversion Projects."
124. Whitson, Farrell, and Alley, "Changes in Rangeland Canopy Cover," 486.
125. Daubenmire, "Plant Succession Due to Overgrazing"; Hanson and Stoddart, "Effects of Grazing upon Bunch Wheat Grass"; Hull and Hull, "Presettlement Vegetation of Cache Valley, Utah and Idaho."
126. Holechek and Stephenson, "Comparison of Big Sagebrush Vegetation."
127. Vale, "Presettlement Vegetation in the Sagebrush-Grass Area"; Johnson, *Rangeland Through Time*.

128. Hull, "Eradication of Big Sagebrush"; Hull, Kissinger, and Vaughn, "Chemical Control of Big Sagebrush in Wyoming"; Cornelius and Graham, "Sagebrush Control with 2,4-D."
129. Blaisdell and Mueggler, "Effect of 2,4-D on Forbs and Shrubs."
130. E.g., Clary, Goodrich, and Smith, "Response to Tebuthiuron by Utah Juniper."
131. Braun et al., "Conservation Committee Report on Alteration of Sagebrush."
132. Hull and Klomp, "Longevity of Crested Wheatgrass in the Sagebrush-Grass Type."
133. Connolly, "Goodman Point Historic Land-Use Study."
134. Marilyn Colyer, botanist, Mesa Verde National Park, Cortez, Colorado, pers. comm., May 21, 2002.
135. Ibid.
136. Fred Blackburn, environmental historian, Cortez, Colorado, pers. comm., May 22, 2002.
137. Ibid.
138. Mike Ferland, Cortez, Colorado, pers. comm., May 8, 2003.
139. Marilyn Colyer, botanist, Mesa Verde National Park, Cortez, Colorado, pers. comm., April 2003.
140. Welch and Criddle, *Countering Misinformation Concerning Big Sagebrush*.
141. E.g., Hemstrom et al., "Sagebrush-Steppe Vegetation Dynamics and Restoration Potential."
142. Saab et al., "Livestock Grazing Effects in Western North America"; Kingery, *Colorado Breeding Bird Atlas*.
143. Welch and Criddle, *Countering Misinformation Concerning Big Sagebrush*.
144. Kerr, "Sage Grouse: The Spotted Owl of the Desert."
145. Braun, "Distribution and Status of Sage Grouse in Colorado."
146. *Durango Herald*, October 29, 1893, and *Telluride Republican*, October 11, 1895, courtesy of Fred Blackburn, Cortez, Colorado.
147. Braun, "Distribution and Status of Sage Grouse in Colorado"; Federal Register, "Notice of Designation of the Gunnison Sage Grouse as a Candidate Species."
148. Young et al., "A New Species of Sage-Grouse from Southwestern Colorado."
149. Gunnison Sage-grouse Rangewide Steering Committee, "Gunnison Sage-grouse Plan."
150. Braun, "Sage Grouse Declines in Western North America."
151. Clifford, "Last Dance for the Sage Grouse?" 8.
152. Braun, "Sage Grouse Declines in Western North America"; Connelly et al., "Guidelines to Manage Sage Grouse"; Oyler-McCance, Burnham, and Braun, "Influence of Changes in Sagebrush on Gunnison Sage Grouse."
153. Oyler-McCance, Burnham, and Braun, "Influence of Changes in Sagebrush on Gunnison Sage Grouse."
154. Bill Fisher, Dolores, Colorado, pers. comm., April 11, 2002; see also Rogers, *Sage Grouse Investigations in Colorado*.
155. Oyler-McCance, "Conservation Strategies for Gunnison Sage-Grouse."

156. E.g., Anonymous, "Gunnison Sage Grouse Conservation Plan Dove Creek, Colorado"; Anonymous, "Gunnison Sage Grouse Conservation Plan San Miguel Basin Colorado."
157. Federal Register, "Notice of Designation of the Gunnison Sage Grouse as a Candidate Species."
158. Anonymous, "Gunnison Sage Grouse Conservation Plan Dove Creek, Colorado"; Dave Harper, Dove Creek game warden, Colorado Division of Wildlife, pers. comm., August 26, 2002.
159. Gunnison Sage-grouse Rangewide Steering Committee, "Gunnison Sage-grouse Plan."
160. Ibid.
161. Scott Wait, Colorado Division of Wildlife, Durango, Colorado, pers. comm., April 24, 2002.
162. Ibid.
163. Dolores County Tax Assessor records.
164. Dave Harper, Dove Creek game warden, Colorado Division of Wildlife, pers. comm., August 26, 2002; C. E. Braun, Grouse, Inc., Tucson, Arizona, pers. comm., July 11, 2002.
165. C. E. Braun, Grouse, Inc., Tucson, Arizona, pers. comm., July 11, 2002.
166. Gunnison Sage-grouse Rangewide Steering Committee, "Gunnison Sage-grouse Plan."
167. Ibid.; San Miguel Basin Gunnison Sage-grouse Working Group Meeting, Norwood, Colorado, pers. comm., June 21, 2005.
168. Anonymous, "Gunnison Sage Grouse Conservation Plan San Miguel Basin Colorado"; C. E. Braun, Grouse, Inc., Tucson, Arizona, pers. comm., July 11, 2002.
169. Donahue, *Western Range Revisited*.
170. U.S. Department of the Interior, Bureau of Land Management, "Dry Creek Basin Coordinated Resource Management Plan."
171. U.S. Department of the Interior, Bureau of Land Management, "Finch Seeding, Project Completion Report."
172. Bob Ball, range conservationist, BLM, Dolores, Colorado, pers. comm, June 6, 2002.
173. Emmerich, "Tebuthiuron-Environmental Concerns."
174. Deadhorse Creek Brush Mow and Reseeding Project Draft Proposal, March 2000, Colorado Division of Wildlife, Montrose.
175. Jim Boyd, Natural Resource Conservation Service, Norwood, Colorado, pers. comm., January 9, 2003.
176. Letter to Bob Ball, dated August 3, 1998, BLM files, Dolores, Colorado.
177. Connelly et al., "Guidelines to Manage Sage Grouse."
178. Bob Ball, range conservationist, Bureau of Land Management, Dolores, Colorado, pers. comm, June 6, 2002; Dean Stindt, BLM, Norwood, Colorado, pers. comm., January 9, 2003.
179. Wenger, Grode, and Apa, "Inventory of Sagebrush Defoliation and Mortality."
180. Art Hayes, BLM, Gunnison, Colorado, pers. comm., May 13, 2002.

181. Anderson and Inouye, "Landscape-Scale Changes in Plant Species"; Young and Eckert, "Historical Perspectives Regarding the Sagebrush Ecosystem"; Beck and Mitchell, "Influences of Livestock Grazing."
182. Clyde Johnson, San Juan BLM Office, Durango, Colorado, pers. comm., January 13, 2003.
183. McCullough, *Metapopulations and Wildlife Conservation*; Bissonette, *Wildlife and Landscape Ecology*.
184. Lee, "Appraising Adaptive Management"; Moir and Block, "Adaptive Management on Public Lands."
185. Ludwig, Hilborn, and Walters, "Uncertainty, Resource Exploitation, and Conservation."
186. U.S. Department of the Interior, Bureau of Land Management, "Dry Creek Basin Coordinated Resource Management Plan," 5.
187. Gunnison Sage-grouse Rangewide Steering Committee, "Gunnison Sage-grouse Conservation Plan." See Web site: http://wildlife.state.co.us/WildlifeSpecies/SpeciesOfConcern/Birds/GunnisonConsPlan.htm.
188. Much of the information in this section is based on the authors' involvement as members of the San Miguel Basin Gunnison Sage-grouse Working Group from 2003 to the present (2006).
189. Gunnison Sage-grouse Rangewide Steering Committee, "Gunnison Sage-grouse Conservation Plan," Executive Summary, pp. 1–2.
190. Garton, "Gunnison Sage-grouse Population Trend Analysis."
191. E-mail discussion among members of Gunnison Sage-grouse working groups and sage-grouse biologists.
192. Atwood, "Notice of Intent to Sue over Endangered Species Act," letter dated April 18, 2006, from Western Environmental Law Center to Mitch King (USFWS), H. Dale Hall (USFWS), and Dirk Kempthorne, Secretary of U.S. Department of the Interior.
193. U.S. Department of the Interior, Bureau of Land Management, *Dry Creek Basin Oil and Gas Environmental Assessment*.

CHAPTER THREE

The Uncompahgre Valley: Making the Desert Bloom

Surrounded by some of the most spectacular parts of Colorado, the natural treasures of the Uncompahgre Valley and its immediate vicinity (see Map 3.1) are easily overlooked. The gray, flattopped mesas and adobe hills appear stark and barren, even though offset by the pastoral feeling of agricultural fields and small, rural communities (see Plate 16). It is a semiarid valley, often reaching 100°F in the summer and receiving only about 8–10" of annual precipitation.[1] Heat, gnats, barren slopes, and mud together make it a challenge to appreciate the adobes, but following a winter of average or above-average rainfall, many flowers

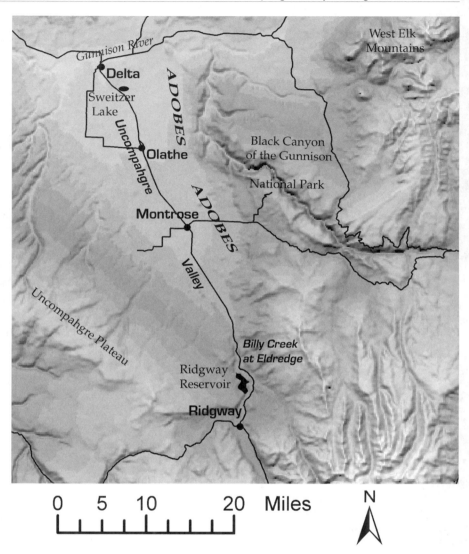

Map 3.1. *Map of the Uncompahgre Valley as covered in this chapter.*

bloom against the bare clays, their beauty highlighted by the harshness. The higher country on the valley margins is a moister and greener landscape and the source of water for the valley.

The adobe hills and mesa slopes are Mancos shale, a sedimentary deposit left by a vast inland sea in the late Cretaceous. This saline marine shale plays a significant role in the valley. The valley is one of the most developed agricultural areas in southwestern Colorado, yet this agriculture is threatened by rapid growth and rural sprawl. Curiously, both agriculture and sprawl are potentially constrained by a limitation of the Mancos shale, whose rich selenium content is a natural but toxic element that threatens native fish downstream.

The valley's original vegetation has been nearly replaced by cultivation and urban development on flatter land. Riparian areas were dominated by cottonwoods and riparian shrubs, but the valley itself was mostly salt-desert shrubland,[2] an inland desert with a few species of salt-tolerant shrubs, grasses, and forbs.

Mancos shale is a harsh environment for plants because rain that falls on the surface becomes tightly bound up by the fine particles of the soil and the salt content makes plant growth difficult. Many plants that live here have special adaptations to withstand the salt and drought.[3] On harsh shale flats and slopes the dwarf shrubs Gardner's saltbush and mat saltbush may grow almost alone—they have glands that secrete the salt the plant absorbs while it is taking up water. A major upland plant community was dominated by the salt-tolerant shrub shadscale saltbush (see Figure 3.1) and the drought-tolerant grass James' galleta (see Plate 6b), with a mixture of other plants (see Table 3.1).[4] In the saline swales and bottomlands with water near the surface was the shrub greasewood, with an understory of Mojave seablite or inland

Figure 3.1. *Shadscale saltbush* (Atriplex confertifolia) *often has some branches that lack leaves and are sharp to the touch. They can be seen along the left side of the photograph.*

Table 3.1. Plants common on adobes in the Uncompahgre Valley.[1]

SHRUBS
  Basin big sagebrush (*Seriphidium tridentatum*)
  Gardner's saltbush (*Atriplex gardneri*)
  Greasewood (*Sarcobatus vermiculatus*)
  Mat saltbush (*Atriplex corrugata*)
  Shadscale saltbush (*Atriplex confertifolia*)
  Wyoming big sagebrush (not in Weber and Wittmann 2001)

FORBS
  Colorado bladderpod (*Lesquerella vicina*)
  Hayden's milkvetch (*Astragalus haydenianus*)
  Mojave seablite (*Suaeda moquinii*)
  Patterson's milkvetch (*Astragalus pattersonii*)
  Singlestem buckwheat (*Eriogonum acaule*)

GRASSES AND GRASSLIKE PLANTS
  Basin wildrye (*Leymus cinereus*)
  Indian ricegrass (*Achnatherum hymenoides*)
  Inland saltgrass (*Distichlis stricta*)
  James' galleta (*Hilaria jamesii*)
  Needle and thread (*Hesperostipa comata*)
  Saline wildrye (*Leymus salina*)

NON-NATIVES
  Field bindweed (*Convolvulus arvensis*)
  Hardheads (Russian knapweed) (*Acroptilon repens*)
  Jointed goatgrass (*Cylindropyrum cylindricum*)
  Prickly Russian thistle (*Salsola australis*)
  Saltlover (Halogeton) (*Halogeton glomeratus*)
  Yellow sweetclover (*Melilotus officinalis*)

1. Common names are from the PLANTS online database, http://plants.usda.gov. Latin names are from Weber and Wittmann, *Colorado Flora*.

saltgrass (see Figure 3.2). The natural vegetation that persists is now found mainly on the adobe hills, where several rare and endangered plants also occur.

On the valley's higher margins are sagebrush shrublands dominated by tall basin big sagebrush (see Figure 2.1) in swales and moister places and by shorter Wyoming big sagebrush (see Figure 2.2) on drier uplands. Upland mesa tops and terraces likely supported grasslands with a mixture of James' galleta, needle and thread (see Figure 2.4a), and Indian ricegrass (see Figure 2.4b). The sagebrush and grasslands gradually merge up into pinyon-juniper and mixed mountain shrub communities. The Black Canyon of the Gunnison National Park is in the heart of the mixed mountain shrub community (see Plate 17), which covers uplands above the pinyon-juniper zone and interfingers with aspen and conifer forests at higher elevations throughout western Colorado. Five

Figure 3.2. *Inland saltgrass (Distichlis stricta) often forms a thick sward beneath greasewood or other salt-tolerant shrubs on saline sites.*

Table 3.2. Plants common in the mixed mountain shrub community.[1]

TREES
  Rocky Mountain Douglas-fir (*Pseudotsuga menziesii* var. *glauca*)
  Rocky Mountain juniper (*Sabina scopulorum*)
  Twoneedle pinyon (*Pinus edulis*)
  Utah juniper (*Sabina osteosperma*)

SHRUBS
  Alderleaf mountain mahogany (*Cercocarpus montanus*)
  Gambel oak (*Quercus gambelii*)
  Mountain big sagebrush (*Serphidium vaseyanum*)
  Mountain snowberry (*Symphoricarpos oreophilus*)
  Utah serviceberry (*Amelanchier utahensis*)

FORBS
  American vetch (*Vicia americana*)
  Hairy false goldenaster (*Heterotheca villosa*)
  Lobeleaf groundsel (*Packera multilobata*)
  Mountain larkspur (*Delphinium ramosum*)
  Nevada pea (*Lathyrus leucanthus*)
  New Mexico groundsel (*Packera neomexicana*)
  Rosy pussytoes (*Antennaria rosea*)
  Small-leaf pussytoes (*Antennaria parvifolia*)
  Tailcup lupine (*Lupinus caudatus*)
  Trailing fleabane (*Erigeron flagellaris*)

GRASSES AND GRASSLIKE PLANTS
  Geyer's sedge (*Carex geyeri*)
  Indian ricegrass (*Achnatherum hymenoides*)
  Muttongrass (*Poa fendleriana*)

NON-NATIVES
  Cheatgrass (*Anisantha tectorum*)
  Common dandelion (*Taraxacum officinale*)
  Crested wheatgrass (*Agropyron cristatum*)
  Kentucky bluegrass (*Poa pratensis*)
  Smooth brome (*Bromopsis inermis*)

1. Common names are from the PLANTS online database http://plants.usda.gov. Latin names are from Weber and Wittmann, *Colorado Flora*.

main shrubs dominate the mixed mountain shrub community (see Table 3.2). Gambel oak is often the tallest and most prominent (see Figure 3.3), with alderleaf mountain mahogany (see Figure 3.4) and mountain big sagebrush (see Figure 3.5) beneath.

This chapter examines the legacies created by irrigation of this valley. Though natural communities were diminished to create productive farmlands, the valley has great potential to provide a sustainable mix of farming and natural landscapes. Groups are working to preserve open space and farmlands and to create new farming options, such as a

Figure 3.3. *Gambel oak* (Quercus gambelii*)*.

local seed industry. Unfortunately, little is being done to protect the remaining natural communities, and both agriculture and natural vegetation face threats from rural subdivision and rapid urban growth.

Figure 3.4. *Alderleaf mountain mahogany* (Cercocarpus montanus).

LEGACY OF PAST HUMAN USES

The Uncompahgre Valley (and Plateau) was home to the powerful Tabeguache Utes when Euro-American explorers first began to penetrate western Colorado. The Tabeguache were one of the last groups of Native Americans to lose control over their territory, but, as Euro-Americans advanced, the Utes were forced to trade territory for beef and other provisions. With the mining boom in the San Juans in the

Figure 3.5. *Mountain big sagebrush (Seriphidium vaseyanum). This high-elevation sagebrush is characterized by a growth form with a rounder or smoother top than related sagebrushes. Basin big sagebrush is taller (Figure 2.1), and Wyoming big sagebrush has a more ragged top (Figure 2.2); both are typical of lower elevations.*

1870s, Euro-Americans began to covet the last of the Tabeguache territory for grazing and agriculture. In 1881 the Tabeguache (then called Uncompahgre Utes) were forcibly removed to the Uintah Reservation in Utah,[5] and ranchers and homesteaders rushed in to the Uncompahgre area.

The valley was an early and major settlement area for Euro-Americans on the Western Slope. The first cattle arrived in 1875 when the Los Pinos Indian Agency was moved to the valley.[6] A road reached Montrose in 1877, and the railroad arrived in 1883.[7] By 1887 Montrose County had 29,700 cattle and 21,160 sheep.[8] While open-range cattle barons flourished in surrounding areas from the 1870s to the 1890s, the valley was quickly claimed by settlers who saw in the Utes' former wintering grounds a desert waiting to bloom. They began growing hay, small grains, and vegetables in the bottomlands and fruit orchards on the nearby mesas.[9] In the late 1800s Montrose became well-known in western Colorado for its apples and pears.[10] The valley produced a food surplus that supplied the booming mining industry of the San Juan Mountains. A well-ordered agricultural landscape soon replaced much of the natural vegetation.

Irrigating the Valley

Settlers soon realized their agriculture was limited only by water, with the sunny climate and clay soils quite favorable for growing crops.[11] The Uncompahgre is a small river with unpredictable flow, but settlers managed to build a maze of diversion canals and bring 30,000 acres into agricultural production by 1903.[12] The river's waters were not enough to convert all of the arable land, so within decades new residents sought more water, looking to the much larger Gunnison River running through a deep canyon near the valley.

From the South Rim of the Black Canyon of the Gunnison, one would never suspect the human feat that lies beneath. The Utes are said to have believed that anyone trying to follow the course of the river through the canyon would never return. Indeed, the 2,000-foot cliffs of dark schist and gneiss and the sweeping views, still largely devoid of permanent human presence, give the impression that surely here nature is much as it was before humans appeared on the scene (see Plate 17). But deep below the surface lies a six-mile tunnel dug by settlers and entrepreneurs from the Uncompahgre Valley.

The Uncompahgre Project was the first Bureau of Reclamation project started and the second one finished.[13] Armed with little more than pick-axes and dynamite, crews worked from both ends, hard-rock miners on the east and coal miners on the shales to the west. The tunnel was completed in 1909, and by 1912 about 76,000 acres of land near Montrose and Delta was irrigated.[14] A swath averaging fifteen miles wide and thirty miles long, from Colona to Delta, is now irrigated.[15] The adobe hills were an exception, and most remained as grazing lands.

Crops grown in the valley have varied, but the largest acreages have always been hay and alfalfa. Hay occupied over 50 percent of harvested acres in Montrose County in 2002, with corn, dry edible beans, barley, and wheat the other major commodities.[16] Many farmers have livestock, which are grazed on federal lands from spring to fall and then winter in the valley.[17] Sugar beets were a major crop from the early 1900s until the valley's Holly sugar factory closed in the mid-1970s.[18] Although small in acreage, vegetables, sweet corn, and melons are the most valuable crops per acre, accounting for sales of over $10 million in Delta and Montrose counties in 2000.[19]

The impacts of irrigation extend well beyond the valley. The Gunnison River, as it runs through the Black Canyon, has been altered by water development. Three large dams were added just upstream of the Black Canyon in the 1960s and 1970s. In the spring of 2003 the U.S. Department of the Interior settled the park's claims to water in the Gunnison River by giving most of its potential water rights to the state of Colorado,[20] leaving in doubt the park's ability to protect its riparian ecosystem. Non-native rainbow and brown trout have become established, and in the reservoirs non-native lake trout and kokanee salmon are now found.[21] Despite this, the solitude and beauty of the Black Canyon remain, and the sparsely vegetated canyon walls exist much as they would without people.

Loss and Decline of the Riparian Plant Community

Along the Uncompahgre River, only small remnants of the natural riparian community remain. The natural vegetation that once lined the large rivers of western Colorado above 6,000 feet in elevation comprises the "Narrowleaf cottonwood/strapleaf willow–silver buffaloberry" plant association. Plant communities, when they acquire a formal name, are called associations.[22] This association is named after the dominant tree, narrowleaf cottonwood (*Populus angustifolia*), and the two shrubs that are abundant or characteristic beneath the trees. Silver buffaloberry (*Shepherdia argentea*) is distinctive because of its gray color and so is easy to see at a distance (see Plate 18). It can be confused with Russian olive (*Eleagnus angustifolia*), a non-native tree that has invaded western Colorado and Utah rivers,[23] particularly at lower elevations. Russian olive is often taller and has leaves that alternate along the stem,

Figure 3.6. *Billy Creek State Wildlife Area along the Uncompahgre River.*

while silver buffaloberry has opposite leaves. Strapleaf willow (*Salix ligulifolia*) has much greener leaves about as wide as those of silver buffaloberry.

The setting for this plant association is broad, open valleys, and the association is now rare because current land uses are concentrated in such settings. These are relatively hot valleys, and livestock concentrate in shady riparian areas near rivers and streams. Riparian areas in general, and this plant association in particular, have been vulnerable to invasion by non-native plants.[24] Excessive livestock grazing in riparian areas tends to remove or alter the shrub layer but also discourages regeneration of cottonwoods and facilitates the invasion of non-native herbaceous species. Dams and major water diversions have been constructed on rivers upstream from most of the desirable agricultural valleys in western Colorado, in some cases almost de-watering the river downstream. Less significant but still contributing has been conversion of river terraces to agricultural crops, sometimes involving clearing of cottonwood groves. These agricultural areas are also, then, sources of weeds that may invade the riparian zone.

One relatively unaltered remnant of this riparian association remains at the Billy Creek Wildlife Area near Eldridge (see Figure 3.6). However, the community is now being degraded because flooding has been reduced since construction of the Ridgway Dam, the last major water project in the Uncompahgre Valley, which stores water to supplement irrigation and municipal water uses. The dam was completed in 1987 and the reservoir filled by 1990, inundating 4.6 miles of the river's riparian zone.[25] Flooding and flow patterns have been altered downstream of the dam, and young narrowleaf cottonwoods, now ten to fifteen years old, have established on the gravel bars. This is known to occur below dams on other rivers throughout the world.[26] Unfortunately, the older established cottonwoods farther from the river may suffer from less frequent flooding and eventually die.

While this might appear to be simply a narrowing of the vegetated river margin in adjustment to the new flow regime imposed by the dam, it is really a symptom of a larger degradation of the riparian vegetation. Periodic natural floods flush out the channel, move the gravels around, and create a mosaic of small ponds, backwater channels, gravel bars, and terraces.[27] Without these periodic floods, this active shifting mosaic of microhabitats along the river will disappear. In the mid-1980s, before the dam was filled, temporary flood channels, away from the margin of the stream itself, contained orchids and other wetland plants. By 2000 these temporary channels were dry and filled with the non-native Kentucky bluegrass. The Billy Creek remnant now has at least thirteen non-native plant species, some of which are invasive and can possibly replace native plants. Without periodic floods, the richness and diversity of the vegetation have been reduced.

Lower- and mid-elevation riparian forests, such as those at Billy Creek, provide important corridors between forest patches for many birds and other animals. The highest diversity and density of breeding birds in Colorado are found in lower-elevation riparian forests, although most of the species that nest there also breed in other habitats.[28] A few birds—such as the yellow-breasted chat, yellow warbler, blue grosbeak, and the now rare western yellow-billed cuckoo—breed mainly in deciduous riparian corridors, even though this habitat is small in area.[29]

Dams can be operated to some extent to offset these adverse downstream ecological effects. A first step is to identify the key hydrologic flows needed to maintain the essential floodplain mosaic.[30] Periodic artificial flows (typically floods) can then be designed and released from reservoirs for the purpose of floodplain restoration and maintenance.[31] Billy Creek reminds us that in and on the periphery of the Uncompahgre Valley, people are still struggling over how much land and water will go to agriculture and housing developments and to what extent water will remain in rivers to maintain their biological diversity. The ecological legacies of this struggle are still being created in places such as Billy Creek and the Gunnison River, and a restoration vision has yet to sprout.

Livestock Legacies in the Mixed Mountain Shrub Community

The South Rim of the Black Canyon of the Gunnison National Park is an inviting place to experience the mixed mountain shrub community, an important part of the natural landscape surrounding the Uncompahgre Valley and truly a community of plants. A plant community is a bit like a human community, in that a repeating set of characters (police, mayor, grocer) occurs from place to place. Five main shrubs dominate this community (see Table 3.2). Gambel oak is the only oak and often the tallest shrub (see Figure 3.3), living to be over 100 years old, based on a count of annual growth rings. Another tall shrub, Utah service-berry (see Plate 17), is distinguished by leaves that are finely toothed, mostly on their upper half. Alderleaf mountain mahogany (see Figure 3.4) is a smaller shrub, with coarse leaves and hairy, curly fruit. Mountain snowberry has leaves that are opposite each other along the stem, and it has white berries in the fall. The sagebrush here is mountain big sagebrush, the typical sage of higher elevations (see Figure 3.5). These shrubs, seen over and over in the community, seem to fit together—the taller oak and serviceberry in the overstory, alderleaf mountain mahogany at midheight, and snowberry beneath. Mountain sagebrush dominates the openings.

Although many birds (see Table 3.3) and mammals are common in the mixed mountain shrublands, none is as strongly restricted to that community as some birds are to sagebrush, pinyon-juniper, or ponderosa pine forests. Of the birds, the green-tailed towhee has the strongest association with mixed mountain shrubs.[32] This robin-sized bird, drab green with a rusty cap, is conspicuous only when singing, often from the top of a tall shrub. None of the many small mammals found in the community is restricted to it, but the nocturnal brush mouse does favor mountain shrublands, relying heavily on acorns from the oaks for food.[33]

Part of the Black Canyon of the Gunnison was made a national

Table 3.3. Common birds of the mixed mountain shrub community of southwestern Colorado.[1]

Blue grouse
Common poorwill
Broad-tailed hummingbird
Dusky flycatcher
Western scrub jay
Blue-gray gnatcatcher
Orange-crowned warbler
Virginia's warbler
McGillivray's warbler
Green-tailed towhee
Spotted towhee
Chipping sparrow
Lazuli bunting

1. Kingery, *Colorado Breeding Bird Atlas.*

monument in 1933, after years of effort by Rev. Mark T. Warner and other Montrose citizens to protect the area. In October 1999 it became a national park. Adjacent ranchers had been using the monument area for both sheep and cattle grazing, but the park staff tried to institute an end to grazing on its lands as early as 1938. However, grazing of sheep, cattle, and sometimes horses continued until the South Rim was fenced in the early 1960s.[34]

Although the park's mixed mountain shrub community now has a thick ground cover of mostly native flowering plants and grasses, some of the legacy of livestock grazing is still evident. The tailcup lupine and mountain larkspur, for example, may be more common because they are poisonous to livestock.[35] Common dandelion is a nonnative species that increases under grazing and remains common here. Other abundant forbs are the white-flowered Nevada pea and trailing fleabane, both native species that seem to persist under grazing.

Beneath the shrubs, Geyer's sedge is common and scattered (see Figure 3.7). Most sedges are found in wet areas, but this dryland sedge is the most abundant understory species—where it has not been lost as a result of overgrazing—throughout the mixed mountain shrub zone. It looks a lot like a grass, but its stem and leaves are triangular in cross section. Two other main grasses are found. Kentucky bluegrass (see Figure 3.8) is scattered among the Geyer's sedge

Figure 3.7. *Geyer's sedge* (Carex geyeri), *reproduced from plate 98 in USDA Handbook No. 374 by Frederick J. Hermann.*

Figure 3.8. *Kentucky bluegrass* (Poa pratensis*)*.

but not in bunches, while muttongrass (see Figure 2.4c) occurs in bunches about a foot in diameter. Mutton-grass and Geyer's sedge are native. Kentucky bluegrass is a common non-native lawn grass very resistant to grazing and trampling because it has underground stems that spread through the soil (see Box—Rhizomes Versus Bunchgrasses, pp. 116–117). Kentucky bluegrass in this area is probably another legacy of the heavy livestock grazing of the past.

BOX—RHIZOMES VERSUS BUNCHGRASSES

Grasses with rhizomes and bunchgrasses are visually distinct (see box figure). To understand the significance of the difference, think about a lawn. Lawn grass is regularly trampled and cut, but it still prospers because a typical lawn grass—Kentucky bluegrass (see Figure 3.8)—and many other grasses have rhizomes. Rhizomes are underground horizontal stems that allow plants to survive and spread even if aboveground leaves and stems are reduced. In contrast, bunchgrasses, such as needle and thread, do not spread vegetatively through underground stems but instead must produce seeds to replace themselves or to spread to new areas.

Grasslands of the Great Plains, which have a long history of herbivory by herds of large animals (bison, pronghorn, elk), had abundant cover of rhizomatous grasses and were less prone to significant alteration by livestock grazing. Grasslands of the Mountain West and Pacific Northwest, which lack this long history of herbivory by large herds of native animals, tend to have more bunchgrasses and fewer or no native rhizomatous grasses.[1]

Bunchgrasses can withstand some grazing, since they store some of the energy produced by photosynthesis in their roots. But each bunchgrass has to survive by itself, not as part of a large organism connected underground by rhizomes. If a bunchgrass is killed by overgrazing, it can only be replaced by a new plant established by seed. If a large area is overgrazed to the point that flowering and seeding of bunchgrasses are prevented, they can be completely lost. This loss of bunchgrasses has occurred throughout the West as a result of overgrazing by livestock.

Rhizomes and bunchgrasses thus have much to do with legacies from livestock grazing. At low elevations in southwestern Colorado's semiarid grasslands and sagebrush and pinyon-juniper country, there was often a mix of the rhizomatous blue grama and James' galleta (see Plate 6), along with some or all of the three common bunchgrasses—needle and thread, Indian ricegrass, and muttongrass (see Figure 2.4). When overgrazing occurs in these ecosystems, it is not surprising that the rhizomatous grasses become predominant and the bunchgrasses may decline or disappear, as in Dry Creek Basin (see Chapter 2). Many bunchgrasses are also disadvantaged by being cool-season grasses that green up early and are grazed heavily by livestock in early spring when forage is limited. Higher elevations in southwestern Colorado—in ponderosa pine, mixed conifer, and subalpine forests and grasslands—lack abundant native rhizomatous grasses. At these higher elevations, when native bunchgrasses are lost through overgrazing by livestock, they often are replaced by the non-native rhizomatous grasses Kentucky bluegrass and smooth brome (see Box—Smooth Brome, pp. 281–282), as well as by common dandelion and other weeds.

NOTE

1. Mack and Thompson, "Evolution in Steppe."

Western wheatgrass (Pascopyrum smithii), *showing rhizomes, on the left and the bunchgrass, needle and thread* (Hesperostipa comata), *on the right.*

WHAT IS HAPPENING NOW?

Rural Subdivision

Today, the most obvious change taking place in the valley is the subdivision of agricultural land for rural residential developments. Remaining natural communities on the adobe lands and mesas are also being consumed by residential development. With a projected annual growth rate of 2.6 percent, the city of Montrose is expected to add 5,000 housing units within its annexed area between 1996 and 2020, doubling the city's housing units.[36] Growth in unincorporated surrounding areas parallels this growth in town. Atypical of agricultural land elsewhere, much of the valley's land is served with potable water from a Bureau of Reclamation program[37] and is easily converted to residential development.

The valley has always been an area with many family-sized farms, operated mostly with family labor, though migrant labor is now also important. There are many benefits to maintaining the small and moderate-sized family farms within the valley. The most important benefit may be that a healthy farm population helps provide a stable social and economic base. Communities dominated by a few large corporate producers tend to have increased income inequality, increased poverty, and decreased retail trade outlets.[38] Family farmers have typically had strong ties to their local communities, and they form a social fabric that cannot be replaced by a few large farmers. When they sell their food locally—as through farmer's markets, which now occur in most towns in southwestern Colorado[39]—nonfarmers learn more about how their food is grown, and entrepreneurship and community identity are enhanced.[40] Relative to subdivisions, the environmental benefits of well-managed farmlands can also be substantial. A high proportion of private land in the valley provides important winter habitat for elk and mule deer (see Map 3.2) as well as valuable open space.

The fate of the still undivided agricultural lands depends to some extent on the health of the ranching and agricultural economy and community. Wayne Cooley, Montrose County Extension agent, explained, "When a farmer has a choice of *losing* $500 per acre growing onions, as the [average farmer] did last year [1999], or selling his acreage for $10,000 per acre for development, the economic choice is pretty easy."[41] Despite excellent climate and secure water, the valley is a testament to the hard times for family farmers under current farm policy and industrialization of agriculture. Because of the distance to markets and the relatively small land area compared with other regions, farmers cannot easily compete in major commodity markets. Farmers in the valley today continue to look for profitable niche markets, such as Olathe's sweet corn, without widespread success to date.

Water is slowly being redirected to support rural housing, subdivisions, and small acreages where mainly recreational horses are kept. Between 1978 and 1997, almost 200,000 acres of the 1.2 million acres of farmland in Mesa, Delta, Montrose, and Ouray counties was converted

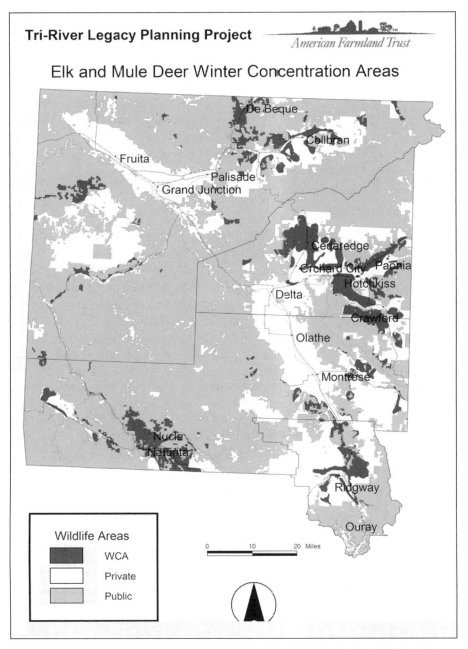

Tri-River Legacy Planning Project
American Farmland Trust

Elk and Mule Deer Winter Concentration Areas

De Beque

Collbran

Fruita

Palisade
Grand Junction

Cedaredge

Orchard City   Paonia

Hotchkiss

Delta

Crawford

Olathe

Montrose

Nucla
Naturita

Ridgway

Ouray

Wildlife Areas

WCA

Private

Public

0   10   20 Miles

Map 3.2. *Elk and mule deer winter concentration areas on private land in the Tri-River Region (Uncompahgre, Gunnison, and Colorado rivers) of western Colorado. Courtesy, James Ferriday and American Farmland Trust, Palisade, Colorado. Wildlife data come from the Colorado Division of Wildlife, Natural Diversity Information Source.*

to other uses, mostly residential subdivisions.[42] Without policy changes, much of the growth will continue to entail land-consuming, scattered rural subdivisions.[43] The natural and cultural landscape is being dramatically altered, but with no new vision guiding the alteration. As land conservation advocate John Wright explained, "The destruction of 'place' is now so institutionalized and bears such a veneer of normality or even inevitability that to challenge it is to appear out of step with the 'real' world."[44] The forces behind rural sprawl are indeed strong, but projects are under way that could help stem sprawl and preserve open space, natural communities, and agriculture.

Native Seed Industry

Improving the economic viability of agriculture is one way to help maintain farmlands and their benefits, and one innovative idea is the development of a native seed industry. This effort is linked to a major restoration effort, the Uncompahgre Plateau project, in the pinyon-juniper and sagebrush ecosystems on the Uncompahgre Plateau (see Chapter 4). Seeding with native grasses and forbs to restore diversity and prevent invasion of non-native weeds, such as cheatgrass (see Box—Cheatgrass, pp. 61–63), will be required in some places. Federal land management agencies now try to use native seeds, but only genetically uniform cultivars of a few North American species developed from seed sources distant from southwestern Colorado have been available. In 2001 the Uncompahgre Plateau project obtained $100,000 in funding from BLM's National Native Plant Material Development project to start a native seed program for the Uncompahgre Plateau region.[45] The goals are to help maintain the species and genetic diversity of the vegetation on the plateau while providing a profitable niche "crop" for farmers in the valley.

Starting a native seed industry is no small undertaking. To get started, small amounts of seed must be collected, typically by hand, from wildlands in the region. These seeds are then planted in fields and expanded until sufficient quantities are available for sale. For the easiest-to-grow grasses, it takes at least three years to produce a marketable "crop" from initial seed. For example, in 1999 Marilyn Colyer, longtime naturalist at Mesa Verde National Park, collected a handful of seeds of a native plant, basin wildrye, to establish a seed source for roadsides and burned areas. Southwest Seeds in Dolores, which specializes in native seeds, planted an area about six by twenty feet with the seed. From that small area, 20 pounds of viable seed were obtained the first year, enough to plant three acres the next year. In the third year the three acres produced 300 pounds of seed, enough to sell some back to the park and to replant eight acres. The eight acres were expected to yield 4,000 to 5,000 pounds of seed by the fifth year.[46] Processing native seeds requires skill and costly machinery, as native seeds are usually smaller and lighter than cultivated grains, and many have bristles and hairs that must be removed (see Figure 3.9).

For most farmers this long return time on investment is prohibitive. Markets are hard to predict five years ahead of time. The Uncompahgre Plateau project obtained a grant to enlist the help of both regional experts on native plant restoration and the government-funded Upper Colorado Environmental Plant Center in Meeker to develop enough viable (foundation) seed to distribute to producers. This will help make farmer entry into the seed industry more feasible. Even with government assistance, however, local native seeds will be more expensive than the uniform cultivars of "native" plants available from major seed producers. Most agree that secure market contracts will be needed to enable farmers to invest in local native seed production. This could be accomplished in part by stipulating that bids require locally produced seed.[47] It is important, however, that the need for a market not be a factor in deciding when and how to manage public lands. To avoid this, a market area larger than the Uncompahgre Plateau is envisioned.

Only recently have land management and other agencies, such as highway departments, begun to require the use of seeds native to the United States. Most highway corridors have been planted to non-native smooth brome and other aliens, while much western public land has been planted to crested wheatgrass (see Boxes—Smooth Brome, pp. 281–282, and Crested Wheatgrass, pp. 85–86). The Uncompahgre native seed project is a possible model for ecosystem restoration projects elsewhere.[48] If successful, it could illustrate the compatibility of ecological and economic activities.

Selenium

In addition to the economic problems facing most family farms in the United States, farmers in the Uncompahgre Valley must also deal with selenium, a difficult and unusual problem shared by only a few other regions. In 1983, deformities and reproductive problems were found in fish and aquatic birds at a wildlife refuge in the San Joaquin Valley of California. Selenium in irrigation drainage was found to be the cause. Studies of around 620 irrigation projects and wildlife areas in the West found the Uncompahgre (irrigation) project area was a major source of selenium to the Uncompahgre, Gunnison, and Colorado riv-

Figure 3.9. *One of the seed-cleaning machines that make up over $1 million in equipment at Southwest Seeds, Dolores, Colorado.*

ers.[49] Mancos shale is the valley's marine deposit that is rich in selenium and salts. In the 1960s about 12,000 acres of Mancos lands on the east side of the valley were reclassified as irrigable.[50] The selenium problem may have begun when these lands were brought into production.[51]

Figure 3.10. *Razorback sucker. Courtesy, Upper Colorado River Endangered Fish Recovery Program, U.S. Fish and Wildlife Service, Denver.*

Fish from Sweitzer Lake, near Delta, where several irrigation canals drain, have selenium levels too high for safe human consumption.[52] Several warm-water fish, including the endangered razorback sucker (see Figure 3.10) living downstream in the Colorado River, could be harmed by high selenium levels contributed by the Uncompahgre River.[53] In 1997 the State Water Quality Control Commission set the standard for protection of aquatic life at five micrograms/liter for selenium; in 2002 the Uncompahgre River downstream of the irrigation project carried about nineteen micrograms/liter.[54]

Thanks to laws such as the Endangered Species Act, the Migratory Bird Act, and the Clean Water Act, the selenium issue is being taken seriously in the valley. The Uncompahgre project is one of five in the United States targeted for remediation work under the National Irrigation Water Quality Program, a federal program set up in the mid-1980s to address the problem of irrigation runoff.[55] In 1998 the Gunnison Basin Selenium Task Force, a group of local stakeholders and agencies from all levels of government, formed to find ways to reduce the selenium load to the river "while maintaining the economic viability and lifestyle of the Lower Gunnison Valley."[56]

Studies have been done on sources of selenium in the valley and on potential remediation approaches. Preventing deep percolation of irrigation water through the Mancos shale is key to reducing selenium in creeks and rivers. Piping irrigation laterals, lining irrigation ditches with a polymer, and improving irrigation methods are measures given high priority by the task force.[57] In 2001, various trees, forages, and annual crops were planted as an experiment northeast of Montrose to see if "phytoremediation" might also help. It was found that a hybrid poplar tree grew well in the valley and concentrated selenium, but it was unclear how the wood product could be marketed profitably without a local processing plant.[58] This new poplar could also be a threat to the high ecological value of native riparian vegetation. Local people and other key stakeholders are strongly opposed to retiring currently productive agricultural ground and returning it to desert.[59] However, it may be in the public interest to identify small areas that are high contributors of selenium that could be voluntarily retired and perhaps become open space.

More important, both for selenium control and protection of natural communities, is limiting development of the still-natural, nonirrigated upland adobes (see Plate 19). Mancos areas not presently irrigated have approximately forty-five times more soluble selenium than alluvial Mancos soils long under irrigation.[60] One new golf course near Delta, for example, negated the selenium reduction effects of a $1.3 million piping project until its water use and storage were altered to address the problem.[61] Upland adobes are experiencing much residential subdivision (see Figure 3.11), often including irrigated lawns and unlined ponds that can contribute high loads of selenium.[62] A recent study of growth and land-use policies in the Uncompahgre and Gunnison basins concluded: "[T]here is sufficient land in the region to absorb the projected population increase, assuming small increases in density of new developments. With guidance and voluntary incentives, growth can be directed away from sensitive lands. Without an effort to redirect development, however, much of the agricultural land and sensitive areas in the region [is] likely to be lost to a highly dispersed, very low-density growth surge."[63]

This study also compared three growth management strategies with what is happening now (status quo). The three strategies were: (1) enact policies that encourage higher density and cluster development, (2) protect sensitive areas (agricultural lands, conservation areas, floodplains), and (3) encourage development within urban growth boundaries and discourage it outside those boundaries. Assuming the same growth rate, expected future landscapes under the scenarios are strikingly different (see Map 3.3). Any of the three strategies maintains much more open agricultural and natural landscape than the status quo and

Figure 3.11. *Rural subdivision on adobes near Montrose, Colorado.*

would save counties millions of dollars in public-service expenses (i.e., taxes needed) over a twenty-five-year period.[64] Growth could also be directed away from the highest-selenium soils. However, in Montrose County a master plan that would have directed growth fell under strong public opposition.[65] Landowners want to retain development options, and directed growth is seen as an infringement on property rights. While local governments have some legal authority to protect the public interest, they rarely have been given the political authority to do so in western Colorado (see Box—Land-Use Legislation and Government Policy, pp. 295–296).

Therefore, the task force is placing emphasis on developing Best Management Practices (BMPs) for residential and commercial development, with an emphasis on educating policy makers and citizens.[66] Central wastewater treatment, low-water landscaping, and proper irrigation are possible BMPs for developments on adobes. The task force is also making the case to citizens that, as taxpayers, they pay for the costly mitigation measures needed to meet water-quality standards.[67] Developers and home buyers are not used to paying the environmental and social costs of rural residential development. And because they reap the benefits of low-cost, unrestricted residential subdivision while the costs are shared by a much wider public, education alone will never

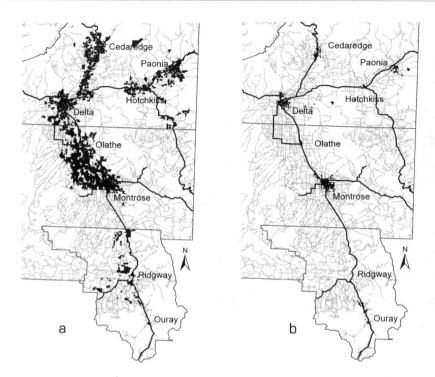

Map 3.3. *Two scenarios for future growth in Delta, Montrose, and Ouray counties: (a) Business as Usual, which continues present trends and policies; and (b) Urban Growth Boundaries, which focuses new growth with boundaries drawn around current towns and cities. Each scenario includes the same number of new residents. From a study by the University of Colorado, Denver (Muller, Bertron, and Yin 2001). Data for the map provided by Brian Muller and Li Yin, based on the maps in Muller, Bertron, and Yin 2001.*

be enough. As Steve Glazer, the High Country Citizens' Alliance representative on the Selenium Task Force, explained, this case shows the need for more integrated management of watersheds and water laws that recognize the public interest in water.[68]

Nonprofit Organizations and Land Protection

Addressing the economic problems of agriculture in places like the Uncompahgre Valley may be essential to maintain rural working landscapes, but it is unlikely to be sufficient. Escalating land values for development are almost certain to outpace agricultural land values, putting pressure on farmers to subdivide no matter how successful the native seeds project and the Selenium Task Force are. As solutions await political consensus, private nonprofit organizations have become important players in tackling the forces of subdivision.

For several years the American Farmland Trust (AFT; see Box—Land Trusts, pp. 128–129) has been working with the counties (Ouray, Montrose, Delta, and Mesa) of the Uncompahgre, Gunnison, and Colorado River basins (the Tri-River Region) to strengthen agricultural land protection. AFT is well-known for the "Cost of Community Services" studies it has conducted for over seventy communities across the United States. These studies show that the costs of local public services, such as roads and fire protection, to rural residential properties are higher than the taxes collected from these properties.[69] The average expenditure per dollar of revenue generated is $1.15 for residential development. The average cost of services per dollar of revenue generated for agricultural land, on the other hand, is only 37 cents.[70] Thus there is a cost of rural sprawl that is borne by the public rather than by homeowners and developers. AFT uses this research to educate the public and officials and to advocate for tax and policy changes to discourage subdivision of commercial ranch and farmlands. The costs and benefits of individual residential development projects vary greatly, depending on distance from existing services, density of the development, types of households, and the natural values of the land developed.[71]

AFT is working with the four Tri-River counties to develop a regional land protection plan, but achieving a political consensus for policy changes that involve regulations or restrictions to guide growth will be a slow and long-term process.[72] Some of these counties also have severe funding limitations for planning or agricultural land protection strategies. Meanwhile, other private land trusts are using conservation easements to protect key pieces of land with the help of willing landowners (see Box—Land Trusts, pp. 128–129).

One of several land trust projects in the Uncompahgre Valley is the Sweitzer Lake area just south of Delta on Highway 50. Three separate conservation easements held by the Black Canyon Regional Land Trust protect 240 acres of wetlands and open space around the lake from development. The area is important habitat for waterfowl, shorebirds, frogs, and other wildlife (see Map 3.4).[73]

Other Threats to Adobes

Today, the remaining undeveloped adobe hills stand as oases of native plants among the roads, canals, houses, and irrigated acres of mostly non-native plants that dominate the Uncompahgre Valley. These

BOX—LAND TRUSTS

As government policies and legal frameworks have been slow to respond to the problem of rural and urban sprawl, voluntary private land
protection efforts have expanded. Over 1,500 land trusts have sprung up
around the United States to offer conservation incentives to willing
landowners.[1] Most land trusts are private, not-for-profit corporations
that hold conservation easements for private property. Under a conservation easement, a property owner gives or sells his or her development
rights to a land trust. The land trust is responsible for enforcing the
development restrictions on the land in perpetuity. Some land trusts also
own lands for conservation, and some assist in transferring land to
public and conservation owners.

The Nature Conservancy alone has protected over 11 million acres
in the United States, much of it through conservation easements.[2]
Regional and local land trusts had protected another 6.25 million acres
by 2000, about a third of that through conservation easements.[3] There are
at least thirty-five land trusts in Colorado, and a dozen operate in
southwestern Colorado.[4] Two of the land trusts active in southwestern
Colorado illustrate their diversity.

The American Farmland Trust (AFT) is a large national land trust
committed to the preservation of farmland and ranch land.[5] Started in
1980, it is also one of the oldest land trusts. AFT has a regional office in
Palisade, Colorado. AFT uses a variety of approaches, including research and policy development, public education, and direct land
protection. In Colorado, AFT often works with local governments to
coordinate planning.

At the other end of the size scale is the Black Canyon Regional Land
Trust (BCRLT). Formed from the merger of two even smaller land trusts
in 2000, BCRLT's mission is to provide open space, protect agricultural
land, and help to physically separate and define the communities of the
Uncompahgre Valley.[6] With an annual operating budget of under
$100,000 in 2002, the BCRLT had over 15,592 acres under conservation
easements, including land surrounding Black Canyon of the Gunnison
National Park.[7] BCRLT considers itself a "working man's land trust."[8]
While wealthy landowners often benefit from tax breaks that come with
the donation of easements, land trusts need to purchase easements from
nonwealthy owners. The number of properties BCRLT is able to put
under easement is limited by funds, not by the lack of landowners who
would like to have conservation easements.

Although some in the West's farming and ranching culture have
criticized even voluntary conservation easements, viewing them as a
loss of private property rights,[9] the common interests of land trusts and
agricultural landowners have become clearer. As land trust scholar John
Wright stated, "There is room for trusts of every ideological and political

stance and for easements that protect land owned by people of all kinds."[10]

On the other hand, many land trusts have few or no criteria for the ecological condition of the lands they purport to protect,[11] and many of the organizations that do have criteria lack sufficient personnel for monitoring and enforcing the agreements in perpetuity.[12] Also, unlike land-use planning and regulation, it is usually impossible to obtain easements at a landscape level, thus limiting ecological gains from easements.[13] Some land trusts may also be abusing the intent of tax breaks and credits for easements by effectively subsidizing wealthy people buying and building on ranch lands, as long as they develop less than the maximum allowed.[14] These new wealthy owners often close off public access across their land to public lands,[15] making it more difficult for people to experience nature. Reform of land trust laws, to prevent abuses and ensure that conservation easements serve the broader public interest, is essential. Conservation easements could lead to a culture where landowners feel they should be paid to do the right thing on their land. Yet without government policies and markets that enable good land stewards to thrive economically and in the absence of regulations and incentives to guide growth, land trusts are presently the main hope for maintaining large areas of privately owned agricultural and natural landscapes.

NOTES

1. Ring, "Write-off on the Range."
2. Tenenbaum, "Land Trusts: A Restoration Frontier?"
3. See the Land Trust Alliance Web site: http://www.lta.org.
4. Rob Molacek, Land Trust Alliance, Grand Junction, Colorado, pers. comm., October 17, 2001.
5. See Web site: http://www.farmland.org.
6. Tony Hoag, former director, BCRLT, Montrose, Colorado, pers. comm., October 10, 2001.
7. Black Canyon Regional Land Trust Newsletter, Summer 2001.
8. Ibid.
9. Schober, "Conservation Easements Contain Pitfalls, Agent Says."
10. Wright, "Patterns and Prospects of Conservation Easement Use," 504.
11. Tenenbaum, "Land Trusts: A Restoration Frontier?"
12. Ring, "Write-off on the Range."
13. Travis, Theobald, and Fagre, "Transforming the Rockies."
14. Ring, "Write-off on the Range."
15. Ibid.

lands are too inhospitable for extensive cultivation, although they had higher livestock grazing pressure in the past and are still grazed in winter. Now, however, new human uses are reaching into the adobes.

Map 3.4. *Two conservation easements held by Black Canyon Regional Land Trust near Sweitzer Lake, Delta County, Colorado. Photo from U.S. Geological Survey, boundaries for easements courtesy Black Canyon Regional Land Trust, Montrose, Colorado.*

Off-road vehicle use has become a popular and controversial sport on the adobes (see Figure 3.12). Transmission lines and pipelines continue to proliferate. Not only do these uses destroy the solitude and open views of the adobes, but roads and corridors also serve as conduits for weed invasions.[74]

Some believe the uplands of the valley were once much more richly covered with grass and that early overgrazing denuded these lands.[75] To test this idea, Dave Bradford, a Forest Service range conservationist in Paonia, and colleagues extensively reviewed early historical reports and photographs.[76] Historical reports clearly describe the adobes and other areas away from the river as dry and sparsely vegetated. The Dominguez-Escalante journals of 1776 describe a well-wooded corridor along the river, with good forage restricted to widely spaced meadows. The description of the valley by Lieutenant Beckwith of the Gunnison expedition of 1853 is typical of early reports: "We traveled 18.25 miles down the Uncompahgre to-day. . . . The country is in all respects like that passed yesterday—cotton-wood, willow and grass in the narrow bottom, and near it heavy sage; but the great mass of the valley land is nearly destitute of vegetation—light, clayey and arid to

Figure 3.12. *Damage from off-road vehicles on BLM public land near Montrose, Colorado.*

such an extent that it is disagreeable to ride over it, as it sends up clouds of dust at every step."[77] Bradford and colleagues' rephotographs of the adobes also show widely spaced plants that have changed very little in size or density since the early 1900s.[78]

The adobes support several species of milkvetch (see Plate 20b) that may limit their value for livestock use. These milkvetches have pea flowers, although later in the summer only pods may still be present. Some milkvetches have a distinctive odor that comes from their tendency to accumulate selenium, which can reach toxic levels in plants such as these. Selenium poisoning causes blind staggers and alkali disease in animals. Blind staggers include impaired vision and wandering in circles, possibly leading to death, while alkali disease is less acute, characterized by emaciation and poor health.[79] About twenty-five milkvetch species in North America are known to accumulate selenium.[80]

The adobe soils are too salty and the slopes too dry for some non-native plants, but with the proliferation of new roads, several non-native plants are gaining ground on the adobes (see Table 3.1). Particularly worrisome is hardheads, more commonly called Russian knapweed (see Plate 21), which arrived in the West as a contaminant of alfalfa seed around 1928.[81] By 1998 it had invaded more than 1.4 million acres of arid land in the western United States.[82] This plant is difficult to eradicate; there is no use trying to pull it up, since its roots can grow to twenty-three feet deep.[83] It can also suppress the growth of neighboring plants.

Another non-native, saltlover or halogeton, first appeared in northern Nevada in the 1930s. It is a red succulent that spreads along the ground (see Plate 20a), is poisonous to sheep, and is now common on more than 10 million acres in the western United States.[84] Russian thistle, a plant of Eurasia as its name implies, has sharp stickers and a drab appearance and became famous as a "tumbling tumbleweed." It disperses by detaching its stem and rolling across the landscape. It appeared first in South Dakota as early as 1877 as a contaminant of flax seed and within twenty-five years had spread across the West.[85]

It is fortunate that the non-native weeds are most common along the roads in the adobes and have not spread over the entire landscape. Some weeds can spread by wind, so tires and disturbed road edges are not the only source of weeds, but they are probably among the most important sources.[86] In June 2000, BLM range conservationist Jim Sazama surveyed an area southeast of Montrose and reported forty acres of Russian knapweed, mainly along roads. He expressed concern that the heavy use of this area by off-road vehicles would spread this noxious species more widely.[87] On primitive and four-wheel-drive roads the large tires of off-road vehicles often contain mud, which can be rich in seeds of weedy species. Utility roads also quickly become lined with Russian knapweed and Russian thistle.

The adobes of the Uncompahgre are home to at least two rare plant species, one ranked by the Colorado Natural Heritage Program as globally vulnerable and the other as globally imperiled. A 2001 survey of adobes north of Montrose found these two threatened plant species had already suffered cumulative 9–11 percent losses to off-road vehicle (ORV) roads and trails.[88] In most ecosystems, noxious weeds and adverse effects on native plants are major reasons for designating travel routes rather than allowing off-road travel. Efforts are under way to designate special ORV use areas within the adobes and to restrict access to some of their best remaining natural communities to prevent weeds from spreading farther and to protect these communities.

The natural value of the valley's adobes has not been widely appreciated. The Natural Heritage Assessment of the Uncompahgre River Basin said: "This zone [semi-desert shrub zone], in our opinion, has historically been the least appreciated landscape in our area. At the same time, it is home to our rarest endemic plants, and deserves our protection. Public education about its unique natural values may be an important prerequisite for protecting this area."[89]

CONCLUDING THOUGHTS

The Uncompahgre Valley is a place that carries difficult legacies and considerable irony. It is one of the places in southwestern Colorado that offers the possibility of a vibrant working landscape of family farms, open space, and wildlife habitat alongside pieces of conserved nature. The ability to achieve this mosaic seems constrained for now by a narrow focus on property rights. To keep the desert blooming will require a major community effort: shared vision, a willingness to allow government to play a role, and personal choices that put long-term community good ahead of short-term personal profit. The land trusts are a start, but they cannot do it alone.

NOTES

1. See Web site: http://climate.atmos.colostate.edu.
2. West, "Intermountain Salt-Desert Shrubland."
3. Ibid.
4. Lyon et al., *Uncompahgre River Basin: Natural Heritage Assessment.*
5. Callaway, Janetski, and Stewart, "Ute."
6. Jocknick, *Early Days on the Western Slope*; O'Rourke, *Frontier in Transition.*
7. Greater Montrose Centennial, *Montrose, Colorado Centennial: 1882–1992.*
8. Denver and Rio Grande Railroad, *Montrose County: Land of Sunshine.*
9. O'Rourke, *Frontier in Transition*; Greater Montrose Centennial, *Montrose, Colorado Centennial: 1882–1992.*
10. Greater Montrose Centennial, *Montrose, Colorado Centennial: 1882–1992.*
11. Ibid.

12. U.S. Department of the Interior, Bureau of Reclamation, *Colorado Bureau of Reclamation Projects.*

13. Marc Catlin, Uncompahgre Valley Water Users Association, Montrose, Colorado, pers. comm., July 6, 2000.

14. U.S. Department of the Interior, Bureau of Reclamation, *Map, Uncompahgre Irrigation Project*; U.S. Department of the Interior, Bureau of Reclamation, *Colorado Bureau of Reclamation Projects.*

15. Marc Catlin, Uncompahgre Valley Water Users Association, Montrose, Colorado, pers. comm., July 6, 2000.

16. See Web site: http://www.usda.ams.gov/statesummaries/CO/County/ Montrose.

17. Wayne Cooley, Montrose County Extension, Montrose, Colorado, pers. comm., July 10, 2000.

18. Mark Catlin, Uncompahgre Valley Water Users Association, pers. comm., Montrose, Colorado, July 6, 2000.

19. Colorado State University Cooperative Extension, *2000 Agricultural Fact Sheet. Tri River Area.*

20. See Web site: http://www.doi.gov/news/030402b.htm.

21. U.S. Department of the Interior, National Park Service, *Visitor Guide for Curecanti National Recreation Area.*

22. Grossman et al., *Terrestrial Vegetation of the United States.*

23. Christiansen, "Naturalization of Russian Olive."

24. Planty-Tabacchi et al., "Invasibility of Species-Rich Riparian Zones"; Stromberg and Chew, "Herbaceous Exotics in Arizona's Riparian Ecosystems."

25. See Web site: http://dataweb.usbr.gov/dams/co82912.htm.

26. Ligon, Dietrich, and Trush, "Downstream Ecological Effects of Dams"; Collier, Webb, and Schmidt, *Dams and Rivers.*

27. Poff et al., "Natural Flow Regime."

28. Kingery, *Colorado Breeding Bird Atlas.*

29. Ibid.

30. Richter and Richter, "Prescribing Flood Regimes to Sustain Riparian Ecosystems."

31. Ligon, Dietrich, and Trush, "Downstream Ecological Effects of Dams."

32. Kingery, *Colorado Breeding Bird Atlas.*

33. Fitzgerald, Meaney, and Armstrong, *Mammals of Colorado.*

34. Beidleman, "History of Black Canyon of the Gunnison National Monument."

35. Glover, *Larkspur and Other Poisonous Plants.*

36. City of Montrose, *Appendix. City of Montrose Comprehensive Plan.*

37. Richard Gibbons, Montrose County planner, Montrose, Colorado, pers. comm., October 2001.

38. Goldschmidt, *As You Sow*; Lobao, *Locality and Inequality.*

39. See Web site: http://www.ams.usda.gov/farmersmarkets/States/ Colorado.htm.

40. Halweil, *Home Grown.*

41. Wayne Cooley, Montrose County Extension, Montrose, Colorado, pers. comm., July 10, 2000.

42. American Farmland Trust, "Tri-River Agricultural Land Protection Project."

43. Muller, Bertron, and Yin, "Tri-River Growth Futures Project."

44. Wright, *Rocky Mountain Divide,* 252.

45. Rick Sherman, Uncompahgre Project technical coordinator, Montrose, Colorado, pers. comm., July 17, 2002; see Web site: http://www.upproject.org/UPP/cpnativeplant_program/accomplishments.htm.

46. Doug Lard, Southwest Seeds, Dolores, Colorado, pers. comm., September 7, 2001.

47. Rick Sherman, Uncompahgre Project technical coordinator, Montrose, Colorado, pers. comm., July 17, 2002.

48. Ibid.

49. Stewart, Crock, and Severson, *Chemical Results from Soils of the Uncompahgre Area.*

50. Uncompahgre Valley Water Users Association, *Information Handout.*

51. Steve Glazer, High Country Citizens' Alliance, Crested Butte, Colorado, pers. comm., July 25, 2002.

52. Karla Brown, facilitator, Selenium Task Force, Colorado State University Cooperative Extension, Montrose, Colorado, pers. comm., July 23, 2002; Butler et al., *Irrigation Drainage in the Gunnison and Uncompahgre River Basins.*

53. See Web site: http://www.seleniumtaskforce.org/history.htm; Butler et al., *Irrigation Drainage in the Gunnison and Uncompahgre River Basins*; Hamilton, "Selenium Effects on Endangered Fish."

54. Mark Catlin, assistant manager, Uncompahgre Valley Water Users Association, Montrose, Colorado, pers. comm., July 6, 2000.

55. See Web site: http://www.usbr.gov/niwqp/prgmstat.htm.

56. See Web site: http://www.seleniumtaskforce.org/history.htm.

57. Karla Brown, facilitator, Selenium Task Force, Colorado State University Cooperative Extension, Montrose, Colorado, pers. comm., July 23, 2002; Butler, *Effects of Piping Laterals on Selenium and Salt Loads.*

58. Fisher, "Uncompahgre River Basin Selenium Phytoremediation."

59. Karla Brown, facilitator, Selenium Task Force, Colorado State University Cooperative Extension, Montrose, Colorado, pers. comm., July 23, 2002.

60. Ibid.

61. Chavez de Baca, "Changing Land Use Effects"; Gunnison Basin Selenium Task Force, "Selenium in Western Colorado."

62. U.S. Department of the Interior, Bureau of Reclamation, "Lining Ponds"; Sonja Chavez, coordinator of Gunnison Basin and Grand Valley Selenium Task Force, Delta, Colorado, pers. comm., July 5, 2005.

63. Muller, Bertron, and Yin, "Tri-River Growth Futures Project" (no pages).

64. Ibid.

65. Karla Brown, facilitator, Selenium Task Force, Colorado State University Cooperative Extension, Montrose, Colorado, pers. comm., July 23, 2002; Richard Gibbons, Montrose County planner, Montrose, Colorado, pers. comm., October 11, 2001.

66. Sonja Chavez, coordinator of Gunnison Basin and Grand Valley Selenium Task Force, Delta, Colorado, pers. comm., July 5, 2005.

67. Gunnison Basin Selenium Task Force, "Selenium in Western Colorado."
68. Steve Glazer, High Country Citizens' Alliance, Crested Butte, Colorado, pers. comm., July 25, 2002.
69. American Farmland Trust, "Fact Sheet: Cost of Community Services Studies."
70. Ibid.
71. Coupal and Seidl, "Rural Land Use and Your Taxes."
72. American Farmland Trust, "Tri-River Agricultural Land Protection Project."
73. Black Canyon Regional Land Trust Newsletter, Montrose, Colorado, Summer 2001.
74. Gelbard and Belnap, "Roads as Conduits for Exotic Plant Invasions."
75. E.g., Marshall, *Where Rivers Meet*; Marshall, *Awesome 'Dobie Badlands*; Larmer, "The 'Dobes Come Alive."
76. Bradford, Reed, and LeValley, *When the Grass Stood Stirrup-High*.
77. Beckwith, *Reports of Explorations and Surveys*, September 16, 1853.
78. Bradford, Reed, and LeValley, *When the Grass Stood Stirrup-High*.
79. James et al., "Selenium Poisoning in Cattle."
80. See Web site: http://www.pprl.usu.edu.
81. Cox, *Alien Species in North America*.
82. Sheley and Petroff, *Biology and Management of Noxious Rangeland Weeds*.
83. Ibid.
84. Cox, *Alien Species in North America*.
85. Ibid.
86. Gelbard and Belnap, "Roads as Conduits for Exotic Plant Invasions."
87. Memo to file, Dry Creek Allotment File, Bureau of Land Management, Montrose, Colorado.
88. Lyon and Denslow, "Gunnison Gorge Survey of Impacts on Rare Plants."
89. Lyon et al., *Uncompahgre River Basin: Natural Heritage Assessment*, 22.

There probably are few if any behavioral
traits that are both unique to humans and
ubiquitous among them, but one possible
candidate is the desire to fiddle with things and
change them for the better.

—Bock and Bock, *View from Bald Hill* [1]

CHAPTER FOUR

The Uncompahgre Plateau: Pinyon-Juniper Restoration

The Uncompahgre Plateau is a tilted-up section
of the Colorado Plateau (see Map 4.1), a province
of red-rock canyons, mesas, ephemeral streams,
pinyons and junipers, cows, rattlesnakes and lizards, and unusual plants. The Colorado Plateau
borders the Rocky Mountains on the west, extending across southeastern Utah into northern
Arizona. Because the Uncompahgre Plateau is
tilted up, reaching nearly 10,000 feet near the crest,
it is topped by less arid Rocky Mountain vegetation, including ponderosa pine forests, mixed
mountain shrublands, and quaking aspen forests,
alternating with bunchgrass parks and meadows.

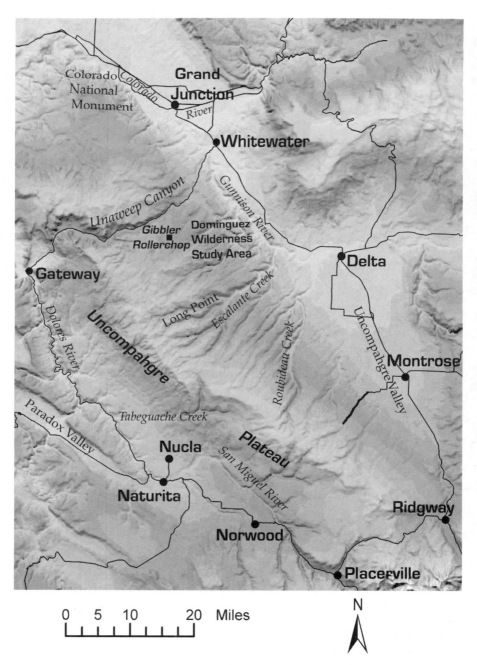

Map 4.1. *Map of the Uncompahgre Plateau and surrounding area with places covered in this chapter.*

One of the earliest Euro-Americans to see the upper plateau was Henry Gannett, topographer for the Hayden expedition, which was on the plateau in 1875, before the country was opened to Euro-American settlement. According to Gannett's romantic, exuberant imagery: "[N]ear the crest, the land is, to the Utes, one flowing with milk and honey. Here are fine streams of clear, cold water, beautiful aspen groves, the best of grass in the greatest abundance, and a profusion of wild fruit and berries, while the country is a perfect flower garden."[2] Between these higher elevations and the adjoining Uncompahgre, Gunnison, San Miguel, and Dolores valleys, much of the plateau is covered by pinyon-juniper woodlands. Twoneedle pinyon and Utah juniper dominate the plateau and the rest of western Colorado and eastern Utah (see Plate 22). Farther west in woodlands of the Great Basin and the Pacific Northwest, other species of juniper and pinyon dominate, as do still others in the Southwest. These woodland trees may grow to only twenty-five feet tall, but they can live for hundreds of years. A tree only a foot in diameter could be 400 years old on the plateau, as trees grow slowly in this semiarid environment.

Few early accounts describe the natural vegetation of the woodlands in any detail. Early stories suggest that native bunchgrasses and desirable shrubs, such as white sage (or winterfat; see Plate 5a), were common in the early days of open-range ranching.[3] However, this was probably not true everywhere, as the topography is dissected and variable in slope, aspect, and soils. Gannett said that below about 7,000 feet on the plateau, "Aspen gives place to piñon and cedar [juniper]. The grasses, fruit, and flowers, to sage, cacti, and bare rock."[4] In contrast, A. C. Peale was near Escalante Forks in 1875, where he noted that the several branches of Escalante Creek all come together: "[T]hese creeks all unite, at an elevation of about 5,600 feet. The ridges between them are timbered, and the valleys are beautifully grassed. Near the heads of the creeks are beautiful little parks, which, in August, were perfect flower-gardens."[5]

Writing about moving cows up to the benches above Escalante Canyon in the fall of 1888, only a few years after the first Euro-American settlers arrived and little more than a decade after Peale's observations in the same area, Jeff Dillard's memory is similar to Peale's: "[W]e started drifting up the bench. Was fine grass; my feet riding along would drag through the grass, all gone to seed. The cattle were full and seemed to want to travel. It was all open country. Little scrub oaks and now and then a grove of thick quaking aspens; several lakes of water."[6] He continued: "[W]e started across to Long Point—good plain Ute trail run across to Long Point and bunch grass was belly deep to our horses all over the country."[7] Thurber's fescue at higher elevations and needle and thread (see Figure 2.4a), or saline wildrye (see Plate 19), down lower are the common native bunchgrasses that may have reached a horse's belly in a good year.

This chapter focuses on the lower elevations of the plateau, the pinyon-juniper woodlands and associated sagebrush and grasslands. The usual division of the landscape is for the pinyon-juniper woodland and black sagebrush to stay up on the rockier slopes and mesas while big sagebrush claims the draws and lower slopes with finer-textured soils. Pinyon-juniper woodland is one of the most widespread ecosystems in the West. Land managers and scientists are struggling to understand how natural vegetation patterns have changed in this ecosystem under the influence of livestock grazing, chaining and other treatments, and climatic fluctuations.[8] On the Uncompahgre Plateau, native grasses and shrubs persist, but it is rare today to find grass that would touch a horse's belly. The plateau has lost native plant diversity as a result of overgrazing by livestock,[9] a source of controversy decades ago. However, an effort is under way to restore the natural landscape using a collaborative learning approach. Little did Jeff Dillard know a century ago that his memory of horse-high grass would today be part of a vision for restoration.

LEGACY OF PAST HUMAN USES

The Uncompahgre Plateau was home to the powerful Tabeguache Utes when Euro-American explorers first began to penetrate western Colorado. After the Tabeguache were forcibly removed to Utah, large open-range cattle herding dominated the plateau until the mid-1890s.[10]

This Was Cattle Country

The first impression one gets traveling across the Uncompahgre Plateau today is of a large, relatively natural landscape (see Plate 23). However, livestock grazing has altered the very fabric of the Uncompahgre Plateau—its vegetation.[11] Large herds wintered in the valleys, while canyon rims and higher elevations were summer range. As more people tried to ranch on the open range, overgrazing became a serious problem.[12]

Estimates of the number of cattle run on the plateau vary widely. The highest estimate of early cattle use comes from a Bureau of Land Management (BLM) range management plan written in the 1940s.[13] It reported that at the peak in the early 1900s, 40,000 cows wintered in the Dominguez, Escalante, and Roubideau drainages. Estimating six and a quarter months of use, the report calculated an annual use of 250,000 animal-unit-months (AUMs). By the time of the 1940s report, only 10,300 AUMs were being used in the same unit, so depleted was the vegetation. But the early estimate was based on an unsubstantiated claim that the Club Ranch near Uravan ran 40,000 head of cattle in the 1890s, and half of those cattle wintered on the Uncompahgre-Gunnison side of the plateau. Other reports suggest the Club Ranch was not nearly that size and that its wintering grounds were the Paradox and San Miguel river valleys.[14]

Although 250,000 AUMs is undoubtedly a high estimate, a more likely number is still impressive. The 1940 range analysis says the five largest ranchers on the north side of the plateau (from whom information was probably closer at hand in the 1940s) alone had 7,800 cattle in the early 1900s, declining to 1,500 head by the 1940s.[15] So for at least a decade or two, the canyons and low mesas running off the plateau into the Gunnison River supported at least five times the number of cattle they supported a few decades later.

Early struggles over management of public lands. One of the major battles over control of public-lands grazing took place on the Uncompahgre National Forest. Forest Service biologist Floyd Reed amassed a wealth of historical photos and documents on this political struggle. Reading through these documents, one is struck by how familiar the arguments over the use of public lands recorded over the years sound today.

Stockmen's associations formed as early as 1897 on the Western Slope of Colorado and eventually supported leasing of federal land to help control overuse, but they strongly resisted government control of grazing practices.[16] In 1925 the U.S. Senate formed a subcommittee to make recommendations on management of public lands and held hearings around the West. The western senators who conducted many of the meetings were openly hostile to the Forest Service.[17] Reed has a letter dated October 27, 1925, to the magazine *Outdoor Life* in which one sportsman complains: "During all the meetings which I attended in Salt Lake City, the stock men showed a bitter hostility toward campers and tourists. . . . [I]f [stockmen] can persuade Congress to pass the law they wish, it will put them in a position whereby they can prevent tourists from camping along the public roads."[18]

Outdoor Life asked the Forest Service to verify or deny the accuracy of this letter. In his response, Assistant District Forester John Hatton assured the editor that the Forest Service recognized the multiple interests on the forest:

Colonel Greeley, the chief forester, appeared before several of the hearings and frequently introduced the suggestion that we have other things to engage our attention besides the livestock and timber uses of the Forest, and urged the stockmen to reflect upon these matters in reaching any final recommendations. . . . Such men as [the sportsman who wrote to *Outdoor Life*] and you will of course help to keep these other necessary matters from being forgotten, and are in a position to assist materially in getting the public, including the stockmen themselves, to take a broader view of these subjects.[19]

Although the feared legislation restricting camping and public use was not passed, the struggle for broad public control of the forests continued.

The Uncompahgre Forest became a focal point of the stockmen's resistance to federal land management agencies. A dispute began in 1938 when the Forest Service conducted a systematic assessment and determined that most of the range was in poor and declining condition. The Forest Service proposed reductions in grazing, including a reduction in the grazing season, which then ran from May 1 to October 31. The stockmen protested, adopting a resolution in 1939 stating: "We emphatically protest the enforcement of the proposed cuts. Instead, we urge a spirit of tolerance and cooperation as best adapted to meet the situation; and insist that further study of conditions and conference with local boards should be made before final action is decided."[20]

The Forest Service did stop its efforts to implement the recommendations, and from 1942 to 1946, stockmen were allowed to demonstrate capacity to improve the range without reductions. In 1947 the Forest Service again conducted assessments and determined that, except for a few pockets, deterioration continued. Again, the Forest Service pressed for reductions. The Uncompahgre Valley Cattle and Horse Growers Association appealed to the secretary of agriculture, who, after a series of hearings and field trips, ruled in favor of the Forest Service.[21] The *Denver Post* (January 8, 1952) called it "the first firm ruling of its kind in the years-long grazing war which pitted the forest service against some of the most powerful ranchers in the west."[22]

Most of the pinyon-juniper lands of the Uncompahgre Plateau are BLM, not Forest Service, lands. BLM lands were unregulated open range until the Taylor Act of 1934, which set up the Grazing Service, which merged with the General Land Office in 1946 to create the Bureau of Land Management.[23] Records of conflict over BLM lands on the plateau are less detailed than those of the Forest Service, but many of the same herds of cattle were moved between lower-elevation BLM lands and higher Forest Service lands. Changes in grazing levels of BLM lands likely mirrored those of the Forest Service. Thus, most observers agree that the pinyon-juniper ecosystem was heavily impacted by grazing in the first half of the twentieth century.

Ecological legacies of livestock grazing. Since the 1950s, both the Forest Service and the Bureau of Land Management have implemented many changes in grazing practices to improve the vegetation, but damage has proven difficult to undo. Floyd Reed's comparison of photos of the plateau's rangelands in the 1940s and those rangelands today shows significant increases in vegetation cover and stabilization of gullies in some areas,[24] but scars of decades of overuse remain. Two Forest Service employees, with wide field experience in other western national forests, said anonymously that they consider the Uncompahgre Plateau to be more damaged by livestock grazing than any other national forest they have seen.

Some legacies of overuse will remain for some time. The moister, higher-elevation sites on the forest were those most able to rebound, but even there non-natives, such as Kentucky bluegrass and common dandelion, have replaced many native plants. Large areas of the drier pinyon-juniper zone are generally perceived to have failed to recover significantly, even with changes in livestock management.

Overgrazing in the pinyon-juniper zone on the plateau may be more severe than elsewhere, but it also occurred elsewhere in the West. In 1936 the secretary of agriculture reported to the U.S. Senate that on over two-thirds of the pinyon-juniper type in the western United States, "the forage is either materially or severely depleted, and on an additional fourth is extremely depleted."[25] Because the land was severely grazed for decades, the more palatable and susceptible bunchgrasses, forbs, and shrubs were greatly reduced and even disappeared from some large areas—a general pattern in the West.[26]

Legacy of Chaining

One response to depleted vegetation was to attempt to increase forage by removing trees. Beginning in the 1940s and continuing into the early 1980s, large areas of pinyon-juniper in the West were chained or otherwise cleared to create grasslands and shrublands (see Figure 4.1). Clearing was typically done by dragging a ship's anchor chain between two tractors or bulldozers, clearing a swath a hundred feet wide.[27]

The primary goal of chaining was to increase forage for livestock.[28] Yet when Bob Welch, then BLM's wildlife biologist for the south end of the plateau, revisited old chainings in the late 1980s, he found that forage

Figure 4.1. *Pinyon-juniper woodland chained a few decades ago. Note the reinvading trees.*

gains had largely disappeared.[29] Earlier documents also indicate the forage gains were quickly lost. A 1984 report on one extensively chained BLM grazing allotment stated, "This area showed [a] downward trend from 1967 to 1979 as the chaining matured and stabilized. . . . The grasses have dropped to a smaller component than originally and are static."[30] Chaining was expensive, yet its benefits were generally short-lived. However, across the West at the time, only a few scientists questioned the value of chaining.[31]

Since chaining at least temporarily converted a site from woodland to non-woodland, it changed the animal communities as well. In north-western Colorado, birds such as the black-throated gray warbler (see Figure 4.2), gray flycatcher, bushtit, and juniper titmouse declined greatly, and the pinyon mouse (see Figure 4.3) was eliminated from chained sites.[32] In Utah, pinyon-juniper woodlands provide essential breeding habitat for blue-gray gnatcatchers, black-throated gray warblers, and gray flycatchers.[33] Yet almost no attention was given to nongame species such as these in designing treatments.[34] Even mule deer, whom chaining was intended to benefit, often did not benefit because large-

Figure 4.2. *Black-throated gray warbler, a pinyon-juniper obligate bird, with nesting material. Courtesy, Dr. Jacob Faust.*

Figure 4.3. *Pinyon mouse. Courtesy, Sevilleta National Wildlife Refuge, New Mexico, and R. B. Forbes.*

scale treatments did not consider their requirements for cover.[35] Fortunately, pinyon-juniper woodlands are vast enough that no animal species dependent on them is currently known to be threatened with extinction, though little is known about impacts on populations locally or regionally.

One problem in restoring forage was that most palatable native species were either missing or so greatly reduced that there was little seed source at the time of chaining to quickly reestablish a ground cover.[36] Without native species, non-native weeds such as cheatgrass (see Box—Cheatgrass, pp. 61–63) can quickly occupy disturbed chained areas. To avoid this and to provide perennial grass forage, many chained sites were planted to the non-native crested wheatgrass, the silver bullet of the day (see Box—Crested Wheatgrass, pp. 85–86). In many old chainings there is now minimal native plant cover and dominance by crested wheatgrass instead, a symbol to many of the failures of this era of management.

WHAT IS HAPPENING NOW?

The Uncompahgre Plateau is still largely undeveloped and publicly owned. Some of the plateau's spectacular canyons seem destined for wilderness protection. In those places grazing is the main human legacy, and recovery will proceed with minimal human intervention. Much of the plateau, however, has been and continues to be fragmented by roads, power lines and pipelines, fences, and vegetation treatments (see Figure 4.4). The desire to fiddle with things, referred to in the opening quote, is still strong, but restoration of the pinyon-juniper woodlands is now a central goal. New mechanical techniques and prescribed burning are being proposed as tools, but uncertainty about how the ecosystem functions and competing objectives complicate restoration efforts.

Protecting a Wilderness Setting: The Dominguez Canyons

A proposed wilderness area may be the best place to introduce the basic natural history of the often underappreciated pinyon-juniper woodlands. The Big and Little Dominguez canyons are spectacular red-rock canyons that drain into the Gunnison River on the northwest side of the Uncompahgre Plateau (see Plate 24). They run through the pinyon-juniper zone. The canyons today are a wilderness landscape—the woodlands have not been extensively harvested, chained, rollerchopped, or subjected to other "treatments." Livestock grazing was once heavy but is now limited, and nature is returning to a wilder, less transformed state than was the case in the twentieth century.

Sparse vegetation, diverse flora. In a dry year or in midsummer, the landscape of the canyons can appear bare except for the pinyons and junipers, but after a wet winter the spring flora is diverse and colorful. We observed twelve native grasses and thirty-eight native forbs along just two miles of trail in 1999. Far fewer species were seen in the drier spring of 2000, but they were there, ready to bloom again when conditions are right. This dramatic annual variability is common in deserts—the southwestern deserts have wildflower Web sites to alert people to exceptional flower years. In Dominguez the blooms are less dramatic, but the scattered colorful plants in spring are striking against the stark, reddish brown soil and rocks of the canyon.

Figure 4.4. *A natural gas pipeline cleared through pinyon-juniper woodland on the Uncompahgre Plateau, with cattle grazing.*

The flora of pinyon-juniper woodlands in western Colorado contains a mix of spring and early summer perennials (see Table 4.1). Many of the plants, such as hoary Townsend daisy (see Plate 25a), boreal sweetvetch (see Plate 25b), and narrowleaf stoneseed (see Plate 26a), are showy. Eaton's penstemon is the classic hummingbird plant, with long red flowers, and is visited by broad-tailed and other hummingbirds. Cacti include the strikingly beautiful kingcup cactus (see Plate 26b) and three pricklypears, including the irritating brittle pricklypear, which releases its pads when touched by a shoe.

Though diverse, the understory is quite sparse in the pinyon-juniper woodland of the canyon walls. It is unlikely that the grass was ever belly-deep here, as early cowboy Jeff Dillard remembered. The specific places Dillard mentioned were at higher elevations on mesa tops with different soils. But surely, large numbers of wintering cattle over decades had some effect. This wilderness study area is still grazed, but the canyons are only a small part of the allotment and now are used only for taking cows up to the higher mesas.[37] Native plants are sparse, there is much bare ground, and the biological soil crust is not well

Table 4.1. Some common plants of the pinyon-juniper woodland on the Uncompahgre Plateau.[1] Riparian species are some common species found along streams, such as Big Dominguez Creek.

	Upland	Riparian
TREES		
Narrowleaf cottonwood (*Populus angustifolia*)	—	X
Rocky Mountain juniper (*Sabina scopulorum*)	X	—
Twoneedle pinyon (*Pinus edulis*)	X	—
Utah juniper (*Sabina osteosperma*)	X	—
SHRUBS		
Alderleaf mountain mahogany (*Cercocarpus montanus*)	X	—
Black chokecherry (*Padus virginiana* subsp. *melanocarpa*)	—	X
Black sagebrush (*Seriphidium novum*)	X	—
Broom snakeweed (*Gutierrezia sarothrae*)	X	—
Gambel oak (*Quercus gambelii*)	X	—
Mountain big sagebrush (*Serphidium vaseyanum*)	X	—
Redosier dogwood (*Swida sericea*)	—	X
Skunkbush sumac (*Rhus aromatica* subsp. *trilobata*)	—	X
Thinleaf alder (*Alnus incana* subsp. *tenuifolia*)	—	X
Utah serviceberry (*Amelanchier utahensis*)	X	—
Water birch (*Betula fontinalis*)	—	X
Willow sp. (*Salix* sp.)	—	X
Winterfat (*Krascheninnikovia lanata*)	X	—
Wyoming big sagebrush (not in Weber and Wittmann 2001)	X	—
FORBS		
Bastard toadflax (*Comandra umbellata*)	X	—
Boreal sweetvetch (*Hedysarum boreale*)	X	—
Carpet phlox (*Phlox hoodii* subsp. *canescens*)	X	—
Eaton's penstemon (*Penstemon eatonii*)	X	—
Fleabane (*Erigeron* sp.)	X	—
Hairy false goldenaster (*Heterotheca villosa*)	X	—
Heartleaf twistflower (*Streptanthus cordatus*)	X	—
Hoary Townsend daisy (*Townsendia incana*)	X	—
Ives' fournerved daisy (*Tetraneuris ivesiana*)	X	—
Longleaf phlox (*Phlox longifolia*)	X	—
Narrowleaf stoneseed (*Lithospermum incisum*)	X	—
Rose heath (*Chaetopappa ericoides*)	X	—
Scarlet gilia (*Ipomopsis aggregata*)	X	—
Scarlet globemallow (*Sphaeralcea coccinea*)	X	—
Sego lily (*Calochortus nuttallii*)	X	—
Spearleaf stonecrop (*Amerosedum lanceolatum*)	X	—
Tansymustard (*Descurainia* sp.)	X	—
Thrift mock goldenweed (*Stenotus armerioides*)	X	—
Toadflax penstemon (*Penstemon linarioides*)	X	—
GRASSES		
Blue grama (*Chondrosum gracile*)	X	—
Indian ricegrass (*Achnatherum hymenoides*)	X	—

. . . .

continued on next page

Table 4.1—*continued*

	Upland	Riparian
GRASSES (continued)		
James' galleta (*Hilaria jamesii*)	X	—
Muttongrass (*Poa fendleriana* subsp. *longiligula*)	X	—
Needle and thread (*Hesperostipa comata*)	X	—
Sandberg's bluegrass (*Poa sandbergii*)	X	—
CACTI		
Brittle pricklypear (*Opuntia fragilis* var. *brachyarthra*)	X	—
Kingcup cactus (*Echinocereus triglochidiatus*)	X	—
Plains pricklypear (*Opuntia polyacantha*)	X	—
Whipple's fishhook cactus (*Sclerocactus whipplei*)	X	—
NON-NATIVES		
Cheatgrass (*Anisantha tectorum*)	X	—
Common dandelion (*Taraxacum officinale*)	—	X
Crested wheatgrass (*Agropyron desertorum*)	X	—
Hardheads (Russian knapweed) (*Acroptilon repens*)	—	X
Kentucky bluegrass (*Poa pratensis*)	—	X
Orchardgrass (*Dactylis glomerata*)	—	X
Saltcedar sp. (*Tamarix* sp.)	—	X
Yellow sweetclover (*Melilotus officinalis*)	—	X

1. Common names are from the PLANTS online database, http://plants.usda.gov. Latin names are from Weber and Wittmann, *Colorado Flora*.

developed (see Box—Biological Soil Crusts. pp. 150–152). This is a wilderness landscape that is wild but recovering.

Fauna of the pinyon-juniper woodland. The fauna in the Dominguez canyons is remarkably diverse. Pinyon-juniper woodland has a fairly high number of obligate bird species—species that depend heavily on a certain habitat (Table 4.2).[38] In Colorado, pinyon-juniper obligates include the gray flycatcher, gray vireo, pinyon jay, juniper titmouse, and black-throated gray warbler (see Figure 4.2), all of which breed almost exclusively in pinyon-juniper.[39] The Townsend's solitaire relies heavily on juniper berries in winter.[40] The pinyon mouse (see Figure 4.3) is the only mammal restricted to pinyon-juniper woodlands.[41]

Much less is known about bird habitat needs within pinyon-juniper woodlands than in other forest types. The woodlands seem common and monotonous to the casual observer, but significant variation exists from place to place. Ron Lambeth, wildlife biologist for the BLM in Grand Junction, is a recognized expert on pinyon-juniper birds. Initial studies by Lambeth show many differences in habitat selected within the pinyon-juniper zone.[42] Gray flycatchers select areas with minimal shrub understory. Black-throated gray warblers are associated with large blocks of mature woodland. Spotted towhee, scrub jay, and Virginia's warbler, which use many types of habitat, select areas with a shrubby understory. The uncommon gray vireo is restricted to lower-elevation sites with fairly widely spaced juniper. In a study in south-western Wyoming, juniper titmouse, Bewick's wren, and gray flycatcher all increased with increasing overstory juniper cover, and both gray flycatcher and juniper titmouse also required the presence of old, dying trees.[43] Knowledge of habitat needs of birds in pinyon-juniper is still limited, but most obligates are associated with mature woodlands, suggesting such woodlands have long been widespread.

BOX—BIOLOGICAL SOIL CRUSTS

It has been said that it is the little things that run the world. In canyon country, much of the ground surface is covered with pedestals of reddish soil with a little mat of tiny organisms on top. The mat has a three-dimensional structure and is mostly composed of cyanobacteria (blue-green algae), green algae, lichens, and mosses (see box figure). The algae bind the soil into a crust, forming a mat; the lichens are scattered about on top; and the mosses appear in patches. These crusts have been called cryptogamic, crypto-biotic, microphytic, or microbiotic crusts, but the simplest name is biological soil crusts. Biological soil crusts are found all over the world; in the United States they are best developed on the Colorado Plateau and in the Great Basin in pinyon-juniper wood-lands, sagebrush shrublands, and nearby salt deserts.[1] Here, aridity limits

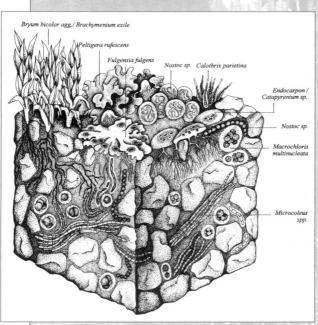

Schematic diagram of a biological soil crust with typical coloniz-ers; Bryum *is a moss;* Macrochloris *is an alga;* Peltigera, Fulgensia, *and* Endocarpon *are lichens; and* Nostoc, Calothrix, *and* Microcoleus *are cyanobacteria. Reprinted from figure 1.1 in Belnap and Lange (2001), with permission of Springer-Verlag, New York.*

grasses, forbs, and shrubs, leaving spaces between them for crust development.[2]

In addition to water deficits, cold deserts are deficient in nitrogen, an essential plant nutrient (the "N" in N-P-K fertilizer). Nitrogen mostly comes from rain (not much in deserts), or it is captured ("fixed") from the atmosphere by specialized organisms (nitrogen fixers). Nitrogen-fixing plants are rare in deserts, but certain cyanobacteria can form thin crusts that fix nitrogen. Lichens, however, are the best of the cold-desert nitrogen fixers.[3]

These crusts also shape water movement and limit soil erosion. Cyanobacteria, fungi, and mosses aggregate soil particles and add organic matter to soils. The uneven, pedestaled surface of crusts in the Colorado Plateau also slows down water movement.[4] Together, in cold deserts these effects of crusts lead to increased infiltration of water into the soil and less surface runoff that erodes soil.[5] Given that it may take thousands of years to create new soil out of bedrock,[6] crusts play a key role in these ecosystems by decreasing soil erosion. Biological soil crusts also benefit associated plants, which usually contain more nitrogen and other essential nutrients when crust is nearby.[7] Crusts also may discourage invasion and domination by non-native plants, such as cheatgrass.[8] This seemingly insignificant group of organisms thus provides a host of "ecosystem services"—key benefits ecosystems provide that are not traded in markets and that do not yet show up on economists' ledger sheets.[9]

Unfortunately, biological soil crusts are easily damaged and recover slowly. Disturbance by livestock, vehicles, human feet, and mountain bikes can destroy crusts. Livestock grazing can significantly damage the important functions of crusts. In Canyonlands National Park south of Moab, Utah, a never-grazed grassland (Virginia Park) had 38 percent cover of biological soil crusts, while an adjacent grassland grazed until 1962 (Chesler Park) had 5 percent cover of soil crusts in the mid-1970s.[10] An experiment showed that fifteen passes with either tennis shoes or lug-soled shoes destroyed the structure of crusts, and after fifty passes biological cover was negligible.[11] Vehicles, which are heavier than humans, more quickly compress soils and turn them over, burying crusts.[12] In the Colorado Plateau region, the best estimate now is that after disturbance, cyanobacteria may recover within 14 to 34 years, mosses within 42 years, and one of the major lichens possibly within 50 years or maybe much longer.[13]

These little crust organisms seem to run the ecosystem, but how can they be kept, given how easy they are to damage and how slow to recover? Livestock grazing when the soil is frozen or snow covered is least damaging, while spring grazing is the most damaging.[14] It is hoped that people can learn to avoid stepping on crusts and will accept concentration of uses (e.g., designated trails and roads) and limitation of livestock grazing to less damaging late fall and winter seasons.[15] If biological soil crusts are recognized and appreciated and if they are monitored as key indicators of ecosystem health,[16] these desert ecosystems can likely be kept healthy and "crusty."

NOTES

1. Evans and Johansen, "Microbiotic Crusts."
2. Ibid.
3. Belnap, "Nitrogen Fixation in Biological Soil Crusts."
4. Belnap et al., *Biological Soil Crusts.*
5. Evans and Johansen, "Microbiotic Crusts."
6. Belnap and Gillette, "Vulnerability of Desert Biological Soils Crusts."
7. Harper and Belnap, "Influence of Soil Crusts on Mineral Uptake."
8. Boudell, Link, and Johansen, "Effect of Microtopography on Seed Bank Distribution."
9. Daily, *Nature's Services.*
10. Kleiner and Harper, "Soil Properties in Relation to Cryptogamic Groundcover."
11. Cole, "Trampling and Recovery of Cryptogamic Soil Crusts."
12. Belnap et al., *Biological Soil Crusts.*
13. Ibid.
14. Memmott, Anderson, and Monsen, "Seasonal Grazing Impact on Cryptogamic Crusts"; Warren and Eldridge, "Biological Soil Crusts and Livestock."
15. Belnap et al., *Biological Soil Crusts.*
16. Rosentreter, Eldridge, and Kaltenecker, "Monitoring and Management of Biological Soil Crusts."

The pinyon-juniper woodland supports a large diversity of snakes and lizards, most of which occur in a variety of arid, upland environments. The colorful collared lizard (see Plate 27) and short-horned lizard ("horny toad") are most distinctive. The sagebrush lizard, plateau lizard, tree lizard, side-blotched lizard, and plateau striped whiptail are common in the dry, open pinyon-juniper woodland and rocky exposures of the Dominguez canyons.[44] The plateau striped whiptail is so self-sufficient it doesn't even need males! This all-female species reproduces by an unusual means called parthenogenesis, which does not require sex. The gopher snake and western rattlesnake are the largest and most conspicuous of the snakes, but a remarkable number of more reclusive species occur in the region's pinyon-juniper woodlands, including the racer, night snake, milk snake, striped whipsnake, and southwestern black-headed snake.[45]

Ribbons of life: Desert streams. Diversity is greatly increased in these canyons by a tiny but critical part of the Dominguez area—the broken ribbon of riparian vegetation along the creeks. Along the upper reaches of the canyons, the streams are lined with dense thickets of willow. A few scattered narrowleaf cottonwoods and a variety of shrubs—including thinleaf alder, black chokecherry, and the red-stemmed redosier dogwood—add to the mix. Skunkbush sumac (see Plate 4) has tangy berries, and the Utes favored this plant's young stems for their high-quality baskets and vessels.[46] Water birch is taller than the willows and has dark bark dotted with rows of white lenticels (small openings in the bark for gas exchange). Sadly, wet places are vulnerable to invasive non-native plants. Orchard grass, Kentucky bluegrass (see Figure 3.8), and yellow sweetclover dominate many areas, having replaced native vegetation. Russian knapweed (see Plate 21) also seems to be increasing in moist areas of canyon country.[47] Fortunately, saltcedar (see Box—Saltcedar, pp. 310–311), another invasive plant, has not overtaken the upper Dominguez canyons.

Table 4.2. Breeding birds associated with pinyon-juniper woodlands of southwestern Colorado.[1]

Turkey vulture
Mourning dove
Northern saw-whet owl
Common nighthawk
Common poorwill
Black-chinned hummingbird
Gray flycatcher*[2]
Ash-throated flycatcher
Gray vireo*
Plumbeous vireo
Western scrub jay
Pinyon jay*
Clark's nutcracker
Common raven
Mountain chickadee
Juniper titmouse*
Bushtit
White-breasted nuthatch
Rock wren
Bewick's wren
Blue-gray gnatcatcher*
Mountain bluebird
Virginia's warbler
Black-throated gray warbler*
Spotted towhee
Chipping sparrow
Black-throated sparrow
House finch
Lesser goldfinch

1. Kingery, *Colorado Breeding Bird Atlas.*
2. * denotes pinyon-juniper obligate.

Even small pockets of riparian vegetation can support birds not found in the drier woodlands. The American dipper, a bird most associated with mountain streams, uses these canyons. Warbling vireo, song sparrow, and red-naped sapsucker all use the riparian area and would not be in the canyon without it.

Toads and frogs provide the chorus for desert washes and canyons. Temporary pools along canyon streams are critical breeding habitat for several western amphibians: the Great Basin spadefoot, red-spotted toad, and canyon tree frog.[48] The Woodhouse toad is more widespread. The red-spotted toad's call is a high, ringing trill, while the Woodhouse toad's call is a lower-pitched "waaah" lasting one to four seconds.[49] These species lay their eggs in temporary pools along the creek, the Woodhouse toad in single- or double-rowed jelly strings, the red-spotted singly or in small clusters. Backcountry recreation, even hiking, can therefore threaten these species.

Most reptiles are denizens of arid upland environments, but a few favor the riparian zone. The Great Plains rat snake is almost always found near streams, and the western terrestrial garter snake, although not restricted to riparian areas, is common there.[50]

Bighorn decline and reintroduction. The natural communities of the Dominguez canyons are diverse, but some of the communities' larger members were extirpated. Whether the Dominguez will ever again have top predators, such as the gray wolf, is an open question. Large predators are still unpopular with many local people. Most other large mammals, however, have recovered. Deer and elk use the canyons, especially in winter, as do mountain lions and black bears.[51] Elk have flourished since reintroduction onto the plateau in 1928 after years of absence.[52]

One large animal that is still struggling is the Colorado state animal, the bighorn sheep. There were once as many as 2 million bighorns across the West, including Canada and Mexico, whereas today only 2–8 percent remain.[53] Archaeologists have found that bighorn bones, present in the Glen Canyon area of Utah during some of the Archaic period, were seven times more common than mule deer bones.[54] Living in open habitats, bighorns were vulnerable to early hunting and quickly became rare. Hunting bighorns was made illegal in Colorado in 1887, but restricted hunting of these majestic animals began again in 1953.[55]

Populations in Colorado recovered to an estimated 7,300 in 1915 but then declined to a low of 2,200 in 1970.[56] Unfortunately, bighorns are very susceptible to diseases of domestic sheep, particularly pneumonia.[57] Efforts to reintroduce bighorns to former habitat have had mixed results, with populations building and then suddenly crashing in some cases, in spite of efforts to treat the bighorns for lungworm and other respiratory diseases.[58] Only 39 percent of 115 reintroductions of bighorn sheep in the Rocky Mountains have been successful.[59] Bighorns in Colorado in 1990 numbered only 6,300.[60]

Hunting and development in lower-elevation habitat have also led to behavioral changes. Bighorns often no longer migrate away from the higher elevations that were once only their summer range.[61] This behavioral change not only restricts habitat but may also reduce the genetic robustness of small, isolated populations and contribute to disease levels.

Dominguez Canyon is one site where an introduced herd appears to be doing well. In 1983, 10 desert bighorn sheep from Lake Mead in

Figure 4.5. *Desert bighorn* (Ovis canadensis nelsoni*). Courtesy, Michael Ward.*

Arizona were released into the Dominguez Wilderness Study Area, and 21 more were transplanted from Nevada in 1985.[62] By 1987 the herd numbered about 65 (see Figure 4.5).[63] Firm evidence is lacking that the desert subspecies of the bighorn sheep (*Ovis canadensis nelsoni*) existed in Colorado.[64] However, it was historically present in adjacent parts of the Colorado Plateau in Utah, and the low-elevation habitat of the plateau suggests that the desert bighorn rather than the Rocky Mountain bighorn (*Ovis canadensis canadensis*) probably is native here.[65]

Fortunately, Dominguez Canyon has always been cattle country, so sheep diseases have not been a threat. The 2002 population estimate was 125–150 bighorns in the Dominguez area and another 75–100 animals elsewhere on the plateau.[66] Some people feel that in a wilderness, nature should be left entirely on its own; in this case, however, it seems human intervention was needed to restore a key member of the natural community.

Restoring the Plateau's Pinyon-Juniper Woodlands

Much of the Uncompahgre Plateau's pinyon-juniper woodland is not destined for wilderness designation because it has been extensively transformed by human uses over the last 100 years. In 2001 a project was begun with a general goal of returning the plateau to a more natural state, including restoring native plants that provide forage for livestock and wildlife. A closer look at this collaborative project illustrates the challenges of meeting multiple human demands while trying to restore natural processes and biological diversity.

The Uncompahgre Plateau project. The Uncompahgre Plateau project (UP project) was one of the new collaborative efforts meant to transform the way decisions are made about management of public lands in the United States. Collaborative management of public lands typically brings together government agencies, private and nongovernmental groups, and interested individuals—ideally using a cooperative, problem-solving approach.[67] The UP project's purpose was to develop a collaborative approach to restore and maintain the ecosystem health of the Uncompahgre Plateau, using the best available science and public input.[68] The need for a long-term, landscape-level view on the plateau was recognized from the outset by the project, and much of its effort was directed at working across various public-agency and private boundaries to create a unified vision for the landscape.

The roots of the UP project date back to 1997 when U.S. Forest Service biologist Floyd Reed (see Figure 4.6) began to organize those interested in declining mule deer populations on the plateau.[69] As scientists and managers at the U.S. Forest Service (USFS) and the BLM began to discuss the situation with the Colorado Division of Wildlife (CDOW), the focus moved to the condition of the vegetation on the plateau. At about the same time, a local group, the Public Lands Partnership (PLP), obtained a large Ford Foundation grant to promote community-based forestry, ranching, and local input in public-land management. In March 2001 the USFS, BLM, CDOW, and PLP signed a Cooperative Agreement and Memorandum of Understanding creating the UP project, encompassing 1.5 million acres of public and private lands.[70]

A technical committee, with one representative from each of the four partners, was set up to decide whether specific management proposals should be supported by the project.[71] One of the goals of the PLP was to bring the public (not just PLP members) directly into the UP project process through collaborative council meetings.[72] The group faced two fundamental challenges. First, it had to forge a cohesive vision for the plateau that encompassed several primary concerns.

- Improving mule deer habitat
- Improving range condition and increasing forage for livestock

Figure 4.6. *Floyd Reed, U.S. Forest Service, discusses the history of management on the plateau during an Uncompahgre Plateau project (UP) field trip, May 25, 2001. Rick Sherman, UP technical coordinator, is seated on the rocks to Floyd Reed's left.*

- Reducing threats of catastrophic wildfire to private land while restoring natural fire to the plateau
- Supporting local economic development and value-added industries
- Preserving and restoring native biodiversity and natural processes

Second, the group needed to make decisions in the face of uncertainty about natural processes on the plateau. The legacies of human uses of the plateau relative to natural changes have yet to be fully sorted out. Unfortunately, the need for a better understanding of this complex landscape has been pitted against a strong desire to move forward quickly.

Initial vision for restoring the pinyon-juniper woodlands. On one of the UP project's first field trips in May 2001, before public meetings were held, the agencies and many local interests seemed to be converging toward a straightforward vision of restoration. Lack of forage for deer and livestock, as well as the perceived increase in catastrophic fire, was believed to be the result of past overgrazing and fire exclusion. Over-

Figure 4.7. *Pinyon and juniper in Wyoming big sagebrush, Monogram Mesa, Dry Creek Basin, southwest of Naturita, Colorado.*

grazing was thought to have released pinyons and junipers from competition with grasses, forbs, and shrubs, allowing those trees to invade adjoining shrublands and grasslands (see Figure 4.7) and to fill in open spaces in the woodland.[73] Fire exclusion—meaning a decline in fire as a result of decreases in fine fuels from livestock grazing, construction of roads that limit fire spread, and intentional suppression of fires—is thought to have occurred throughout the West. In some parts of the Great Basin and the Pacific Northwest, surface fires (not in tree crowns) are thought by some to have maintained open savanna woodlands by thinning small, young trees while merely scorching or scarring older trees.[74] The increased tree cover, after overgrazing and fire exclusion, was thought to be the primary factor that suppressed the shrubs, grasses, and forbs needed by deer and livestock.

The solution was to use mechanical treatments and prescribed fire, rather than wildfires, to remove trees and set the landscape back more to shrubs, grasses, and forbs.[75] Wildfires produce smoke disturbing to valley residents and are difficult to control. The mechanical treatments would provide jobs, the increased forage would better support surrounding ranches and a larger mule deer herd, and the ecosystem would be restored to a more natural state.[76] Thus, UP project members seemed to have arrived at a vision for restoration that met everyone's needs.

However, these explanations of tree expansion and declining forage were based on very few data from the plateau or nearby areas; and as nearby research was brought to bear and new scientific studies were completed, the explanations were challenged. In western Colorado, evidence suggests that low-intensity surface fires were rare or absent in pre-Euro-American pinyon-juniper woodlands.[77] High-intensity fires are natural in these woodlands in Mesa Verde National Park[78] and on the Uncompahgre Plateau,[79] as in other parts of the West.[80] Pinyon-juniper fires typically burn very hot and rapidly in the crowns of trees, consuming much of the foliage and even some of the branches and trunks (see Plate 28).[81] Thus, exclusion of fire cannot explain increases in tree density in pinyon-juniper woodlands on the Uncompahgre Plateau, since surface fires were rare or absent before Euro-American settlement.[82]

The practice of putting out small fires or a decrease in the number or size of fires as a result of overgrazing could conceivably have reduced the amount of area burned by stand-replacing crown fires, allowing some areas to become abnormally old. However, the time between fires was likely so long that this effect is not very important. The "fire rotation," or time it takes to burn over a pinyon-juniper landscape one time, is 400–600 years in the plateau's pinyon-juniper zone,[83] so only 8–13 percent of the plateau's woodlands burns on average in a fifty-year period. Intentional fire suppression was not very effective until widespread use of slurry bombers after World War II. Because of the long fire rotation and ineffectiveness of fire suppression until the mid-twentieth century, the suppression of stand-replacing crown fires since Euro-American settlement is likely to have affected only a small part of the plateau's woodlands.

Livestock grazing alone could be a primary factor responsible for invasion of pinyons and junipers into adjoining sagebrush and grassland areas, as it has been in other parts of the West.[84] Recent research on the Uncompahgre Plateau, however, documents that sagebrush and grasslands have not been substantially reduced by tree invasion, as was initially thought to be occurring widely on the plateau. A study of aerial photographs found that mean pinyon-juniper cover did not change significantly between A.D. 1937 and 1994, and there was no significant expansion of pinyon-juniper into grasslands or shrublands.[85] Any expansion of pinyon-juniper that might have occurred over this period may have been offset by mechanical treatments that removed pinyons and junipers.[86] In fact, tree-ring dating in a sample of woodlands across the plateau suggests that post-settlement trees do now occupy some sagebrush and grassland areas.[87] While these trees appear to be invading, they could simply represent a slow natural return of woodland trees following temporary removal by fire or drought.[88] Some "invaded" areas have evidence of previous woodlands, but others do not. The story is not simple, but the evidence suggests that expansion of pinyon-juniper is minor or lacking.

In addition to invasion, tree density may have increased in the plateau's woodlands since Euro-American settlement, but that increase did not generally result from overgrazing or fire exclusion. Research shows that on the Uncompahgre Plateau and in nearby areas, pinyons in particular began increasing in density more than 200 years ago, long before Euro-American settlement, so livestock grazing and fire exclusion cannot be the primary explanation (see Figure 4.8).[89] In some cases, livestock grazing contributed to the density increase, but only small trees (< 2" diameter). The most likely explanations of density increases (or decreases) are past fluctuations in climate (i.e., wet periods, droughts) and disturbances by native insects and disease.[90] Pinyons in particular are known from paleoecological research to have expanded during past wet periods and contracted during dry periods.[91] By the summer of 2003, following the 2002 drought, extensive mortality of pinyon was evident on parts of the plateau, suggesting that drought alone can decrease tree density. The tree expansion that began 220–250 years ago may thus represent recovery following a drought.[92]

The effects of human land uses (livestock grazing and fire exclusion) on pinyon-juniper woodlands over the last century have taken place against this backdrop of longer-term natural fluctuations and events.[93] Careful study may be needed to unravel what has happened in a particular place. However, the overstory tree component of pinyon-juniper woodlands on the plateau today may be generally within the range of natural variability (see Box—Range of Natural Variability, pp. 161–162) and in no need of restoration, in contrast to the initial vision of the UP project.

Forage decline on the deer winter range. Although tree populations may not generally require restoration on the plateau, there is little doubt that the forage base for native herbivores (deer, elk) and livestock was degraded by past overgrazing (reviewed earlier in this chapter) and requires restoration. The Uncompahgre Partnership began as a project to reverse the decline in mule deer on the plateau that has been occurring over much of the West since the 1960s.[94] In spite of many studies, a 2001 report to the Colorado legislature said the decline in mule deer

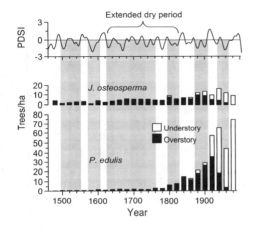

Figure 4.8. *Period of origin of living Utah juniper* (J. osteosperma) *and twoneedle pinyon* (P. edulis) *and their density (trees/ha) on the Uncompahgre Plateau. Overstory trees are > 2" in diameter, understory trees are < 2" in diameter. The top graph shows an index of drought, called the Palmer Drought Severity Index, in which negative numbers indicate drought periods. From Shinneman (2006).*

BOX—RANGE OF NATURAL VARIABILITY: RESTORATION ON A DYNAMIC EARTH

Even if natural systems are valued primarily for uses provided for people rather than for the inherent value of their continued existence, an important framework is the "range of natural variability" (RNV), or "historical range of variability," of ecosystems.[1] A definition of RNV is "the ecological conditions, and the spatial and temporal variation in these conditions, that are relatively unaffected by people, within a period of time and geographical area."[2] The key concept is that RNV represents how the ecosystem would operate with little effect from people, except where people were a key part of ecosystems over evolutionary time. In the United States the few hundred years of pre-Euro-American history are usually considered the most relevant for understanding RNV, as the ecology of the continent was significantly changed by the arrival of Euro-American people.[3] Earlier periods are also relevant; most studies assess conditions and processes over the last few thousand years, since this is often the longest period during which present ecosystems have been in place or been comparatively stable.

Maintaining an ecosystem within its RNV usually costs less and requires fewer external inputs and subsidies than maintaining an ecosystem outside its RNV.[4] For people who value nature in its own right and want to minimize the adverse effects of land uses on ecosystems and species, RNV also provides a frame of reference for assessing whether impacts are minimized. If the past is not understood, land uses may inadvertently decrease the viability of species and ecosystem processes and lead to undesirable outcomes (e.g., high soil erosion rates).

One past mistake has been a failure to understand that keeping an ecosystem outside its RNV may lead to unexpected and undesirable outcomes. Foresters in the 1950s and 1960s thought it would be beneficial to convert a mosaic of old-growth and younger forests to a uniform landscape of young, rapidly growing trees—a condition outside the RNV. In the Pacific Northwest, this led to significant declines in species viability (e.g., spotted owl). In the southern Rocky Mountains, forest disease, insect problems, and vulnerability to high-intensity fire may have been increased by uniform landscapes of young forests.[5]

Climate does change, evolution is ongoing, and it would be foolish to restore and then maintain ecosystems exactly as they occurred at a single particular moment in the past (e.g., right before Euro-American settlement). However, restoring some or all of those conditions is often a useful and necessary way to move ecosystems back within the RNV, even if those exact conditions are not expected to remain constant. For example, restoration of native bunchgrasses that are important components of many ecosystems in southwestern Colorado would serve both preservation and utilitarian goals. The Ponderosa Pine Partnership is using the RNV of forest structure to set goals for tree harvesting in southwestern Colorado (see Chapter 5), and an understory of native grasses would aid in restoring the desired fire regime. Even if the management goal is not restoration of pre-Euro-American conditions, RNV provides a framework for understanding the implications of maintaining ecosystems in other conditions.[6]

Scientists with a diversity of values have endorsed the value of RNV in management. Kauffman and colleagues suggest that "[s]cientifically, the most sound basis for ecosystem management is to assure that the variation characterizing ecosystems includes the range of conditions that are expected at various scales in ecosystems uninfluenced by humans."[7] Ecosystems are complex, and this complexity has repeatedly led to surprises. In the case of ecosystems, one who ignores history is condemned not to repeat it but to face unexpected and often undesirable consequences for people and the rest of nature.

NOTES

1. Landres, Morgan, and Swanson, "Use of Natural Variability Concepts."
2. Ibid., 1180.
3. Ibid.
4. Ibid.
5. Veblen, "Disturbance Patterns in Southern Rocky Mountain Forests."
6. Landres, Morgan, and Swanson, "Use of Natural Variability Concepts."
7. Kaufmann et al., *Ecological Basis for Ecosystem Management*, 5.

numbers in Colorado and elsewhere is richly speculated but not well understood.[95] It is extremely difficult to separate the influence of habitat change, predation, competition from elk, hunting policies, and other factors.

Recent reviews of mule deer predation studies in the West present a complicated picture.[96] Predators do not appear to suppress deer populations when deer are near the habitat's carrying capacity.[97] Where predators have been controlled, predation rates sometimes go down, but mortality of deer from starvation and other causes tends to go up in response.[98] Predators are often taking young that would not survive anyway. Tracking of radio-collared fawns on the plateau has shown that coyotes kill 12–13 percent of fawns in their first six months, while bears and mountain lions take another 5–14 percent.[99] Disease and starvation claim as many as 30 percent of fawns some years.[100] A four-year CDOW study has documented that poor winter range conditions contributed to subsequent poor survival of fawns.[101] Weakened fawns are more susceptible to both disease and predation, confounding the influence of predation.[102]

Reduced forage has impacted deer herds, but construction of rural subdivisions in the winter range, as well as competition with elk and livestock, are all likely having some additional effect. Most of the deer herd winters on the southern half of the plateau, where a large portion uses private land rapidly being subdivided for housing.[103] Elk numbers on the plateau more than tripled in the 1980s and have remained near an unprecedented 9,000 animals since 1990. Deer populations have fluctuated widely over time but declined steadily during the 1990s, from 51,000 in 1988 to a low of 28,000 in 1997 and 1998 (see Figure 4.9). These trends occurred across Colorado, and it is thought that elk might be outcompeting deer because they are larger, have a broader diet, and tend to better survive harsh winters.[104]

Livestock grazing that was exceptionally heavy in the past may have created much of the degradation problem on the winter range, and restoration is unlikely to succeed without further changes in grazing. Forage gains after treatments in the 1970s and 1980s were lost by the late 1980s because of subsequent overgrazing.[105] This would likely happen again today without additional changes. Although the number of livestock and the length of use have declined over the past two decades on some allotments, the lower elevations of the pinyon-juniper zone still tend to be used heavily during the peak spring growing season for cool-season grasses and forbs. These native grasses and forbs have never recovered from past overgrazing.[106]

Thus, the loss and degradation of mule deer habitat have many causes—subdivision of private lands, high elk numbers, and livestock grazing at levels that prevent recovery of the forage base. All these causes, although recognized, are much more politically difficult to address than the supposed expansion of pinyon-juniper woodlands, and

UNCOMPAHGRE PLATEAU DEER & ELK POPULATION ESTIMATES

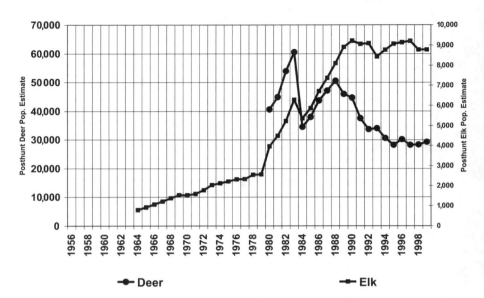

Figure 4.9. *Modeled estimates of elk and mule deer populations on the Uncompahgre Plateau. Note the smaller numbers for elk on the right-hand axis. Data provided by Bruce Watkins, Colorado Division of Wildlife, Montrose.*

finding creative new solutions to these problems has not been a focus of the UP project.

Toward a new vision for restoring pinyon-juniper woodlands. A revised vision for restoring the ecosystems of the pinyon-juniper zone on the plateau has not yet emerged following new scientific studies of the woodland and the deer decline. The UP project initiated a pilot project in two watersheds, Dry Creek and Spring Creek, which offers the opportunity to work through competing ideas about degradation and restoration. The Dry Creek–Spring Creek project was formulated within the context of the original UP model of degradation and so was focused primarily on applying treatments to remove aging woody vegetation. However, the project does include attention to findings from scientific studies on the plateau and some new concerns about biological diversity.

In developing the restoration and management plan for the Spring Creek–Dry Creek watersheds, the agency team invited researchers, members of the Black Canyon Audubon Society, and others to meet to discuss the goals of restoration in the project area. Naturalists and re-searchers emphasized that pinyon-juniper obligates need large blocks of mature and old-growth pinyon-juniper woodlands, which must be considered when planning vegetation treatments for deer and for fire protection. About 22 percent of sampled woodlands in one study and 56 percent in another qualified as ancient, and an additional 18–39 per-cent were old growth[107] (see Box—Ancient Pinyon-Juniper Woodlands, p. 166), suggesting that much of the plateau had old-growth or ancient woodlands prior to chaining. Unfortunately, good information is not available on the amount of old growth that has been treated (chained or prescribed burned). Old growth on flat sites with deep soils (see Figure 4.10) was targeted for chaining because of the sites' accessibility and productivity, and large areas of such woodland now appear to be scarce.[108] Based on this information, the project has added protection and restoration of old pinyon-juniper woodlands as one of its goals.

Perhaps the most innovative aspect of the UP project is its approach to restoring native plants on the plateau. The UP project has supported research to determine which species are missing and need active resto-ration, such as planting, and which species might be common enough to recover on their own.[109] Scientists collected native plants from the pla-teau and are experimenting with techniques to grow them for eventual larger-scale production in the Uncompahgre Valley (see Chapter 3). Some areas on the plateau itself might also be designated for production and collection of native seed.

Barriers to the UP project's goal of ecosystem restoration include social attitudes toward high-intensity fire (see Plate 28), which occurs naturally in the plateau's pinyon-juniper woodlands.[110] This problem is intimately linked with the housing development that is decreasing the area of available winter range. As the West began to experience the worst drought in generations and large fires began to destroy homes, in 2000 Congress poured funds into a National Fire Plan intended to protect homes in the "wildland-urban interface."[111]

As part of the Dry Creek–Spring Creek project, land managers are substantially altering pinyon-juniper woodlands to lower fire risk, par-ticularly within 0.5–1.0 mile of private land. However, the evidence that such efforts will lower risk to homes is weak—private landowners themselves can do the most to lower fire risk simply by clearing fuels within the "home ignition zone," the 100–200 feet immediately sur-rounding a house.[112] Nonetheless, agency fire managers are under pub-lic pressure to put fires out before they reach private property. Much of the burden for fire protection for private landowners who choose to build in fire-prone areas near public land is thus shifted to public-land

BOX—ANCIENT PINYON–JUNIPER WOODLANDS

Pinyon-juniper woodlands that are 400 years old or older can be considered "ancient,"[1] while woodlands 200–400 years old are "old growth."[2] Ancient and old-growth pinyon-juniper woodlands have clear biological value. The understory flora in these woodlands can comprise hundreds of species, including several rare species,[3] but many species of fungi, moss, and microbes are also present.[4] Among the birds, the pinyon-juniper obligates (e.g., black-throated gray warbler, pinyon jay) are more common in old growth. Pinyon jays depend on woodlands old enough to produce pinyon nuts. But the old-growth woodland also contains birds that fly above the trees, eating insects (white-throated swift), as well as birds that "flycatch" from dead branches (gray fly-catcher) and birds that are "bark gleaners," such as the white-breasted nuthatch, which crawls down tree trunks poking about for insects.[5]

Counting the insects, thousands of species benefit from these seemingly unproductive ecosystems. The stability and age of pinyon-juniper woodlands are their strengths, providing secure and reliable habitat for a variety of species for thousands of years and even featuring the same tree in the same place for as much as 600–700 years.

Some people argue that mature woodlands also produce the highest potential economic value in the form of pinyon nuts.[6] Lanner's book on the pinyon, *The Piñon Pine: A Natural and Cultural History*,[7] has an excellent discussion of pinyon nuts, which were an important food source for Native Americans (see Figure 1.3) and still support a small industry.[8] But the United States now imports 8 million pounds of pine nuts annually from twenty-eight countries.[9] An online historical vignette from the early days of the pinyon nut industry describes the challenges of working with this irregular but bountiful resource.[10] The pinyon nut might be part of a viable and more sustainable local economy, which could allow the woodland's biological diversity to be perpetuated while providing economic value for people.

NOTES

1. Romme et al., "Ponderosa Pine Partnership."
2. Mehl, "Old-Growth Descriptions for Major Forest Cover Types."
3. Floyd and Colyer, "Beneath the Trees."
4. Belnap, "Magnificent Microbes: Biological Soil Crusts."
5. San Miguel and Colyer, "Mesa Verde Country's Woodland Avian Community."
6. Kline, "Piñon/Socioeconomic Potential of Piñon Woodlands."
7. Lanner, *Piñon Pine: Natural and Cultural History*.
8. Dunmire and Tierney, *Wild Plants and Native Peoples of the Four Corners*.
9. See Web site: http://www.pinenut.com.
10. See Web site: http://www.nau.edu/library/speccoll/exhibits/traders/trade/pinon.html.

Figure 4.10. *Old-growth pinyon-juniper woodland on level site with deeper soils on the Uncompahgre Plateau.*

Figure 4.11. *A rollerchopper, which is pulled over relatively young pinyon and juniper to crush trees and other woody vegetation to ground level and chop them up.*

managers. Publicly funded fire protection may even increase the chance that development will occur in the winter range, adversely affecting deer herds and the overall health of the plateau. To what extent should public-land managers subsidize fire protection for development, knowing that development is degrading the winter range?

As part of this effort to lower fire risk but also in an attempt to increase forage, a good deal of land will be mechanically treated as part of the Dry Creek–Spring Creek project. Mechanical treatments today include hydroaxing, which chops up woody plants individually, and rollerchopping. A rollerchopper (see Figure 4.11) is a heavy drum with blades that crush and chop the vegetation, with substantial ground disturbance. The Gibbler site on the north end of the plateau was chained in the mid-1960s. By 2001, pinyons and junipers had grown up again, and about 500 acres were rollerchopped (see Plate 29) "to increase forage for wildlife and livestock."[113] The project is also a "fuels reduction program to reduce continuous fuels to insure that large fires do not happen in this area."[114]

At Gibbler, if rollerchopping eventually will increase forage, that increase had not occurred by 2003. The rollerchopped area that year had about 4 percent cover of native grasses and 3 percent cover of crested wheatgrass, compared with 13 percent cover of native grasses in the untreated woodland near the road.[115] Rollerchopping also did not decrease fuels but instead increased small, dead woody fuels (those less than about three inches in diameter), the fuels that most participate in a fire.[116] Only if the area were subsequently burned would fuels really be decreased; otherwise, rollerchopping may actually increase fire risk, at least for a number of years. Finally, the biological soil crust (see Box—Biological Soil Crusts, pp. 150–152), which had about 4 percent cover in the untreated woodland, was decreased to only a trace by rollerchopping.[117] Both bare ground and a decreased biological soil crust can allow increases in non-native invasive weeds. Rollerchopping might have potential as part of a program to restore native plants in degraded woodlands and sagebrush on the plateau, but realizing this potential will require more care in livestock management, native plant establishment, protecting the soil crust, and weed control than has been the norm to date.

A central challenge for the UP project is to create a new strategy for restoration that is science-based, integrates what has been learned from past efforts, does not require destroying ancient woodlands, and leads to new land uses that are ultimately sustainable without ongoing subsidies such as repeated mechanical treatments. Only short-term economic gain came from chaining. Rollerchopping, prescribed burns, and fuel reduction without broader changes in land use promise no better outcome.

Challenges to collaborative learning. One of the most important promises of more open, collaborative decision making is the potential for improved understanding of the situation through collaborative learning.[118] This goal is both laudable and lofty, as society has not generally taken a holistic, cooperative, long-term view, especially in the West.[119] Hunters, ranchers, hikers, wildlife biologists, range scientists, public managers, foresters, and environmentalists each view restoration through a different lens. Any single, narrow lens can produce understandings that are incomplete or erroneous, leading to mistakes. Science is not immune. The chaining of pinyon-juniper woodland, for example, was supported by the science of the day, using a rather narrow lens.[120] Bringing together multiple lenses, at least theoretically, should improve society's understanding of a place, but it requires a certain amount of openness and curiosity.

The UP project has made some progress toward a more collaborative approach. Ideas challenging the need for large-scale removal of pinyon and juniper trees have been published in the UP newsletter.[121] The technical committee has supported studies to try to resolve some of the uncertainty about vegetation changes and their causes on the plateau. The interaction among agency managers, the public, and scientists is still quite limited, however.

The first technical coordinator of the UP project, Rick Sherman, described the task of keeping all parties committed to a management process that is more open and therefore slower and less predictable as similar to "turning the aircraft carrier."[122] A collaborative learning approach asks not only that the various agencies coordinate and cooperate among themselves—no small hurdle in itself—but also that managers and decision makers find time and ways to directly involve the public and outside scientists.

In tension with the needed time for learning is a sense of urgency and desire to change things for the better, alluded to in this chapter's opening quote. As Sherman explained, "People [in the agencies] don't like pushing paper; this project excites them because they feel they can actually do something worthwhile on the ground."[123]

On-the-ground projects in the past have involved manipulating vegetation, generally making it younger or thinner. Now that science suggests this is not the central problem, other, more difficult issues require attention. Changing livestock management may be the most important action needed, but that has proven frustratingly difficult for managers. Similarly, reducing elk herds would be controversial. One of the emerging criticisms of the collaborative approach is its naive attitude toward power relations. Strategic behavior and unequal power relations do not disappear in a collaborative setting.[124] Powerful interests continue to exert a strong influence on how issues are framed and on what can and cannot be addressed, thus limiting collaborative learning and change.

Moreover, many agency personnel and local people deeply believe the plateau's vegetation requires further manipulation. In a culture of active management, they find it hard to consider the possibility that restoration in some places might require slowly and carefully reestablishing native plants or slowly regrowing mature and old-growth woodlands to offset a deficit created by past manipulations.

It is the premise of this book that a diversity of people and their perspectives must contribute to a search for a deeper, less narrow understanding of the natural world. No clear vision emerged from early meetings of the UP project, but some community members felt they had been somewhat successful in opening public-land management in the region to greater local input. On the other hand, the emphasis on face-to-face meetings made it difficult for nonlocal people with interest in the plateau to participate. This is a significant problem because collaborative agreements worked out among local groups, individuals, and agencies may be challenged by urban and national interests, either because they have not been involved in the group learning process or because their values have been inadequately considered.[125]

CONCLUDING THOUGHTS

The expansive undeveloped, lightly populated Uncompahgre Plateau is as important for the current human economy as it was for the Tabeguache Utes. There is widespread agreement that the plateau requires restoration, but competing perceptions, values, and goals have thwarted a unified vision. Few appreciate the pinyons and junipers or the diverse natural communities of these woodlands. A perception persists that the woodlands have grown too old and dense, although ecological studies suggest otherwise. So woodlands are still cleared or thinned in hopes of protecting housing and infrastructure from natural fires and in pursuit of increased forage. The formation of a native seed industry to support restoration and the development of plans to protect and even restore some old-growth woodlands are encouraging signs. The UP project struggles to address difficult issues but has achieved some collaborative success, in spite of a lack of unified vision. However, without better collaborative learning where people "fiddle with things" together and work through competing ideas and values, management will continue to be by experts, too heavily influenced by agency culture and the scientific paradigms and politics of the day.

NOTES

1. Bock and Bock, *View from Bald Hill*, 16.
2. Gannett, "Report of Henry Gannett," 340.
3. Dillard, "Up from Texas"; Curtis, *Riding Old Trails*; Marshall, *Red Hole in Time*.
4. Gannet, "Report of Henry Gannett," 340.
5. Peale, "Report of A. C. Peale," 44.
6. Dillard, "Up from Texas," 72.
7. Ibid., 73.
8. Shinneman, "Determining Restoration Needs."
9. Ibid.
10. O'Rourke, *Frontier in Transition*.
11. Shinneman, "Determining Restoration Needs."
12. O'Rourke, *Frontier in Transition*; Marshall, *Red Hole in Time*.
13. U.S. Department of the Interior, Bureau of Land Management, "Range Management Plan, Escalante Unit."

14. Rockwell, *Uncompahgre Country;* Marshall, *Red Hole in Time.*
15. U.S. Department of the Interior, Bureau of Land Management, "Range Management Plan, Escalante Unit."
16. U.S. Department of Agriculture, Forest Service, "Grand Mesa—Uncompahgre Forest History."
17. Voigt, *Public Lands Grazing.*
18. U.S. Department of Agriculture, Forest Service, "Information Packet" (no pages).
19. Ibid.
20. Ibid.
21. Ibid.
22. Ibid.
23. Voigt, *Public Lands Grazing.*
24. Floyd Reed, U.S. Forest Service, Delta, Colorado, pers. comm., October 12, 2001.
25. Wallace, *Western Range,* 100.
26. Ibid.
27. Arnold, Jameson, and Reid, *Pinyon-Juniper Type of Arizona.*
28. Lanner, "Eradication of Pinyon-Juniper Woodland."
29. Data collected by Bob Welch in 1988, on file at Bureau of Land Management, Montrose, Colorado.
30. Highway 90 Allotment Evaluation, September 27, 1984, on file at Bureau of Land Management, Montrose, Colorado (no pages).
31. E.g., Lanner, "Eradication of Pinyon-Juniper Woodland."
32. Sedgwick and Ryder, "Effects of Chaining on Non-game Wildlife."
33. Webb, "Importance of Pinyon-Juniper Habitat to Birds."
34. Lanner, "Eradication of Pinyon-Juniper Woodland."
35. Terrel and Spillett, "Pinyon-Juniper Conversion"; Howard et al., "Effects of Cabling on Mule Deer and Lagomorph Use."
36. Clary, "Effects of Juniper Removal on Herbage Yields."
37. Gary Thygerson, BLM, Grand Junction, Colorado, pers. comm., October 2001.
38. Paulin, Cook, and Dewey, "Pinyon-Juniper Woodlands as Sources of Avian Diversity."
39. Kingery, *Colorado Breeding Bird Atlas.*
40. Ibid.
41. Fitzgerald, Meaney, and Armstrong, *Mammals of Colorado.*
42. Ron Lambeth, BLM, Grand Junction, Colorado, pers. comm., October 18, 2001.
43. Pavlacky and Anderson, "Habitat Preferences of Pinyon-Juniper Specialists."
44. Hammerson, *Amphibians and Reptiles of Colorado.*
45. Ibid.
46. Dunmire and Tierney, *Wild Plants and Native Peoples.*
47. Based on authors' observations in 1999.
48. Hammerson, *Amphibians and Reptiles of Colorado.*
49. Ibid.

50. Ibid.
51. U.S. Department of the Interior, Bureau of Land Management, "Final Wilderness Environmental Impact Statement."
52. U.S. Department of Agriculture, Forest Service, "Grand Mesa–Uncompahgre Forest History."
53. Singer, "Bighorn Sheep in Rocky Mountain National Parks."
54. Hartley, *Rock Art on the Northern Colorado Plateau.*
55. Bear and Jones, *Bighorn Sheep in Colorado*
56. Fitzgerald, Meaney, and Armstrong, *Mammals of Colorado.*
57. McCutchen, "Desert Bighorn Sheep."
58. Hinshaw, *Crusaders for Wildlife.*
59. Singer, "Bighorn Sheep in Rocky Mountain National Parks."
60. Fitzgerald, Meaney, and Armstrong, *Mammals of Colorado.*
61. Ibid.
62. Harley Metz, Bureau of Land Management, Grand Junction, Colorado, pers. comm., October 24, 2001.
63. U.S. Department of the Interior, Bureau of Land Management, "Final Wilderness Environmental Impact Statement."
64. Fitzgerald, Meaney, and Armstrong, *Mammals of Colorado.*
65. McCutchen, "Desert Bighorn Sheep."
66. Bruce Watkins, Colorado Division of Wildlife, Montrose, pers. comm., January 4, 2002.
67. Wondolleck and Yaffee, *Making Collaboration Work;* Daniels and Walker, *Working Through Environmental Conflict.*
68. See Web site: http://www.UPproject.org/; accessed May 11, 2006.
69. Rick Sherman, Uncompahgre Plateau project technical coordinator, Montrose, Colorado, pers. comm., October 8, 2001, and July 17, 2002; UPDATE, a publication of the Uncompahgre Plateau project (Montrose, Colorado), Fall 2001.
70. Ibid.
71. Ibid.
72. Mary Chapman, project coordinator, Public Lands Partnership, Montrose, Colorado, pers. comm., October 24, 2001.
73. Cottam and Stewart, "Plant Succession Since Settlement in 1862"; Johnsen, "One-Seeded Juniper Invasion"; West, "Successional Patterns and Potentials of Pinyon-Juniper Ecosystems."
74. West, "Successional Patterns and Potentials of Pinyon-Juniper Ecosystems."
75. Uncompahgre Ecosystem Restoration Project. Field trip and handout, Montrose, Colorado, May 21, 2001.
76. Ibid.
77. Floyd, Romme, and Hanna, "Fire History in Mesa Verde National Park"; Eisenhart, "Historic Range of Variability on Uncompahgre Plateau"; Shinneman, "Determining Restoration Needs."
78. Floyd, Romme, and Hanna, "Fire History in Mesa Verde National Park."
79. Eisenhart, "Historic Range of Variability on Uncompahgre Plateau"; Shinneman, "Determining Restoration Needs."

80. Baker and Shinneman, "Fire and Restoration of Piñon-Juniper Woodlands."
81. Hester, "Pinyon-Juniper Fuel Can Really Burn."
82. Eisenhart, "Historic Range of Variability on Uncompahgre Plateau"; Shinneman, "Determining Restoration Needs."
83. Ibid.
84. E.g., Miller and Rose, "Fire History and Western Juniper Encroachment."
85. Manier et al., "Canopy Dynamics on a Semi-arid Landscape."
86. Ibid.
87. Shinneman, "Determining Restoration Needs."
88. Erdman, "Pinyon-Juniper Succession After Natural Fires on Mesa Verde."
89. Eisenhart, "Historic Range of Variability on Uncompahgre Plateau"; Shinneman, "Determining Restoration Needs."
90. Shinneman, "Determining Restoration Needs."
91. Betancourt et al., "Influence of History and Climate"; Petersen, "Warm and Wet Little Climatic Optimum."
92. Shinneman, "Determining Restoration Needs."
93. Eisenhart, "Historic Range of Variability on Uncompahgre Plateau."
94. Gill, *Declining Mule Deer Populations.*
95. Ibid., v.
96. Ballard et al., "Deer-Predator Relationships"; ibid.
97. Ballard et al., "Deer-Predator Relationships."
98. Gill, *Declining Mule Deer Populations.*
99. Pojar, "Understanding Recruitment in Mule Deer Herds."
100. Ibid.
101. Watkins, Olterman, and Pojar, "Mule Deer Studies on the Uncompahgre Plateau"; Bishop et al., "Effect of Nutrition and Habitat Enhancements."
102. Gill, *Declining Mule Deer Populations;* Pojar, "Understanding Recruitment in Mule Deer Herds."
103. Kufeld, *Mule Deer Population on East Side of Uncompahgre Plateau;* Watkins, Olterman, and Pojar, "Mule Deer Studies on the Uncompahgre Plateau."
104. Gill, *Declining Mule Deer Populations.*
105. Data collected by Bob Welch in 1988, on file at Bureau of Land Management, Montrose, Colorado.
106. Shinneman, "Determining Restoration Needs."
107. Eisenhart, "Historic Range of Variability on Uncompahgre Plateau"; ibid. Eisenhart's estimate is based only on pinyon ages; Shinneman's estimate, which includes junipers, suggests that Eisenhart's stands are likely > 100 years older. If this were added, the percentage of old growth would be much higher, closer to the value reported by Shinneman.
108. Shinneman, "Determining Restoration Needs."
109. Ibid.
110. Eisenhart, "Historic Range of Variability on Uncompahgre Plateau"; Baker and Shinneman, "Fire and Restoration of Piñon-Juniper Woodlands"; Shinneman, "Determining Restoration Needs."
111. U.S. Department of Agriculture, Forest Service, and U.S. Department of the Interior, *Report to the President in Response to Wildfires of 2000.*

112. Cohen, "Preventing Disaster."
113. U.S. Department of the Interior, Bureau of Land Management, "Environmental Assessment for Gibbler Roller Chopping."
114. Ibid.
115. Paulson and Baker, observation and visual estimates of cover, June 29, 2003.
116. Paulson and Baker, observation of fuels on Gibbler rollerchop, June 29, 2003.
117. Paulson and Baker, observation and visual estimates of cover, June 29, 2003.
118. Wondolleck and Yaffee, *Making Collaboration Work.*
119. Limerick, *Legacy of Conquest.*
120. Lanner, "Eradication of Pinyon-Juniper Woodland."
121. Baker and Paulson, "Importance of Research on Natural Disturbance," 1, 10–13.
122. Rick Sherman, UP project technical coordinator, pers. comm., October 8, 2001.
123. Ibid.
124. Walker and Hurley, "Collaboration Derailed"; Singleton, "Collaborative Environmental Planning in the American West."
125. Kenney, *Arguing About Consensus.*

Pagosa lies in the heart of that splendid pine forest, which covers a tract one hundred and thirty miles east and west by from twenty to forty miles north and south. Here the trees grow tall and straight, and of enormous size. No underbrush hides their bright, clean shafts, and curiously enough, it is only in special locations that any low ones are to be found. These monarchs of the forest seem to be the last of their race, and, like the Indians, are doomed very soon to disappear. They are of immense value, for they form a huge storehouse of the finest lumber in a country poorly supplied in general with such material.

—Ingersoll, *The Crest of the Continent*[1]

CHAPTER FIVE

To many people, including Ernest Ingersoll, one of the earliest Euro-Americans to see the country, the ponderosa pine forest is southwestern Colorado's most beautiful forest. This forest ecosystem is found across the western United States, and in western Colorado it is best developed along the southern base of the San Juans from 6,000 to 8,500 feet elevation (see Maps 0.1, 5.1). The forest almost certainly varied in understory and size of trees more than Ingersoll's opening quote portrays. However, numerous early writings and photos indicate that ponderosa pine forests often had large, widely spaced trees and an

Ponderosa Pine Forests, Grasslands, and Aspen Forests of the Southern San Juan Mountains

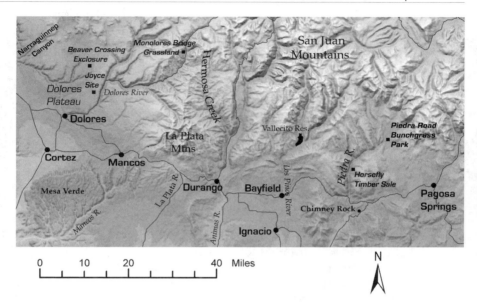

Map 5.1. *Map of region of ponderosa pine forests of the southern San Juan Mountains with places described in this chapter.*

understory of bunchgrasses (see Box—Rhizomes Versus Bunchgrasses, pp. 116–117) and scattered shrubs (see Plate 30). Unfortunately, Ingersoll's prediction in the quote came true shortly after his visit in 1874. Today, very few of the towering pines remain. In many forests native bunchgrasses are also gone or greatly reduced as a result of overgrazing by livestock and replacement by non-native plants. The beauty of an old-growth pine forest with a bunchgrass understory has seemingly faded from society's collective memory.

Very little ponderosa pine forest anywhere escaped logging of the large trees, until recently considered the wisest use. Many U.S. houses were built with lumber from old-growth pine forests, including those of southwestern Colorado. Logging and livestock grazing, accompanied by suppression of fire, created today's relatively uniform landscape of young trees (see Figure 5.1). These young forests will need a century or more to regain their old-growth qualities.

Quaking aspen forests occur adjacent to, or intermixed with, the pine forests or at slightly higher elevations (see Plate 31). In the San Juan Mountains aspen is extensive, since its major competitor to the north, lodgepole pine, is absent. Commercial logging came more recently to the aspen forests, following depletion of the large pines and development of new products that can use aspen (e.g., particle board, paneling).

Figure 5.1. *Dense, young ponderosa pine forest, now typical of the ponderosa pine zone.*

People have begun to rethink the ponderosa pine landscape and its meaning and value. The Ponderosa Pine Partnership is learning how to restore the forest's old-growth character while harvesting products from the forest. The bunchgrasses in the forests and parks await similar attention. Restoration is not a focus in the aspen forest, as aspen was less extensively harvested than the ponderosa pine forest. However, aspen forests are very important for biological diversity, and how aspen is harvested is also worth considering. Logging, though, is no longer the primary threat to the forests of the ponderosa pine zone. Expanding rural subdivisions, with accompanying roads and weed invasions, are perhaps the most significant threat, but innovative options for housing developments exist.

LEGACY OF PAST HUMAN USES

Early Euro-American Exploration and Settlement

The first non-Indian movement into the San Juan region was by traders and miners from Spanish settlements in New Mexico, but little evidence remains of their early activities in Colorado.[2] The first regular incursions of Europeans into southwestern Colorado were along an established Ute path that became the Old Spanish Trail in the early 1800s.[3] The trail's original southern route skirted the pine zone, passing near present-day Durango, Dolores, and Dove Creek. Large numbers of horses and mules were traded over this route between California and New Mexico.[4] The goal was to get the animals to Santa Fe quickly, so grazing probably occurred only near the trail. Fur trappers entered the region by 1832 or earlier.[5]

The first formal U.S. (as opposed to Spanish) expedition into far southwestern Colorado was Macomb's 1859 U.S. Army expedition along the Old Spanish Trail. J. S. Newberry, reporter for the expedition, was especially impressed with the Pagosa Springs area. He called it "evenly turfed over" and "a verdant meadow of the finest grass," adding that "[o]n every side are hills covered with gigantic pines or the slender Oregon spruce."[6] The latter is Douglas-fir, and the forest is visible in a painting done by the expedition (see Plate 32). The Pine River, he reported, "is a clear, cold trout-stream. . . . The bottom-lands are wooded with willows, cottonwood, alder . . . and scattered trees of yellow [ponderosa] pine, the latter of which mark[s] its course in the open sage-covered country through which it flows."[7] West of the La Plata Mountains, Newberry crossed the "Great Sage Plain" of the Montezuma Valley, where he reported sparse forage and lack of wildlife but much broken pottery and other evidence of the Ancestral Puebloans.

Within two decades of this report Euro-Americans settled rapidly, spurred by the discovery of precious minerals around present-day Silverton, where a mining industry began in the early 1870s.[8] By 1877, when Lieutenant C.A.H. McCauley was sent to survey the San Juan region, he found small numbers of settlers squatting on Ute lands along most of the rivers flowing south from the San Juans. Animas City (now the north end of Durango) already had thirty-eight buildings, and Animas Park north of Durango and nearby areas had 11,000 sheep and 5,000 head of cattle.[9] Wightman Road, connecting booming Silverton to Animas City, was completed shortly after McCauley's survey. The railroad, completed in 1882, provided the critical connection to the miners, spurring further development of the agricultural lands surrounding the mountains.[10] Legacies of hunting, early grazing, and logging are still evident in the ponderosa pine zone.

Hunting

Euro-Americans reported plentiful game during the early years of settlement.[11] Many settlers relied on wild game for food, and game animals were plentiful enough to allow market hunting—but only for a very brief period. Within a few years virtually all game species were gone or had become rare. Deer, which had wintered in large numbers on the lower Piedra River, and turkey, which were also common there, had virtually disappeared by 1904.[12] Some species, such as the "hundreds of prairie chickens" (most likely Gunnison sage-grouse) reported in Piedra Park as late as 1896,[13] have never returned. Elk had to be restocked throughout Colorado, and twenty-three were shipped from Jackson Hole, Wyoming, to Hermosa in 1913 to restock one of the last remaining herds in the region.[14] Game laws were eventually passed, but little enforcement occurred in the early years.[15]

Predators experienced heightened hunting rather than protection in the early 1900s. In response to requests by livestock producers and farmers, the legislature passed bounties on most predators, including hawks.[16] The gray wolf and grizzly bear were rare by the 1930s and then disappeared, although one grizzly survived until it attacked a hunter in the southern San Juans near Platoro in 1979.[17] Fur-bearing animals were also late to receive protection, as trapping was a source of income for rural families. Beavers were trapped out in much of the West before Euro-American settlement, altering streams on which they were keystone species. The beaver and most other fur-bearing animals have recovered and now have viable populations. The river otter, once common in the larger rivers of the ponderosa pine zone, was eliminated from Colorado but was reintroduced in southern Colorado and is recovering well.[18]

Effects of Livestock Grazing on the Bunchgrasses of the Ponderosa Pine Zone

One of the earliest widespread impacts of Euro-American settlement in the ponderosa pine zone was the grazing of domestic livestock. In a 1903 survey of the proposed San Juan Forest Reserve, which extended from the Needle Mountains to the New Mexico line, Coert Dubois reported that sheep grazed from the alpine to the lower forests and that an estimated 268,100 sheep spent the summer months on the proposed reserve, mostly east of the Pine River.[19] Cattle dominated the country below 10,000 feet in elevation west of the Pine River, where Dubois estimated about 20,000 head were present. With the establishment of the San Juan National Forest in 1905, grazing began to be regulated.[20] Today, about 16,000–22,000 head graze the entire San Juan National Forest, indicating that stocking rates have declined since Dubois's report.[21]

Figure 5.2. *Dense grassland of Parry's oatgrass* (Danthonia parryi), *insert illustrating the flowers.*

The graceful Arizona fescue (see Plate 33a), the sturdier mountain muhly (see Plate 33b), and the dense Parry's oatgrass (see Figure 5.2) were likely the main bunchgrasses over the ponderosa pine zone in southern Colorado; the first two were also dominant in Arizona and New Mexico.[22] In describing early settlement north of Dolores, R. York said: "During the first few years or until about 1885, practically the only kind of hay cut for market was wild grass, principally mountain bunch grass. This was cut with both mowers and scythe and baled in either small hand balers, or horsepower 'ground hog' balers."[23] However, the bunchgrass was lost, and Dubois described the transformation: "In low gulches and flats where large herds of cattle have been ranged year after year, the bunch grass is pulled up by the roots and gradually dies out. On overstocked cow ranges the white roots of bunch grass can be seen all over the ground."[24] Dubois's descriptions of the early cattle days agree with those of David Lavender in the San Miguel–Dolores country. Lavender said vegetation was removed to almost nothing year after year until institutions were established in the early 1900s to control grazing.[25] These institutions and policies were not fully successful in preventing the loss of bunchgrass, as extensive losses occurred after the period 1910–1915.[26]

Today, it is difficult to find healthy native bunchgrasses in the forests[27] or openings and parks of the ponderosa pine zone. Over most of the area non-native forbs, such as common dandelion, and two non-native grasses, Kentucky bluegrass (see Figure 3.8) and smooth brome (see Box—Smooth Brome, pp. 281–282), have replaced the native bunchgrasses. These two grasses are rhizomatous rather than bunchgrasses, which confers resistance to livestock grazing (see Box—Rhizomes Versus Bunchgrasses, pp. 116–117).

Livestock grazing has also affected forest structure (e.g., density of trees). Tree density has increased in some ponderosa pine forests since Euro-American settlement.[28] Some of that increase may have resulted from rare climatic episodes in the early 1900s favorable to ponderosa pine regeneration,[29] but livestock grazing may have been the trigger in two ways. First, grazing reduced the grassy fuels that fed surface fires. There is clear evidence that ponderosa pine forests in the Southwest experienced surface fires that killed young trees, helping to maintain a rather open forest.[30] Reduced fire allowed young trees to survive that might otherwise have been killed by such fires. More important, loss of bunchgrasses, which compete with young trees for moisture, allowed more young trees to regenerate and survive.[31] This conclusion is supported by two studies of relicts of ponderosa pine forest never grazed by domestic livestock (see Box—Remnants and Relicts, pp. 183–184).

BOX—REMNANTS AND RELICTS

Relicts of natural vegetation are sites that never experienced modern land uses because they are in inaccessible areas, such as on topographically isolated mesas, or that by accident were never used. Remnants are areas that have been used since Euro-American settlement but that have received light use or later protection from use because of changes in ownership or accidents in fencing, road construction, or other changes. For example, in a northern Utah valley, scientists used remnants in unplowed corners of croplands, on steep slopes where livestock graze only lightly, and in inaccessible areas to try to understand the vegetation in the valley before Euro-American settlement.[1] Researchers seek remnant and relict areas that native herbivores can access and where natural processes (e.g., fire) have not been altered, but such areas cannot always be found.

Data on the composition and abundance of plants in remnants and relicts can help us understand and manage the effects of land uses and can provide information useful in restoration. In much of the West it is lower-elevation ecosystems—including sagebrush, pinyon-juniper woodlands, and ponderosa pine forests—where land uses have been most pervasive. It is here where remnants and relicts are rarest but most useful in sorting out land-use legacies.

Sagebrush and pinyon-juniper relicts, never grazed by domestic livestock or chained or otherwise treated, have been found on steep-sided mesa tops that must be accessed by helicopter.[2] These relicts usually contain more abundant native bunchgrasses (e.g., muttongrass) and palatable forbs than are found in comparable nearby areas grazed by livestock.[3] Cover of native grasses is seldom high (e.g., 5–15 percent cover) even in relicts of these semiarid communities, but they typically have more abundant biological soil crusts (see Box—Biological Soil Crusts, pp. 150–152) than areas subject to livestock grazing.

Scientists have studied two relicts of ponderosa pine forests in the West, one in Zion National Park, Utah,[4] and the other in central Washington.[5] Both relicts have abundant native bunchgrasses and both had few fires in the last century, yet neither has dense, young trees. Comparable mesas nearby also had few fires but were grazed by livestock and have high densities of young trees. These studies concluded that the loss of competition from bunchgrasses as a result of overgrazing has been the primary cause of tree-density increases in ponderosa pine forests since Euro-American settlement.

Important remnants and relicts have been formally protected on public lands—in some cases by designation as U.S. Forest Service or BLM Research Natural Areas (RNAs), BLM Areas of Critical Environmental Concern (ACECs), or State Natural Areas.[6] In more populated places in the world, few remnants and relicts can be found, as much of the original vegetation has been cultivated or extensively transformed. In these places it is impossible to know what has changed or been lost except through historical accounts, old photographs, and other records. In southwestern Colorado, people are fortunate to have some important remnants and relicts to help them understand legacies.

NOTES

1. Hull and Hull, "Presettlement Vegetation of Cache Valley."
2. E.g., Jameson, Williams, and Wilton, "Vegetation and Soils of Fishtail Mesa."
3. Ibid.; Mason et al., "Vegetation and Soils of No Man's Land Mesa Relict Area."
4. Madany and West, "Livestock Grazing–Fire Regime Interactions."
5. Rummell, "Effects of Livestock Grazing on Ponderosa Pine Forest."
6. The Bureau of Land Management designated an ACEC to protect riparian vegetation on the San Miguel River (see Chapter 7). U.S. Forest Service RNAs are listed online (see Web site: http://nhp.nris.state.mt.us/rna/), and the Colorado Natural Areas Program maintains an online database of state and federal Research Natural Areas (see Web site: http://parks.state.co.us/cnap).

Logging the Ponderosa Pine Forests

With the mining industry under way in the San Juans in the 1870s, small-scale logging to supply mining camps and new settlements began. Commercial logging for nonlocal markets did not begin until railroad logging started in the 1890s near Pagosa Springs.[32] By 1918 the largest pines had been removed from forests around Pagosa Springs, and logging began to move west.[33]

In his detailed history of railroad logging along the Denver and Rio Grande Railroad near Dolores, Gordon Chappell described this era that strongly shaped the forests of today. In 1924 the New Mexico Lumber Company won the Forest Service bid for 400 million board feet of timber on 118,391 acres of the plateau north and west of Dolores. A typical 2,000-square-foot house today uses 16,000 board feet of lumber,[34] so 400 million board feet is enough for 25,000 houses. According to Chappell, it was expected to take eighteen years to cut the timber at an annual rate of 22 million board feet. The mill was constructed at McPhee (six miles west of Dolores and now under McPhee Reservoir). By 1929 the company had 500 employees and over fifty miles of railroad track. Large-scale logging declined, but it continued through the Depression, with trucks replacing railroads in 1933. Harvests in the late 1930s were estimated at 12 million board feet a year. After fire destroyed the second mill at McPhee in 1948, the site was abandoned.[35]

After World War II, forests in the western United States were again intensively harvested, this time to meet the postwar building boom. A San Juan Forest history states that "between 1944 and 1966 annual harvests [from national forests] quadrupled."[36] In 1966, 89 million board feet were harvested from the entire San Juan National Forest.[37] High-grade logging, harvesting the largest and healthiest trees, had depleted the older forest near the railroads but continued on the rest of the forest until the early 1980s.[38] Also, "sanitation-salvage" harvesting removed old and diseased trees or trees with signs of insect infestation, trees now known to be an important part of old-growth forests.[39] The landscape today contains a uniform forest of relatively young trees with few or no snags, dead trees, or old trees (see Figure 5.1).

Most logging of the Dolores Plateau was done under Forest Service management. William Romme and Robert Bunting detail how the Forest Service's ideal of maximizing forest growth rates led to the elimination of old-growth forests: "In 1920, the 'Timber Sale Policy of the Forest Service' read: 'It will be necessary in some instances to cut more than the annual growth for a time because of the presence of large quantities of over-mature stumpage which is in danger of deterioration

Figure 5.3. *Logging ponderosa pine in the early days. Photo by Morris Long. Courtesy, Galloping Goose Historical Society, Dolores, Colorado.*

and retards the production of which the land is capable.'. . . Idealized numbers, theoretical modeling, and practical politics thus became the basis for calculating what was to be an allowable cut."[40] This focus on maximizing timber production persisted for decades.[41] Thus, under Forest Service stewardship, old-growth ponderosa pine forests were liquidated in the name of conservation.[42]

Forestry science into the 1980s reflected the dominant conservation ethic of the time, as science usually does. The ethic was strongly utilitarian. Railroad logging books, such as Chappell's, and the photo collections of logger-photographer Morris Long (held at the Rio Grande Southern Railroad Museum in Dolores) include few photos of the forest itself. Almost all photos are of large logs, machinery, and logging operations (see Figure 5.3). Newspaper accounts from that period revel in the size of the resource and describe with pride the power of people and industry.

As timber was depleted, forestry science turned its sights toward increasing wood production through more aggressive manipulation of the landscape. On the forest's drier margins, where pines were widely scattered among Gambel oak, large areas were clear-cut and then plowed to remove the oak's competing root systems.[43] One can still see the irregular furrows from this plowing (see Figure 5.4). Pine seedlings were hand-planted, but few of the young trees survived; those that did are not growing well. A thick ground cover of Kentucky bluegrass and

Figure 5.4. *Furrows remain visible two decades after this area was logged and plowed to remove Gambel oaks. Non-native grasses and weeds dominate the vegetation, and the planted pines that survived are stunted.*

a few other species has replaced the native diversity of grasses, forbs, and shrubs. Also lost is the natural structure of this ecotone between forest and oak shrubland.

The railroad and truck loggers and subsequent timber sales left little old-growth ponderosa pine in southwestern Colorado.[44] On the west side of the San Juan National Forest, the only old growth on level ground is at McPhee Park, a forty-acre site on the Dolores Plateau a mile south of the Dolores-Montezuma county line. This area was left to preserve an example of the pre-logging forest. Another uncut stand of ponderosa pine is in steep-sided Narraguinnep Canyon, a Research Natural Area about twenty miles northwest of Dolores. The largest remaining old-growth ponderosa pine forest in the southern San Juans is along Hermosa Creek north of Durango.

WHAT IS HAPPENING NOW?

Today, new approaches are emerging that may reshape the way the ponderosa pine forest and associated ecosystems are managed. Diminishing supplies of large trees, rising environmental concerns, and public interest in recreation and other forest uses led to declining harvests on the San Juan National Forest in the 1990s. In 1992 the chief of the Forest Service declared that the national forests would turn away from an industrial wood-production model and begin to focus on management of the entire ecosystem. Ponderosa pine forests have been among the first ecosystems to receive this new focus, and the Ponderosa Pine Partnership, discussed here, illustrates a promising restoration approach in this region. Protection and restoration are not yet common in the parks and grasslands of the pine zone, but remnant native bunchgrass parks—the grassland equivalent of remnant old-growth forests—offer models for restoration. Aspen stands have only recently been the focus of wood extraction, so in this case the goal may be to avoid creating negative legacies. Patch clear-cutting has been the method of choice for logging aspen but may adversely affect biodiversity. Finally, the subdivision of private land in and adjoining the ponderosa pine zone is proceeding rapidly. The way a growing human population is accommodated could strongly shape the possibilities for maintaining and restoring the nature of the region.

Ponderosa Pine Restoration

The 1992 San Juan Forest Plan Amendment emphasized the health of forest ecosystems, and the annual harvest on the forest declined from about 44 million to about 24 million board feet.[45] With the rise of roadless areas as a significant environmental issue, the annual harvest was reduced further, to about 16 million board feet by 2000.[46] Perhaps as significant as the reduced level of logging was a new vision of how logging could be part of forest restoration. A major project for restoring the forest was the Ponderosa Pine Partnership.

The Ponderosa Pine Partnership. Innovative approaches often come when one is between a rock and a hard place. Such was the case with the Ponderosa Pine Partnership. Dwindling timber, a competitive market, and increasing public value placed on nontimber uses of the forest were leading to a crisis in the local logging and milling industries by the early 1990s. Montezuma County commissioners approached the staff at the San Juan National Forest in Dolores about a bigger role for the county in forest planning. Eventually, a broader range of interests (including academics, State Forestry, the timber industry, and citizen groups) became involved, and in 1993 the Ponderosa Pine Partnership was formed with a goal of engaging local industries to aid in forest restoration.[47]

To provide a scientific foundation for restoration, Bill Romme, then a biology professor at Fort Lewis College, was hired to study the pre-logging structure of ponderosa pine forests that had been mature or old-growth forests at the time.[48] The characteristics of old-growth forests are identified by studying surviving unlogged stands, evidence from stumps on logged areas, and data and photographs from historical sources.[49] The qualities of old growth (see Table 5.1) include a certain number of large, old, living trees (some of which have rotten or deformed tops) and a number of dead trees that are standing as snags, as well as down and decomposing on the forest floor. Romme found that much of the pre-logging forest contained clumps of trees differing in age, with small openings among the clumps but trees much larger on average than they are today (see Figure 5.5). The three forests used to estimate the characteristics of the pre-logging forest in the Dolores area had average stump diameters of 20", 26", and 27", respectively,[50] which would likely qualify them as old growth.

The ponderosa pine forest landscape today, unlike the pre-Euro-American forest, is deficient in large, old trees and snags and is relatively homogeneous and dense. Live trees in ponderosa pine forests in the Dolores area in the late 1990s averaged only 8" in diameter. Romme and colleagues also found that in the pre-logging forests, surface fires had periodically burned through the forests, maintaining a rather open understory.[51] The problem was how to accelerate a return to conditions closer to old growth. In many ways simply the passage of time will return the forest to an old-age condition. However, there are worries that the uniform, dense forest of today is more vulnerable to crown

Table 5.1. Minimum structural attributes of old-growth ponderosa pine forests in the Southwest and Rocky Mountains. Ponderosa pine forests in southwestern Colorado are located on the border between these two regions.

| Criterion | Popp, Jackson, and Basse (1992)—Southwest | | Mehl (1992) |
	Low-Growth Sites	High-Growth Sites	Rocky Mountains
Live trees per acre	20 trees 14" dbh[1] or 12 trees 18" dbh	20 trees 20" dbh or 14 trees 24" dbh	10 trees 16" dbh
Live tree ages	180 years	180 years	200 years
Variation in tree diameter	Not determined	Not determined	Yes
Basal area (square feet per acre)[2]	70	90	Not specified
Total canopy cover (percent)	40	50	Not specified
Decadence (dead, broken, or deformed tops; bole or root rot)	Not determined	Not determined	Yes
Standing dead trees per acre	1 tree 14" dbh and 15 feet high	1 tree 14" dbh and 25 feet high	2 trees 10" dbh
Down trees per acre	2 pieces 12" dbh and 15 feet long	2 pieces 12" dbh and 15 feet long	No minimum
Trees in upper canopy slow-growing	—	—	Yes
Wide range of tree vigor	—	—	Yes

1. Tree size is often measured as diameter at breast height (about 4.5 feet), or dbh.
2. Basal area is the sum of the areas of the circular cross sections of each tree.

Figure 5.5. *Second-growth ponderosa pine forests of the post-logging landscape. Note the size and spacing of old stumps.*

fires and insect outbreaks and may not return to old-growth conditions without assistance.

Hermosa Creek Trail: A remnant old-growth forest. For additional understanding of old growth, it is useful to look at the characteristics of one of the few remaining areas of old-growth ponderosa pine in the region, along Hermosa Creek north of Durango (see Figure 5.6). Few forests with trees this size, stature, and age have survived. The oldest trees here are relatively few, but they are 275–375 years old. The other large trees are 150–250 years old, and another age group is 70–110 years old.[52] Hermosa Creek is also an area of high plant diversity, especially at lower elevations. An inventory of the watershed in 1993 found 191 plant species, including a few rare ones.[53] Eight species of trees and 24 species of shrubs are found in the first few miles of trail. This forest is more diverse than many pine forests because it is along a canyon with a mix of drier south-facing slopes and moister north-facing slopes, as well as areas along streams ("riparian" areas) (see Table 5.2).

This is also one of the most bird-rich areas in southwestern Colorado (see Table 5.3). Ponderosa pine supports more breeding bird species than any other coniferous forest type in Colorado.[54] The number of

Figure 5.6. *Old-growth ponderosa pine along Hermosa Creek Trail.*

Table 5.2. Common native plants of ponderosa pine forests in southwestern Colorado.[1]

TREES
  Douglas-fir (*Pseudotsuga menziesii*)
  Ponderosa pine (*Pinus ponderosa*)
  Quaking aspen (*Populus tremuloides*)
  Southwestern white pine (*Pinus strobiformis*)
  White fir (*Abies concolor*)

SHRUBS
  Creeping barberry (*Mahonia repens*)
  Gambel oak (*Quercus gambelii*)
  Hairy false goldenaster (*Heterotheca villosa*, formerly *Chrysopsis*)
  Mountain snowberry (*Symphoricarpos rotundifolius*)
  Oregon boxleaf (*Paxistima myrsinites*, formerly *Pachistima*)
  Rocky Mountain maple (*Acer glabrum*)
  Saskatoon serviceberry (*Amelanchier alnifolia*)
  Utah serviceberry (*Amelanchier utahensis*)
  Woods' rose (*Rosa woodsii*)

FORBS
  Alpine false springparsley (*Pseudocymopterus montanus*)
  Arizona mule-ears (*Wyethia arizonica*)
  Aspen pea (*Lathyrus leucanthus*)
  Bastard toadflax (*Comandra umbellate*)
  Canadian white violet (*Viola scopulorum*)
  Fendler's meadow-rue (*Thalictrum fendleri*)
  Hookedspur violet (*Viola adunca*)
  Richardson's geranium (*Geranium richardsonii*)
  Small-leaf pussytoes (*Antennaria parvifolia*)
  Virginia strawberry (*Fragaria virginiana* subsp. *glauca*)
  Western yarrow (*Achillea lanulosa*)
  White sagebrush (*Artemisia ludoviciana*)

GRAMINOIDS
  Arizona fescue (*Festuca arizonica*)
  Geyer's sedge (*Carex geyeri*)
  Mountain muhly (*Muhlenbergia montana*)
  Muttongrass (*Poa fendleriana* subsp. *longiligula*)
  Parry's oatgrass (*Danthonia parryi*)
  Prairie Junegrass (*Koeleria macrantha*)
  Western wheatgrass (*Pascopyrum smithii*, formerly *Agropyron*)

1. Common names are from the PLANTS online database, http://plants.usda.gov. Latin names are from Weber and Wittmann, *Colorado Flora*.

breeding bird species recorded for any given ponderosa forest ranges from twenty-three to forty-seven.[55] This large number is surprising, since the forest canopy is usually dominated by one tree, but a mature ponderosa pine forest offers a large and structurally diverse set of habitats. Pineland dwarf mistletoe (see Plate 34), for example, is a common

Table 5.3. Breeding birds strongly associated with ponderosa pine forests in southwestern Colorado.[1]

Chipping sparrow	Northern pygmy-owl +	Western bluebird + *
Evening grosbeak	Northern saw-whet owl +	Western tanager
Flammulated owl +[2]	Plumbeous vireo	Western wood peewee
Grace's warbler *	Pygmy nuthatch + *	White-breasted nuthatch +
Lewis's woodpecker +	Steller's jay	Wild turkey
Mountain chickadee +	Violet-green swallow +	Williamson sapsucker +

1. Kingery, *Colorado Breeding Bird Atlas*.
2. + denotes cavity nester; * denotes ponderosa pine obligate or near-obligate species.

parasite of ponderosa pine that adds to canopy complexity and bird diversity (see Box—Forest Health, pp. 290–291).

A key feature of old-growth forests for many birds, mammals, and insects is an abundance of snags, standing dying trees, and dead trees (see Figure 5.7). The tiny pygmy nuthatch drills its own nest holes, which requires that a tree bole be fairly rotten.[56] In winter, pygmy nuthatches roost communally in tree cavities, probably for warmth. Most resident birds of ponderosa pine forests nest in cavities.[57] Violet-green swallows, western bluebirds, house wrens, and other birds rely on cavities built by other birds.[58] In a study in ponderosa pine in Arizona, published in 1983, forty-nine birds, ten mammals, several amphibians and reptiles, and numerous insects were found to use tree cavities.[59] Diverse, healthy bird populations may help keep insect pests at endemic, as opposed to epidemic, population levels.[60] One bat, the long-legged myotis, lives mostly in ponderosa pine in Colorado, where it roosts under loose pine bark—a short-lived habitat on any given tree.[61] Thus, the creation of snags and dead trees is an important part of restoration that will influence how quickly the faunal diversity typical of old growth returns. Unlike the present young forests of the ponderosa pine zone, Hermosa Creek has many snags and other old-growth features (see Table 5.1).

While it was a common perception in the 1950s and 1960s that fire "destroyed" the forest, by the 1970s ecologists and forest managers were realizing that many forests, including ponderosa pine, contain species adapted to fire. The bark of the larger ponderosa pine trees is like baklava, with numerous flaky layers that peel off when the trunk is dry. The bark is thick, so heat penetrates only a little, but the layers are separated by air, which slows the transfer of heat. Also, if the bark catches fire, it can drop off the trunk like a flaming cornflake. Ponderosa have few limbs near the ground, perhaps because low limbs would let fire climb into the canopy where it could be fatal. Other plants in the

Figure 5.7. *Snags in a ponderosa pine forest on Archuleta Mesa near Chimney Rock (see Plate 30).*

community, such as Gambel oak (see Figure 3.3), can resprout from roots or underground stems after fire. About 3,500 acres in the Hermosa Creek drainage were prescribe-burned in 1989, with funds from the

Colorado Division of Wildlife,[62] to replace tall oaks with shorter sprouts more accessible to deer and elk.

While the forest overstory retains most of its natural qualities, livestock grazing has impacted the understory vegetation at Hermosa Creek. Historically, this allotment had heavy use. The lower reach of Hermosa Creek is in the Dutch Creek allotment, about 10,000 acres of which is used for cattle grazing; the pine zone is grazed in early summer each year.[63] Keeping cattle well distributed is difficult, given the steep terrain. The non-native Kentucky bluegrass and common dandelion have generally replaced native bunchgrasses in grazed parks and riparian areas. The replacement is a significant legacy because, as discussed earlier, a healthy native forest understory may be as critical as fire in maintaining the forest. A healthy old-growth ponderosa pine forest has large trees, periodic fire, and native bunchgrasses, as well as snags and dying trees.

Restoration in action on the Dolores Plateau. Using sites such as Hermosa Creek and Bill Romme's restoration prescription as guides, the Ponderosa Pine Partnership began working to restore the nearly homogeneous landscape of logged forest on the Dolores Plateau to a more natural state. The initial logging was set up as an experiment. In 1996, five stands were thinned to reduce the density of small trees, leaving uneven-aged clumps of trees, typical of unlogged ponderosa pine forests. Prescribed burning was conducted to reintroduce fire. The vegetation and the bird community were monitored before and periodically after treatment to see whether ecological objectives were met. It may be some years before the ecological success of the treatments is clear, but it was soon clear that the prescription required modification from an economic perspective.[64]

Dennis Lynch, an economist from Colorado State University, was hired to study the economics of the restoration program. One of the dilemmas of restoration is that it is difficult to market and profit from small-diameter wood, which is much of the product from restoration. Based on experience from the first experiments, Lynch learned that a site needs some harvestable larger-diameter trees to make a sale profitable—specifically, at least six harvestable trees, at least 12" in diameter, per acre.[65] So the Joyce site, a site that had been logged but had somewhat larger trees, was chosen for a new restoration test. Logging was completed in 1997 using the new profitability criteria, and a profit of $16,719 was made for the ninety-nine-acre sale, in contrast to an average net loss on the first demonstration sites.[66]

The restored Joyce site forest can be compared with the unrestored forest across the road (see Figure 5.8a, b). Many of the smaller trees

Figure 5.8. *(a) Joyce site after 1997 restoration logging and prescribed fire, and (b) the untreated forest across the road; both from 2001.*

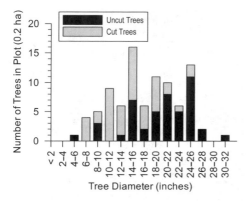

Figure 5.9. *A comparison of the size (diameter) of trees that were cut and those that were left (not cut) on the Joyce site.*

have been cut, leaving a more open, clumped forest dominated by the largest trees. We tallied trees that were cut and not cut, by diameter, and found that 34 percent of harvested trees were at least 16" in diameter and 11 percent were at least 20" (see Figure 5.9). The San Juan Citizens Alliance, a local environmental group, supports the restoration efforts but would like an upper limit of 16"–18" on the trees that can be taken.[67] However, Phil Kemp says that in some cases they must take trees even 20" in diameter or larger to restore the open old-growth structure because there are too many trees that size on some sites.[68] We dated cut 20" in diameter trees on the Joyce site and found they were 85–95 years old in 2001, having germinated in about 1905–1915. Thus, these trees may be valuable because they are large, but they are not old growth.

Restoration logging was able to proceed because trust had been built by Romme's scientific work, the inclusive group process, and Phil Kemp's (of the Forest Service's Dolores District) (see Figure 5.10) willingness to discuss everyone's concerns on the ground throughout the process. Kemp said it is not difficult to find sites that have enough large trees to meet Lynch's criteria and still leave sufficient large trees for restoration.[69] Thus, adaptive management led to development of a modified prescription for restoration harvesting in the pine zone.

The prescription provides a model for restoration forestry in the general area, but unlogged ponderosa pine forests varied markedly in density, and not all forests should be restored to one low-density standard.[70] Moreover, even in the relatively small region of the southern San Juan Mountains, the forest understory varies considerably. The classic southwestern ponderosa pine forest has an understory typically dominated by Arizona fescue and mountain muhly, probably the understory type Ingersoll described in this chapter's opening quote. In the San Juan Mountains, this type may not have been as common as it was in the Southwest. Leslie Stewart, a range conservationist with years of experience on the Dolores Plateau, believes this understory was somewhat limited on the Dolores Plateau.[71]

Figure 5.10. *Phil Kemp, silviculturalist for the U.S. Forest Service, Dolores, Colorado. Courtesy, Carla G. Harper, Montezuma County Federal Lands Program. Cortez, Colorado.*

Many other sites, including the Joyce site, likely had Gambel oak in the understory. The natural role of the oak understory was an issue early in the ponderosa pine restoration project. Some proposals were made to eradicate large areas of Gambel oak with fire to restore a grassy understory. Game biologist Scott Wait argued that on rolling and steep areas, oak was the natural understory and provided essential cover and forage for turkeys and deer.[72] The question of where the understory was naturally grass and where it was oak will need to be resolved, as trying to replace oak with grass through frequent burning in areas where oak was the natural understory could be futile. Moreover, the natural frequency of fire in ponderosa pine forests is presently uncertain, and, until resolved, it is premature for these forests to be burned at short intervals.[73]

Some mortality or damage from fire is a natural source of snags valuable to wildlife, and because of a snag deficiency, 14–18 imitation snags were created on the ninety-nine-acre Joyce site by cutting off the tops of live trees. The number of created snags is likely too few for restoration to be considered complete. Linnea Hall and colleagues estimated that 2 large snags per acre (or 200 snags on this ninety-nine-acre site) "may be necessary to maintain populations of cavity-nesting species,"[74] a number consistent with Mehl's criterion for snag density in old-growth forests (see Table 5.1).

One problem with all types of disturbance, including restoration, is the likelihood of weed invasion. Thirty-eight noxious weeds are known from southwestern ponderosa pine forests (see Box—Noxious Weeds, pp. 200–201), and both logging and forest restoration can provide ample disturbance for their spread.[75] For example, on the Horsefly timber sale near the Piedra River, sites logged in 1999 and 2000 were heavily disturbed by equipment during wet conditions. Although the sites were

BOX—NOXIOUS WEEDS

A weed is any plant that crowds out the plants people want in a particular place or that grows where it is unwanted. In this book, the concern is the replacement of native plants by non-natives. Little is known about the spread of plants by Native Americans, so non-native plants are considered those not present before Euro-American influences. Not all non-native plants are invasive—capable of invading and replacing natural vegetation—but many are. Most of the non-native plants found in the West are from parts of Eurasia with a similar semiarid climate.[1] They become invasive here because their natural insect predators and diseases are not present, and they are adapted to natural disturbances or the disturbances people create.

Some non-native plants would invade naturally, but the rate of anthropogenic invasions far exceeds the natural rate.[2] About 2,100 non-native plant species are now present in the United States, 11 percent of the total flora.[3] Non-native species cause more than $137 billion in economic losses annually, mainly to agriculture, in the United States.[4] About 40 percent of federally threatened and endangered plant and animal species are at risk primarily because of effects of non-native species.[5] Many of the non-native weeds found in the West arrived as contaminants in agricultural seed mixes.[6] Other weeds arrived on ship ballast released in ports, in shipments of bulk commodities (e.g., wool and cotton), and in containerized freight.[7] Many harmful invasives were introduced intentionally. Escaped ornamentals alone have caused billions of dollars in damage.[8] Purple loosestrife, yellow toadflax, and oxeye daisy were all introduced as ornamental plants.

The worst of the invasive non-native weeds have been legally recognized as "noxious weeds"—plants that are a serious threat to economic, environmental, and other public interests. Federal, state, and most local jurisdictions have their own lists of noxious weeds. Listed noxious weeds in Colorado[9] that are a problem in the southwestern part of the state are presented in Box Table 1. A good educational brochure for information on noxious weeds in southwestern Colorado is "Noxious Weed Gang Taking Over the West," published by the San Juan Mountains Association.

A few increasingly effective weed-control programs are countering the expansion of weeds. La Plata County has an especially innovative weed program. County weed manager Rod Cook uses global positioning and geographical information systems to locate and map noxious weed infestations. Letters are sent to property owners who have weeds, along with a map of weed locations and information about the weeds. The county also offers a weed identification program, information on weed control, and a cost-share program.[10] Such programs require adequate county funding.

Single control methods rarely work for weeds. Large invasions require some combination of biological, chemical, cultural, and physical control, supplemented by restoration of native plants.[11] Preventing invasion is the most effective method; this is done by maintaining healthy plant communities and by early detection and control of weeds. Weeds are a growing threat in southwestern Colorado, and many believe success in preventing and controlling weed invasions in the next decade will be crucial to the future of natural communities there.

NOTES

1. U.S. Congress, Office of Technology Assessment, *Harmful Non-Indigenous Species.*
2. Lodge and Shrader-Frechette, "Nonindigenous Species."
3. Cox, *Alien Species in North America and Hawaii.*
4. Pimentel et al., "Costs of Nonindigenous Species."
5. Wilcove et al., "Quantifying Threats to Imperiled Species."
6. Cox, *Alien Species in North America and Hawaii.*
7. U.S. Congress, Office of Technology Assessment, *Harmful Non-Indigenous Species.*
8. Reichard and White, "Horticulture as a Pathway."
9. See Web site: http://www.ag.state.co.us/DPI/rules/noxious.html.
10. See Web site: http://www.co.laplata.co.us/weeds.
11. Sheley and Petroff, eds., *Biology and Management of Noxious Rangeland Weeds.*

Box Table 1. State-listed noxious weeds that are problems in southwestern Colorado.[1]

Common Name	Latin Name	Common Name	Latin Name
Canada thistle	*Breea arvense*	Oxeye daisy	*Leucanthemum vulgare*
Cheatgrass	*Anisantha tectorum*	Purple loosestrife	*Lythrum salicaria*
Common tansy	*Tanacetum vulgare*	Redstem filaree	*Erodium cicutarium*
Dalmatian toadflax	*Linaria genistifolia* subsp. *dalmatica*	Russian knapweed	*Acroptilon repens*
Dame's rocket	*Hesperis matronalis*	Russian thistle	*Salsola australis*
Diffuse knapweed	*Acosta diffusa*	Saltcedar	*Tamarix* spp.
Halogeton	*Halogeton glomeratus*	Scentless chamomile	*Matricaria perforata*
Hoary cress	*Cardaria draba*	Scotch thistle	*Onopordum acanthium*
Houndstongue	*Cynoglossum officinale*	Spotted knapweed	*Acosta maculosa*
Leafy spurge	*Tithymalus esula* & *T. uralensis*	Yellow star-thistle	*Leucantha solstitialis*
Musk thistle	*Carduus nutans* subsp. *macrolepis*	Yellow toadflax	*Linaria vulgaris*

1. State of Colorado, Department of Agriculture website:http://www.ag.state.co.us/DPI/weeds/statutes/weedrules.pdf. Common names are from the PLANTS online database, http://plants.usda.gov. Latin names are from Weber and Wittmann, *Colorado Flora.*

seeded with short-lived annuals and a few native species, the year after logging, large areas were covered by non-native plants and noxious
weeds not previously obvious on the site. Once established, weeds can
be almost impossible to control, and more care is needed to prevent
soil disturbance and weed spread during logging.[76] If non-natives become dominant, only the trees, not the ecosystem as a whole, have
been restored.

Old trees, like good wines and strong cheeses, are acquired by aging. When the trees again are giants, will society have the wisdom to
avoid another short-term harvesting boom? Can a way be found to
keep the forest in its majestic old-age condition once it has been restored? This depends on whether the economic attraction of the boom
can be foregone. Some people will always walk among tall, majestic
pines that are the work of ages and dream of a few years of bountiful
harvest. But the next time, society will have been through this before.

Will the marriage of ecology and economy last? It is too early to say
whether the marriage of ecology and economy will last. The Ponderosa
Pine Partnership has not stopped the decline of traditional local logging and milling operations. Between 1985 and 2001, the number of
mills in Montezuma County, where Cortez and Dolores are located,
declined from twenty to four.[77] Much of the decline occurred before the
partnership began, but some mills have since closed.[78] Persistent problems include inconsistent supplies of wood; competition from large-
scale, high-tech mills in Olathe (since closed) and Montrose; mill owners nearing retirement; and low wood prices.[79]

The market price of wood products is important. According to the
study by Lynch and colleagues, a 13 percent rise in prices for the small-
diameter wood on the demonstration sales would have increased average profit margins from less than 1 percent to about 7 percent.[80] As is
the case with most products, wood prices do not reflect the costs of
preventing environmental damage during production. Until a tariff was
recently reimposed, low-cost imported Canadian wood produced with
fewer environmental restrictions drove down the price of wood in the
United States. Had the Joyce restoration been conducted in May 2001,
just before the tariff was reimposed, it would not have had a net profit.[81]
Loggers can do little to change markets, so they look for other ways to
compete, but it is challenging to do so without using ecologically un-
sound practices to cut costs and boost profits.

Becoming more efficient and adding value to wood products locally are two ways to increase profit. Of forty-five businesses in
Montezuma County engaged in wood acquisition, processing, sales,

and distribution in 1998, 53 percent were conventional sawmills, of which fewer than half did any secondary processing to add value.[82] Value can be added, for example, by kiln drying, treating, or planing rough-sawn lumber. Even more value can be added by milling the lumber into marketable products, such as paneling or furniture. Efficiency can be increased by turning sawmill waste material, which is about 50 percent of the raw log, into a marketable product such as landscape mulch, compost, or wood pellets.[83] These strategies usually require investment in equipment, and this has been a barrier to change in the industry.

According to Tim Reader of the Colorado State Forest Service in Durango, logging and milling businesses have been unwilling to invest in value-added ventures at least in part because of inconsistent supplies of wood from Forest Service lands.[84] This problem is tied to the lack of a long-term (e.g., five-year) timber sale plan or budget and in some cases to frequent appeals of timber sales. Phil Kemp has worked hard to ensure a small but consistent volume of timber sales (1,000–2,000 acres/year) in the Dolores District of the San Juan Forest, mostly as restoration or thinning projects. Because the forest restoration program in the district has been well accepted by local environmental groups, few appeals have occurred there in recent years.[85]

Considerable public and private time and energy have gone into making this marriage of ecology and economy work, but under the 2000 National Fire Plan, larger trees can be harvested to pay for thinning operations, with little public input. Will the Forest Service continue its careful assessments to ensure ecologically based restoration now that laws are less restrictive and a perceived fire crisis exists? If it does, what types and levels of forest products can be consistently supplied from public lands if restoration, followed by maintenance of a more natural forest, is the driving force? What changes are needed in Forest Service administration to ensure the supply? What can local wood products industries do to capture as much economic and social value as possible from products the forest can supply? Given their strong influence on surface fires and forest structure, can restoration of bunchgrasses be integrated into forest restoration?

Future of Native Bunchgrasses

Restoration of ponderosa pine forests is relatively new, and attention has yet to be given to the native grasslands associated with these forests. Grasslands within the forest are an important part of the broader ecosystem, and remnants of these native grasslands can serve as models for restoration, just as Hermosa Creek serves as a model for pine restoration. Range conservationists may be aware of remnant sites and may monitor them, but more explicit recognition and protection of grassland remnants are needed as part of ecosystem management in the pine zone. A program similar to the Ponderosa Pine Partnership may also need to be developed to restore the native bunchgrass parks and forest understories.

Lessons from Beaver Crossing exclosure. Small exclosures that keep livestock out can provide information on the effects of grazing and on whether livestock exclusion may allow degraded grasslands to be restored. An example in a large meadow on the Dolores Plateau is the Beaver Crossing exclosure, constructed in 1949 after many years of heavy livestock grazing. The meadow is in the Beaver Crossing allotment managed by the Forest Service. This allotment, a major staging and gathering area for cattle since early ranching days, illustrates the problems faced in perpetuating natural vegetation.

The effects of fifty years of rest from livestock grazing can be seen by comparing the vegetation on both sides of the exclosure fence, but the contrast is visually subtle (see Plate 35). Forest Service range conservationist Leslie Stewart studied the fence-line contrast in 1995. Stewart concluded that "trend appears to be downward outside the exclosure based on more bare soil and less litter," as well as changes in species composition.[86] Litter is the fine, dead vegetation left at the end of a year's growth. Several known increasers are, as expected, more common outside the exclosure than inside it, while decreasers show the opposite trend (see Box—Increasers and Decreasers, pp. 205–206). Increasers include hairy false goldenaster (*Heterotheca villosa*), Parry's rabbitbrush (*Chrysothamnus parryi*), woolly cinquefoil (*Potentilla hippiana*), and yellow owl-clover (*Orthocarpus luteus*). Decreasers include mountain muhly (*Muhlenbergia montana*) and needle and thread (*Hesperostipa comata*). Because this grassland is a gathering pasture, it has been grazed in both spring and fall. This may explain the decrease outside the exclosure in both needle and thread (see Figure 2.4a), a cool-season bunchgrass that grows in the spring and produces seed by early summer, and mountain muhly (see Plate 33b), a warm-season bunchgrass that grows and produces seed later in the summer.

The stocking rate on this allotment has been consistently above the grazing capacity. Stocking rate, a measure of the intensity of grazing use, is often expressed as the land area used per cow-calf pair for a month, called an animal-unit-month (AUM). In excellent range condition, about 2–3 acres of ponderosa pine bunchgrass range can provide forage for a cow-calf pair for a month.[87] In poor conditions, as on this

BOX—INCREASERS AND DECREASERS

There is little doubt that overgrazing can lead to a loss of native plants and their replacement by invasive non-native species, such as cheatgrass, Kentucky bluegrass, or smooth brome. Along the way to that degraded endpoint the original native plants decrease, some weedy natives increase, and some other plants—often non-native—invade. Plants in these categories are determined by comparing sites, grazed at various levels by livestock, with remnants or relicts (see Box—Remnants and Relicts, pp. 183–184), where the "potential plant community" is still present. Rangeland in excellent condition has lots of decreasers and few increasers or invaders, while land in poor condition has mostly invaders (see box figure). Examples of plants in these categories in southwestern Colorado are presented in Box Table 2. This simple conceptual framework, developed in the late 1940s,[1] served as the basis for determining the condition of rangelands for several decades.

Reassessments of range-condition concepts in the last decade have challenged this simple framework, suggesting instead that plant communities degrade in more complex ways that include thresholds, multiple pathways, and alternative degraded states.[2] Individual plant species, as a result, may not always fit into simple categorization as increasers, decreasers, or invaders. The original reassessment by a committee sponsored by the National Academy of Sciences addressed this complexity by suggesting that "the similarity of current plant composition and biomass production to that of a climax plant community . . . or potential natural community . . . should not be used as the primary standard of rangeland health."[3] The group, however, then went on to propose a radical change, defining health as comprising simply three things: degree of soil stability and watershed functioning, integrity of nutrient and energy cycles, and presence of functioning recovery mechanisms (e.g., vigorous plants of several ages). The committee omitted further mention of using the vegetation of undisturbed sites, where natural communities still exist, as a standard of rangeland health. Some modernization of criteria might have been warranted, but this particular revision omits native biological diversity as a key criterion.

The effect of this change may be to allow a site to be given a range-condition rating of excellent or properly func-

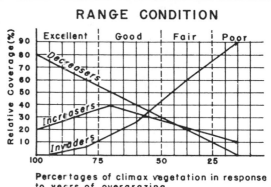

Reprinted from E. J. Dyksterhuis (1949), figure 1, with permission of the Society for Range Management.

tioning, even though it is dominated entirely by non-native plants or native increasers, if those assemblages of plants stabilize the soil, cycle nutrients, and are vigorous. This is a utilitarian approach that assumes people understand ecosystems well enough to be able to successfully transform them into new states that still function properly, an unfounded assumption in semiarid settings. Moreover, for those who care about native species and natural communities of plants and animals, this change leaves out one of the most important criteria of land health: the presence on a site of native plants and animals in natural proportions. If perpetuating native biological diversity is to remain a goal, the composition and abundance of plants in undisturbed communities should remain a standard in any assessment of land health. Therefore, it remains important to recognize common increasers and decreasers (e.g., see Box Table 2). Large areas of public lands that have been in "poor" or "fair" range condition could receive "excellent" or "properly functioning" ratings under the new criteria. If so, these criteria sanction degradation of native biological diversity on public lands by domestic livestock grazing.

NOTES

1. Dyksterhuis, "Condition and Management of Range Land."
2. Busby et al., *Rangeland Health*; Pyke et al., "Rangeland Health Attributes and Indicators."
3. Busby et al., *Rangeland Health*, 88.

Box Table 2. Some common plants that are examples of decreasers, increasers, and invaders in southwestern Colorado plant communities grazed by domestic livestock.[1]

Native Decreasers	Native Increasers	Non-Native Invaders
SHRUBS		
Antelope bitterbrush	Broom snakeweed	
Willow species	Rabbitbrush species	
Winterfat	Woods' rose	
FORBS		
American vetch	Colorado false hellebore	Canada thistle
Paintbrush species	Hairy false goldenaster	Common dandelion
Penstemon species	Lupine species	Gypsyflower
	Milkvetch species	Halogeton
	Orange sneezeweed	Musk thistle
	Pussytoes species	Oxeye daisy
	Subalpine larkspur	Prickly Russian thistle
	Thrift mock goldenweed	Yellow sweetclover
	Western yarrow	Russian knapweed
	Yucca species	Yellow toadflax
GRASSES		
Arizona fescue	Blue grama	Cheatgrass
Indian ricegrass	Fendler's threeawn	Kentucky bluegrass
Muttongrass	James' galleta	Orchardgrass
Needle and thread	Sand dropseed	Smooth brome
Parry's oatgrass		Timothy
Thurber's fescue		

1. Common names are from the PLANTS online database, http://plants.usda.gov. Latin names are from Weber and Wittmann, *Colorado Flora*.

Figure 5.11. *Arizona mule-ears* (Wyethia arizonica)*, an unpalatable, weedy native plant.*

allotment, 8–15 acres are required.[88] Stocking rates on this allotment (then part of the Biggs Common allotment) exceeded this requirement between 1940 and 1967, as an average of only 5.7 acres were available per cow-calf pair.[89] In 1965 a range allotment plan was written in which the allotment's grazing capacity was found to be only 43 percent of the level of grazing at that time.[90] After 1972, stocking rates fluctuated, but in 1998 the stocking rate on the Beaver Crossing unit was still 5.13 acres per cow-calf pair per month.[91] Range condition remains poor, and the stocking rate remains well above grazing capacity.

Poor range condition often leads to weed problems. A major weed in this area is the yellow-flowered Arizona mule-ears (see Figure 5.11), an unpalatable native plant. Between 1955 and 1967, 1,680 acres in this area were treated with 2,4-D to control mule-ears. Although relatively unsuccessful in controlling mule-ears, the program may have contributed to the loss of the sharp-tailed grouse population on the Dolores Plateau because aspen, mountain shrub, and riparian areas were also sprayed with this brush-killing herbicide.[92] As recently as 1985, parts of this allotment were sprayed with herbicide to reduce mule-ears.[93]

Poor range condition can also lead to a decision to start over by plowing or disking the site and replanting. This extreme action indicates severe overuse. For example, a fifty-acre park was reseeded in August 1984 on the allotment (see Plate 36). Before disking, the allotment record said the "meadow . . . is composed of undesirable species with little forage value."[94] Unfortunately the seed mix was entirely non-native grasses.

If these grasslands were restored to native bunchgrasses and grazed moderately, forage production could be two to three times what it is now in its poor condition,[95] with benefits for biological diversity in the grasslands and adjoining pine forests. But is restoration of the bunchgrass parks possible? Even after fifty years of rest from grazing, the vegetation in the exclosure remains in poor condition, although it is better than that outside. Some scientists suggest overgrazing can force vegetation into a new stable state that may not reverse simply with rest from grazing.[96] However, native bunchgrass cover (especially Arizona fescue) increased by a factor of 5 in six exclosures on ponderosa pine–bunchgrass range protected for about twenty-five years in New Mexico.[97] Moreover, in 68 percent of twenty-two exclosures on ponderosa pine–bunchgrass ranges in Colorado, Wyoming, and South Dakota, grasses were more abundant inside exclosures.[98] Rest may not always work, but sometimes it can.

If rest is insufficient, a prescription needs to be developed—like that of the Ponderosa Pine Partnership—that will move the vegetation more rapidly toward recovery. The situation is similar, as both forest and grassland were overused and are in a depleted condition. Just as it will take a century or more to fully restore ponderosa pine to its old-growth condition, grassland recovery may require decades or even centuries. As in the forests, research is needed to understand the native grasslands, but in grasslands there are no stumps or tree rings. The few remnant native grasslands will be especially important models for restoration.

Monolores Bridge Bunchgrass Park: An Arizona fescue–mountain muhly remnant. Arizona fescue and mountain muhly not only were the understory of pine forests, but they also formed grassland openings in the ponderosa pine zone. Such grasslands were probably common along south-facing slopes and on benches of the Dolores River before overgrazing and development converted most areas to non-native species. Today, only small patches of this grassland remain. One remnant grassland is located at the Monolores Bridge between Dolores and Telluride (see Plate 37), where it is part of the Tenderfoot allotment. The site apparently escaped the intense livestock grazing pressure that extirpated bunchgrasses elsewhere because Arizona fescue and mountain muhly are still dominant over much of the area.

Unfortunately, this grassland is now under heavy grazing pressure and appears to be degrading. In 2001 the flora still contained many native plants, but the Arizona fescue displayed the ring formation typical of overgrazed bunchgrasses (see Figure 2.7), and the mountain muhly was heavily grazed.[99] Parry's rabbitbrush and musk thistle were taking over parts of the grassland, and the grazing increasers woolly cinquefoil and small-leaf pussytoes were very common (see Box—Increasers and Decreasers, pp. 205–206). This is a small area that should not be essential to the permittee. Perhaps with complete rest, some moist years, and control of non-native plants, this could be restored to healthy grassland. If restored and preserved, this remnant would be of considerable value as a reference area for restoring other grasslands in the area.

Piedra Road Bunchgrass Park: An oasis of grass diversity. Another grassland of the ponderosa pine zone is dominated by Parry's oatgrass, a bunchgrass often also found in the understory of open ponderosa pine forests. It also dominates some open grasslands from the ponderosa pine zone to much higher elevations (see Figure 5.2). A remarkably diverse remnant of this grassland, probably typical of the grassy parks in the Pagosa Springs area, is found along Piedra Road at the Hinsdale-Archuleta county line. A fence, long in place, separates Forest Service land from private property to the north. The south side of the fence lies over a ridge from the main part of the allotment and water, so cattle probably did not graze as heavily here. This type of accident of fencing and distance to water often explains where remnant vegetation is found. The Nature Conservancy purchased the property south of the fence and transferred it to the Forest Service in 1993. Since 1998, after five years of rest, the site has been grazed by cattle early in the season, until about mid- to late July.[100]

Looking up and down the valley from this site, one can imagine what Lieutenant C.A.H. McCauley saw here on an 1877 government survey of ranching and farming potential: "In the aggregate there are over 40,000 acres on the water-shed of this river that are of the highest value for the rearing of cattle and sheep, being all superior summer and fall ranges."[101] He observed that several ranches were already started, but with only cabins erected. About three miles west on Weminuche Creek, a little lower in elevation, McCauley also observed: "In the valley of the Weeminuche [sic], the western tributary of the Piedra, a most lovely section, luxuriant grasses are passed over, which were fully 3 feet in height."[102] The tall grass was probably Arizona fescue (see Plate 33a), also the tallest grass in this remnant.

The fence-line contrast (see Plate 38) offers striking evidence of the transformation and loss of the native bunchgrass community that likely dominated the entire valley when McCauley surveyed the area. The upshot is that the five native bunchgrasses that make up the bulk of vegetation on the south side of the fence are replaced on the north side of the fence largely by the non-native Kentucky bluegrass, the common grass of lawns in towns (see Table 5.4). Squirreltail, a native grass, is also more abundant on the north side of the fence, perhaps because it is resistant to grazing. In 2001 Peggy Lyon, a botanist with the Colorado Natural Heritage Program, found 21 native species of plants (4 grass

Table 5.4. Differences in cover of major plants across the fence at Piedra Road Bunchgrass Park (percentage cover south and north of the fence that follows the county line east of the road).[1]

	South	North
GRAMINOIDS		
Parry's oatgrass (*Danthonia parryi*)	35	tr[2]
Arizona fescue (*Festuca arizonica*)	15	tr
Idaho fescue (*Festuca idahoensis*)	5	tr
Pine dropseed (*Blepharoneuron tricholepis*)	5	tr
Mountain muhly (*Muhlenbergia montana*)	2	—
Squirreltail (*Elymus elymoides*, formerly *Sitanion hystrix*)	tr	3
FORBS		
Woolly cinquefoil (*Potentilla hippiana*)	4	tr
White sagebrush (*Artemisia ludoviciana*)	3	1
Tobacco root (*Valeriana edulis*)	1	tr
Western yarrow (*Achillea lanulosa*)	tr	3
NON-NATIVES		
Butter and eggs (*Linaria vulgaris*)	—	tr
Kentucky bluegrass (*Poa pratensis*)	2	80
Smooth brome (*Bromopsis inermis*, formerly *Bromus*)	tr	—
Timothy (*Phleum pratense*)	tr	—

1. Common names are from the PLANTS online database, http://plants.usda.gov. Latin names are from Weber and Wittmann, *Colorado Flora*.
2. A dash indicates a species is absent, and "tr" indicates a trace amount (< 0.5% cover).

species and 17 forb species) that occurred only on the south side of the fence.[103] Thirteen native species of plants (4 grass species and 9 forbs) were about equal on the two sides of the fence, with none on the north side of the fence that were not also on the south side of the fence. Even plants that are typically increasers, such as woolly cinquefoil, became rare or disappeared under heavy grazing. Livestock grazing led to replacement of the diverse assemblage of native plants in the bunchgrass community by the non-native Kentucky bluegrass and a very small percentage (and small coverage) of the original native flora.

This replacement is evident over most of the 40,000 acres McCauley identified as good grazing land in 1877. Scattered patches of Parry's oatgrass and Arizona fescue remain on the hillsides in valleys near Pagosa Springs, but Kentucky bluegrass, smooth brome (see Box— Smooth Brome, pp. 281–282), and weedy plants are now dominant—a significant legacy. It is not known exactly when the replacement occurred, but the unregulated heavy livestock use between McCauley's survey and World War I was likely a major contributor. Degradation and loss probably continue today.[104] Yellow toadflax (see Plate 39), a noxious weed (see Box—Noxious Weeds, pp. 200–201), is expanding in

Figure 5.12. *A fence-line contrast with a private horse pasture, illustrating how over-grazing opens bare ground for invasion by non-native species.*

the region and has begun to invade grasslands and forest along the nearby Piedra Canyon Trail. Subdivision has potentially major impacts, particularly where horses are kept on insufficient acreage (see Figure 5.12).

Ann Shepherdson, range conservationist with the Forest Service in Pagosa Springs, believes restoring native grasses here is possible and would actually be good for ranchers, as well as assist in restoring native biological diversity.[105] In drought years she thinks native bunchgrasses provide more reliable forage than Kentucky bluegrass does. During drought, native bunchgrasses can compete with Kentucky bluegrass and gain ground if rested or only lightly grazed.[106] Smooth brome is more aggressive and competitive and may be harder to replace with native plants.

It is exciting to have this remnant grassland at the county line. It is hoped that the Forest Service will fence this grassland so it can be protected from livestock use in perpetuity. It is important for people to be able to see this remnant of the country as it once was, as McCauley and the early ranchers saw it—full of promise. The promise seen now is as a source of seeds and a model when native bunchgrass communities become part of the vision for restoring ponderosa pine landscapes.

Aspen Forestry: Time for Reassessment

Clear-cutting has been discredited for most types of forestry, but in aspen it remains the method the Forest Service prefers. Just as old-growth ponderosa pine was liquidated a few generations ago because of perceptions that it was overmature or decadent, old-growth aspen could suffer the same fate. Although some researchers and interest groups believe aspen is in decline because conifers are taking over former aspen stands as a result of fire suppression,[107] research in the San Juans suggests that aspen overall is stable or increasing and that logging and burning are not needed to restore aspen.[108] Allowing aspen to grow to an old-growth stage does not maximize wood production. It is important, therefore, to understand the noneconomic value of mature aspen, assess the impacts of logging in this ecosystem, and think about new possibilities for managing aspen ecosystems.

The Horsefly timber sale just east of the Piedra River is an example of the type of aspen forestry that predominates today. This was a mixed ponderosa pine and aspen sale, with the ponderosa pine portion following many of the guidelines of restoration forestry developed by the Ponderosa Pine Partnership. Aspen was harvested in seven "patch cuts" (small clear-cuts). The bid went to the Western Excelsior mill in Mancos in 1997.[109] By the summer of 2001 all the aspen had been harvested, but only three of the six ponderosa pine units had been cut, demonstrating the relative value of aspen compared with small-diameter wood available on the pine units.[110]

The first patch cut of aspen was a stand of about ten acres of very large aspen. The entire stand was clear-cut in 1998. Based on a count of tree rings on stumps, the largest trees were about 120 years old when cut. This aspen stand seemed to be regenerating in 2001.[111] Aspen regenerate occasionally from seed after fires[112] but more often by sprouting from horizontal roots that connect a "clone" of aboveground trees; clones sometimes cover an entire hillside.[113] However, aspen regeneration has failed after clear-cutting in parts of northern Arizona,[114] on the Uncompahgre Plateau,[115] and elsewhere in Colorado.[116] Glenn Crouch found that six to ten years after clear-cutting, in fifteen stands northeast of Dolores "successful restocking of the study area is questionable."[117] Failed regeneration occurs in particular places: where water tables are high; where a thin, organic-rich surface layer occurs in the soil; and where slopes are less than 10 percent.[118]

Elk browsing can also play a role in regeneration failure. Elk regularly use aspen sprouts and bark for food; in winter they may bite aspen trunks seeking the nutritive inner bark, which has high food value.[119] The bites offer an entry point for fungi and other aspen dis-

Figure 5.13. *Uncut quaking aspen* (Populus tremuloides*) forest showing lush understory and elk bite on aspen trunks.*

eases[120] that may increase mortality of established stems.[121] Aspen are susceptible to many diseases.[122] Heavy elk browse on young sprouts leads to repeated branching, a failure to grow high enough to resist elk browsing, and possible mortality.[123] Elk at high density can prevent regeneration of aspen after clear-cutting and fires.[124] Where elk are abundant, as in winter ranges and some parks, aspen may be threatened.[125] However, where predators of elk are present or hunting of elk is sufficient, aspen may regenerate successfully.[126] Successful regeneration, even on favorable sites, may require reductions in elk populations by predation, hunting, fencing, or other management to keep livestock out.[127]

Two years after clear-cutting this aspen stand, sprouts were about four feet high, but nearly all had tops lost to elk browsing.[128] Cattle and elk droppings were abundant in the clear-cut, and elk bite on aspen trunks was evident in most uncut stands nearby (see Figure 5.13). By the third year after the cut, the aspen sprouts had grown about another two feet. Elk browsing was less obvious, but much of the new growth was dead from an unidentified disease.

Small patches of weeds were found throughout the site, and cheatgrass was dominant in some highly disturbed areas where aspen had not regenerated (see Plate 40).[129] Cheatgrass has not usually been considered a problem in aspen forests, and its abundance here is a significant concern. Another aspen clear-cut nearby had three other noxious weeds: Canada thistle, musk thistle, and common mullein. While generalizations about clear-cut logging effects on aspen forests should not be drawn from just one area, there is reason to worry that clear-cutting will increase noxious weeds.

It appears that the oldest stands in this area were targeted for clear-cutting. The harvested stands may not qualify as old growth, which requires a minimum of 20 trees per acre that are 14" in diameter and at least 100 years old,[130] but these stands were close. Foresters in the past were attracted to the higher volumes of wood available from larger trees, but they also viewed old forests as unproductive, labeling them "overmature."[131] Clear-cuts were seen as a way to "regenerate" these "overmature" stands, leading to thrifty, faster-growing forests.[132] However, today society may consider "overmature" to be a label reflecting an outdated wood-production focus, as old forests are now recognized to have intrinsic habitat value because of their age.[133]

Aspen is an important habitat for a wide range of wildlife, supporting a greater richness of bird species and numbers than any other mountain habitat in North America.[134] Hugh Kingery explains the qualities that make aspen forests attractive to many breeding birds: "The ecosystem typically contains a profuse, diverse understory of shrubs, grasses, and herbaceous plants, including the Colorado columbine. Foliage-dwelling insects are plentiful in the aspen forest ecosystem, and the structure provides openings for insectivores that feed on the wing. The thick ground cover provides opportunities for ground nesters, and older forest stands, depending on their condition[,] provide many cavities."[135]

In addition to the Colorado blue columbine, other dominant plants of the aspen understory include the yellow-flowered mountain goldenbanner, the grassy-looking Geyer's sedge (see Figure 3.7), and Fendler's meadow-rue (see Table 5.5). Ungrazed, these plants form a tall, lush ground cover (see Figure 5.13).

The red-naped sapsucker breeds almost exclusively in mature aspen forests,[136] where it may be a keystone species,[137] a species many other species in an ecosystem depend upon in one way or another for survival. Sapsuckers are unusual among woodpeckers in drilling sap wells, neat rows of small holes in the bark that fill up with sap and attract insects. Many other birds, as well as numerous insects and even small mammals, utilize the high-energy sap.[138] Probably more important for other species is the sapsucker's provision of nest sites. In aspen, as in ponderosa pine forests, many birds and mammals nest in tree

Table 5.5. Common native plants of aspen forests in southwestern Colorado.[1]

TREES
  Quaking aspen (*Populus tremuloides*)

SHRUBS
  Gambel oak (*Quercus gambelii*)
  Mountain snowberry (*Symphoricarpos rotundifolius*)
  Woods' rose (*Rosa woodsii*)

FORBS
  Alpine false springparsley (*Pseudocymopterus montanus*)
  Colorado blue columbine (*Aquilegia coerulea*)
  Fendler's meadow-rue (*Thalictrum fendleri*)
  Fireweed (*Chamerion danielsii*, formerly *Epilobium angustifolium*)
  Mountain goldenbanner (*Thermopsis montana*)
  Porter's licorice-root (*Ligusticum porteri*)
  Rocky Mountain iris (*Iris missouriensis*)
  Western yarrow (*Achillea lanulosa*)

GRAMINOIDS
  Geyer's sedge (*Carex geyeri*)

FERNS
  Hairy brackenfern (*Pteridium aquilinum*)

1. Common names are from the PLANTS online database, http://plants.usda.gov. Latin names are from Weber and Wittmann, *Colorado Flora*.

Table 5.6. Breeding birds associated with aspen forests of southwestern Colorado.[1]

Black-capped chickadee +[2]	House wren +	Sharp-shinned hawk
Blue grouse	Mountain bluebird +	Tree swallow +
Broad-tailed hummingbird	Northern flicker +	Violet-green swallow +
Cooper's hawk	Northern pygmy-owl +	Warbling vireo
Downy woodpecker +	Red-naped sapsucker * +	Western tanager
Dusky flycatcher	Orange-crowned warbler	Western wood-peewee
Hairy woodpecker +	Purple martin + ·in Colorado, an aspen obligate)	Yellow-rumped warbler

1. Kingery, *Colorado Breeding Bird Atlas*.
2. * denotes an aspen-forest near obligate; + denotes cavity nesting.

cavities (see Table 5.6). The red-naped sapsucker drills a new nest cavity every year, leaving behind its old cavities for species—such as mountain chickadees, house wrens, and mountain bluebirds—that require cavities but cannot drill their own. Sapsuckers strongly prefer living trees with heart rot for nesting cavities, and these occur mainly in older stands.[139] Black-capped chickadees, which excavate their own cavities, also require aspens with a rotten center.[140] Thus, stands of aspen at least 80 years old support more diverse bird communities than younger stands.[141] In 1880, before logging began, half of all aspen stands in the southern San Juans were over 70 years old, and most of those were over 120 years old, so there was ample habitat for the old-growth community.[142]

With a potential continuation of, or increase in, aspen harvesting, is this logging creating a new legacy that will be a future concern? Aspen clear-cutting is not favorable to native birds, may increase non-native weeds, and is prone to regeneration failure. No ecological need exists to clear-cut aspen forests, as these forests are not in decline.[143] Of course, timber products are still in demand, and people use wood products as part of daily life, so production will always be a part of forestry. However, society's relationship with aspen is now more complex and contested than it was previously.

To protect the ecological value of aspen forest, new approaches to use are needed. Value-added industries (e.g., paneling, furniture) would help increase the economic viability of communities in the region without placing excessive demands on aspen forests.[144] Some of these industries already exist. The harvest of aspen stands should be avoided in roadless areas, on sites where aspen will not regenerate, or in stands containing the oldest and biggest trees, which have special value to society and nature as protected old growth. Harvesting methods are needed that minimize the possibility of noxious weeds. By concentrating aspen harvesting into fewer areas adjacent to existing roads, noxious weeds could be minimized and other aspen stands left to support native biological diversity.[145] Livestock grazing techniques are needed that better perpetuate native biological diversity and that do not encourage noxious weeds. Clear-cutting can be replaced with variable retention harvesting systems that more closely mimic natural disturbance effects.[146] Harvesting and grazing in new ways may not maximize wood and forage production but could be less damaging to the native flora and fauna. Aspen forestry could become part of a new land ethic rather than a divisive and controversial issue with possibly significant future legacies.

Rural Sprawl and a Cohousing Alternative

A recent and long-term impact on the ponderosa pine zone is the sale and subdivision of lands formerly managed as large ranches (see Box—Rural Sprawl and Its Ecological Impacts, pp. 217–219). The four southern San Juan counties (Dolores, Montezuma, La Plata, Archuleta) increased in population by over 20 percent from 1993 to 1999, with the largest, La Plata, adding almost 7,000 people.[147] Unfortunately, more land is consumed for housing than population growth alone requires

BOX—RURAL SPRAWL AND ITS ECOLOGICAL IMPACTS

Communities across the West are grappling with the effects of rapid growth, as affluent professionals, baby-boomer retirees, and vacation-home builders flock to the amenity-rich Rocky Mountain states from all other parts of the country.[1] Population increased in the Mountain West by 25 percent in the 1990s, and growth rates are predicted to remain high.[2] Many of the migrants are choosing rural areas with natural amenities such as mountains, natural areas, and recreational opportunities[3]—areas that abound in southwestern Colorado. Low-density rural development in Colorado has expanded at three times the rate of population growth.[4] The resulting rural sprawl has social and economic costs, but we focus here on the ecological costs.

Rural sprawl results when large private ranches are divided into multiple homesites, commonly thirty-five-acre "ranchettes." Although this book describes many negative impacts of livestock grazing on natural communities, ranching could be reformed to better coexist with the natural world. Widespread rural subdivision, on the other hand, has inherent negative impacts, many of which cannot be overcome, not even by the most conscientious homeowner. The lower elevations around mountains provide critical winter range for big game, valleys are the most productive farmland, and streamside (riparian) habitat supports two-thirds of Colorado's plant and animal species.[5] Yet these are the very lands where sprawl is concentrated because they are largely private and are preferred as locations for homesites.

A major impact of rural sprawl is increased road density and capacity. In one study of foothills subdivision, road density was eight times higher on subdivided ranches than on intact ranches.[6] Faster roads and heavier traffic from rural commuters prematurely end many animals' lives. Even in the remote, high-elevation habitat of the lynx, at least six and possibly eight of the forty-five lynx reintroduced into southwestern Colorado that had died by 2003 were hit by cars.[7] Many animals avoid roads, so roads block their migration and dispersal across the landscape. Most insidious, roads fragment the landscape, increasing edges that favor generalist species such as skunks and coyotes and reducing large habitat blocks needed by more specialized species.[8]

Non-native invasive plants are often carried on automobile tires, boots, and shoes or on horses or other animals, and they invade relatively intact native vegetation along new roads.[9] The spread of noxious and invasive weeds may be one of the biggest impacts of rural sprawl, as people new to the country often do not recognize an emerging problem until it is very costly to correct.[10] Many new residents do not realize how many acres a horse requires in most of the nonirrigated rangeland of the West. Severely overgrazed pastures (see Figure 5.12) retain little of the natural community and are magnets for invasive weeds, which favor disturbed ground.

Housing development has a much bigger impact than the actual footprint of homesites, with exurban developments reducing native biodiversity across the landscape.[11] In a study in Pitkin County, Colorado, human-tolerant species—such as American robin, black-billed magpie, and brown-headed cowbird—increased within 500 feet of rural houses, whereas human-sensitive species—such as black-capped chickadee, black-headed grosbeak, and orange-crowned warbler—declined.[12] In the Yellowstone region, nest success of a common bird, the yellow warbler, declined for 3.6 miles around homesites as a result of increased cowbird parasitism and increased density of nest predators.[13] The effect of human presence is increased by security lights, fences, noise, and cats and dogs.[14] In Wisconsin, rural cats were found to average ninety-one kills a year per cat.[15] Cats from homes near canyons outside San Diego killed an average of twenty-four rodents, fifteen birds, and seventeen lizards each year and eliminated several species from moderately sized habitat fragments.[16] Some animals, such as raccoons, may increase with new food sources, but when larger animals begin raiding garbage or start dining on pets, they become problem animals that often are destroyed.

Finally, the proximity of private homes to public lands has begun to impinge upon the management of public lands.[17] It is politically difficult to maintain natural disturbances, such as forest fires, or even to restore lands through prescribed burns. While homeowners can reduce some of their impacts by the choices they make, there is considerable irony to building a house in the woods to be with nature.

NOTES

1. Riebsame, Gosnell, and Theobald, "Land Use and Landscape Change I."
2. Masnick, "America's Shifting Population."
3. Hansen et al., "Ecological Causes and Consequences of Demographic Change."
4. Theobald, "Fragmentation by Inholdings and Exurban Development."
5. Riebsame, Gosnell, and Theobald, "Land Use and Landscape Change I."
6. Mitchell, Knight, and Camp, "Landscape Attributes of Subdivided Ranches."
7. See Web site: http://wildlife.state.co.us/T&E/lynx.asp.
8. Theobald, Gosnell, and Riebsame, "Land Use and Landscape Change II"; Theobald, Miller, and Hobbs, "Effects of Development on Wildlife"; Miller et al., "Urbanization, Avian Communities, and Landscape Ecology."
9. Baker and Knight, "Roads and Forest Fragmentation in the Southern Rocky Mountains."
10. An excellent source of information on the weed problem in southwestern Colorado is *Noxious Weed Gang: Taking Over the West*, published by the San Juan Mountains Association and available at many county and federal land management offices in southwestern Colorado.
11. Maestas, Knight, and Gilgert, "Biodiversity Across a Rural Land-Use Gradient."

12. Odell and Knight, "Songbird and Mammal Communities Associated with Exurban Development."
13. Hansen et al., "Ecological Causes and Consequences of Demographic Change."
14. Knight, Wallace, and Riebsame, "Ranching the View."
15. Coleman and Temple, "On the Prowl."
16. Crooks and Soulé, "Mesopredator Release and Avifaunal Extinctions."
17. Riebsame, Gosnell, and Theobald, "Land Use and Landscape Change I."

because of a significant demand for acreage for rural homes and hobby ranches. In La Plata County, 80 percent of population growth is occurring outside town boundaries.[148] In 1999 alone, 387 permits were issued for new septic systems in La Plata County,[149] and population is projected to continue to grow at about 2 percent annually through 2020.[150]

In La Plata County, as in adjacent counties, much of the lower-elevation ponderosa pine forest and many associated grassland parks are privately owned and experiencing rapid subdivision. Lower elevations provide essential habitat for wildlife (see Box—Rural Sprawl and Its Ecological Impacts, pp. 217–219). Romme suggests that "by 2020—if current trends continue—approximately one-fourth of the county's waterfowl breeding areas, one-third of the waterfowl winter concentration areas, one-quarter of the elk severe winter range, and one-third of elk winter concentration areas will lie within subdivisions. . . . [M]uch of the wildlife and native biodiversity that we now value in La Plata County, and often take for granted, could become quite scarce within the next human generation."[151]

Policies that encourage in-fill and higher-density development can greatly alter the impact of population growth in a region (Chapter 3, see Map 3.4). In 2003, Durango considered annexing 245 acres north of town to help support a "new urban" development that would include 800 homes (including townhomes and apartments), retail and professional offices, parks, and open space.[152] That project was not approved, in part because of adverse impacts on the river corridor, but a new node of development on the southeastern edge of Durango is expected to be developed by the Southern Ute Tribe. Appropriately placed high-density developments would help absorb population, but policy tools are needed to stem sprawl outward from these developments. So far, even rapidly growing La Plata County has placed few restrictions on development.

One voluntary effort to develop rural land in an ecologically sensitive manner is the Heartland Cohousing Project outside Bayfield, Colorado. Cohousing is a movement to design communities that foster neighbor-

hood communication and cooperation—qualities more typical of neigh-
borhoods in the past.[153] The Heartland Cohousing Project was started
by Mac and Sandy Thompson and a small group of people interested in
developing a cohousing community in an earth-friendly manner. A 360-
acre ranch that had been slated for eleven 35-acre homesites was purchased, and the cohousing community was clustered in a meadow (see
Plate 41), leaving about 250 acres of undeveloped land.[154] The land is in
important deer and elk winter range, which is much less impacted than
it would have been if eleven houses and associated roads had been
built across the landscape, yet the development contains more than
twice as many homes. All houses were constructed with sustainably
harvested wood (either certified or logged locally by a group member), are superinsulated, and have passive-solar features; several are
duplex townhouses. There is a community building, greenhouse, and
garden space; and equipment is shared to the extent possible. The
project's lots and homes sold quickly, suggesting there is demand for
this type of housing.[155]

Cohousing has some barriers to overcome. One problem is that creating such a development is a multimillion-dollar real estate project.
The novelty and uncertainty of this approach probably discourage some
developers. Neighbors of Heartland were concerned about a "group of
hippies" moving in next door.[156] Around the world, however, rural vil-
lages are the norm, and Americans are unusual in spacing themselves
across the landscape. Many people would probably appreciate the sense
of community, balanced with privacy and surrounded by common open
space, clustered cohousing development can offer.

CONCLUDING THOUGHTS

New residents are coming, and it is again a time of rapid change in the
pine zone. Intensive logging and grazing during early settlement by Euro-
Americans and throughout the twentieth century left significant legacies. Now a new restoration forestry, developing out of the Ponderosa
Pine Partnership, provides a model for a smaller, sustainable wood-
product economy in the region if value-added products can be developed. A value-added industry could allow substantial old-growth forest
to be maintained while providing forest products, particularly if the
few remaining old-growth forest remnants (e.g., Hermosa Creek) are
protected to provide models and inspiration for restoration and sustainable management. Aspen forests and bunchgrass parks await a similar
vision for protection, restoration, and sustainable use. Ironically, as restoration and sustainability are emerging, the pine zone faces a new

destructive force in expansive retirement and second-home development. A house on a large lot in the pine forest consumes the forest's beauty and degrades its ecological value. High-density development, clustering, and cohousing offer alternatives. A new approach to housing in the pine zone is needed, and time is short.

NOTES

1. Ingersoll, *Crest of the Continent,* 124.
2. Blair, *Western San Juan Mountains.*
3. Simmons, *Ute Indians of Utah, Colorado and New Mexico.*
4. Hafen and Hafen, *Old Spanish Trail.*
5. York, "Forest History."
6. Newberry, *Report of the Exploring Expedition from Santa Fe,* 74.
7. Ibid., 79.
8. Nossaman, *Many More Mountains, Vo . I.*
9. Ruffner, *Annual Report upon Explorations and Surveys.*
10. Nossaman, *Many More Mountains, Vol. I.*
11. York, "Forest History."
12. Ibid.
13. Ibid.
14. Fitzgerald, Meaney, and Armstrong, *Mammals of Colorado;* York, "Forest History."
15. Hinshaw, *Crusaders for Wildlife.*
16. Ibid.
17. Ibid.; Fitzgerald, Meaney, and Armstrong, *Mammals of Colorado.*
18. Fitzgerald, Meaney, and Armstrong, *Mammals of Colorado;* Stein, "Otter's Comeback a Splashing Success."
19. Dubois, "Report on Proposed San Juan Forest Reserve."
20. O'Rourke, *Frontier in Transition.*
21. Rodebaugh and Blumenfeld, "Ranchers Watch Grazing Dwindle in National Forest."
22. Smith, *Effects of Cattle Grazing on Ponderosa Pine–Bunchgrass Range.*
23. York, "Forest History," 129.
24. Dubois, "Report on Proposed San Juan Forest Reserve," 11.
25. Lavender, *One Man's West.*
26. Zier and Baker, "A Century of Vegetation Change in the San Juan Mountains."
27. Romme et al., "Ponderosa Pine Forests of Southwestern Colorado."
28. Covington and Moore, "Southwestern Ponderosa Forest Structure."
29. Savage, Brown, and Feddema, "Role of Climate in Pine Forest Regeneration Pulse."
30. Covington and Moore, "Southwestern Ponderosa Forest Structure."
31. Pearson, "Herbaceous Vegetation in Regeneration of Ponderosa Pine"; Savage and Swetnam, "Fire Decline Following Sheep Pasturing."

32. Chappell, *Logging Along the Denver & Rio Grande;* Romme and Bunting, "History of the San Juan National Forest."
33. Chappell, *Logging Along the Denver & Rio Grande.*
34. See National Association of Homebuilders Web site: http://www.nahb.com.
35. Chappell, *Logging Along the Denver & Rio Grande.*
36. Romme and Bunting, "History of the San Juan National Forest," 43.
37. York, "Forest History."
38. Phil Kemp, silviculturalist, U.S. Forest Service, Dolores, Colorado, pers. comm., May 25, 2000.
39. Block and Finch, *Songbird Ecology in Southwestern Ponderosa Pine Forests;* Romme et al., "Ponderosa Pine Forests of Southwestern Colorado."
40. Romme and Bunting, "History of the San Juan National Forest," 27.
41. Ibid.
42. Ibid.
43. Phil Kemp, silviculturalist, U.S. Forest Service, Dolores, Colorado, pers. comm., May 25, 2000.
44. Romme et al., "Old-Growth Forests of San Juan Natural Forest."
45. Phil Kemp, silviculturalist, U.S. Forest Service, Dolores, Colorado, pers. comm., May 25, 2000.
46. Ibid.
47. Preston and Garrison, *Ponderosa Pine Partnership.*
48. Ibid.
49. Kaufmann, Moir, and Bassett, eds., *Old-Growth Forests.*
50. Romme et al., "Ponderosa Pine Forests of Southwestern Colorado."
51. Ibid.
52. Ibid.
53. Romme et al., "Biological Diversity in the Hermosa Unit."
54. Kingery, *Colorado Breeding Bird Atlas.*
55. Hall, Morrison, and Block, "Songbird Status and Roles."
56. Kingery, *Colorado Breeding Bird Atlas.*
57. Szaro and Balda, *Selection and Monitoring of Avian Indicator Species.*
58. Kingery, *Colorado Breeding Bird Atlas.*
59. Ffolliott, "Snag Policies on Southwestern Ponderosa Pine Forests."
60. Hall, Morrison, and Block, "Songbird Status and Roles."
61. Fitzgerald, Meaney, and Armstrong, *Mammals of Colorado.*
62. Morrison, "Prescribed Burn Plan for Hermosa Drainage."
63. Dutch Creek Allotment file, San Juan National Forest, Durango, Colorado.
64. Romme et al., "Ponderosa Pine Partnership: Ecology, Economics, and Community Involvement."
65. Lynch, Romme, and Floyd, "Forest Restoration in Southwestern Ponderosa Pine."
66. Romme et al., "Ponderosa Pine Partnership: Ecology, Economics, and Community Involvement."
67. Mark Pearson, San Juan Citizens Alliance, Durango, Colorado, pers. comm., November 28, 2001.
68. Phil Kemp, silviculturalist, U.S. Forest Service, Dolores, Colorado, pers. comm., May 25, 2000.

69. Ibid., July 12, 2001.
70. Dubois, "Report on Proposed San Juan Forest Reserve"; Romme et al., "Ponderosa Pine Forests of Southwestern Colorado"; Allen et al., "Ecological Restoration of Southwestern Ponderosa Pine."
71. Leslie Stewart, U.S. Forest Service, Dolores, Colorado, pers. comm., July 11, 2001.
72. Scott Wait, Colorado Division of Wildlife, Durango, pers. comm., December 3, 2001.
73. Baker and Ehle, "Uncertainty in Surface-Fire History."
74. Hall, Morrison, and Block, "Songbird Status and Roles," 77.
75. Sieg, Phillips, and Moser, "Exotic Invasive Plants."
76. Ibid.
77. Carla Harper, Montezuma County Federal Lands Program, Cortez, Colorado, pers. comm., December 7, 2001.
78. Ibid.
79. Ibid.; Tim Reader, Colorado State Forest Service, Durango, pers. comm., December 4, 2001.
80. Lynch, Romme, and Floyd, "Forest Restoration in Southwestern Ponderosa Pine."
81. Romme et al., "Ponderosa Pine Partnership: Ecology, Economics, and Community Involvement."
82. Reader, "Survey of Montezuma County Forest Products Businesses."
83. Ibid.
84. Tim Reader, Colorado State Forest Service, Durango, pers. comm., December 4, 2001.
85. Phil Kemp, silviculturalist, U.S. Forest Service, Dolores, Colorado, pers. comm., May 25, 2000; Mark Pearson, San Juan Citizens Alliance, Durango, Colorado, pers. comm., November 28, 2001.
86. Beaver Crossing Exclosure Trend Study, 1995, on file at U.S. Forest Service, Dolores, Colorado.
87. Costello and Schwan, "Conditions and Trends on Ponderosa Pine Ranges."
88. Ibid.
89. Calculated from data in the Beaver Crossing grazing allotment file, U.S. Forest Service, Dolores, Colorado.
90. Booth, "Demonstration Range Allotment Plan: Biggs C&H Allotment," Biggs allotment file, U.S. Forest Service, Dolores, Colorado.
91. Anonymous, "Land Use History—Range."
92. Ibid.
93. Beaver Crossing Allotment—Inspection Summaries, Draft, U.S. Forest Service, Dolores, Colorado, May 1999.
94. Memo in Biggs allotment file, U.S. Forest Service, Dolores, Colorado.
95. Smith, *Effects of Cattle Grazing on Ponderosa Pine–Bunchgrass Range*.
96. Laycock, "Stable States and Thresholds of Range Condition."
97. Potter and Krenetsky, "Plant Succession with Released Grazing."
98. Costello and Turner, "Vegetation Changes Following Exclusion of Livestock."

99. Baker and Paulson, field observations, July 25, 2001.
100. Ann Shepherdson, U.S. Forest Service, Pagosa Springs, Colorado, pers. comm., September 4, 2001.
101. Cited in Ruffner, *Annual Report upon Explorations and Surveys*, appendix SS, 1769.
102. Ibid.
103. Peggy Lyon, Colorado Natural Heritage Program, Ridgway, Colorado, pers. comm., August 14, 2001.
104. Based on Baker's work with The Nature Conservancy from 1980 to 1985 and recent field observations.
105. Ann Shepherdson, U.S. Forest Service, Pagosa Springs, Colorado, pers. comm., September 4, 2001.
106. Smith, *Effects of Cattle Grazing on Ponderosa Pine–Bunchgrass Range.*
107. Bartos, "Landscape Dynamics of Aspen and Conifer Forests"; Club 20, *Decline of Aspen.*
108. Manier and Laven, "Changes in Landscape Patterns"; Zier and Baker, "A Century of Vegetation Change in the San Juan Mountains."
109. Bob Dressel, U.S. Forest Service, Bayfield, Colorado, pers. comm., December 5, 2001.
110. Ibid.
111. Paulson and Baker, field observations, July 8, 2001.
112. Quinn and Wu, "Quaking Aspen Reproduce from Seed."
113. Shepperd, *Growth, Development, and Clonal Dynamics of Aspen.*
114. Rolf, "Aspen Fencing in Northern Arizona."
115. Johnston, "Multiple Factors Affect Aspen Regeneration."
116. Jacobi and Shepperd, *Fungi Associated with Sprout Mortality in Aspen Clearcuts.*
117. Crouch, *Aspen Regeneration in 6- to 10-Year-Old Clearcuts*, 4.
118. Johnston, "Multiple Factors Affect Aspen Regeneration."
119. White, Olmsted, and Kay, "Aspen, Elk, and Fire in Rocky Mountain National Parks."
120. Hinds, "Diseases."
121. Baker, Munroe, and Hessl, "Effects of Elk on Aspen in Rocky Mountain National Park."
122. Jacobi and Shepperd, *Fungi Associated with Sprout Mortality in Aspen Clearcuts.*
123. Baker, Munroe, and Hessl, "Effects of Elk on Aspen in Rocky Mountain National Park"; White, Olmsted, and Kay, "Aspen, Elk, and Fire in Rocky Mountain National Parks."
124. White, Olmsted, and Kay, "Aspen, Elk, and Fire in Rocky Mountain National Parks"; Rolf, "Aspen Fencing in Northern Arizona."
125. Baker, Munroe, and Hessl, "Effects of Elk on Aspen in Rocky Mountain National Park"; Kay, "Is Aspen Doomed?"
126. White, Olmsted, and Kay, "Aspen, Elk, and Fire in Rocky Mountain National Parks"; Ripple and Larsen, "Aspen Recruitment, Elk, and Wolves in Yellowstone."

127. Johnston, "Multiple Factors Affect Aspen Regeneration"; Rolf, "Aspen Fencing in Northern Arizona."
128. Paulson and Baker, field observations, July 13, 2000.
129. Ibid.
130. Mehl, "Old-Growth Descriptions for Major Forest Types in Rocky Mountain Region."
131. Jones, Winokur, and Shepperd, "Management Overview."
132. Ibid.
133. Romme et al., "Old-Growth Forests of San Juan National Forest."
134. DeByle and Winokur, Aspen: Ecology and Management; Turchi et al., "Bird Species Richness in Relation to Isolation of Aspen Habitats."
135. Kingery, Colorado Breeding Bird Atlas, 30.
136. Kingery, Colorado Breeding Bird Atlas, 256.
137. Vance, "Sapsucker."
138. Ibid.
139. Hart and Hart, "Heartrot Fungi's Role in Creating Picid Nesting Sites."
140. Kingery, Colorado Breeding Bird Atlas, 348.
141. Hart and Hart, "Heartrot Fungi's Role in Creating Picid Nesting Sites."
142. Romme et al., "Aspen's Ecological Role in the West."
143. Manier and Laven, "Changes in Landscape Patterns"; Zier and Baker, "A Century of Vegetation Change in the San Juan Mountains."
144. Rodebaugh, "Aspen Agreement."
145. Ibid.
146. Perera, Buse, and Weber, Emulating Natural Forest Landscape Disturbances.
147. Operation Healthy Communities, Pathways to Healthier Communities.
148. Romme, "Creating Pseudo-Rural Landscapes in the Mountain West."
149. Operation Healthy Communities, Pathways to Healthier Communities.
150. See Web site: http://laplatacountycolorado.org/business/population_table.htm; accessed May 8, 2006.
151. Romme, "Creating Pseudo-Rural Landscapes in the Mountain West," 148–149.
152. Miller, "Panel Urges River Trails Annexation."
153. See Web site: http://www.cohousing.org.
154. Mac and Sandy Thompson, Bayfield, Colorado, pers. comm., December 6, 2001.
155. Ibid.
156. Ibid.

> On earth, man is not a visitor who does not
> remain; this is our home planet and we belong
> here. Leopold speaks of man as both "plain
> citizen" and as "king." Humans too have an
> ecology, and we are permitted interference with,
> and rearrangement of, nature's spontaneous
> course; otherwise there is no culture. When we
> do this there ought to be some rationale showing
> that the alteration is enriching, that natural
> values are sacrificed for greater cultural ones.
> We ought to make such development sustain-
> able. But there are, and should be, places on
> Earth where the nonhuman community of life is
> untrammeled by man, where we only visit and
> spontaneous nature remains.
> —Holmes Rolston III[1]

CHAPTER SIX

The Upper Animas River Watershed: Mining and Wilderness

Long ago wracked by violent volcanism and broken by mineral-bearing fractures, the upper
Animas River Valley and surrounding high country around Silverton today bear the legacy of the
oldest and longest hard-rock mining in western
Colorado (see Figure 6.1). At 9,300 feet, Silverton
is the seat of a highly unusual county, one whose
historical economy was almost exclusively based
on mining. Although grazed by sheep, San Juan
County has no acreage in agriculture, and even
the sheep are not popular among the miners' descendants. In recent decades the economy has un-
dergone a complete transformation from mining

Figure 6.1. *Looking northeast toward Silverton. Mineral Creek is on the left, Cement Creek is in the center, and the upper Animas is on the right. Photo by W. Cross, taken August 23, 1900. Courtesy, U.S. Geological Survey, Photographic Library, Denver, Colorado.*

to tourism. The tourism is based largely on the colorful legacy of early exploitation: the mining and railroad history. It is also based in part on the spectacular high peaks and mountain valleys with their Jeep roads and displays of wildflowers, as well as on the Weminuche Wilderness.

The Animas River, ironically, links and mixes these two—mining and wilderness. One of only a few undammed large rivers in the region, the Animas is a wild but polluted torrent flowing in part from the mined landscapes of the upper Animas near Silverton and in part from the wilds of the Weminuche (see Map 6.1). The Animas River Canyon, carved by the river, is a focus of the tourist train and the key entry point to the Needle Mountains portion of the wilderness. The canyon also has a valuable riparian ecosystem with narrowleaf cottonwood and blue spruce elsewhere endangered by dams, livestock grazing, and invasive non-native plants.[2]

Map 6.1. *A map of the area and some sites covered in this chapter.*

0   5   10 Miles

N

    In the high country around Silverton is a beautiful mosaic of subalpine forests of Engelmann spruce and corkbark fir and high meadows of Thurber's fescue and Parry's oatgrass. Subalpine willow-dominated wetlands, alternating with beaver ponds, cover flatter riparian settings.[3] Alpine vegetation caps the peaks and is filled with flowers. Even this far south, it shares almost a third of its flora with that of the Arctic.[4]

    The mountains are derived from a mix of forces. Ancient pre-Cambrian rocks of gneiss, schist, and granite have been warped and uplifted into the towering Needle Mountains. After long periods of deposition of sedimentary rocks, volcanic eruptions alternated with deposition for millions of years beginning about 40 million years ago in the Miocene, leading to a striking mixture of colored peaks, as at Red Mountain Pass. The colored rocks are oxides of iron-laden deposits that were not the target of mining, but these colors may hint at where silver and gold deposits are to be found.[5] And found they were—the Silverton caldera, a giant collapsed volcanic summit that extends to Red Mountain Pass, yielded millions of dollars in silver and gold.[6]

    Silverton is both burdened and enriched by the legacies of mining. Recently, a local collaborative group has developed plans for addressing pollution from the former mines and their wastes, but the Animas River will carry a permanent legacy. Was the wealth generated from Silverton's mines the clear, sustainable gain for culture that Holmes Rolston suggested should remain after such a rearrangement of nature's spontaneous course? The legacies of natural disturbances, such as floods in Animas Canyon and large fires in the subalpine forest, differ from those of the mining boom in that they enhance rather than diminish natural diversity. Could natural disturbances serve as guides for human activities? And finally, what do the human pressures on the popular Weminuche Wilderness teach us about the meaning of wilderness?

LEGACY OF PAST HUMAN USES

Mining in the Upper Animas Watershed

Silverton's mineral-rich geology has profoundly shaped the natural world and its modern human society. In 1874, after the Brunot Treaty, approximately 2,000 miners entered the Silverton district.[7] In 1882 the railroad was completed through Animas Canyon from Durango. This connection to mills, markets, and supplies allowed greatly expanded mining production, which continued in characteristic boom-and-bust cycles until the last mine, the Sunnyside, closed in 1991. The population of Silverton, the only town in San Juan County, reached a high mark of 5,000 in 1910. In 2000 there were about 500 full- and part-time residents, making it the eighth-least-populated county in the United States.[8]

Legacies of early mining practices. The early miners' remarkable exertions to extract and process precious minerals left multiple and significant impacts on the landscape. Old cabins and even boardinghouses are perched at tree line, high above Baker's Park where Silverton is located. Over 1,500 patented mining claims are now privately owned (see Map 6.2), and almost as many unpatented mines surround Silverton.[9] The surface area impacted by mines, tailings, and roads is visibly obvious, though in many places native vegetation is reclaiming old sites.

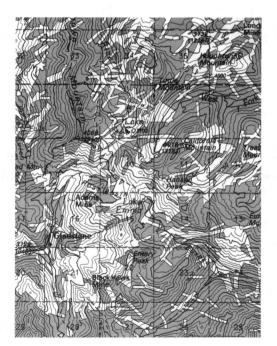

One of the earliest and longest-lasting impacts of the mines was on aquatic life and water quality. The separation of target ores from the rock—whether done by hand, as in the early days, or by mechanical milling operations—left behind piles of waste rock high in nontarget minerals. For example, when silver was the target mineral, zinc-rich rocks were discarded as waste. These pul-

Map 6.2. *Patented mining claims in the Eureka area upstream of Silverton, from U.S. Geological Survey 1:100,000-scale map for Silverton, Colorado.*

Figure 6.2. *Draining mine adit upstream of Silverton.*

verized mine tailings were left at the surface or in mined-out areas, where they are exposed to precipitation and groundwater seepage (see Figure 6.2). Mine tunnels were sometimes dug thousands of feet into the mountains.[10] Water draining from mine adits (the opening at the surface) increased the amount of dissolved minerals carried by water entering streams. High metal content is toxic to aquatic life, and metal concentrations are high enough in many Colorado streams to strongly affect aquatic communities.[11]

The impact of mine drainage was not well-known during the early mining era, but sediment from dumping mill tailings into streams was recognized as an early problem. By the turn of the twentieth century, pollution of the Animas River downstream to Durango had become a major public issue. On August 7, 1901, the *Durango Democrat* editorialized, "Silverton's method of dumping is purely criminal and absolutely without excuse, a wanton assault on human health. There is no mill in San Juan that can not flume the tailings to some point instead of directly into the river."[12] But the economic influence of the mining industry overwhelmed concern for the Animas.[13]

Over time, milling became much more efficient at extracting metals, but this also meant that much larger volumes of lower-grade ore were being processed—with an accompanying increase in fine sediments, which were still fairly high in minerals.[14] Farmers in the Animas Valley, forty-five miles south, began to complain that mining sediments from Silverton were filling their irrigation ditches. Durango gave up on the Animas as a water source and built a diversion from the Florida River to supply its water. Fine sediments with high levels of copper, lead, and zinc still influence the stream channel at least as far as Durango.[15] At Durango, 80 percent of metals in the bed sediments are from the tributaries of the Animas River above Silverton.[16]

Impacts on aquatic life were not well-known at the time, but an oral interview recorded this recollection by Lester Short, an early Durango resident: "The Animas River at that time, you didn't do anything with the Animas River. The mill tailings were running into it. I've seen it run plum green, and of course Durango was dumping its raw sewage into the river, so down here (Sunnyside on Florida Mesa south of Durango) why you didn't even swim in the Animas. There wasn't any fish in it, there wasn't anything, it was really a dead river."[17] Even today, only the non-native brook trout (see Plate 42)—the trout most tolerant of zinc—persist in the streams around Silverton, although stocked brown trout, which are also more tolerant of metals than are the native cutthroat, are now plentiful in the river above Durango.[18]

Tailings continued to be dumped directly into streams until about 1935, when the U.S. Supreme Court ruled against a Central City company for dumping tailings. Although mine operators at the time argued that tailings were benign at worst and possibly even beneficial as a soil resource, in 1935 the largest mill in the area began to use tailings ponds to settle and capture sediments. Mining wastes in streams after this were not chronically high, but much of the damage had already been done: "Total production for the entire one hundred twenty-one year period (1871–1991) is estimated at 17,400,000 tons with an estimated 7,500,000 tons discharged directly into the watershed as mill tailings."[19]

Eureka and the Sunnyside mill. Several miles upstream of Silverton is the site of the former town of Eureka and the remains of the Sunnyside mill. It is hard to believe that a town with a post office, a restaurant, boardinghouses, saloons, and general stores once occupied this site,[20] but a historical photograph and rephoto capture the history of boom and bust (see Figure 6.3a, b). The most prominent landmark today is the foundation of the old mill. This was the second Sunnyside mill, the first having opened in 1899. Built in about 1918, the mill closed in 1930 and was dismantled in 1948.[21] About seventy-five years after closure, nature has only begun to revegetate the floodplains and hillside. The former town now has native narrowleaf cottonwoods and spruce, but downstream of the mill the gravel and boulder bed of the floodplain remains remarkably bare (see Figure 6.4). Only scattered plants and a few small Engelmann spruce have taken hold.

What explains this absence of recovery on the floodplain? The mine waste is the likely explanation. The stream is much more level below

Figure 6.3. *The town of Eureka (a) in about A.D 1928 by Walker Art Studios and (b) in A.D. 2002. (a) Courtesy, San Juan County Historical Society, Silverton, Colorado.*

Eureka than above it, which has allowed sediments from mining to accumulate. Mills above Eureka, from the 1880s to 1930, dumped tailings directly into the river, increasing sediment deposition on the streambed by 50–4,700 times the pre-mining rates.[22] Wastes accumulated here, raising the bed by three feet.[23] These bed sediments have high concentrations

Figure 6.4. *Tailings-filled floodplain just downstream of Eureka, 2002.*

of zinc,[24] one of the most important metals limiting aquatic life in the Animas River system. Metals are mobilized during snowmelt and high runoff and are replenished from mine sources surrounding Eureka.

In recent decades, mining operators have had to meet stricter discharge requirements and remediate their impacts. *Remediation* and *reclamation* are mining terms meaning that the effects of mining are partly cleaned up. But the legacy of mining on water quality, stream communities, and the landscape remains a serious environmental issue. How the Silverton community is dealing with this legacy is discussed in "What Is Happening Now?" later in this chapter.

Intentional Species Introductions

Early overhunting decimated large carnivores and game animals in the upper Animas area as elsewhere.[25] However, the sparsely settled upper Animas area is again home to many of the species native to the region, including the lynx, which was reintroduced in the San Juan Mountains beginning in 1999[26] (see Chapter 7 for more of the lynx story). Several intentional introductions of non-native species in the upper Animas region have altered its native diversity.

"Enhancing" nature with new game animals. Unlike elk and deer, bighorn sheep, once common in the upper Animas, never recovered from

the unregulated hunting of the late 1800s (see Chapter 4 on the bighorn sheep decline). So in 1964 about 100 mountain goats, which are native to the Pacific Northwest, were introduced into the Needle Mountains near Chicago Basin.[27] They have flourished to the point of being a nuisance to campers. The goats have spread throughout the Needle Mountains but do not appear to be dispersing beyond them.[28]

Mountain goats can be strong competitors with bighorn sheep because they have a broader diet than the bighorns and are less sensitive to declines in food availability.[29] Bighorn sheep have not recovered across their range, largely because of introduced diseases that periodically kill large numbers.[30] Herds often recover slowly from these die-offs, and then as population increases, disease spreads and populations crash again. Modeling indicates that bighorn populations will not recover from these periodic die-offs where they share habitat with mountain goats; bighorns will persist only under heavy hunting to keep populations low enough to prevent the disease cycle and to keep mountain goats from outcompeting them.[31]

Heavy hunting would be politically difficult to institute in a popular area such as Chicago Basin, where mountain goats are habituated to people. So the presence of mountain goats could lead to the loss of native bighorns there. Meanwhile, bighorns are being transplanted to Animas Canyon—at considerable cost—in continued attempts to restore them to their former range.[32] Rather than learn from this mistake, in 1993 the Colorado Wildlife Commission declared mountain goats native to Colorado, even though scientific evidence clearly shows otherwise.[33]

Perhaps the most wide-reaching impact of game animal introductions has been with fish. Game fish have been widely introduced across the United States, greatly impacting native fish populations.[34] Little is known about the native fish in the upper Animas River, much less the nongame fish and macroinvertebrates[35] that inhabited the Animas River before mining began. It is possible that the high-elevation lakes, and possibly even the Animas River above the falls at Cascade Creek, never had native fish. In an early survey of the region undertaken in 1877, the only reference to fish mentions these falls as a barrier: "Near the beginning of the 'Box' Canon of the river there is descent above the average, and falls and rapids of the river interpose too great for the agility of the trout. While this fish of superior size and flavor may be taken in the Park below, none can be found in the Grand Canon [Animas Canyon] nor in Baker's Park above."[36] Early news articles from Silverton indicate that trout were rare or nonexistent in the Silverton area until they were stocked.[37] A native fish that may have reached into Animas Canyon is the endangered sculpin, which persists below Animas Canyon today.[38]

In 1885 non-native eastern brook trout (see Plate 42) were stocked in the Animas above Silverton, where water quality was reported as exceptionally pure.[39] Miners and early settlers quickly introduced rainbow and brook trout into numerous lakes and streams. Fishing in high-elevation lakes has become very popular, and in the 1960s the Colorado Division of Wildlife (CDOW) began to regularly stock non-native trout in most high-elevation lakes in the San Juans. However, in 1994 CDOW began a policy in the Weminuche Wilderness of only stocking cutthroat trout native to the Colorado River drainage.[40] More recently, CDOW began restoring native cutthroats in selected drainages where non-native trout can be eliminated or controlled. Restoring high-elevation lakes to fish-free status would be radical and unpopular; any unique aquatic communities that may have existed without fish have probably already been lost.

The Lime Creek burn and the introduction of lodgepole pine. Introduction of a tree may have much more far-reaching impacts in the upper Animas watershed than either mountain goats or non-native trout. In 1879 the Lime Creek fire burned 26,000 acres of spruce-fir forest west of Animas Canyon around Molas Pass. There has been much speculation that Utes started the fire, but despite a highway sign stating that it was human-caused, there is no clear evidence for this.[41] Fires were extensive during 1879 throughout western Colorado.[42]

The spruce forest failed to regenerate decades after the fire, so civic-minded folk from Durango decided to plant trees, beginning in earnest in about 1940. Spruce seedlings were in short supply, so they obtained seedlings of lodgepole pine.[43] Lodgepole pine is not native to this part of the San Juan Mountains; its natural distribution extends from Canada south only into the mountains southeast of Gunnison. Large patches of spruce and planted lodgepole can be seen in the vicinity of Molas Pass along Highway 550 and around Little Molas Lake (see Plate 43). Unlike spruce, whose cones are killed by fire, lodgepole pinecones are opened by fire, enabling them to reseed rapidly following fire. Thus, lodgepole pine might be expected to eventually spread beyond the area where it was planted, particularly when there are future fires in this area.

There is reason to be concerned about this non-native tree. In northern Sweden, where lodgepole pine has been grown since the 1970s in large plantations for wood production, Swedish scientists are now considering control or eradication of the species.[44] A scientific assessment suggested that significant ecological effects on native Swedish forests were likely if lodgepole pine is left in the landscape. The scientists also suggested ways to limit the possible spread of lodgepole pine into native Swedish forests, recognizing that the tree can be extremely invasive in some places. In New Zealand, for example, the government has been attempting to control lodgepole pine, which spread to about 250,000 acres after introduction.[45]

The spread of lodgepole pine forests at the expense of spruce-fir forest in the San Juans could affect a variety of species. Introduced trees typically bring new pathogens, insects, and other organisms that may affect native trees and other plants, which may lack natural defenses.[46] Lodgepole pine would likely have a negative effect on several birds in the region. In Colorado, the boreal owl, three-toed woodpecker, golden-crowned kinglet, and pine grosbeak all depend heavily on spruce-fir forests. Some birds, such as crossbills, are highly specialized to exploit a single common tree species for food.[47] White-winged crossbills in Colorado have bills specialized to exploit spruce, not pine.[48] Conversely, most birds that use lodgepole pine also use a wide variety of other forests, so the spread of lodgepole is unlikely to benefit other species.[49]

Large stand-replacing fires occur naturally in spruce-fir forests at infrequent intervals, and the slow regeneration of spruce after the 1879 fire was almost certainly a natural phenomenon.[50] Some parts of the burn area still have not regenerated to spruce and fir (see Figure 6.5); it is not uncommon for it to take 50–100 years before trees return to high-elevation burned sites. Parts of the burn may remain as meadows, which is also not uncommon.[51] Some subalpine meadows, which are rich in plant species and offer important forage for wildlife, owe their existence to infrequent natural fires and delayed tree regeneration.

Replanting the forest was a plantation approach, rooted in an agricultural view of forest management with a focus on trees rather than the entire ecosystem. Laments over the loss of forests to natural fires, insects, and diseases are still common, as if these were tragedies not only for the people impacted by them but also for the natural world. However, mortality of trees as a result of these natural agents has been part of the forest ecosystem for millennia—so much so that burned, diseased, dead, and dying trees support considerable native biological diversity.[52]

The lodgepole pine forests in this region are a utilitarian legacy—a legacy that is still unfolding. Lodgepole could simply fail and disappear because it is not adapted to the San Juans, or it could remain where it is right now. More likely, it could spread farther in the San Juans, transforming much more of the landscape. As in Sweden, society may still have a choice about whether to remove lodgepole pine before it becomes infeasible.

Figure 6.5. *The Lime Creek burn (a) in about* A.D. *1915 (photographer unknown) and (b) in* A.D. *2000. (a) Courtesy, San Juan County Historical Society, Silverton, Colorado.*

WHAT IS HAPPENING NOW?

The major forces influencing the natural landscape of the high country surrounding Silverton today differ noticeably from those of other places covered in this book. Rather than population growth and subdivision of agricultural lands, San Juan County experienced a 26 percent decline in population between 1990 and 2002.[53] Ghosts of the past and premonitions of the future hang in the air of the San Juan high country. The ghost is the environmental legacy of the hard-rock mining industry; the premonition is the rapidly growing recreational use of public lands, which make up most of the upper Animas watershed. Mining itself has not made a comeback to date, but mining tourism and wilderness recreation are beginning to flourish.

Inheritance of a Mined Landscape

The mining history of Silverton and the surrounding high country is a paradoxical mix of blessing and bane. The historical landscape of the early mining industry is a source of pride and community identity and a major tourism resource. Less visible and less welcome are the lasting impacts of pollution on the watershed's streams and waters. Most of the mining companies that caused the pollution came and went long before there was much appreciation for the damage they were doing. Left behind are many orphaned mine sites, with small absentee owners who never profited from the mining, and one major mining company (Sunnyside Gold Corporation, a subsidiary of Echo Bay Mining Company) trying to finish its reclamation work and responsibilities in the basin.[54]

Animas Forks: From mining to tourism. Approaching what was once the mining community of Animas Forks in midsummer, one is struck most immediately by the wildflowers rather than the signs of a mined landscape. Tall, pinkish purple fireweed and yellow-flowered tall blacktip ragwort line the rocky roadside. The wildflower display on the meadows around Animas Forks is one of the most spectacular and diverse accessible to two-wheel-drive vehicles above Silverton (see Plate 44). One can easily find fifty species of flowers and grasses in the subalpine meadows here (see Table 6.1). Long patches of grayleaf willow run up the mountainside. These stripes and patches of willow characterize the tree-line area in the San Juan Mountains but are not so common farther north.

The San Juan Mountains are the first major mountains encountered by moist tropical air of the North American Monsoon, flowing north

Table 6.1. Some common plants of alpine meadows near tree line and subalpine meadows in southwestern Colorado.[1]

SHRUBS
  Diamondleaf willow (*Salix planifolia*)
  Grayleaf willow (*Salix glauca*)

FORBS
  American bistort (*Polygonum bistortoides*)
  Beautiful cinquefoil (*Potentilla pulcherrima*)
  Brook saxifrage (*Saxifraga odontoloma*)
  Colorado blue columbine (*Aquilegia coerulea*)
  Colorado false hellebore (*Veratrum tenuipetalum*)
  Columbian monkshood (*Aconitum columbianum*)
  Common yarrow (*Achillea lanulosa* subsp. *alpicola*)
  Elephanthead lousewort (*Pedicularis groenlandica*)
  Fendler's meadow-rue (*Thalictrum fendleri*)
  Fireweed (*Epilobium angustifolium*)
  Giant red Indian paintbrush (*Castilleja miniata*)
  Hairy false goldenaster (*Heterotheca villosa*)
  Heartleaf arnica (*Arnica cordifolia*)
  Heartleaf bittercress (*Cardamine cordifolia*)
  Ledge stonecrop (*Rhodiola integrifolia*)
  Meadow deathcamas (*Zigadenus venenosum*)
  Owl's-claws (Orange sneezeweed) (*Helenium hoopesii*)
  Parry's primrose (*Primula parryi*)
  Richardson's geranium (*Geranium richardsonii*)
  Rocky Mountain goldenrod (*Solidago multiradiata*)
  Ross' avens (*Geum turbinatum*)
  Seep monkeyflower (*Mimulus guttatus*)
  Showy alpine ragwort (*Ligularia amplectens*)
  Sickletop lousewort (*Pedicularis racemosa*)
  Silky phacelia (*Phacelia sericea*)
  Splitleaf Indian paintbrush (*Castilleja rhexifolia*)
  Subalpine fleabane (*Erigeron peregrinus*)
  Subalpine larkspur (*Delphinium barbeyi*)
  Tall blacktip ragwort (*Senecio atratus*)
  Tall fringed bluebells (*Mertensia ciliate*)
  Twinflower sandwort (*Minuartia obtusiloba*)
  Varileaf cinquefoil (*Potentilla diversifolia*)
  Virginia strawberry (*Fragaria virginiana* var. *glauca*)
  Western Indian paintbrush (*Castilleja occidentalis*)
  Whipple's penstemon (*Penstemon whippleanus*)
  White marsh marigold (*Caltha leptosepala*)

GRASSES
  Parry's oatgrass (*Danthonia parryi*)
  Thurber's fescue (*Festuca thurberi*)
  Tufted hairgrass (*Deschampsia cespitosa*)

1. Common names are from the PLANTS online database, http://plants.usda.gov. Latin names are from Weber and Wittmann, *Colorado Flora*.

from the Gulfs of Mexico and California between about July 1 and September 15 each year.[55] This moist, unstable air leads to afternoon cloudiness, with thundershowers and lightning, but it can also rain for days. These mountains are, as a result, much wetter in the summer than mountains to the north in Colorado. Trees grow faster, meadows are more lush, and waterfalls and rushing streams are more abundant.

The road to Animas Forks is part of the Alpine Loop National Back Country Byway, an old mule road built by miners in the late 1800s to connect Silverton, Lake City, and Ouray. Although wildflowers and spectacular mountain scenery are major attractions, remnants of the early mining era, including eleven town sites along the route, are a major draw for many. Most area guidebooks include some of the many photographs taken during the mining era.

That this high, remote mountain country, which is snow-free for only a couple of months a year, once hosted a booming economy and small towns is hard to imagine. A retake of an early photograph of Animas Forks shows how the town disappeared after the mine became inactive (see Figure 6.6). In 1885 the town had 450 people. The large Gold Prince mill (not visible in the photograph) was built in 1904 and closed in 1910.[56] Trees that have grown up on the lower part of the hillside just left of the town site in the photo had eighty-five to ninety annual tree rings when we cored them in 1998. They sprouted around 1910, about the time the mill closed. At the town site a small mine opening is still visible, and lots of metal pieces and debris are lying around. Clearly, this area was heavily impacted, but it is now mostly a profusion of wildflowers and other native plants, with virtually no non-natives. This suggests that even at this high elevation, moist areas disturbed by logging, construction, and trampling can recover after episodes of human disturbance.

For the community of Silverton, these remnants of nineteenth- and early-twentieth-century mining are important economic assets. More than a quarter of San Juan County's labor force is engaged in "arts, entertainment, recreation, accommodation and food services."[57] The San Juan County Historical Society is working hard to preserve its cultural landscape, including its old mine buildings and other sites (see Figure 6.7). This resource has an unexamined complexity, however. As in the Canyons of the Ancients, where nature has strongly reclaimed sites that were once hubs of ancient Puebloan activity, it is the juxtaposition of nature and society across time on this land that fascinates and draws people at some deep level.

Unlike most historical cultural resources, old mines carry a high price. An estimated 80–90 percent of the Animas River floodplain between

Figure 6.6. *Animas Forks (a) taken as late as* A.D. *1885 (photographer unknown) and (b) same spot in* A.D. *2003. (a) Courtesy, San Juan County Historical Society, Silverton, Colorado.*

Figure 6.7. *The Mayflower Gold mill, just upstream of the Sunnyside mine tailings (see Figure 6.8).*

Silverton and Animas Forks has been altered by mining and related human activities.[58] The legacy of the Gold Prince mine and others remains in the river itself. The headwaters of the Animas River are so heavily laden with metals that no aquatic life exists until downstream, where Eureka Gulch and other tributaries begin to dilute the heavily contaminated waters.[59] The scope of the pollution is huge, but the community has tried an innovative approach to address the legacies of its mining history.

Stakeholder decision making: A new model for mined-land cleanup? The story of cleanup on the upper Animas is a complex tale of government action and local resistance and collaboration combined with scientific uncertainty. It is an important tale because mining has had a significant impact on streams in many parts of Colorado and the West. The stream pollutants that are the focus of the story (e.g., lead, zinc, manganese, aluminum, iron) are mostly metals that are left behind by mining or that drain out of mine tunnels but that can also leach into streams naturally from highly mineralized geologic formations. There is the rub— how much is natural? The upper Animas is a key place to understand the story because here the regulatory government agencies tried an alternative approach: they empowered a local group of citizens and other stakeholders to study the problem, then propose and help implement a cleanup plan. Many people are watching this process to see whether it will be a model for future cleanup of mining-affected streams in other areas.

To understand the story, the responsible government agencies and groups must be introduced. First is the Environmental Protection Agency (EPA), the federal agency that regulates water quality under the federal Clean Water Act and that could potentially oversee cleanup. Second is the state of Colorado's Water Quality Control Commission (WQCC), called here the Water Commission, which consists of nine members appointed by the governor. The Water Commission develops specific water-quality policies and regulations under the Colorado Water Quality Control Act, which generally mirrors the Clean Water Act. Third is the state of Colorado's Water Quality Control Division (the Water Division), which serves as professional staff and handles enforcement of regulations for the Water Commission. Finally is the local group, the Animas River Stakeholders Group (the Stakeholders Group), an ad hoc volunteer group whose members include local people, mining companies, and various government agencies.

Many historic mining districts have lost local control of cleanup, having come under the control of the Comprehensive Environmental Response, Compensation and Liability Act, also known as Superfund. Under Superfund, the EPA or any other entity or individual can sue current or past owners and operators of sites and require cleanup of hazardous substances. Superfund enables EPA to force a former mine owner or current landowner to remediate. EPA may also do the cleanup itself and charge the landowner or other responsible parties for the cost, when they can be located and have assets.

One advantage of Superfund is that it usually provides significant federal funding for cleanup, which helps if former owners cannot be found and current property owners lack the financial means for remediation. However, loss of control over private property and a drop in property values usually associated with Superfund make it unpopular with local communities that might come under Superfund designation.[60] In Silverton there is also concern that the mining district's cultural resources would be damaged or destroyed under Superfund.

The Stakeholders Group was formed in 1994 with initial funding from a Clean Water Act Section 319 grant and other EPA funding.[61] The Water Division proposed to upgrade water-quality standards and classification for the Animas River to bring it into compliance with state regulations and the Clean Water Act.[62] The standards proposed included water-quality goals that must be reached within a certain time period, so they are called "goal-based" standards.

The Stakeholders Group questioned whether the river segments around Silverton could be reclaimed sufficiently to achieve the standards proposed by the Water Division. Some stakeholders also were concerned about setting standards too high, thereby precluding future small-scale mining. The Stakeholders Group wanted a cooperative approach that would avoid the regulatory inflexibility and litigative atmosphere typical of Superfund. After a hearing in 1994, the Water Commission gave the Stakeholders Group six years (three years and a three-year extension) to gain a better understanding of the basin and to produce a Use Attainability Analysis.[63] The purpose was to determine (1) the sources of metals entering streams in the upper Animas River watershed, (2) the biological impacts of various metals, and (3) what levels of reclamation are feasible.

In 1994 relatively little was known about either the water quality needed to support various components of aquatic life or the specific sources of water pollution in the upper Animas Basin.[64] Historical records from the early mining period, before human impacts were large, suggest great variation in water quality within the basin. Stocked trout thrived in the Animas River above Cement Creek in the early days.[65] An 1885 news article suggested, however, that highly mineralized Cement Creek (see Plate 45) prevented trout movement below its confluence with the Animas.[66] Mineral Creek was also reported in this article to be too mineralized for trout.

The Use Attainability Analysis was completed in 2001.[67] A product of many hours of volunteer and contracted work, the report incorporates large volumes of data collected at considerable expense over the six-year period. As a consequence of this process, pollution sources and biological impacts in the upper Animas Basin are much better understood than in most Colorado mining districts.

With completion of the Use Attainability Analysis, the Stakeholders Group laid out its position on the level of remediation needed and the water-quality standards attainable for the basin's streams. At a cost of almost $30 million, the Stakeholders Group proposed to remediate thirty-four draining mine adits and thirty-two mining waste sites that account for 90 percent of the identified mining sources of metals. The Stakeholders Group noted that even this level of remediation would be difficult because few funding sources are available to achieve it.[68]

The water-quality standards the Stakeholders Group proposed were the current conditions minus the expected reduction in metals when all proposed remediation projects are complete. For many stream segments and metals, the standards are not improvements over current levels.[69] For the upper Animas Canyon, the stream segment that reflects the water quality leaving the entire mining district, the standards for zinc, iron, and copper are about a 20 percent improvement over current conditions.[70] Bill Simon, coordinator of the Stakeholders Group, acknowledged that the percentage improvement is small numerically but said it is all that is feasible given the high contribution of metals from natural sources.[71] The more important measure of success, he argued, is improvement within the aquatic community. The Stakeholders Group believes the introduced brook trout, which are tolerant of zinc, will become healthier and that macroinvertebrates will increase with even the small proposed reductions in metals.[72]

The Water Division, however, challenged the Use Attainability Analysis primarily on the grounds that the Stakeholders Group had failed to address a large source of metals, which the latter called "groundwater."[73] Because it was impossible to distinguish mining and natural contributions of metals to groundwater, the Stakeholders Group excluded this major source of metals from remediation consideration. The Water Division's position was that while human and natural sources may not be easily separated, the historical use of dynamite in the region had greatly fractured the mountains and clearly increased metal loadings, so the goal should be to improve water quality in the most effective way, not to remediate only known human-caused sources.[74] The Water Division also argued that (1) the method used to estimate metals coming from mine waste piles underestimated their contribution, (2) the metal loading coming from the Sunnyside tailings (see Figure 6.8) was not measured, and (3) Jeep roads built with mine wastes (still practiced by San Juan County) were not addressed.[75] Essentially, the Water Division believed higher water-quality standards could be attained.

The Water Division suggested one alternative cleanup approach: to use treatment plants at key points, removing both natural and human-caused metals, so that higher water-quality standards could be achieved downstream.[76] Drawbacks of this approach are that, first, since the sources of pollution are not reclaimed, treatment can never end, and second, sludge (also a toxic material that must be safely stored) is produced indefinitely. Treatment plants would also disturb the stream channel and vegetation wherever they are placed.

In spite of the Water Division's concerns, the Water Commission accepted the Stakeholders Group's recommendation with relatively few changes. This was the first case in the state in which biological standards were adopted for some stream segments.[77] Brook trout must be maintained in the stream segments in which they now exist.[78] Two stream

Figure 6.8. *Looking upstream at the Sunnyside mine tailings piles.*

segments, the upper Animas Canyon (down to Deer Park Creek) and the main stem of Mineral Creek, were downgraded from Aquatic Life Class 1 status to Class 2 status in response to the Use Attainability Analysis finding that these segments naturally could not support the high level of aquatic life of a Class 1 stream. The commission did agree with the Water Division that the Stakeholders Group must further study the Sunnyside tailings' contribution to metal loadings in the stream.

The Animas River Stakeholders Group's willingness and ability to tackle such a complex problem as watershed-scale mine reclamation are remarkable and encouraging, but from the standpoint of water quality and natural stream community restoration, was this process a success? It is difficult for an outside observer to judge, since different expert parties do not agree on what is feasible. The outcome would have been more satisfying and credible if the Water Division had been more closely involved in the Use Attainability Analysis. Unfortunately, the Water Division has limited resources to take part in a process such as the Stakeholders Group, especially because its staff is located hours away in Denver. Thus, the "stakeholder" whose mission it was to push for the highest achievable standards did not play a large role in the process and in the end was critical of the outcome. Had all the entities worked together on the Use Attainability Analysis, there would probably still be uncertainty but not competing claims about what can be accomplished.

Local working groups' inability to effectively include distant stakeholders remains one of these groups' biggest weaknesses.

Ultimately, the value of the Stakeholders Group's work will depend on the future political and economic climate. It is encouraging that the Stakeholders Group has remained very active since the water standards were accepted, seeking and obtaining funding to conduct numerous remedial actions. Monitoring of water quality and macroinvertebrates had shown mixed results as of 2005.[79] However, if efforts continue, the wealth of knowledge already accumulated on sources of metals and biological tolerances, and the skills and relationships built within the working group, will be invaluable in restoring the upper Animas Basin.

Yet society must address a larger question: At what point are the costs of cleanup too high relative to potential gains for the environment? Is the increase in invertebrates and brook trout that will be achieved with the proposed $30 million cleanup worth the cost and effort, or would that money be better spent on restoration or preservation elsewhere? Philosopher Robert Frodeman, who has studied the upper Animas and other mine reclamation projects, suggests that motivations for cleaning up mined landscapes are deep and not strictly economic: "There is on the part of many an intuition that there has been something wrong with the way we have behaved. We have mistreated the natural world, and we are under some type of obligation to correct our mistakes."[80] While this may be true, resources are limited and mistakes were many. Mined landscapes present society with difficult choices.

A Role for Land Trusts in Historic Mining Districts?

One of the difficulties of cleaning up the landscape of historic mining districts, such as the upper Animas, is that many of the people who have inherited small mined land claims have no funds for restoration. Recently, a small, innovative land trust (see Box—Land Trusts, pp. 128–129) was formed to address this issue. Started in 1999 by Ridgway mayor Pat Willits, the Trust for Land Restoration (TLR)[81] is opening new paths for land protection trusts. Willits, who formerly worked for The Nature Conservancy in western Colorado, had noted the reluctance of land trusts to work with lands that have significant liability as a result of past mining activities, especially liability under the Clean Water Act. Many private lands deserving and needing protection in the Rocky Mountains have such a history. The TLR has worked to find ways for itself, other land trusts, and government agencies to negotiate complicated liability issues on mined lands.[82]

To educate itself about the legal landscape, TLR took on some difficult land conservation projects on abandoned mine lands in Colorado. Its approach has been to work with counties to identify mine lands that are environmentally significant and that also have a manageable liability risk. TLR then helped to purchase those properties, carry out the needed mine site cleanup, and transfer the properties to the county or another government entity. It has freely shared its lessons with other land trusts and government agencies.[83]

The work of TLR helped bring about a major change in federal law in 2002 that makes it easier for land trusts to restore and protect mined landscapes. Brownfields law has helped fund and facilitate the reclamation of contaminated industrial sites for economic reuse, mostly in poor urban areas. The new brownfields legislation added scarred mine lands to the types of sites considered brownfields and added open space as a legitimate economic reuse.[84] Good Samaritan legislation, which would exempt individuals and entities who are trying to clean up abandoned mine sites from certain liabilities and would help efforts to remediate lands with mining liability, has also been proposed. Such legislation has been controversial because some versions would exempt not only nonprofit groups but also companies that benefited from the mining.[85] Good Samaritan legislation introduced in 2006 would grant Samaritan status to the Animas River Stakeholders Group for a ten-year pilot program.[86]

The Weminuche Wilderness

In spite of the mining legacy, the San Juan high country is now some of the region's wildest land. A substantial part of the Animas River watershed is in the officially designated 500,000-acre Weminuche Wilderness area. It is no coincidence that the mountains that became wilderness never produced rich mineral finds. Numerous small mines dot the wilderness's high country, but the gold and silver veins were not extensive,[87] and large mines, mills, and permanent settlements did not become part of this landscape. Mining camps were located in the Needle Mountains in the heart of the Weminuche in the late 1800s but were short-lived.[88]

A large portion of what became the Weminuche Wilderness was officially designated San Juan and Rio Grande primitive areas as early as 1932.[89] Exploration for molybdenum in Chicago Basin in 1960 fortunately produced no high-grade ore,[90] or the area could have been transformed beyond reclamation. The Climax Molybdenum Company, which held mining claims around Chicago Basin, has removed mountainsides above Leadville in its production of molybdenum. Instead, by declaring the Weminuche Wilderness in 1975, society decided to allow this area to continue its return to a wilder and more natural state.[91]

Wilderness, according to the 1964 Wilderness Act, is "an area where the earth and its community of life are untrammeled by man, where man himself is a visitor who does not remain." But the Wilderness Act also stipulates that wilderness areas should be administered for the "use and enjoyment of the American people" while protecting their wilderness values.[92] Today, people are only visitors, but as the number of visitors increases, they can significantly alter a wilderness.

Wilderness under stress: Chicago Basin. Most of the wilderness in southwestern Colorado does not suffer the impacts typical of wilderness areas near large population centers, but one area in the heart of the Weminuche may foreshadow future trends. Chicago Basin is an internationally known climbing and hiking destination, famous for its spectacular setting at the base of Windom, Sunlight, and Eolus peaks (see Figure 6.9). These Fourteeners, mountains over 14,000 feet tall, are sought by climbers eager to conquer the tallest peaks in the western United States. Access to the trailhead via the historic Durango-Silverton narrow-gauge train is easy and attractive for backpackers (see Figure 6.10). Chicago Basin has become one of the most popular wilderness destinations in western Colorado, hosting about 17,000 visitor-days in 2000, mostly in July and August.[93]

Campsites are a problem in Chicago Basin. Many of the groups coming into the basin are not experienced in wilderness travel. They arrive late after a six-mile uphill struggle, looking for a place to camp. The trail runs near Needle Creek, and every flat spot with a view has become a campsite. Many are within 100 feet of the stream where camping is banned. Fecal contamination of the stream has not been studied, but wilderness managers believe it is a serious problem.[94] Campsites exist in the trees away from the trail, but few search for or find them. Almost every summer morning, wilderness rangers must move people off illegal campsites too near the stream. In response, the Forest Service closed a dozen campsites (mostly those too near water) in September 2001, hoping campers will start using new campsites farther from the stream.[95]

Wilderness managers use a conceptual and planning framework called "Limits to Acceptable Change" to negotiate a path between the sometimes contradictory goals of wilderness use and preservation. One of these goals must be given ultimate priority over the other—in wilderness management, wilderness values are usually the ultimate goal,

Figure 6.9. *Meadow in Chicago Basin, Weminuche Wilderness.*

and minimum criteria are set beyond which these values cannot be compromised by the competing goal of public access.[96] Wilderness management, then, moves beyond the ideals and philosophy of wilderness to the nuts and bolts of what is allowed where.

Figure 6.10. *Needleton train stop with backpackers unloading.*

Chicago Basin (and the Needle Creek drainage leading to it) was designated a semi-primitive management area in the San Juan–Rio Grande Forest Wilderness Management Plan.[97] Wilderness is usually managed for pristine or primitive condition. Pristine areas provide maximum solitude and are places where "natural processes and conditions have not and will not be *measurably* [emphasis added] affected by human use."[98] Most of the area of the Weminuche is designated as pristine. Most established trails and destinations along them are, in contrast, designated as primitive areas. Primitive areas offer moderate solitude and are places where "natural processes and conditions have not and will not be *significantly* [emphasis added] affected by human activity."[99] Semi-primitive areas, in contrast, "are managed to protect natural conditions while providing for use and enjoyment of the recreational and natural features."[100]

Each category of wilderness (pristine, primitive, semi-primitive) has a narrative description of the desired condition and associated numeric standards and guidelines. The standards and guidelines for the semi-primitive category clearly bend the definition of wilderness as "untrammeled." Up to six campsites per linear mile are allowed in semi-primitive management areas, and 40 percent of these can be of larger size classes with significant impacts on vegetation. The crowding guideline specifies that a hiker will encounter no more than twelve other parties in an eight-hour period and will not be within sight or earshot of more than three other campsites. Visitation to Chicago Basin continues to increase, and the impacts of use surpass even some of the lenient standards of a semi-primitive area.[101]

This was not Aldo Leopold's idea of wilderness, but few wilderness advocates would want to see a place such as Chicago Basin excluded from wilderness designation because of its popularity. Campsite density and condition class are above thresholds, and the Forest Service could begin implementing a quota permit system.[102] This appears unlikely in the near future, however. Public comment during preparation of the forest's Wilderness Management Plan included significant opposition to limiting access to the wilderness through quotas or other means.[103]

To date, the Forest Service has relied heavily on the education of visitors to minimize impacts to the ecosystem, although some restrictions have also been put in place. A ban on campfires in Chicago Basin has been helpful in minimizing ecological impacts. Camping at Twin Lakes, which had been a high-elevation camp for climbers, is now banned, although the fragile alpine tundra will likely require years to heal (see Plate 46).

One might expect that maintaining naturalness in a wilderness would be low-cost, if not free. Do not do anything, and nature will prevail. But enforcing regulations, monitoring use and impacts, maintaining trails, and controlling weeds are all required to ensure that an area's many visitors do not seriously compromise its wilderness qualities. To adequately protect just the westernmost portion of the Weminuche (where Chicago Basin is located) requires seven rangers for the summer months (mid-June through September). Salary, training, uniforms, supplies, and travel for rangers cost about $140,000 in 2001.[104] So compared with the $8–$9 million budgeted for forestry on the entire forest,[105] wilderness management is cheap. Still, some years wilderness management's budget is only $80,000–$100,000, and fewer rangers are hired.[106] To fill the gap, one innovative group coordinates a volunteer program.

Innovative volunteer programs. The San Juan and Rio Grande national forests have found wilderness volunteers highly successful in reducing the impacts of visitors, thus minimizing the need for policing. A Wilderness Information Specialist program was started in 1989 as a way to implement the newly adopted fire ban in Chicago Basin; it is now an integral part of wilderness protection in the Weminuche Wilderness. A

Figure 6.11. *Ghost Rider volunteer talking to visitors in the Weminuche Wilderness. Courtesy, Kathe Hayes, San Juan Mountains Association, Durango, Colorado.*

Ghost Riders program provides similar volunteers on horseback to work with fellow equestrians (see Figure 6.11), and a Cultural Site Steward-ship program has recently begun enlisting volunteers to "adopt" An-cestral Puebloan and other cultural sites on public lands in southwest-ern Colorado.[107] All of these programs and others are operated by the San Juan Mountains Association (SJMA), a nonprofit, nonpolitical group that works in partnership with the Forest Service and other land man-agement agencies in southwestern Colorado. The SJMA's mission is to promote community stewardship of natural and cultural resources through educational programs and volunteer opportunities.[108]

Wilderness Information Specialists (WISes) volunteer to spend a week or several weekends in the Weminuche each summer. They must have their own backpacking gear and transportation and attend a one-day training session, where they learn wilderness regulations. Each volunteer wears a uniform and serves as a goodwill ambassador on the trail. Volunteers emphasize "the authority of the resource" rather than regulations.

A typical day for a WIS volunteer involves hiking a trail in the wilder-ness area; offering information about the weather, water, and wildlife to visitors; and picking up litter. WIS volunteers hand out tiny brochures and discuss Leave No Trace Outdoors Principles with campers. These principles were developed as a way to visit and camp in the wilderness with the least amount of impact. If a WIS volunteer encounters a group that refuses to follow regulations, he or she reports the situation to a ranger. As volunteers and visitors become skillful in using the wilderness as lightly as possible, this becomes a community norm.[109]

The WIS program places seventy-five to eighty volunteers in the field each year. Funding for the small staff comes from membership, fund-raising events, local businesses, and grants from sources such as the Colorado State Historical Society. The SJMA has been a model for community stewardship programs on public lands and has won numerous awards, including a $10,000 award from the El Pomar Foundation for Excellence in Environmental Education.[110]

The meaning of wilderness. It is interesting to note the difference between the wilderness *experience* and the naturalness of a wilderness area. Naturalness is the way the nonhuman world would proceed without human intervention. Wilderness experience is compromised only by the perception of excessive human presence and influence. The number of other visitors, signs, and regulations encountered influences one's wilderness experience. Wilderness managers, therefore, avoid the use of signs that would indicate areas along streams where people should not camp, even though doing so means moving campers from those areas every morning.

How much human presence is too much varies depending upon one's background. Obvious alterations of the natural environment—clear-cuts, for example—are recognized as human in origin and diminish the wilderness experience for most people. On the other hand, most visitors do not recognize non-native plants and noxious weeds. The trail up to Chicago Basin has patches of weedy non-native species, including white clover. The invasion of non-native weeds into the natural world may have no effect on most people's wilderness experience, although the presence of non-natives diminishes the physical wilderness (and the wilderness experience of those who recognize them). Similarly, if one does not recognize that 150 years ago bighorn sheep, not mountain goats, were in Chicago Basin, one will not perceive any loss in wilderness value as a result of that change. Yet the wilderness value of naturalness has been compromised.

Perhaps the most insidious impact on the naturalness of the Weminuche Wilderness is that of nearby oil and gas development and coal-burning power plants on air quality. Nitrates in rainfall at high elevations in the San Juan Mountains are at much higher levels than occur naturally. Nitrates create acid rain, impacting the entire ecosystem of higher elevations. A major source of these nitrates appears to be coal-fired power plants in northwestern New Mexico. The Four Corners plant, which powers 300,000 homes from Texas to California, is large and not very clean; among power plants it was the number-one producer of nitrogen oxide in 2004.[111] The nearby San Juan Generating Station is also a big producer of nitrogen oxide, carbon dioxide, and mercury. Mercury contamination has resulted in advisories limiting fish consumption from San Juan Basin lakes and reservoirs. A visible haze obscures the mountains at times, yet more power plants are slated to be built in the region.[112] Over 10,000 natural gas wells planned in the San Juan Basin of southern Colorado and New Mexico would further reduce air quality.[113] More than wilderness values are under threat. Nearer the source of emissions, in northern New Mexico, ozone levels are already high enough to damage children's lungs, aggravate asthma, and increase susceptibility to respiratory infections.[114]

Most people would probably agree that the actual naturalness of a place, not just one's perception of it, is an important wilderness value. Of course, any understanding of naturalness and human impacts is a perception, but some perceptions are more informed and accurate than others. Can major human impacts to the naturalness of a wilderness area—alteration of entire plant communities through acid rain deposition, for example—be ignored simply because most visitors do not perceive the change? Unfortunately, even local threats, such as noxious weeds, are effectively ignored because the limited resources for management are spent according to public pressure. That is why it is important for a critical mass of people to be literate about the natural world and advocate that wilderness retain its naturalness. Without that political constituency, people's enjoyment will take precedence over "untrammeled" wilderness.

Nature's Own Legacies in the Animas River Canyon

Some of the most natural places are not official wilderness and even have a substantial human presence. The Animas River Canyon is one of those places (see Figure 6.12). Animas Canyon, which extends from Cascade Creek to Elk Park—about thirteen miles—contains the most extensive reach of mid-elevation riparian vegetation in a relatively natural state in southwestern Colorado.[115] River floodplains are obvious places for farms, ranches, towns, and transportation routes. Livestock spend disproportionate time in riparian areas for shade, the comparatively moist and lush forage, and water, leading to degradation of the

Figure 6.12. *Animas River near Needleton.*

riparian environment—a widespread problem in the West.[116] The Animas River Canyon has largely escaped these impacts. There were a few early homesteads, including a dairy herd in Elk Park in Animas Canyon, but after transportation was established between Silverton and Durango, these isolated homesteads quickly disappeared.[117]

The train route from Durango to Silverton through the canyon was completed in 1882. The track constrains the river somewhat, is a source of weeds, and alters river-flow patterns in places; and the train has been responsible for some fires. Needleton at one time had a store and supplied miners in Chicago Basin. A placer mining claim at Needleton was patented and then sold, eventually becoming the cabin sites that are there today. People who come to fish, raft, hike, ride horses, or engage in other activities bring non-native plants and other influences, although to date, these effects appear comparatively minor. Pack animals have overgrazed some meadows and forest areas. The legacies are thus numerous, but the river vegetation as a whole remains remarkably natural.[118]

Relatively undisturbed riparian vegetation has considerable scientific value, and the canyon is a good place to understand the effect of floods on such vegetation.[119] By dating trees growing in patches along the river, one can determine when they were born. Patches are then mapped by decade of origin (see Map 6.3). All of the area presently containing riparian forests has been affected by floods over the last two centuries, and most patches of forest originated after periods of high river flow or known floods within the past 150 years. A new patch is likely created when floodwaters cut across a forested gravel bar, perhaps especially if logs, boulders, or debris serve as battering rams during a flood. Flows large enough to originate a single new stand along the reach occur about every 10 years, and flows large enough to create several new stands at once occur about every 15 years.[120] Many people may think of floods as disasters, and they are in some ways, but floods also maintain diversity along the riparian corridor.

The Animas River has experienced some exceptional floods in the past century. The huge floods on the river occurred in 1911 and 1927. During early October 1911 a tropical Pacific cyclone came onto land, swung across Arizona, and hit the San Juans, producing continuous rain for days. Needle Creek apparently exploded in flood, spitting large boulders into the Animas that then plowed into riparian forests downstream. A flood of this magnitude (about 25,000 cubic feet per second) has an estimated recurrence of once per 1,000 years.[121] Another flood, this one in June 1927, was approximately a 250-year flood (20,000 cubic feet per second), and it apparently removed much of the young vegetation established after the 1911 flood.[122] The Animas is a lively river even during a normal year, but much of the present landscape was shaped by these 1911 and 1927 floods, and revegetation has been slow.

A short distance down from the Needleton train stop is a boulder bar on which most of the trees date back to just after the 1927 flood. It was probably a mature forest before that flood. Photos of this site were taken in 1986 and 2001 to record vegetation change over time (see Figure 6.13). Visible in the photos are the main trees on the bar—narrowleaf cottonwood and blue spruce. The underground part of narrowleaf cottonwood may survive some floods and simply resprout afterward, but blue spruce must recolonize from seed. These two trees dominate early in the process of revegetation (or "plant succession") after a disturbance such as the 1927 flood. Since 1927 the vegetation has recovered very slowly, and almost no change occurred in the fifteen years between these photographs. The magnitude of the 1911 and 1927 floods may have exceeded the forest's capacity to regenerate and regrow quickly, and it is unclear whether these boulder bars will ever return to the pre-flood forest, yet they remain dominated by a diversity of native riparian plants.[123]

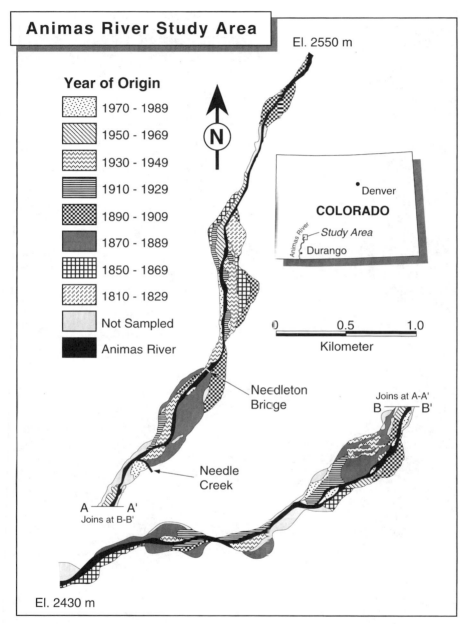

Map 6.3. *Patches of riparian vegetation originated during different periods along the Animas River in Animas Canyon. Reproduced from Baker and Walford (1995)*, An-nals of the Association of American Geographers *85:323, with permission of Blackwell Publishers, Cambridge, Massachusetts.*

Figure 6.13. *Rephotograph on a gravel bar on the Animas River downstream of Needleton train stop on the train side of the river in (a)* A.D. *1986 and (b)* A.D. *2001.*

Nature is usually considered resilient and capable of recovery from natural disturbances, with disturbances caused by people more likely to create legacies because those disturbances have often been more intense and qualitatively different from natural disturbances. Mining the upper Animas and depositing the metal-laden waste in the channel is an example. The exceptional floods of 1911 and 1927 created legacies that may be long-lasting in Animas Canyon but not in a way that clearly diminishes the ecosystem. We are left with a beautiful, diverse mountain river, still flowing under the spontaneous power of nature. Could the upper Animas have been mined, unquestionably with significant "rearrangement of nature's spontaneous course," in a way that left the river and uplands more diverse and alive?

CONCLUDING THOUGHTS

The extraction of the upper Animas's great mineral wealth enriched some individuals and the then-young United States, but it is questionable whether cultural gains were greater than the losses of the natural community, a criterion suggested by Holmes Rolston in the chapter's opening quote. The legacies of a century of hard-rock mining may be irreparable, at least in the river and its aquatic communities. Ironically, the most lasting contribution to the local economy and culture is the historical landscape of mining. Yet that landscape represents human cleverness and ambition, not wisdom. Rolston's equation was here seemingly turned on its head, minimizing the apparent cultural gain while leaving sizable legacies.

Today, people are trying to rebalance that equation. The Animas River Stakeholders Group began the process of learning about the nature of this place and making conscious choices about its future. In addition to restoration, the opportunity exists here to leave room for Rolston's "spontaneous nature." With elevations ranging from 9,000 to 14,000 feet, this is a place not well suited to a large human population, and nature in a wilderness state once again claims much of the landscape. An economy based primarily on appreciation of the natural world may be the most sustainable and most ethical human presence.

NOTES

1. Rolston, "Wilderness Idea Reaffirmed," 377.
2. Baker, "Changes in Riparian Vegetation.'
3. Ibid.
4. Baker, "Alpine Vegetation of Wheeler Peak, New Mexico."

5. Chronic and Williams, *Roadside Geology of Colorado*.
6. Ibid.
7. Benham, *Silverton and Neighboring Ghost Towns*.
8. See Web site for STATS Indiana, USA Counties in Profile: http://www.stats. indiana.edu/uspr/a/usprofiles/08/us_over_sub_pr08111.html.
9. Animas River Stakeholders Group, *Use Attainability Analysis*.
10. Jones, "History of Mining and Milling Practices."
11. Clements et al., "Heavy Metals Structure Benthic Communities."
12. Cited in Black, "Historical Accounts of Water Quality" (no page).
13. Animas River Stakeholders Group, *Use Attainability Analysis*, chapter 7, 9.
14. Jones, "History of Mining and Milling Practices."
15. Church, Fey, and Blair, "Pre-Mining Bed Sediment Geochemical Baseline."
16. Church et al., *Source, Transport, and Partitioning of Metals*.
17. Cited in Black, "Historical Accounts of Water Quality," B-17.
18. Simon, Horn, and Wegner, "Review of Animas Fisheries"; Moore, "Animas Trout Making a Comeback."
19. Jones, "History of Mining and Milling Practices," 12.
20. Reidhead, *Tour the San Juans*.
21. Ibid.
22. Vincent, Church, and Fey, "Geomorphological Context of Metal-Laden Sediments."
23. Church, Fey, and Blair, "Pre-Mining Bed Sediment Geochemical Baseline."
24. Church et al., *Source, Transport, and Partitioning of Metals*.
25. Hinshaw, *Crusaders for Wildlife*.
26. Colorado Division of Wildlife, *Wildlife in Danger*.
27. Bronaugh, "Field Study of Mountain Goat."
28. Scott Wait, wildlife biologist, Colorado Division of Wildlife, Durango, Colorado, pers. comm., August 5, 2002.
29. Dailey, Hobbs, and Woodward, "Diet Selection by Mountain Goats and Mountain Sheep."
30. Hinshaw, *Crusaders for Wildlife*.
31. Hobbs et al., "Criteria for Introductions of Large Mammals."
32. Sluis, "Bighorn Sheep Released in San Juans."
33. Fitzgerald, Meaney, and Armstrong, *Mammals of Colorado*.
34. Rahel, "Homogenization of Fish Faunas."
35. Macroinvertebrates are any animals without a visible backbone—mostly aquatic insects but also clams, snails, and crayfish.
36. Ruffner, *Annual Report upon Explorations and Surveys*, 1800.
37. Black, "Historical Accounts of Water Quality."
38. Simon, Horn, and Wegner, "Review of Animas Fisheries."
39. Ibid.; *La Plata Miner*, March 21, 1885, cited in Black, "Historical Accounts of Water Quality."
40. Mike Japhet, Colorado Division of Wildlife, fish biologist, Durango, Colorado, pers. comm., December 6, 2001.
41. Nossaman, *Many More Mountains. Vol. 2*.
42. Veblen, "Disturbance Patterns in Southern Rocky Mountain Forests."

43. Nossaman, *Many More Mountains, Vol. 2.*
44. Engelmark et al., "Ecological Effects and Management."
45. Ledgard, "Spread of Lodgepole Pine in New Zealand."
46. Engelmark et al., "Ecological Effects and Management."
47. Benkman, "Evolution of Crossbill Diversity."
48. Benkman, "White-Winged Crossbill"; Kingery, *Colorado Breeding Bird Atlas.*
49. Kingery, *Colorado Breeding Bird Atlas.*
50. Stahelin, "Natural Restocking of High Altitude Burns."
51. Ibid.
52. E.g., Castello, Leopold, and Smallidge, "Pathogens, Patterns, and Processes"; Bennetts et al., "Influence of Dwarf Mistletoe on Bird Communities."
53. See Web site for STATS Indiana, USA Counties in Profile: http://www.stats. indiana.edu/uspr/a/usprofiles/08/us_over_sub_pr08111.html.
54. Animas River Stakeholders Group, *Use Attainability Analysis*, chapter 4.
55. Adams and Comrie, "North American Monsoon."
56. Reidhead, *Tour the San Juans.*
57. See Web site for the U.S. Department of Commerce, Bureau of the Census, 2000 Census: http://factfinder.census.gov Summary File 3, table QT-P30, Industry by Sex—Percent Distribution.
58. Blair, "Progress Report on Surficial Deposits and Geomorphology."
59. Owen, "Water Quality and Sources of Metal Loading."
60. Animas River Stakeholders Group, *Use Attainability Analysis*, chapter 2.
61. State of Colorado, Water Quality Control Division, *Total Maximum Daily Load Assessment.*
62. Animas River Stakeholders Group, Meeting Summary, April 20, 2000, on file at Silverton Public Library, Silverton, Colorado.
63. Animas River Stakeholders Group, *Use Attainability Analysis.*
64. Barb Horn, aquatic biologist, Colorado Division of Wildlife, Durango, pers. comm., November 19, 2001.
65. Simon, Horn, and Wegner, "Review of Animas Fisheries."
66. *La Plata Miner*, March 21, 1885, cited in Black, "Historical Accounts of Water Quality."
67. Animas River Stakeholders Group, *Use Attainability Analysis.*
68. Prehearing Statement of Animas River Stakeholders Group, March 2001, Water Quality Control Commission Hearing, document at Silverton Public Library, Silverton, Colorado.
69. Animas River Stakeholders Group, *Use Attainability Analysis*, table 12.1; see Web site: http://www.cdphe.state.co.us/op/regs/100234tables.pdf.
70. See Web site: http://www.cdphe.state.co.us/op/regs/100234tables.pdf.
71. Bill Simon, coordinator, Animas River Stakeholders Group, Silverton, Colorado, pers. comm., November 28, 2001.
72. Barb Horn, aquatic biologist, Colorado Division of Wildlife, Durango, pers. comm., November 19, 2001.
73. Responsive Prehearing Statement of Water Quality Control Division, March 2001, WQCC Hearing, document at Silverton Public Library, Silverton, Colorado.

74. Sarah Johnson, Water Quality Control Division, Denver, Colorado, pers. comm., December 5, 2001.

75. Responsive Prehearing Statement of Water Quality Control Division, March 2001, WQCC Hearing, document at Silverton Public Library, Silverton, Colorado.

76. Rebuttal Statement of Water Quality Control Division, March 2001, WQCC Hearing, document at Silverton Public Library, Silverton, Colorado.

77. Peter Butler, Friends of the Animas River representative to Animas River Stakeholders Group, Durango, Colorado, pers. comm., November 23, 2001.

78. Animas River Stakeholders Group, *Use Attainability Analysis*, chapter 11.

79. Bill Simon, coordinator, Animas River Stakeholders Group, Silverton, Colorado, pers. comm., July 17, 2005.

80. Frodeman, "Sense of the Whole," 133.

81. See Web site: http://www.restorationtrust.org.

82. Pat Willits, Trust for Land Restoration, Ridgway, Colorado, pers. comm., July 30, 2002.

83. Ibid.

84. Rob Molacek, Land Trust Alliance, Grand Junction, Colorado, pers. comm., October 17, 2001; Pat Willits, Trust of Land Restoration, Ridgway, Colorado, pers. comm., July 30, 2002.

85. Stephanie Odell, Upper Animas Project manager, U.S. Forest Service and Bureau of Land Management, Durango, Colorado, pers. comm., November 21, 2001.

86. Rodebaugh, "Mine, River Cleanup—With a Twist."

87. Cross et al., "Description of Needle Mountains."

88. Boucher, *Walking in Wilderness*.

89. Ibid.

90. Schmitt and Raymond, *Geology and Mineral Deposits of the Needle Mountains*.

91. For an excellent account of the controversy generated in setting aside the half-million-acre Weminuche from logging, road building, motorized vehicles, and (eventually) mining, see Boucher, *Walking in Wilderness*.

92. Wilderness Act of 1964 (Public Law 88-577), Sec. 2 (a), (c), Congressional Record 110, Part 16, pp. 20626–20627.

93. Estimate based on trailhead registration data, Nancy Berry, wilderness specialist, U.S. Forest Service, Durango, Colorado, pers. comm., November 11, 2001.

94. Laura Johnson-Boudreux, Durango, Colorado, pers. comm., November 20, 2001.

95. Nancy Berry, wilderness specialist, U.S. Forest Service, Durango, Colorado, pers. comm., November 20, 2001.

96. Brunson, "Managing Naturalness."

97. U.S. Department of Agriculture, Forest Service, *Wilderness Management Direction*.

98. Ibid., II-29.

99. Ibid., II-32.

100. Ibid., II-35.

101. Ibid.
102. Ibid.
103. Nancy Berry, wilderness specialist, U.S. Forest Service, Durango, Colorado, pers. comm., November 20, 2001.
104. Ibid.
105. Linda Knipp, Budget Officer, San Juan National Forest, Durango, Colorado, pers. comm., December 5, 2001.
106. Nancy Berry, wilderness specialist, U.S. Forest Service, Durango, Colorado, pers. comm., November 20, 2001.
107. Kathy Hayes, volunteer services coordinator, San Juan Mountains Association, Durango, Colorado, pers. comm., November 29, 2001.
108. San Juan Mountains Association, *Echoes of the Land* [Durango, Colorado] (Spring 2001).
109. Kathy Hayes, volunteer services coordinator, San Juan Mountains Association, Durango, Colorado, pers. comm., November 29, 2001.
110. Ibid.
111. Rodebaugh, "Four Corners Emissions Rate Among Worst in United States."
112. Ibid.; Crane, "Planned Power Plant Causes Concern."
113. Associated Press, "Wells Create Fears of Increased Pollution."
114. University of New Mexico, Community Environmental Health Program, "Ozone and Your Health in the Four Corners"; see Web site: http://www.sanjuancitizens.org/hot_topics/ozone%20broch%20UNM-pdf.pdf; accessed May 10, 2006.
115. Baker, "Recent Changes in Riparian Vegetation."
116. Briggs, *Riparian Ecosystem Recovery in Arid Lands.*
117. Boucher, *Walking in Wilderness.*
118. Baker, "Recent Changes in Riparian Vegetation."
119. Baker, "Size-Structure of Riparian Woodlands"; Baker and Walford, "Multiple Stable States."
120. Baker, "Climatic and Hydrologic Effects on Regeneration."
121. Baker and Walford, "Multiple Stable States."
122. Ibid.
123. Ibid.

Plate 1. *Ancestral Puebloan Holly Ruin in Hovenweep Nationøl Monument.*

Plate 2. *Pale desert-thorn* (Lycium pallidum)*. Courtesy, Utah Native Plant Society, Salt Lake City.*

Plate 3. *Two color phases of the plains pricklypear* (Opuntia polyacantha).

Plate 4. *Skunkbush sumac* (Rhus aromatica *subsp.* trilobata*). Native Americans used this plant for many purposes.*

Plate 5. *(a) Winterfat* (Krascheninnikovia lanata) *and (b) broom snakeweed* (Gutierrezia sarothrae).

Plate 6. *Two common warm-season grasses: (a) blue grama* (Chondrosum gracile) *and (b) James' galleta* (Hilaria jamesii).

Plate 7. *Cropland north of the Sand Canyon area showing red loess soil of the Great Sage Plain.*

Plate 8. *Dolores bench grasslands near hanging flume overlook.*

Plate 9. *Dolores bench grasslands site, May 18, 2002. The short foreground shrubs are broom snakeweed, and the patches of gray are the cacti tulip pricklypear (*Opuntia phaeacantha*), which has large pads, and plains pricklypear, which has small pads.*

Plate 10. *Sand Canyon Pueblo. Painting by Glenn Felch. Courtesy, Crow Canyon Archaeological Center, Cortez, Colorado.*

Plate 11. *Antelope bitterbrush* (Purshia tridentata*)*.

Plate 12. *(a) Whipple's fishhook cactus (*Sclerocactus whipplei*) and (b) thrift mock goldenweed* (Stenotus armerioides*).*

Plate 13. *Wyoming big sagebrush and a few basin big sagebrush with native bunchgrasses at Goodman Point, May 2002.*

Plate 14. *Overgrazed Wyoming big sagebrush in Dry Creek Basin, illustrating the near absence of understory forbs and grasses.*

Plate 15. *Fragmented nature of Dry Creek Basin as a result of conversion to agricultural fields and eradication of sagebrush and other native shrubs.*

Plate 16. *Uncompahgre Valley and adobes looking south from Dry Cedar Creek; San Juan Mountains in the distance.*

Plate 17. *South Rim of Black Canyon of the Gunnison National Park with typical mixed mountain shrub community. The white flowering shrub in the lower right foreground is Utah serviceberry (*Amelanchier utahensis*). The grayish brown shrubs on the hillside are Gambel oak (*Quercus gambelii*).*

Plate 18. Silver buffaloberry (Shepherdia argentea) is the grayish shrub shown here on the right along the Uncompahgre River, Colorado.

Plate 19. *Natural vegetation on a hillside draw in Mancos shale adobes southeast of Montrose. The tall brownish foreground bunchgrass is saline wildrye* (Leymus salina). *Short shrubs on the little ridge are shadscale saltbush* (Atriplex confertifolia), *Gardner's saltbush* (Atriplex gardneri), *and mat saltbush* (Atriplex corrugata).

Plate 20. *(a) A young plant of saltlover (halogeton)* (Halogeton glomeratus*) and (b) the selenium-accumulating plant Hayden's milkvetch* (Astragalus haydenianus*). Note the red stem on Hayden's milkvetch.*

Plate 21. *Russian knapweed, also known as hardheads* (Acroptilon repens), *in flower.*

Plate 22. *Twoneedle pinyon* (Pinus edulis) *on the left and Utah juniper* (Sabina osteosperma) *on the right.*

Plate 23. *Roubideau Canyon on the Uncompahgre Plateau.*

Plate 24. *Big Dominguez Canyon looking downstream from Cactus Park trailhead.*

Plate 25. *(a) Hoary Townsend daisy* (Townsendia incana) *and (b) boreal sweetvetch* (Hedysarum boreale).

Plate 26. *(a) Narrowleaf stoneseed* (Lithospermum incisum) *and (b) kingcup cactus* (Echinocereus triglochidiatus).

Plate 27. *Collared lizard, a denizen of rocky canyons with sparse ground cover.*

Plate 28. *High-severity fires such as this are natural in pinyon-juniper woodlands on the Uncompahgre Plateau. Plant succession leads to recovery of native plant diversity in the burned woodland, as here in the Cone Mountain fire, which burned south of Gateway, Colorado, in A.D. 2000, three years before the photo was taken. The orange flower is scarlet globemallow (Sphaeralcea coccinea subsp. dissecta), and the grass is Indian ricegrass (Achnatherum hymenoides).*

Plate 29. *Gibbler rollerchop site in September 2001, the year of treatment.*

Plate 30. *Old-growth ponderosa pine on Archuleta Mesa near Chimney Rock. This inaccessible mesa top is thought to have had no domestic livestock for at least sixty years. The dominant understory vegetation includes needle and thread grass* (Hesperostipa comata)*, antelope bitterbrush* (Purshia tridentata)*, and Gambel oak* (Quercus gambelii).

Plate 31. *Fall aspen near McClure Pass.*

Plate 32. *Pagosa Springs as it appeared when painted by a member of the Macomb expedition in* A.D. *1859 (Newberry 1876).*

Plate 33. *(a) Arizona fescue (*Festuca arizonica*) and b) mountain muhly (*Muhlenbergia montana*).*

Plate 34. *Pineland dwarf mistletoe* (Arceuthobium vaginatum *subsp.* cryptopodum) *parasitic on ponderosa pine.*

Plate 35. *Fence line of Beaver Crossing grazing exclosure, constructed in 1949. Differences between inside exclosure* (right) *and outside are subtle even after almost sixty years.*

Plate 36. *A fifty-acre park in the ponderosa pine zone on the Biggs allotment after it was disked and reseeded to non-native grasses in August 1984. Photo from allotment file, U.S. Forest Service, Dolores, Colorado.*

Plate 37. *Arizona fescue–mountain muhly* (Festuca arizonica–Muhlenbergia montana) *grassland remnant at Monolores Bridge.*

Plate 38. *Looking north from the Parry's oatgrass–Arizona fescue* (Danthonia parryi–Festuca arizonica) *grassland in the foreground at upper Piedra Valley that Lieutenant C.A.H. McCauley described cn his visit in* A.D. *1877 (Ruffner 1878). Beyond the fence is a pasture dominated by non-native Kentucky bluegrass* (Poa pratensis).

Plate 39. *Butter and eggs, or yellow toadflax* (Linaria vulgaris),
*a state-listed noxious weed that is replacing native plant communities in the ponderosa pine
zone and becoming common in rural subdivisions.*

Plate 40. *Cheatgrass on disturbed area of an aspen clear-cut, Horsefly timber sale, July 2001, 8,300 feet elevation.*

Plate 41. *Heartland cohousing near Bayfield, Colorado. Single and duplex homes face inward toward a central walkway.*

Plate 42. *Brook trout. Copyright Richard Grost. Courtesy, Richard Grost.*

Plate 43. *Non-native lodgepole pine* (Pinus contorta) *forests planted after the Lime Creek burn of 1879 are the trees with a lighter shade of green, while native Engelmann spruce* (Picea engelmannii) *and corkbark fir* (Abies arizonica) *are a darker shade of green. The view is looking up at the Molas Creek cirque, a recommended hiking area.*

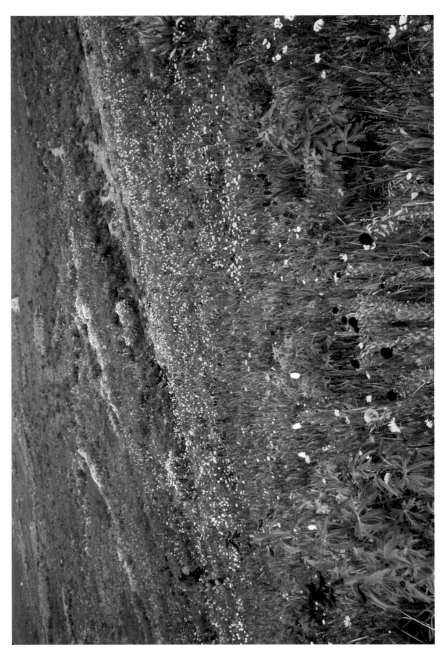

Plate 44. *Diversity of alpine flowers at Animas Forks.*

Plate 45. *Cement Creek, illustrating the iron-oxide stain.*

Plate 46. *Twin Lakes in Chicago Basin; damage from previous campsite in foreground.*

Plate 47. Subalpine larkspur (Delphinium barbeyi) near the start of Lizard Head Trail.

Plate 48. San Miguel River (right) entering the Dolores River.

Plate 49. *Looking east across Lizard Head Pass, showing sheep corrals.*

Plate 50. *Thurber's fescue* (Festuca thurberi) *under active grazing by sheep. Note bare ground between grass clumps.*

Plate 51. *Owl's-claws (orange sneezeweed)* (Helenium hoopesii) *in the alpine above Little Molas Lake.*

Plate 52. *Oxeye daisy* (Leucanthemum vulgare) *invasion on a road bank.*

Plate 53. A large gully in Wilson Meadows. Note the person at the far end of the gully for scale.

Plate 54. *Telluride and the Valley Floor in the distance on the left.*

Plate 55. *The Nature Conservancy's Canyon Preserve, showing diverse deciduous riparian trees and shrubs.*

Plate 56. *Looking upstream on the San Miguel River at Tabeguache Preserve.*

Plate 57. *Saltcedar, or tamarisk* (Tamarix ramosissima*), in bloom.*

Plate 58. *Faces of the Old and New West.*

City and county land-use planners and conservationists . . . have their hands full. They are wrestling with the musculature of Western cultural and historical geography. While money is certainly a central motivation of developers, it's as if the quiet of the land bothers them, and they turn to the buzz and clatter of platted civilization to blot out the silence. To others, the powerful beauty of the landscape is a catalyst which stimulates intense life experiences and the urge to save geographic rarities. Both options still lie before us. For in the West, you can stand on a rimrock and see a hundred years in either direction, or you can choose not to see at all.

—John B. Wright, *Rocky Mountain Divide*[1]

San Miguel River: The Old West and New West Join in a Watershed Vision

These words from geographer John Wright aptly capture the San Miguel River from several angles. In a literal sense, this is truly a country of vistas, stretching over eighty miles from the spectacular peaks and high-country meadows where the San Miguel originates near Telluride (Plate 47), through impressive red-rock canyons, to its destiny in the desert slick-rock country where it feeds the Dolores River (see Plate 48). Culturally and economically, it would be easy to divide the landscape— Naturita, Nucla, and Norwood represent the Old West and Telluride and the Mountain Village ski resort represent the New West (see Map 7.1). But

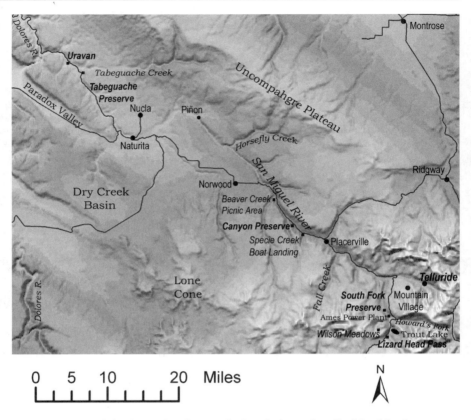

Map 7.1. *Map of the San Miguel watershed and places described in this chapter.*

as more people are choosing to see, the futures of these two ends of the river are inescapably linked. A century of boom-and-bust economies has left ecological legacies and lessons, including mine-scarred land, dead tributaries, invasive non-native plants, and reduced biodiversity. Still, as one of the West's last major free-flowing rivers, the San Miguel has the potential to be restored for future generations.

The river itself is simply the thread uniting a watershed that includes an impressive array of ecosystems, geology, and climates, beginning with 14,000-foot peaks and ending in the hot, dry Colorado Plateau. The San Juan Mountains are the result of volcanism about 18–35 million years ago.[2] However, older sedimentary rocks, such as the Cretaceous Mancos shale, surround and dot the volcanic high country.[3] The river is slowly transporting boulders and gravel left by retreating glaciers, which once reached down to about 8,500 feet in elevation.[4]

Figure 7.1. *Narrowleaf cottonwood* (Populus angustifolia) *on the left and Rio Grande cottonwood* (Populus deltoides *subsp.* wislizeni) *on the right.*

The riparian vegetation changes along the river length, beginning with willow-dominated wetlands called carrs. Willows are only 2–3 feet high near tree line, but willows up to 10 feet tall form broad carrs lower in the subalpine and montane zones.[5] Carrs' dense cover and ample insects provide favorite breeding habitat for Lincoln's, fox, song, and white-crowned sparrows and for McGillivray's and Wilson's warblers.[6] Engelmann spruce and corkbark fir dominate subalpine forests in general, as well as riparian forests along steep subalpine streams. At about 8,500 feet in elevation, narrowleaf cottonwood and blue spruce take over along rivers, extending down to the mountain front near 6,000 feet.[7] Below 6,000 feet, where rivers cut through canyon country with pinyon-juniper woodlands, sagebrush, and semiarid grasslands, the broad-leafed Rio Grande cottonwood (see Figure 7.1) is the main riparian tree.

Like many places in the West, this watershed features mining boomtowns gone bust, with some towns rising again from the ashes. In this chapter, mining and high-elevation sheep grazing are highlighted as legacies of early Euro-American land uses. A more questionable legacy is fire suppression in high-elevation forests, habitat of the recently re-introduced lynx population. The San Miguel region is also a fitting place to examine the impacts of the New West economy, with its influx of wealth and subdivision of rural land for second and vacation homes. Most important, there is a hopeful story here of people harnessing new economic and social forces to protect and restore the San Miguel River and its watershed.

LEGACY OF PAST HUMAN USES

Mining Along the San Miguel

Three types of mining occurred along the San Miguel River. High elevations experienced the same hard-rock mining boom as the upper Animas (see Chapter 6). Surface scars and huge piles of waste remain as reminders of decades of hard-rock mining for gold, silver, and other metals. Along the middle reaches of the river, placer mining altered the river channel. Near the river's mouth, where it joins the Dolores River, the surrounding rocks hold uranium, radium, and vanadium in places where mining dominated the economy for several decades until the nuclear industry declined.

The hard-rock mining era and its legacies. Hard-rock mining dominated the high elevations of the San Miguel watershed. The first hard-rock mining claim in the area was filed in 1875 above present-day Telluride. Telluride grew rapidly in the 1880s,[8] especially after toll roads were built in the mid-1880s.[9] By 1890 the town had ninety businesses, five lawyers, four doctors, and three dentists.[10] In 1891 Otto Mears completed the short-lived Southern Rio Grande Railroad linking Telluride to Ridgway, Rico, and Durango.[11]

The Smuggler and Sheridan mines flourished during the 1880s silver boom, while two other big mines, the Liberty Bell and the Tomboy, took off in the mid-1890s with gold production.[12] Telluride's population reached its maximum around 1900, when San Miguel County had over 5,000 residents.[13] The Telluride area was rich with minerals, but the mining industry was tumultuous, as markets for silver and gold alternately peaked and collapsed.

The boom-and-bust economy fostered rapacious use of natural resources. Demand for building material and fuel led to depletion of nearby forests (see Figure 7.2). Some of these harvested forests have not grown back. By 1899 the large mining companies had implemented new con-

Figure 7.2. *Marshall Basin mining area east of Telluride in* A.D. *1895. Photo by C. Whitman Cross. Courtesy, U.S. Geological Survey, Photographic Library, Denver, Colorado. This is a cropped portion of the original photograph.*

centration techniques that entailed crushing the rock and either heating it or applying chemicals, such as cyanide or mercury, to extract the desired metals.[14] Tailings and effluents were dumped directly into the river, along with raw sewage, dead animals, and garbage.[15]

Hard-rock mining began to decline in the upper San Miguel Basin in 1917,[16] and by 1928 all the major mines had closed.[17] After World War II, hard-rock mining resurged, but dumping tailings into the river was no longer acceptable, so waste rock accumulated in large tailings piles and ponds that remain prominent around Telluride and Ophir (see Figure 7.3).[18] The Idarado mines and mill, the last to operate near Telluride, closed in 1978, and an expensive and controversial cleanup project was nearing its end in 2002 under the supervision of the Colorado Department of Public Health and Environment.[19] As at Silverton, most difficult to remediate are hundreds of mine adits (openings) in the high country, many of which still drain toxic heavy metals and acidic waters into the upper streams of the watershed.

Figure 7.3. *Mine tailings in Howards Fork, which flows into the San Miguel River.*

Placer mining along the San Miguel River. Downstream from Telluride, placer mining was common along the San Miguel, although it never prospered.[20] Western rivers emanating from the mountains typically have sediments that originated from the same ore-bearing rocks targeted by hard-rock mining. Thus, small particles of precious metal, especially gold, can be reclaimed from these sediments. Large-scale placer

Figure 7.4. *Placer mining on the San Miguel River, A.D. 1888. This was probably in the area upstream of Piñon. Courtesy, Denver Public Library, Western History Collection, Denver, Colorado.*

mining dislodged sediments from stream banks and the riverbed with high-powered water hoses (see Figure 7.4), stripping the riparian vegetation. Placer mining altered stream channels, destabilized stream banks, degraded wetlands, and left weedy gravel bars.

Placer mining left sediments no longer connected to the channel, but the connection can be restored: "Reconnecting channel to floodplain is important because natural flooding improves riparian plant habitat, enables cottonwood regeneration, . . . redistributes nutrients, creates and recharges backwater habitat for native fish rearing. Reconnecting channel to floodplain also provides for lateral channel migration, which allows the channel to absorb energy, drop sediment, and to create and maintain riparian plant and aquatic habitat."[21]

Commercial placer mining is no longer common, but its legacies are a focus of restoration efforts on the San Miguel and other rivers. A few miles downstream of Placerville is the former Dory Placer mine at Specie Creek, an active mine until the late 1980s when it closed and defaulted on its reclamation bond. The bond was insufficient to cover reclamation, leaving the Bureau of Land Management (BLM) and the state with a steep, unstable slope and significant trash, including a wrecked trailer.

The mine had used cyanide to leach gold from gravels, compounding the cleanup.[22] To reclaim the area, the slope was recontoured with heavy equipment, and The Nature Conservancy subcontracted to bring in an Americorp team to revegetate the slope.[23] The site remained an ugly scar, however, until BLM obtained a grant to construct the boat landing and parking areas.

The 1872 Mining Law leaves most federal land open to mining claims, and small-scale, "recreational" placer mining still takes place along the San Miguel, as indicated by small posts containing claim documents. The Telluride Gravel site just downstream of Telluride, however, has had the biggest impact on the streambed in recent years. Removal of the riverbed materials at that site resulted in downcutting and a lowering of the water table. The channel is so destabilized that tons of excess sediment from the site are flushed into the river during high water flows.[24]

Placer mining also required the transport of water through flumes. An awesome example is the thirteen-mile flume built along the walls of the lower San Miguel and Dolores River canyons to bring water to placer claims near Mesa Creek (see Figure 7.5). Using almost 2 million board feet of lumber, the flume was completed in 1891 but was used less than a year before the placer was deemed impossible to mine hydraulically.[25]

Uravan: Radioactive boom and bust. In the lower reaches of the San Miguel a soft yellow ore called carnotite was discovered in the late 1800s. When Madame Curie isolated radium from the uranium in the carnotite in 1910, western Colorado was the only known source of carnotite, and a period of mining booms and busts began along the lower San Miguel.[26] Mills for processing carnotite into radium and later vanadium were constructed at Uravan and near Naturita.[27]

The largest boom period coincided with the Cold War and the nuclear arms race. During World War II the Manhattan Project led to exploration of the Colorado Plateau for uranium for the atomic bomb.[28] After World War II the Atomic Energy Commission encouraged prospecting for uranium by bulldozing hundreds of miles of roads—still a legacy— into remote country and offering bonuses for high-grade ore finds.[29] During the 1950s thousands of prospectors combed the area, setting up mining camps of tents, trailers, and tar-paper shacks, similar to the gold camps of a century before.[30] The uranium industry collapsed in the area after 1980 when the market for uranium sagged,[31] but it restarted in 2005 when the price for uranium rose again.[32]

At the former town of Uravan, it is hard to imagine that a large uranium processing mill and a company town, where 700–1,000 people

Figure 7.5. *Remains of hanging flume along the lower San Miguel River near the confluence with the Dolores River.*

lived, were so recently located there (see Figures 7.6a and 7.7a). Unlike the mining camps, Uravan had stores, tennis courts, a swimming pool, and a recreation center.[33] Today, local people remember this history proudly, but the toll—not counting the remaining nuclear weapons stock—included health and environmental costs not appreciated during the uranium boom.[34]

Ventilation in mines was poor, and exposure to radon at both mines and mills was high until regulations were established in the late 1960s.[35] Early uranium workers suffered from an increased incidence of lung cancer. The first suspected death, in 1956, was a uranium miner from Nucla.[36] By 1967 six Nucla miners had died of cancer, but locals, fearing a further collapse of the industry, resisted the idea that radiation was the cause. A *Wall Street Journal* article quoted a local miner: "Those fellows who died from cancer probably had weak lungs and shouldn't have been in the mines in the first place."[37] Toxic wastes from the mill also flowed into the river and contaminated the groundwater. Three years after the mill closed in 1984, the 450-acre mill and town became a Superfund site.[38]

Umetco Minerals Corporation, a subsidiary of Union Carbide, as part of its Remedial Action project with the Environmental Protection

Figure 7.6. *(a) The original town of Uravan, Colorado (unknown date), and (b) in* A.D. *2002. (a) Courtesy, Rimrocker Historical Museum, Naturita, Colorado.*

Agency, dismantled 260 buildings in Uravan, leaving only the board-inghouse (see Figure 7.6b). The mill buildings were dismantled (see Figure 7.7b) and deposited, along with other radioactive materials and

Figure 7.7. (a) U.S. Vanadium mill at Uravan, Colorado (unknown date), and (b) in A.D. 2002. (a) Courtesy, Rimrocker Historical Museum, Naturita, Colorado.

soils, in a large pit dug into Club Mesa above the river. The pit and 1.8 million cubic yards of tailings have been stabilized and capped with soil and rock.[39] Drainage from the pit, tailings, and hillside is collected in large evaporation ponds to prevent seepage of heavy metals (lead, arsenic, cadmium, vanadium) and radioactive materials (uranium, radium, and liquid wastes) into the river and groundwater.[40] Treatment of groundwater continues, but metals and radioactive materials still impact aquatic life downstream from Uravan.[41]

Many pass this site with a single-mindedness directed at the canyon scenery or the next town. But much here is worth reflection. In the span of little more than a century, this place supported four distinct economies. In 1881, thousands of years of occupation by hunting-and-gathering people ended as the Tabeguache Utes were forced from their land. Soon thereafter, the famous Club Ranch headquarters (discussed in Chapter 2), a potent symbol of the open-range cattle industry, was built here on the banks of the San Miguel. Half a century later the hayfields and ranch buildings of Club Ranch were replaced by the town of Uravan, an equally significant symbol of another era—the atomic age. For another half century the search for vanadium and uranium transformed the land and held the region in its sway. More recently, this portion of Highway 141, which runs along the lower San Miguel and Dolores rivers, was designated as part of the Unaweep/Tabeguache Scenic Byway. The beautiful landscape and rich human history now support a small tourism-based economy. Yet the tension between those who would return to the high-paying jobs of the uranium era and those supporting a new economy based on the region's natural beauty and history is likely to resurface for some time.

High-Country Sheep Grazing at Lizard Head Pass and Wilson Meadows

The legacies of grazing are as significant along the San Miguel as in any part of western Colorado. Norwood was at the heart of the early cattle industry based on open-range grazing of the Uncompahgre Plateau, San Miguel Basin, and Lone Cone. Placerville (see Figure 7.8) was once a large livestock shipping point.[42] High-elevation meadows of the watershed were grazed by pack animals and cattle to supply the mining camps as early as the 1870s,[43] but sheep predominated in the high country through most of the twentieth century, leaving their distinct imprint on the plant communities.

The Lizard Head Pass area typifies the high-elevation sheep country of the San Miguel watershed. The sheep corrals at the pass (see Plate 49) are the only conspicuous sign of the grazing history. Sheep were brought to Lizard Head very early (see Figure 7.9), and the area was long managed under Forest Service permits. The Lizard Head al-

Figure 7.8. *Placerville, A.D. 1887, by Charles Goodman. Courtesy, Denver Public Library, Western History Collection, Denver, Colorado.*

lotment, south of Lizard Head Pass, has a documented history of problems long unaddressed.[44] The first memo indicating damage, dated September 22, 1949, reads: "All the high range on this allotment is in bad shape[,] also that portion on the Uncompahgre Forest—it looks like the permitted number of 1000 for 80 days is just too many sheep."[45] In 1957: "Country in head of Slate Creek around Lizard Head is in very poor condition, both from a watershed and range standpoint[,] and should be closed to grazing. Bad gullies are present over all this country and all are actively cutting. Not a suitable area for sheep grazing (or cattle)."[46] In 1967: "Area at the head of Lizard Head Creek is in extremely poor condition. The soil is a Mancos Shale and very unstable. Roads and sheep trailing [have] contributed to some of the gullies and [are] causing a great deal of damage on the already damaged area. The area should not be used by sheep or at least rest-rotation. It will never recover under present management."[47] In a memo dated July 22, 1968, Norwood District ranger E. R. Browning wrote that the critical area involved places where exposed shale was bare and eroding. The obligation of permitted sheep was still 1,000 sheep for 90 days, longer than the 1949 season. Browning also felt the problem was overstocking.[48]

Figure 7.9. *Sheep grazing a high mountain meadow in the San Juan Mountains, August 26, 1915. Photo by J. F. Hunter. Courtesy, U.S. Geological Survey Photographic Library, Denver, Colorado.*

Reports like these were repeated for several other allotments around Lizard Head.

In the 1980s recreationists and other residents began to complain about range conditions and conflicts with herders. Near Trout Lake, the Old West may have ended the way it began—with a gun: "In fact his [the permittee's] herder was threatened by a Trout Lake resident with a rifle who said that he was going to shoot any sheep that went any further toward Hope Lake. Shots were fired in the air. Sheep were removed."[49] Recognizing the overuse and rising conflicts, the Forest Service closed several allotments, and by the early 1980s the Lizard Head allotment was used mainly just for loading at the corrals and trailing through the allotment. Allotments on Sheep Mountain east of the pass remained active sheep-grazing areas, despite continued poor range condition.

The legacy of sheep grazing at high elevations is usually distinct from that of cattle. Sheep tend to select forbs over grasses, so they often reduce or deplete native forbs but can allow native bunchgrasses to persist.[50] Grasslands grazed by cattle tend to have lost their dominant bunchgrasses, as cattle are more likely to eat the entire grass plant.[51] The grassland at Lizard Head Pass still supports a diversity of plants (see Table 7.1). The dominant native grass is Thurber's fescue, a tall bunchgrass with narrow leaves (see Plate 50), which forms subalpine grasslands from central New Mexico to southern Wyoming.[52] One sign of past stress on this native grass is the presence of the common non-native smooth brome (see Box—Smooth Brome, pp. 281–282). It is likely a legacy of overgrazing, as smooth brome was planted by the Forest Service in the past to stem erosion.

If sheep impacted the grasses on this site, forbs were probably greatly reduced and have not recovered fully. Browning's July 22, 1968,

BOX—SMOOTH BROME

There has been an attitude of attempting to remedy the symptoms of poor land management rather than addressing the cause(s). One of these ill-founded solutions has been the introduction of exotic plants. Smooth brome was examined as a potential forage because production of native grasses was apparently declining. Little or no attempt was made to determine why it was declining.[1]

Smooth brome (see box figure) was introduced to the United States as a forage grass in 1884 from its native habitat in Eurasia and was widely planted on degraded grazing lands and abandoned agricultural lands across the Great Plains and the West.[2] Smooth brome is an invasive non-native plant, usually ranked below the most invasive but still a serious concern in many areas, particularly the U.S. Great Plains and Canada.[3]

Yet many horticultural and agricultural extension Web sites promote smooth brome. For example, Purdue University's Center for New Crops and Plants Products says: "The root system is strong and interlaced, making the plant excellent for erosion control. Smooth brome is among the best of the pasture and hay grasses, being both highly

Smooth brome (Bromopsis inermis). *Note the wide, flat blade, which often has a slight marking in the shape of the letter "W."*

palatable and nutritious."[4] There is no mention of the negative threats The Nature Conservancy's Invasive Plants Web site includes: "It forms a dense sod that often appears to exclude other species, thus contributing to the reduction of species diversity in natural areas. Within the Rocky Mountain range of the native *Bromus pumpellianus*, hybrid introgression is occurring."[5]

Hybrid introgression means smooth brome's genes are mixing with the genes of this native brome, threatening the persistence of a native plant. Smooth brome is absent, too, from the definitive book *Weeds of the West*.[6] The value of this grass for forage and revegetation of disturbed sites seems to have trumped concern for its invasive properties.

Smooth brome has replaced native communities across North America, including in southwestern Colorado. The last remnants of the original fescue prairies in Canada and prairies in the United States are being invaded by smooth brome because of its high seed production and its ability to spread vegetatively by rhizomes.[7] Burning can successfully control smooth brome in mixed and tall-grass prairies in the U.S. Great Plains, but burning reduces native plants too much to be effective in fescue prairies, where more expensive herbicide control is required.[8] Southwestern Colorado's fescue grasslands are also vulnerable to smooth brome invasion.

Smooth brome might be a symbol of a conflict of values: forage production on the one hand and protection of native vegetation on the other. Yet it appears more to be a tragedy of inertia—using this established grass is simple and convenient. However, the U.S. government's enormous research capabilities could be directed at restoring native grasses that offer as much or better forage and are also important components of native ecosystems. Smooth brome could then be on the noxious weed list where it belongs.

NOTES

1. Romo, Grilz, and Driver, "Invasion of Canadian Prairies," 132.
2. Lorenz, "Introduction and Early Use of Crested Wheatgrass."
3. Ibid.; Wilson and Belcher, "Plant and Bird Communities of Native Prairie."
4. See Web site: http://www.hort.purdue.edu/newcrop/Crops/Smooth-brome.html.
5. See Web site: http://www.tnc.weeds.ucdavis.edu/esadocs/documents/bromine.html.
6. Whitson et al., *Weeds of the West*.
7. Grilz and Romo, "Water Relations and Growth of *Bromus inermis*."
8. Ibid.

memo stated: "The Fescue Parks have been picked clean between the clumps."[53] Another report on the Lizard Head area from October 19, 1989, said, "FETH [Thurber's fescue] plants had been utilized to about

Table 7.1. Common plants of subalpine grasslands and forests of the Lizard Head area.[1]

	Grassland	Forest
TREES		
Corkbark fir *(Abies arizonica)*	—	X
Engelmann spruce *(Picea engelmannii)*	—	X
Quaking aspen *(Populus tremuloides)*	—	X
SHRUBS		
Grayleaf red raspberry *(Rubus idaeus* subsp. *melanolasius)*	—	X
Mountain snowberry *(Symphoricarpos rotundifolius)*	—	X
Red elderberry *(Sambucus microbotrys)*	—	X
Shrubby cinquefoil *(Pentaphylloides floribunda)*	X	—
Trailing black currant *(Ribes coloradense)*	—	X
FORBS		
American vetch *(Vicia americana)*	X	—
Beautiful cinquefoil *(Potentilla pulcherrima)*	X	—
Colorado false hellebore *(Veratrum tenuipetalum)*	X	—
Fendler's meadow-rue *(Thalictrum fendleri)*	X	—
Giant red Indian paintbrush *(Castilleja miniata)*	—	X
Orange sneezeweed *(Helenium hoopesii)*	X	—
Showy goldeneye *(Heliomeris multiflora)*	X	—
Splitleaf Indian paintbrush *(Castilleja rhexifolia)*	—	X
Subalpine larkspur *(Delphinium barberyi)*	X	—
Sulphur Indian paintbrush *(Castilleja sulphurea)*	—	X
Tall fleabane *(Erigeron elatior)*	X	—
Towering Jacob's-ladder *(Polemonium foliosissimum)*	X	—
Virginia strawberry *(Fragaria virginiana* subsp. *glauca)*	X	—
GRAMINOIDS		
Slender wheatgrass *(Elymus trachycaulus)*	X	—
Thurber's fescue *(Festuca thurberi)*	X	—
NON-NATIVES		
Common dandelion *(Taraxacum officinale)*	X	—
Kentucky bluegrass *(Poa pratensis)*	X	—
Oxeye daisy *(Leucanthemum vulgare)*	X	—
Smooth brome *(Bromopsis inermis)*	X	—

1. Common names are from the PLANTS online database, http://plants.usda.gov. Latin names are from Weber and Wittmann, *Colorado Flora.*

75% and the forb component was missing."[54] The grasslands at the pass have been rested from livestock grazing since the late 1980s, but the forb species present (see Table 7.1) are the survivors of sheep grazing. Some, such as beautiful cinquefoil and Virginia strawberry, appear to be increasers (see Box—Increasers and Decreasers, pp. 205–206).[55]

One reason sheep were able to claim the high country in the San Juans was the presence of subalpine larkspur (see Plate 47), which is poisonous to cattle but can be eaten by sheep.[56] Orange sneezeweed (see Plate 51), in contrast, is especially poisonous to sheep, although cattle are also susceptible,[57] and it is often common on subalpine grasslands grazed by sheep. Around the Lizard Head Pass area, in swales and wetter areas, are large patches of Colorado false hellebore (see Figure 7.10), which is also poisonous to sheep and cattle.[58] This plant has substantially increased in the San Juan Mountains over the past century.[59]

High-elevation grasslands have few noxious weeds compared with lower elevations. However, the oxeye daisy (see Plate 52), now a state-listed noxious weed (see Box—Noxious Weeds, pp. 200–201), was introduced as an ornamental plant and is spreading at moderately high elevations. Many people still do not recognize this pretty flower as a weed, but it can crowd out native plants, destroying the diversity of subalpine meadows. Although it can invade native plant communities, it is still associated mainly with disturbed ground.

Mountain grasslands provide important habitat for a number of animal species. For example, although the grassland at Lizard Head has a legacy of sheep grazing, in its recovering state it serves as habitat for the savannah sparrow, which has nested there in recent years. The savannah sparrow, an inconspicuous bird with a boldly striped head and faint insect-like song, breeds mostly in moist mountain meadows. It is a Colorado Species of Special Concern because of the loss of its grassland breeding habitats to agriculture.[60]

From Lizard Head Pass, a trail goes over the divide to Wilson Meadows in the San Miguel watershed. Wilson Meadows is a large subalpine carr with some areas of sedge meadow. The primary willow is the two-foot-tall planeleaf willow, which dominates the highest-elevation willow carrs in western Colorado.[61] Wilson Meadows was seriously altered by domestic sheep grazing, and recovery of the native community has only begun. It was part of the Basin allotment, which has not been used since 1989 after a long history of overuse and gradual declines in permitted grazing (see Figure 7.11). The level of sheep grazing in the allotment declined from the 1930s to the 1950s. While declining use in the 1940s suggests that vegetation condition must have been poor earlier, the first reports of overuse of this site are from April 3, 1964: "A range analysis summary prepared for 1960 indicates that ⅔ of the allotment is unusable, and 1042 acres are in very poor condition. . . . Particularly severe trailing and damage in Wilson Meadows was noted. Forage conditions are poor. Least desirable plants appear to make up the major percentage of plant composition. Present plant density and composition is insufficient to retain soil in place."[62] On August 30, 1967, the file indicated: "Bray [permittee] is to rake in 50 lbs. of BRIN on bare spots in Wilson Meadows."[63] BRIN is the abbreviation for smooth brome (see

Figure 7.10. *The large-leafed plant is Colorado false hellebore (*Veratrum tenuipetalum*).*

Box—Smooth Brome, pp. 281–282). The need for the use of this plant in revegetation indicates the degraded condition of Wilson Meadows in the 1960s.

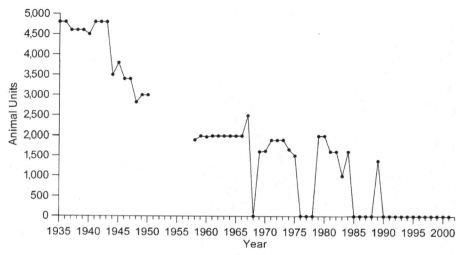

Figure 7.11. *Historical trends in sheep grazing in animal months (e.g., 800 sheep for 2.5 months = 2,000 animal-months), 1935–2000, for the Basin allotment, which is west of the highway on the north side of Lizard Head Pass and includes Wilson Meadows.*

Today, Wilson Meadows is recovering from a century of sheep grazing, and recovery is slow. Forb diversity is relatively low, although the floral display of the purple elephanthead lousewort (*Pedicularis groenlandica*) can be spectacular. Willows are very short or absent from much of their former area. At Wilson Meadows the damage goes beyond changes in the plant community. Gullies are deep and still eroding upstream (see Plate 53).[64] No scientific knowledge indicates how long recovery might take in a high-elevation setting such as this, where elk still graze heavily in the summer. It could be several decades before the natural plant communities and stream channel are restored.

Fire Suppression, Old-Growth Forests, and Native Predators in the High Country

Health is a nearly universal desire for people, and who would not want forests to be healthy too? Recent legislation, the Healthy Forests Restoration Act of 2003, suggests that many western forests are unhealthy as a result of fire suppression. Fires were intentionally suppressed in many forests, but fire suppression likely had little effect on high-elevation subalpine forests, such as those on Lizard Head Pass.[65] As in pinyon-juniper woodlands, fire suppression has only been effective for a few decades, while the mean time between fires is long—300

Figure 7.12. *Conifers beneath old aspen on Lizard Head Trail.*

years or more in subalpine forests.[66] Also, large fires in subalpine forests are rare, since these forests are moist and would require exceptionally dry conditions to allow fires to become large.[67] During very dry conditions, a bit of extra fuel from a few decades of fire suppression probably has a minor effect.

The trail between Lizard Head Pass and Wilson Meadows runs through a remarkably diverse and interesting subalpine forest, where the impacts of fire suppression can be considered. The mature forest here has quaking aspen, Engelmann spruce, and corkbark fir. In many places the aspen forest contains smaller conifers beneath the canopy (see Figure 7.12)—considered by some to be a sign of fire suppression,[68] since repeated fires would kill the conifers and favor aspen, which can resprout after fire. Using an increment borer to extract tree-ring cores to date a few trees, we learned that the taller and larger aspens were about 135 years old in 1998, having originated in the 1860s. This is moderately old for quaking aspen in the southern Rockies. The aspen showed evidence of rapid early growth, followed by slower growth, typical of trees that spring up after a fire.[69] Beneath the canopy were conifers that were a third to half the height of the aspen in 1998. Most were corkbark fir, with only a few Engelmann spruce—generally about 45–50 years old in 1998, having originated around 1950.

While the aspen almost certainly resprouted after a fire, it is less easy to understand the burst of fir regeneration around 1950. Does it take almost a century for conifers to successfully invade an aspen forest? The intensity of sheep grazing on this allotment declined starting around 1940 and leveled off in the 1950s (see Figure 7.11). This reduction in grazing pressure could have encouraged a conifer invasion; tree invasions have occurred after grazing reductions in other areas.[70] However, a wet period or a dry period in the 1950s could also have encouraged trees to regenerate.

Now that conifers are present beneath the aspen, are they likely to take over the aspen forest? This is a commonly cited concern about aspen forest health.[71] If conifers that are about 50 years old today continue to grow as they did over the past 50 years, it will take about another century for them to reach the height of the aspen canopy. But what might happen during the next century? Aspen do not often live to be 235 years old, so they may begin to die and fall, opening the canopy and thus perhaps enhancing the height growth of the conifers or smaller aspen. Even if the conifers win the race to the canopy, another fire might occur, killing the conifers and allowing the aspen to resprout. Although the average interval between fires in conifer-dominated subalpine forests may be 300 or more years,[72] the average interval between fires in lower-elevation aspen forests in this area is about 140 years,[73] so a fire could occur again at any time. Of course, predictions about future forests often fail, particularly for forests that grow, burn, and reburn on the scale of centuries. What we see in the forest today, looking back at its history, suggests it is a diverse and interesting place and a "healthy" forest. It will not stay exactly as it is today, however, and in 30–50 years perhaps a new direction will be evident.

By then, the forest might be "old growth." In a few places along the Lizard Head Trail, the forest is made up of large Engelmann spruce (up to three feet in diameter) and some especially large aspen that are 150 to 170 years old. While not ancient, these old forest areas are approaching old-growth spruce-fir forest; to qualify, trees must be more than 200 years old.[74] Some corkbark fir trees are dead or dying, possibly as a result of the fir engraver—a small beetle that attacks these trees, leaving intricate galleries under the bark (see Figure 7.13). Such dead or dying trees are an essential feature of healthy old-growth forests (see Box—Forest Health, pp. 290–291).

Old-growth forest has an abundance of downed trees, stumps, and large-diameter snags[75] that provide important habitat for the American marten[76] and the lynx.[77] Marten are uncommon but not rare. Lynx, on the other hand, had become rare if not extirpated in Colorado. So for many people the news in 2003 that reintroduced lynx had moved into the Lizard Head area was very exciting. Sixteen kittens were born in

Figure 7.13. *Galleries left beneath the bark of a corkbark fir* (Abies arizonica) *by a small beetle, the fir engraver, which was experiencing an outbreak in parts of the San Juan Mountains in* A.D. *2002.*

2003 and thirteen in 2004 (see Figure 7.14).[78] The lynx is a denizen of boreal forests, and the conifer forests of the Colorado Rockies are at the southern edge of its range (see Map 7.2).[79] Until 1970 the lynx was a nonprotected predator in Colorado, and the last known lynx in Colorado was killed near Vail in 1974.[80] In 2000 the lynx was listed as threatened in the contiguous United States under the Endangered Species Act.

In 1999, Colorado began a lynx reintroduction program in the San Juan Mountains. These mountains have large wilderness areas dominated by spruce-fir forests, which lynx and their prey, the snowshoe hare, seem to prefer. More than half of the 166 lynx released from 1999 to 2004 survived,[81] a reasonable rate for a reintroduced population. Those that died were killed on highways, by predators, or intentionally by humans. It is too soon to know whether southwestern Colorado has enough habitat and snowshoe hares to support a viable breeding population, but the birth of kittens holds out hope that lynx reintroduction may succeed.[82]

Old-growth forests are essential for both marten and lynx. We saw a marten along the trail in this area during one of our visits. Marten rely on the complex forest floor structure created by large downed trees to escape predators and provide subnivean spaces (the space between the snow and the ground) in winter for resting.[83] One of the marten's main prey species, the red-backed vole, also requires this subnivean habitat.[84] Both martens and lynx den in well-forested areas with many downed logs and large stumps to provide cover for kittens.[85] All of the lynx dens found in 2003 were in areas with extensive downed wood.[86]

BOX—FOREST HEALTH

The concept of forest health has been controversial and remains so today because people value the forest in different ways. Values might be characterized as a split between utilitarian and ecosystem perspectives, but value differences are likely complex.[1] This value conflict became political with the passage in 1995 of the emergency salvage logging rider, Public Law 104-19, which expedited logging to remove dead and dying trees from public forests.

Utilitarians focus on the value of forests in providing products for human use, including timber, forage, recreation, and other uses. From this perspective, diseased or dying trees suggest a forest health problem. The ecosystem perspective views the forest as a complex system satisfying multiple objectives, not as focused solely on immediate products for people. Ecosystems sustain biological diversity and provide indirect services such as clean water and nutrient cycling. Sick and dying trees are not necessarily a forest health problem, as insect outbreaks, disease, and tree deaths are often normal processes in ecosystems. Forest health problems, from this perspective, are invasive non-native weeds and pathogens, forest fragmentation as a result of logging and roads, overgrazing, nonsustainable logging, and other impacts of land uses.[2]

Southwestern Colorado's forests are still relatively free of non-native diseases and insects, but native insects and disease have long been part of the region's forest ecosystems. Native insects that have occasional outbreaks and kill trees over large areas include the mountain pine beetle in ponderosa pine forests, the western spruce budworm and Douglas-fir beetle in mixed conifer forests, the spruce beetle and fir engraver in subalpine forests, and the western tent caterpillar in aspen forests.[3] Spruce budworm in the San Juan Mountains erupts during wet periods about every twenty-five to forty years.[4] The spruce beetle has periodic outbreaks that kill spruce over large areas—an outbreak in the 1850s–1880s affected subalpine forests throughout western Colorado, and the spruce beetle may be as important as fire in structuring these forests.[5] Patches or even large areas of dead trees have long been a part of southwestern Colorado forests.

Disease, insects, and parasites are important to biological diversity in forests.[6] In Colorado ponderosa pine forests, dwarf mistletoe (see Plate 34) is a common native parasite that reduces tree growth and can kill trees; however, the number and diversity of native birds are positively correlated with the level of dwarf mistletoe.[7] Researchers studying dwarf mistletoe in these pine forests say that "while dwarf mistletoe has traditionally been viewed as a forest pest because of reductions in timber volume, we suggest that in areas where management goals are not strictly focused on timber production, control of dwarf mistletoe may not be justified, practical, or even desirable. . . . [W]e suggest that eradication efforts be reconsidered given that dwarf mistletoes have been a part of these forest ecosystems for thousands, and possibly millions, of years."[8]

NOTES

1. Jenkins, "Forest Health, Crisis of Human Proportions."
2. Peters, Frost, and Pace, *Managing for Forest Ecosystem Health.*
3. Schmid and Mata, *Natural Variability of Insect Populations.*
4. Ryerson, Swetnam, and Lynch, "Western Spruce Budworm Outbreaks."
5. Baker and Veblen, "Spruce Beetles and Fires."
6. Castello, Leopold, and Smallidge, "Pathogens, Patterns, and Processes in Forest Ecosystems."
7. Bennetts et al., "Influence of Dwarf Mistletoe on Bird Communities."
8. Ibid., 899.

Figure 7.14. *Lynx kittens, taken in the San Juan Mountains in 2003. Photo by Grant Merrill. Courtesy, Colorado Division of Wildlife, Denver, Colorado.*

The Healthy Forests Restoration Act might envision that a legacy of fire suppression is evidenced by diseased and downed trees in old-growth forests, but in the subalpine forest these are actually the marks of a healthy forest. The needs of native forest predators and their prey illustrate how misguided "fuels reduction" projects are that would remove habitat features critical to these native species.

WHAT IS HAPPENING NOW?

Telluride's Latest Boom

San Miguel County reached a low point in population in 1970, with only 553 people in Telluride and fewer than 2,000 residents in the entire county.[87] Idarado, the last of the upper-basin mines, wound down; the uranium mill at Uravan closed; and the county returned to its agricultural base. A new wave of immigrants arrived in the 1970s, attracted by a new ski area—opened in 1972—and an empty niche. They brought a strong counterculture that remains the foundation for Telluride's unique

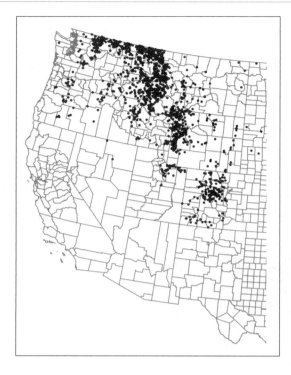

Map 7.2. *Trapping, visual, and track records of lynx in the western United States from 1842 to 1998. Data provided by Kevin S. McKelvey, USDA Forest Service, Missoula, Montana.*

(for western Colorado) political character.[88] These newcomers formed an "intentional community"—that is, people came not because of economic opportunity but for the chance to create an alternative, egalitarian town.[89]

Linda and Phil Miller arrived with this first wave in the 1970s when Phil was working for the Forest Service on a wilderness proposal for the Sneffels Range. Linda says the "radical goals and philosophy" of that early core group included food co-ops, community child care, a community radio station (KOTO), and preservation of the town's natural environment and historical character.[90] The town began to host its famous Telluride Film and Bluegrass festivals and became known as a place where celebrities could walk the streets without causing commotion.[91]

In 1979 two entrepreneurs purchased and expanded the ski area and began development of Mountain Village, an upscale ski resort above Telluride. With the opening of the Telluride Regional Airport to commercial flights in 1985, a new wave of immigration began, attracted by the ski resort, natural and cultural amenities, and rural property. In the 1990s, real estate values soared as increasingly wealthy immigrants arrived. Multimillion-dollar homes began filling the mesas along the San Miguel River. In 1999, three ranches on Deep Creek Mesa and Beaver Mesa were subdivided into thirty-five-acre lots. In 2000, nineteen real estate transactions involving these lots averaged over $3 million each.[92]

As the countryside is being subdivided, Telluride struggles to maintain its historical small-town boundaries and feel. Restored old buildings and new construction fill the narrow town site. Between 1990 and

Figure 7.15. *Entrance gate to a house near Telluride, Colorado.*

2000, Telluride's population grew from 1,309 to 2,221, while the county grew from 3,653 to 6,594 residents. The median price of condominiums in 2005 was $567,500 in Telluride and Mountain Village. Average house prices in 2005 were $1.49 million in Telluride and $3.2 million in Mountain Village.[93]

The juxtaposition of an egalitarian, alternative culture and extreme wealth creates a town with contradictions. The economy of the town and county is now based on construction, real estate, and the ski resort.[94] The marked social and economic disparities are hardly visible; no slums or trailer parks mar the area's beauty. Each morning, however, construction and service workers, unable or unwilling to pay high housing prices, follow narrow highways into Telluride from homes an hour or more away in Dolores, Cortez, Norwood, and Montrose. The young and international workers who take the low-paying jobs, such as tending landscaped gates of multimillion-dollar mansions (see Figure 7.15) and cooking and cleaning for the lodging industry, crowd into apartments and dormitories in town. Ironically, in the midst of this housing crunch, only about 60 percent of homes in the county are occupied as permanent residences.[95]

In spite of these overwhelming economic forces or perhaps because of them, citizens of the San Miguel watershed are working to preserve their natural landscapes and communities by steering and, at times, resisting the forces of change. We wondered what enabled these people to shape the future when surrounding places seem overrun by it? What we found was an activist political climate and a set of individuals who together have the skills and perspectives needed to create a vision for the watershed and make it a reality.

Innovative Local Government Initiatives

Both the town of Telluride and San Miguel County are noted for their activist local governments. Longtime residents say that Telluride's egalitarian and radical spirit has eroded with the influx of money and the resort and second-home culture, but this erosion is not apparent in reading the *Telluride Daily Planet*.[96] Local elections, at least in recent years, have been hotly contested and debated, with candidates taking divergent positions on key land-use and planning issues that will determine Telluride's future.

For most of its length, the San Miguel River flows through San Miguel County. The San Miguel County Commission, at the time we wrote this book, reflected the diversity that shapes the New West. Art Goodtimes of the Green Party is a charismatic writer who hand-weaves during public meetings. Vern Ebert, a Republican, is an army colonel who has retired to one of the county's exclusive subdivisions. Elaine Fisher, who initially cleaned houses in Telluride, became the town's mayor and represents the Telluride District on the commission as a Democrat. The commission as a whole tends to be moderate and pragmatic, placing a premium on holding the county together with forward-looking approaches to planning.

The innovative policies of Telluride and San Miguel County include real estate transfer taxation, deed-restricted affordable housing, active programs for the creation and protection of open space, and, in the case of the county, creative planning. Telluride taxes all real estate transfers at 3 percent. These taxes paid for the public swimming pool, town-park improvements, and a renovated downtown streetscape,[97] designed with wide sidewalks and gathering areas to encourage mingling of residents.[98]

Common folk may be able to walk the streets of Telluride comfortably, but living there is another matter. In spite of the presence of 766 affordable housing units managed by Telluride, Mountain Village, and the county, a 2000 assessment found that 940 workers commuted from outside the county each day, and 75 percent of residents and workers surveyed felt that housing is the "most critical" or "one of the most serious" problems of the area.[99] The town and county have incentives and requirements for new developments to include housing with deeds restricted to those who work in the county, but the problem remains unresolved.

The housing shortage impinges on discussions of growth management and land-use planning, but it has not dampened residents' support of open space. In 1993, Telluride residents voted to devote 20 percent of the town's revenue to the Open Space Fund. These funds allowed the joint purchase (with the San Miguel Conservation Foundation) of a 320-acre parcel of forest adjoining the town park.[100] The Bear Creek Preserve is now an important natural area and heavily hiked open space.

San Miguel County's Open Space Commission purchases development rights for lands with significant wildlife, riparian, or agricultural value, using funds from the Great Outdoors Colorado program (funded by the state lottery) and a county mill levy. Under this Purchase of Development Rights program, the landowner agrees to a conservation easement with a land trust (see Box—Land Trusts, pp. 128–129) of the landowner's choosing. The Gunnison sage-grouse (see Chapter 2) is being helped by this program. Sagebrush habitat south of Norwood is important to the San Miguel Basin subpopulation, and some of that habitat has recently been protected from development under the Open Space program.[101] Still, the program is small relative to the rapid rate of subdivision of the county's more scenic ranch lands.

County planning codes and practices may be the most critical tools for implementing a vision that includes natural areas and open space. San Miguel County uses legal powers under state law to place modest restrictions on development to protect wildlife habitat, wetlands, and riparian areas (see Box—Land-Use Legislation and Government Policy, pp. 295–296). Although planning regulations can help guide the future

BOX—LAND-USE LEGISLATION AND GOVERNMENT POLICY

What the U.S. experience shows . . . is the importance of understanding private property as a symbol as well as an economic and political institution, and paying careful attention to the way private ownership is described. Ownership *rights* need to marry ownership *responsibility*. Talk of property as individual enclave needs to be matched with community-focused talk about owning as belonging.[1]

Federal and state laws have long recognized a basic right of local governments to regulate land use for the public good. But courts have also recognized private property rights under the Fifth Amendment of the U.S. Constitution, which states that private property shall not be taken for public use without just compensation. Courts' interpretations of the "takings" clause have varied from state to state and over time. Rulings are influenced by a judge's view of government regulation and whether he or she views land more as a private commodity or a community resource.[2]

Subdivision of rural private land has profound community impacts but few regulations. Typical of many states today, Colorado state law exempts parcels of 35 acres or more from subdivision regulations. Local governments have some tools to discourage "galloping 35s," but few counties use them, probably because sentiment for strong private property rights runs deep in many rural counties. Counties can zone land for particular uses, and some counties have zoned parts of their jurisdictions for larger minimum lot sizes, typically 80 acres. Counties can also use incentives to encourage clustering of development on a small portion of a subdivided land area. Especially promising is the Areas and Activities of State Interest law, commonly called House Bill 1041. This law grants local governments authority to develop guidelines for areas of "state interest," which include natural hazard areas and areas with important historical, archaeological, or natural resource values.[3] So far, counties have utilized these "1041 powers" sparingly.

San Miguel County is a leader in the use of 1041 powers, using them mainly to develop guidelines and policies that limit and mitigate development on hazardous sites, important wildlife habitat such as elk calving areas, historic sites, and wetlands.[4] A county cannot stop development of private lands but can adopt regulations and guidelines for development in areas of "state interest."[5] For example, in San Miguel County, dogs over a certain size are not allowed in elk calving areas. San Miguel County also defined the Telluride/Ophir High Country Area, a historic mining zone within which regulations restrict the size of buildings, limit lighting, and prevent road improvements—thus protecting the broader public interest in this important historic area and tourist attraction. Regulations in the zone had to be carefully crafted to allow limited development so as not to provoke a legal takings challenge.

Because of local governments' reluctance to use H.B. 1041 and other tools, many open-space advocates believe raising the exemption limit to 160 acres, as Montana has done, would help greatly in reducing sprawl. Counties would then have more opportunity to direct development for the community good.

NOTES

1. Freyfogle, "Community and Market," 410 (original emphasis).
2. Ibid.
3. Panos, "H.B. 1041 as a Tool for Municipal Attorneys."
4. San Miguel County Land Use Code, Land Use Policies, County Planning Office, Telluride, Colorado.
5. Green, "Areas and Activities of State Interest Act."

of the San Miguel watershed and its communities, their ability to regulate development is still limited.[102] Thus, local activism is also playing an important role in shaping the San Miguel's future.

Grassroots Resistance to Large-Scale Development: Saving the Valley Floor

The town of Telluride is surrounded by large corporate landowners. Mountain Village, which lies out of view to the south, was developed as an exclusive resort community around the Telluride Ski and Golf Company's development—until recently owned by Hideo Morita, the son of Sony's founders.[103] Just east of Telluride, up valley, are the mines, mills, and reclaimed tailings piles of Idarado Mining—now a subsidiary of Newmont Gold Company, the world's largest gold company. To the west, the 857-acre Valley Floor is owned by Neal Blue, CEO of General Atomics, who purchased it in 1983 from Idarado.[104] Both Idarado and Blue proposed to develop their properties, but the people of Telluride resisted.

In 2000 and 2001, Idarado proposed that Telluride annex 405 of the 3,500+ acres of the mine lands east of town. Luxury homes and condominiums would have been built, along with affordable housing on 175 acres. Over 2,220 acres of high-country mining claims would have been donated to a land trust and eventually transferred to the Forest Service.[105] Opponents argued that the development would double the size of the town, cause traffic congestion, and change the town's character irrevocably. Also, it was not clear who would build the affordable housing.

Others argued that the deal was too favorable to Idarado, which the state of Colorado had to sue for cleanup of the Idarado mine and mill sites under Superfund.[106] It took ten years of negotiations and court procedures for the state and Idarado to reach an agreement, but in 2006, Idarado had completed most remediation projects and was approaching compliance.[107] The proposed development would have enabled Idarado to recoup some of the millions spent on cleanup while transferring hard-to-develop, high-elevation mined lands, with high liability under the Clean Water Act and Superfund, to the public. Telluride voters rejected the proposal for annexation in November 2001. Idarado then approached the county, and the Board of County Commissioners accepted a modified proposal for development of thirty-seven homesites. The proposal includes sale and transfer to the Forest Service of 2,500 acres of high-country land.[108]

Even more contentious has been the relationship of the town with its neighbor to the west. The wide, undeveloped Valley Floor defines

Figure 7.16. *Save the Valley Floor demonstration, July 2000. Courtesy, Melanie J. McCloskey Photography, Salt Lake City.*

the western edge of town (see Plate 54) and provides a beautiful entrance to Telluride, as well as unofficial open space. In reaction to the threat of development, a Save the Valley Floor campaign was launched. In July 2000, 750 people formed a human chain along Valley Floor to encourage the town council to condemn the property and retain it as public open space (see Figure 7.16).[109]

For two years the council vacillated, and the public hotly debated the merits, dangers, and costs of condemnation. Condemnation would mean a long and expensive legal process that some thought would cost over $60 million.[110] People with a strong belief in the market and property rights argued that the town should negotiate with the owner instead. Some also thought development could provide affordable housing and would be good for Telluride's economy.[111] The Sheep Mountain Alliance, a local environmental group, led the campaign for condemnation. The group's members argued that an economy based on resort and residential development was not sustainable and that affordable housing could not keep pace with new service jobs the development created. They argued that it was the rightful role of government to protect the valley for the benefit of the people of Telluride.[112]

A broad spectrum of residents supported condemnation. With many wealthy residents willing to contribute, the Sheep Mountain Alliance raised over $5 million before the vote to show that funding would be forthcoming if condemnation proceeded.[113] In June 2002, voters approved (609 to 385) a citizen-written ordinance to condemn 570 acres of Valley Floor on the south side of the highway.[114] In late 2003 Neal Blue's San Miguel Valley Corporation (SMVC) rejected the town's offer to buy the property for $19.5 million, and the council began proceedings for condemnation.[115] In December 2005 the Telluride City Council postponed its court date and supported a negotiated deal with SMVC to annex the land and develop only a portion of it with twenty-two homes, a school, and other services. On February 14, 2006, voters rejected (609 to 429) the deal and directed the council to resume condemnation.[116] Few towns have taken on such a challenge as this plucky little town did, as it resisted a fate others might see as inevitable.

Preserving the San Miguel's Natural Diversity

The San Miguel is an unusually natural river despite its extensive mining history. In the 1980s The Nature Conservancy (TNC) funded an inventory to identify natural vegetation along rivers and streams as part of its Rivers of the Rockies initiative. One of the authors (Baker), working on this project and his dissertation in 1985, noticed that long reaches of the San Miguel appeared relatively free of invasion by non-native plants, heavy grazing by domestic livestock, significant mining in the channel, diversion for agricultural use, and other direct impacts. Particularly valuable ecologically is the simple fact that the river lacks a major dam. Impacts in the channel downstream from Telluride are fewer than those along most other rivers this size. So, with some excitement, Baker mapped places where the vegetation was least altered, sampled it, took photographs, and put together a set of preserve designs for TNC.

Identifying remnants is easy compared with the effort required to protect those remnants. Approaching a landowner to discuss a possible sale or conservation easement requires another set of skills. Over the next several years, TNC was able to acquire several miles of the river. Sydney Macy, then TNC's director for Colorado, negotiated a complex deal to transfer land along the lower San Miguel to TNC as part of Umetco's Superfund settlement for its uranium mill at Uravan. David Adamson, TNC's Colorado director for development, arranged purchases of the South Fork Preserve at Illium and the San Miguel River Canyon Preserve downstream from Placerville just before prices soared.[117]

Other purchases required both perseverance and luck. In 1992 TNC's
Pat Willits began visiting the owners of 350 acres of land adjacent to the
Umetco property TNC had acquired. The family was not interested in
selling, but Willits kept visiting. Finally, in 1996 family dynamics had
changed, and TNC was able to buy the ranch to add to the Umetco
property, creating the seven-mile-long San Miguel at Tabeguache Creek
Preserve (see Map 7.1).[118] This preserve protects a rare and ecologically
significant low-elevation cottonwood community.

To purchase land for protection, one must know the land and relate
to the people who own it. Serendipity can also play a role. Willits tells
of one such purchase: "I met a Nucla family by accident at the Ouray
Hot Springs with my one-year-old daughter in my arms. I had seen
their name on ownership maps and talked my way into getting a tour
of the property."[119] It turned out that the land was not important to the
ranching operation and therefore may eventually have been developed.
TNC helped purchase and transfer the land to BLM ownership. Were it
not for landowners willing to sell for conservation, donors providing
funds to purchase the land, and the patient skills of people such as
Macy, Adamson, and Willits, these ten miles of riparian preserve would
likely now be filled with houses, as is most private land along the river.

South Fork Preserve. The South Fork Preserve is a 1.5-mile reach of
the South Fork of the San Miguel River only a few miles from Telluride.
Although it is small (about sixty-seven acres), the preserve includes the
best reach of a particular type of riparian ecosystem found only in this
part of Colorado. The vegetation here is very natural, with little evidence of the livestock grazing that has altered this ecosystem along
most rivers. It is not "pristine," as this was a placer mining claim and
bits of old iron can be found here and there, suggesting past mineral
exploration and other uses. A few non-native plants are also present.
Yet few sites of this type remain in such an undisturbed state.

Riparian ecosystems in southwestern Colorado change distinctively
with elevation because the dominant trees have elevational limits probably related to tolerance to temperature.[120] In southwestern Colorado,
narrowleaf cottonwood dominates the riparian zone from about 6,000
feet in elevation (e.g., at the Tabeguache Preserve) up to about 8,500
feet, where it mixes—as it does here—with blue spruce (see Figure
7.17). Blue spruce continues on up by itself to over 10,000 feet in elevation. Blue spruce is not always blue, and it is sometimes difficult to
distinguish from its cousin, Engelmann spruce. Blue spruce has longer
cones (about 3"–4" rather than 1"–2"), and its young twigs lack the little
hairs Engelmann has (a hand lens is needed to see this).

Figure 7.17. *The Nature Conservancy's South Fork Preserve. Blue spruce and narrow-leaf cottonwood are the dominant trees at this elevation.*

The cottonwood-spruce community at South Fork Preserve is characterized by a diverse shrub understory, with twinberry honeysuckle most prominent. This shrub, with opposite leaves and paired flowers, has blackish fruits in late summer that are truly awful in taste. This small area contains at least seven native tree species, fifteen shrubs, forty forbs, and eleven grasses, sedges, and rushes for a total of at least seventy-three native plants. Some of the common ones are presented in Table 7.2. This is a high level of plant diversity for such a small area—typical upland forests nearby would have only twenty to forty species. In western Colorado, highest plant species richness may occur in riparian forests along subalpine streams at this elevation or a little higher.[121] Why are so many plants present in this area? In part, it is simply that this is a moist setting favorable to plants, but the river is also continually reshaping the environment, which prevents a particular species from monopolizing the system. Also, periodic floods create diverse physical settings, including boulder and gravel bars interwoven with small side channels, as well as finer-textured terraces covered with forest.

In 2001–2002 a group of volunteers, including a Colorado Youth Corps group from Durango and International Adventure Tours from Moab, helped TNC construct a viewing platform and boardwalk. Local

Table 7.2. Plants mentioned in the text and common trees, shrubs, and non-native plants at The Nature Conservancy's South Fork, Canyon, and Tabeguache preserves.[1]

	South Fork	Canyon	Tabeguache
TREES			
Blue spruce (*Picea pungens*)	X	X	—
Douglas-fir (*Pseudotsuga menziesii*)	X	—	—
Narrowleaf cottonwood (*Populus angustifolia*)	X	X	—
Rio Grande cottonwood (*Populus deltoides* subsp. *wislizenii*)	—	—	X
SHRUBS			
Basin big sagebrush (*Seriphidium tridentatum*)	—	—	X
Drummond's willow (*Salix drummondiana*)	X	—	—
Gambel oak (*Quercus gambelii*)	—	—	X
Greasewood (*Sarcobatus vermiculatus*)	—	—	X
Mountain snowberry (*Symphoricarpos rotundifolius*)	X	—	—
Narrowleaf willow (*Salix exigua*)	—	X	X
Park willow (*Salix monticola*)	—	X	—
Redosier dogwood (*Swida sericea*)	—	X	—
Rocky Mountain maple (*Acer glabrum*)	X	X	—
Rubber rabbitbrush (*Chrysothamnus nauseosus*)	—	—	X
Skunkbush sumac (*Rhus aromatica* subsp. *trilobata*)	—	—	X
Strapleaf willow (*Salix ligulifolia*)	—	—	X
Stretchberry (*Forestiera pubescens*)	—	—	X
Thinleaf alder (*Alnus incana* subsp. *tenuifolia*)	X	X	—
Twinberry honeysuckle (*Distegia involucrate*)	X	X	—
Utah serviceberry (*Amelanchier utahensis*)	X	X	X
Water birch (*Betula fontinalis*)	—	X	X
Woods' rose (*Rosa woodsii*)	X	X	X
NON-NATIVES			
Canada thistle (*Breea arvense*)	—	—	X
Cheatgrass (*Anisantha tectorum*)	—	—	X
Kentucky bluegrass (*Poa pratensis*)	X	X	X
Orchardgrass (*Dactylis glomerata*)	X	X	X
Russian olive (*Eleagnus angustifolia*)	—	—	X
Saltcedar (*Tamarix ramosissima*)	—	—	X
Siberian elm (*Ulmus pumila*)	—	—	X
Smooth brome (*Bromopsis inermis*)	—	X	X
Yellow sweetclover (*Melilotus officinale*)	—	X	X

1. Common names are from the PLANTS online database, http://plants.usda.gov. Latin names are from Weber and Wittmann, *Colorado Flora*.

businesses donated materials. A trail through the preserve was placed to avoid trampling in the wet areas on the riverbank. Volunteers also cut weeds in the preserve each year.[122]

Unfortunately, the water quality of the river itself is much less natural, and there is concern for the hydrologic regime. About a mile upstream of the preserve, the Howard Fork joins the Lake Fork to create the South Fork. Howard Fork contains numerous old mines and tailings piles and is contaminated with heavy metals (zinc, copper, lead) at levels sufficient to warrant designation as a Superfund site.[123] Howard Fork is mostly devoid of fish and native insects, but there is considerable interest in cleaning up the mine waste.[124] Also currently under study are winter releases of water from the Ames Power Plant, which appear to be creating ice flows that scour the channel and banks downstream for about twenty miles.[125]

Important to this preserve is continuation of natural flooding. Diversions and storage of runoff in Trout Lake and Hope Lake may diminish spring runoff, affecting the riparian zone at South Fork Preserve. These are small dams, and the San Miguel is still a wild river capable of major floods. On August 8, 2001, about four inches of rain in forty minutes in the upper watershed led to a flash flood that affected over seventy miles of the river.[126] Periodic floods are a normal ecosystem process that reshapes the floodplain and provides new opportunities for native plants. This preserve has stimulated interest in preservation and restoration upstream and down, and it is also a beautiful and important spot on its own.

The Canyon Preserve and BLM's Area of Critical Environmental Concern. A few miles downstream from Placerville is The Nature Conservancy's San Miguel River Canyon Preserve. This stretch of the river, through a spectacular red-rock canyon, is lined with a beautiful riparian forest (Plate 55). Here, narrowleaf cottonwood is near the middle of its elevational range and is associated with a much higher diversity of smaller trees and large shrubs, including Rocky Mountain maple, thinleaf alder, water birch, and redosier dogwood (see Table 7.2). Riparian areas at this elevation are not very prone to replacement by non-native trees and shrubs, but when the canopy is opened or the soil is disturbed, many non-native grasses and forbs can invade. At nearby recently disturbed areas, non-native plants (Kentucky bluegrass, orchardgrass, Canada thistle, and yellow sweetclover) are common. This area's proximity to both the road and recreational use means non-native seeds will continue to arrive. However, in the preserve the trees are dense, and non-natives are a small part of the mostly native understory.

While protection of private land is crucial, much of the river corridor from Deep Creek (between Placerville and Telluride) to Piñon (just above Naturita) is public land managed by the BLM. In the early 1990s individuals in the BLM's Montrose office began working with TNC and the San Miguel County Planning Office to protect and restore BLM lands along the San Miguel. TNC proposed that a large section of BLM's riparian corridor be declared an Area of Critical Environmental Concern (ACEC).[127] An ACEC highlights areas where special management attention is needed to protect important historical, cultural, or scenic values; fish and wildlife resources; or other natural systems or processes.

The response to this initiative was quick and impressive. Jim Ferguson, BLM biologist at Montrose, took on the huge task of amending the Resource Management Plan so the ACEC designation would be possible. TNC helped conduct field trips for decision makers and the public and helped Montrose BLM obtain $1 million from the Land and Water Conservation Fund to purchase key pieces of land along the river. BLM recreation planner Karen Tucker, recognizing the growing recreational pressures on the river corridor, worked with Ferguson to combine the 22,000-acre ACEC with an 11,000-acre buffer to create a Special Resource Recreation Management Area, which has high priority for BLM recreational funds.[128]

Thus, at a time when the clash between public and private interests seems to have grown in the West, concern for the San Miguel's future encouraged many supportive and productive relationships among the BLM, TNC, and local citizens. Because of the efforts of a few dedicated people, the beautiful canyon of the San Miguel River will be better protected and managed.

Tabeguache Preserve: A dynamic riverine landscape. The Tabeguache Preserve begins about six miles downstream from Naturita and continues for seven miles to the point where Tabeguache Creek meets the San Miguel River just above the Uravan town site. It is a good place to think about cottonwoods and floods. This beautiful preserve is not pristine, as the imprints of ranching and mining are numerous. Much of the understory vegetation is Kentucky bluegrass, orchardgrass, yellow sweetclover, and other non-native plants (see Table 7.2). The jewels of the Tabeguache Preserve are the trees of the riparian ecosystem.

No other place known in Colorado contains well-reproducing Rio Grande cottonwoods with a relatively low incidence of saltcedar (see Box—Saltcedar, pp. 310–311) on a river that is essentially free-flowing. The preserve is found near the upper elevational limit of Rio Grande cottonwood, which dominates lowland rivers in western Colorado, eastern Utah, and into New Mexico.[129] It is also at the lower elevational limit of narrowleaf cottonwood (see Figure 7.1).

The arrangement of the two cottonwoods can tell much about the natural flood regime of the San Miguel. Looking upstream from near the downstream end of the preserve (see Plate 56), a gravel bar across the river is dominated by small narrowleaf cottonwood, but the larger, older trees behind the bar are mostly Rio Grande cottonwood. Through-out the preserve these two cottonwoods are arrayed in a mosaic. Gravel bars upstream of this stop have more narrowleaf cottonwood, while bars downstream have more Rio Grande cottonwood. Narrowleaf wil-low occupies the river edge of the bars.

Over time, the river meanders across the bottom of the valley, leaving behind bars while cutting into banks on the other side, occasionally flooding across a bar and opening a new channel. This leads to a dy-namic, slowly shifting mosaic of riverine landforms—from bare sand-bars to older terraces—that support a mosaic of cottonwoods, willows, and other plants.

Within the older stands are few young cottonwoods. There may be a few sprouts here and there, but the stand consists mostly of trees of similar size. Cottonwoods in particular seem to regenerate as a cohort, groups of individuals born at about the same time, especially after a flood or a wet period.[130] The older forests here are perhaps a century old. In 2002 the younger stand on the bar across the river in Plate 56 was likely fifteen to twenty-five years old, and the intermediate-sized stand farther upstream was probably sixty to seventy-five years old.

Cottonwoods may also die together as a cohort when the river blasts through an old stand or slowly erodes away the bank, gradually toppling the old trees. The river is sufficiently dynamic that few spots escape a flood every century or so, which may be why cottonwoods are rarely over 150 years old. Events that dramatically shift the mosaic somewhere along the river might come only every decade or two, typi-cally when very deep snowpack high in the watershed melts quickly or when the melt is accompanied by high rainfall.[131]

Cottonwoods may undergo expansions and contractions as climate fluctuates. In the late 1800s, narrowleaf cottonwoods in western Colo-rado expanded into broader and warmer valleys such as this one. This expansion was discovered by comparing historical photographs taken in the late 1800s with modern retakes done in 1985–1986 (see Figure 7.18). Cool, wet weather in the late 1800s may have allowed narrowleaf cottonwood regeneration in open, hot valleys where it normally would fail as a result of late-summer heat and drought.[132] What might the place in Plate 56 look like in 100 years? Will the cottonwoods on the bar be grown up, the willow gone, the old cottonwoods in the back re-placed by a new channel? If global warming continues, narrowleaf cot-tonwood may decline here where it is at its lower elevation limit, and Rio Grande cottonwood may expand. The preserve will provide an opportunity to better understand how the changing climate and flood regime affect riparian ecosystems.

Figure 7.18. *A rephotographic pair illustrating the expansion of narrowleaf cotton-wood* (Populus angustifolia) *in western Colorado. This photo shows the town of Aspen in Pitkin County, Colorado: (a) original photograph by William H. Jackson, probably* A.D. *1890–1891. Courtesy, Colorado Historical Society, Denver. (b) Rephoto reprinted from plate 104 in Baker (1987).*

The natural flood regime and riparian trees may be the most sig-nificant aspects of this protected area, but low-elevation riparian for-ests such as this also support a higher diversity of birds than any other habitat in Colorado (see Table 7.3).[133] In May, when birds are defending breeding territories, the mature cottonwood stands support a chorus of birds. Migrating birds also depend heavily on riparian corridors through desert terrain. Bald eagles roost and hunt along the river in winter, and a few stay to breed nearby. Common mergansers, spotted sandpipers, and other waterbirds breed along the river. People tend to view floods as destructive, and they are when they wash away build-ings or valuable land, but floods are a way of life for cottonwoods, willows, and the birds and animals that depend on them.

Recognizing Connections: The San Miguel Watershed Coalition

The protection of natural communities is important, but it is only part of the story of restoration of the San Miguel watershed. Stretching from alpine wilderness areas and mined high country to irrigated farms

Table 7.3. Breeding birds of lower-elevation riparian habitats of southwestern Colorado.[1]

American crow	Blue grosbeak	Lazuli bunting
American goldfinch	Bullock's oriole	Mourning dove
American kestrel	Canada goose	Northern flicker
Bank swallow	Common merganser	Rough-winged swallow
Belted kingfisher	Downy woodpecker	Western screech owl
Black phoebe	Great blue heron	Wood duck
Black-billed magpie	Great-horned owl	Western kingbird
Black-capped chickadee	House wren	Yellow warbler
Black-chinned hummingbird	Lewis's woodpecker	Yellow-breasted chat

1. Kingery, *Colorado Breeding Bird Atlas;* Partners in Flight, *Land Bird Conservation Plan.*

and canyons of the Colorado Plateau, the watershed encompasses about 1 million acres (see Map 7.3). It includes over 6,000 residents and is the source of many of their livelihoods.[134] In the 1990s many of those people came together, as they recognized that the forces of the New West were upon them and that the future of their communities, the land, and the river required a collective effort.

According to Pam Zoline of the nonprofit Telluride Institute, the rapid changes taking place at both ends of the watershed motivated seventy people to travel to Mountain Village through a May blizzard for the first meeting of the Friends of the San Miguel River Task Force.[135] West-end ranchers, Telluride locals, and their wealthy new neighbors met—many for the first time. In 1993 the newly formed San Miguel Watershed Coalition initiated a watershed-wide planning process facilitated by the Telluride Institute and the National Park Service's Rivers, Trails, and Conservation Assistance Program. At the start, the group knew little about the watershed or what questions to ask. Zoline, whose father started the original Telluride ski area, said, "It took a couple of years of blood, sweat and tears, but there was lots of common ground, and we found the distance between us was not insurmountable."[136]

In 1998 the group released a collaborative planning framework, the San Miguel Basin Watershed Plan. After five years of gathering both scientific and local knowledge, the group had a much clearer picture of the watershed and the threats it faced. The coalition, coordinated from its inception until 2001 by Linda Luther of Placerville, had already achieved much. The coalition's key concept is the unity of the watershed, and unity requires people who work well across institutional and social boundaries.

Some accomplishments of the coalition. The coalition has documented historical and new threats to the integrity of the watershed. Some of

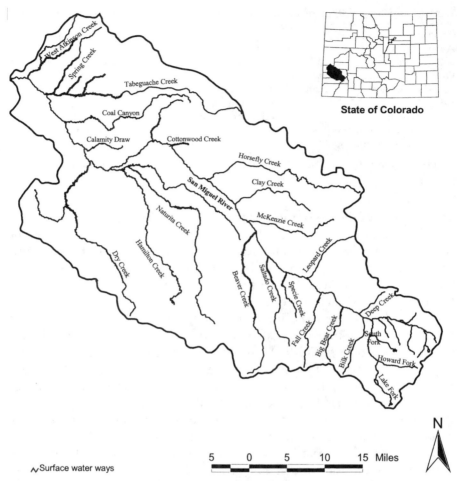

State of Colorado

N

5   0   5   10   15 Miles

∿Surface water ways

Map 7.3. *San Miguel River watershed. Reprinted from Willits (2001), map 1. Map by Chris Hazen and the Telluride Institute, with permission of Pat Willits.*

the historical problems identified were abandoned mine sites draining heavy metals into the river, old placer mines and gravel operations that had altered the stream channel and riparian vegetation, and sediment and salinity runoff from arid, overgrazed uplands.[137] At the same time, new demands, particularly recreation along the sensitive riparian corridor, needed management.

The coalition identified dispersed camping and vehicle-assisted recreation as the most pressing threat to the watershed.[138] River rafting had also grown in popularity and required boat launches, as well as parking and camping areas. A limit on the number of commercial raft-

Figure 7.19. *Norwood high school students learning about fly-fishing insects and aquatic ecology along the San Miguel River. Courtesy, April Montgomery, Naturita, Colorado.*

ing permits, in conjunction with stricter camping regulations and education on low-impact camping, has reduced the impacts of those who float the river. To provide access points that minimize damage, BLM's Karen Tucker obtained major grants to build the Beaver Creek picnic area and the Specie Creek boat launch. The length of camping stays was reduced. The coalition also hired local resident Leigh Sullivan to serve as the "River Ranger." She recruits and supervises volunteers, implements site projects, and provides environmental education.[139]

The San Miguel Watershed Education project uses the San Miguel River as a living classroom (see Figure 7.19), and the Norwood Hill area was developed to assist that program. By involving students from all three area school districts in hands-on monitoring of the river and restoration activities, it is hoped the next generation will develop a holistic view of the watershed.[140] By 2005 the coalition was hosting regular collaborative forums and educational programs to pursue specific issues in depth. The coalition monitors water and air quality and recreational use and abuse. It also coordinates restoration projects.[141]

Two ambitious projects are crucial for the long-term protection of the San Miguel's unique riparian communities. The first is elimination of non-native trees that have begun to invade the riparian corridor.

Mallory Dimmitt of TNC in Telluride has led the effort to eliminate saltcedar (see Box—Saltcedar, pp. 310–311), Russian olive, and Siberian elm. Saltcedar (see Plate 57) has been mapped in over 100 miles of river and tributaries in the watershed. Eradication is hard work, involving cutting the trees and immediately applying an herbicide to the stumps (see Figure 7.20). Volunteers handle some of the lighter infestations, but a six-person construction crew from Norwood has been hired to do the bulk of the work during the fall and spring. Private landowners are comfortable giving the local crew access, and the work is an economic boost to Norwood in the off-season.[142] The cost of removing saltcedar along the San Miguel and its tributaries is estimated to be over $600,000. Funding for the first three years came from the Terra Foundation of Boulder, Monsanto, BLM, the National Fish and Wildlife Foundation,

BOX—SALTCEDAR

We simply do not agree that vast areas now infested by saltcedar cannot be returned to habitats dominated by native riparian species.[1]

For anyone who feels hopeless about the world, this is a story of unexpected hope in the face of what seemed a decade ago an impossible foe— saltcedar, an introduced tree that has taken over much of the low-elevation riparian habitat in the West. Saltcedar, also called tamarisk (see Plate 57), was probably first introduced into the United States from Eurasia by nurserymen in the early 1800s as an ornamental.[2] About five species of saltcedar escaped from cultivation by 1900 in several southwestern states, but not until the 1920s was its presence widely noticed.[3] From 1920 to 1960 saltcedar expanded by about 22,500 acres on average per year,[4] galloping up the Colorado River at about twelve miles per year.[5] By 1987 it occupied about 1.5 million acres in the Southwest alone[6] and was still expanding up rivers to as high as 7,000 feet in elevation.[7] Saltcedar may possess sufficient genetic diversity to allow it to move farther up in elevation and farther north into colder climates.[8] Remarkably, some nurseries were still selling it as recently as 2002.

Saltcedar is a monster among weeds. Dams, overgrazing, and other intense human uses of rivers have aided the spread of saltcedar, but it also appears capable of invading relatively undisturbed riparian vegetation.[9] Saltcedar establishes on moist, bare sediment on the margins of rivers, lakes, and reservoirs. Growing up to thirteen feet tall in a single season and capable of flowering the first year and producing a half million seeds per plant, saltcedar quickly forms dense stands that become near-monocultures.[10] These dense stands support a much lower density and diversity of native plants, birds, and mammals than uninfested stands.[11] Seven bird species are in serious decline and two others have been extirpated by saltcedar invasion along the lower Colorado River.[12] Anyone who has crawled through a saltcedar stand knows that it feels sterile, with a thick mat of fallen leaves and a dense mass of arching stems. The mat of dead leaves and litter is very flammable relative to a comparatively moist cottonwood-willow stand, and fires recur with alarming frequency, as often as every ten to twenty years.[13] Saltcedar resprouts quickly after fire, but cottonwoods often fail to regenerate—much less reach old age—where saltcedar dominates.[14]

Can saltcedar be stopped? Cutting the stems seems to stimulate growth, as does burning, and killing it by flooding requires twenty-four to thirty-six months.[15] However, hand application of the herbicide Triclopyr (trade name Garlon) to cut stems was used successfully to remove the 80 percent cover of saltcedar from the Coachella Valley Preserve in southern California.[16] Bosque del Apache National Wildlife Refuge in New Mexico successfully killed saltcedar using Imazapyr (trade name Arsenal), then replanted native trees and shrubs on about 400 acres.[17] Floods have in some cases removed large areas of saltcedar and led to regeneration of native riparian plants.[18] Restriction of livestock grazing to winter may allow native riparian trees and shrubs to increase.[19] Promising biological control agents—insects from the native habitat of saltcedar in Eurasia—are still awaiting approval, largely because of concern for the southwestern willow flycatcher, an endangered bird.[20] Today, considerable optimism exists that saltcedar can be controlled and riparian areas restored.

NOTES

1. Dudley et al., "Saltcedar Invasion of Western Riparian Areas," 363–364.
2. Robinson, *Introduction, Spread, and Areal Extent of Saltcedar.*
3. Ibid.
4. Ibid.
5. Graf, "Fluvial Adjustments to the Spread of Tamarisk."
6. Brotherson and Field, "Tamarix: Impacts of a Successful Weed."
7. Everitt, "Ecology of Saltcedar."
8. Sexton, McKay, and Sala, "Plasticity and Genetic Diversity May Allow Saltcedar to Invade Cold Climates."
9. Dudley et al., "Saltcedar Invasion of Western Riparian Areas."
10. Di Tomaso, "Impact, Biology, and Ecology of Saltcedar."
11. Ibid.
12. Dudley et al., "Saltcedar Invasion of Western Riparian Areas."
13. Di Tomaso, "Impact, Biology, and Ecology of Saltcedar."
14. Ibid.
15. Brock, "Tamarix spp. (Salt Cedar)."
16. Martin, "Tamarisk Control in Southern California."
17. Taylor and McDaniel, "Restoration of Saltcedar (*Tamarix* sp.)–Infested Floodplains."
18. Dudley et al., "Saltcedar Invasion of Western Riparian Areas."
19. Hughes, "Tamarisk . . . Maybe Not Invincible."
20. Dudley et al., "Saltcedar Invasion of Western Riparian Areas."

Figure 7.20. *Crew member spraying cut saltcedar in the San Miguel watershed. Courtesy, Sheila Grother, Weed Manager, San Miguel County, Colorado.*

Colorado's Wetlands Initiative, and as mitigation for the Bureau of Reclamation's Central Utah project.[143]

A second project critical to the long-term protection of the river involves in-stream flow rights. The one thing a river needs to maintain its unique natural communities is water. Nothing in Colorado law currently prevents the complete appropriation of water, resulting in a dry riverbed (see Figure 7.21). The river's water is allocated to users in order by the year their water rights were claimed. The oldest, most senior right for San Miguel water is a large appropriation far downstream—the Colorado Cooperative Ditch (CC Ditch), which allowed the establishment of Nucla as an agricultural cooperative in 1894.[144] This large senior water right protects much of the river because junior water-right holders upstream must leave at least enough water in the river to meet the CC Ditch right during irrigation season. Every month there are new applications for San Miguel River water, mostly for small amounts to irrigate small areas, to fill stock or fish ponds, or for domestic use.[145] Eventually, the river could be overallocated, so the coalition made it a priority to obtain in-stream flow rights for the river.

Figure 7.21. *Lower San Miguel River, seen here from Naturita, was de-watered to a trickle in July 2002 by upstream irrigation and other uses during this drought year.*

In-stream flow rights are held by the state of Colorado and are controversial, as water always is in the West. Traditional water users make up the Colorado Water Conservation Board, so a strong case must be made that a river's natural values warrant an in-stream flow right. The effort to do an assessment and make the case for the San Miguel was led by Dennis Murphy, hydrologist for the Montrose BLM Office.[146] Assessment and negotiation took several years, as landowners and county commissioners in Montrose County objected to in-stream flow rights and San Miguel County commissioners supported them. Finally, in 2002 the Colorado Water Conservation Board decided to apply to the state engineer for a significant in-stream flow right for the San Miguel River from Fall Creek (just below Telluride) to just upstream of Horsefly Creek (below Norwood). The in-stream flow right was protested by one landowner and Tri-State Power,[147] and in July 2005 the right still had not been negotiated. The coalition hopes to apply for a similar in-stream flow assessment for the lower San Miguel, which has the rare cottonwood community of the Tabeguache Preserve. Unfortunately, powerful interests currently block even minimal protection of the lifeblood of the San Miguel River.

Positive futures do not just happen. These stories show the power of ordinary people with a vision. A faceless bureaucracy did not make the difference on the San Miguel, nor will one person be remembered for saving the river. Rather, many individuals, each with particular talents and skills, worked together to envision and make possible a restored watershed. Because of these individuals' hard work, the San Miguel may hold more natural beauty and ecological and social integrity for generations to come.

Where the Dolores and San Miguel rivers meet. Just downstream from Uravan, the San Miguel empties into the Dolores River, and here one can see the importance of the efforts of the San Miguel Watershed Coalition. The Dolores River was largely a free-flowing river until about 1986, when McPhee Reservoir was completed upstream near the town of Dolores. The contrast between the flows of the two rivers can be large or modest, depending upon the time of year. In May 2003 the Dolores appeared to flow upstream for several hundred yards where the high spring flow of the San Miguel met the almost empty Dolores channel. Although the Dolores is naturally the bigger river, when McPhee Reservoir is being filled for agriculture on the Great Sage Plain, the Dolores River may dwindle to a trickle. The San Miguel is now often the more significant river at the confluence.

The variety of age classes of cottonwoods observed at Tabeguache Preserve is missing along much of the Dolores. There are few or no young cottonwoods, and only a few remaining older trees are scattered along the river, mostly on high terraces. These terraces are effectively isolated from the river, as McPhee Dam significantly diminishes floods. The Dolores runs through a deeper canyon than the San Miguel, which may also lead to fewer trees. The most striking contrast, though, is how abundant saltcedar (see Box—Saltcedar, pp. 310–311) is along the Dolores compared with the San Miguel. Both Rio Grande cottonwood and saltcedar are affected by the pattern of river flow. Saltcedar is favored by continued low stream flows, and saltcedar has claimed the Dolores.

People need water, but in desert environments damming a river plays out downstream for long distances, even hundreds of miles. We need to come back to the confluence now and then to remind ourselves of how valuable that water is to both people and nature. The Dolores and San Miguel rivers do not represent stark, divisive choices—one favoring people, the other nature. Along the San Miguel River, people are searching for and finding ways to meet the needs of both people and nature, and this is a tangible source of hope. And perhaps there is hope for the Dolores River too. In 2003 the Dolores River Coalition formed with an incipient vision of "a larger[,] more natural river flow" and "sustainable local economies."[148]

NOTES

1. Wright, *Rocky Mountain Divide*, 40.
2. Chronic and Williams, *Roadside Geology of Colorado*; Ellingson, "Volcanic Rocks."
3. Larsen and Cross, *Geology and Petrology of the San Juan Region.*
4. Chronic and Williams, *Roadside Geology of Colorado.*
5. Baker, "Classification of Riparian Vegetation."
6. Kingery, *Colorado Breeding Bird Atlas.*
7. Baker, "Classification of Riparian Vegetation."
8. Fetter and Fetter, *Telluride*; Telluride Consulting, *Profile: An Economic Study of Telluride.*
9. Wyckoff, *Creating Colorado.*
10. Rockwell, *Uncompahgre Country*; Smith, "A Country of Tremendous Mountains."
11. Wyckoff, *Creating Colorado.*
12. Lavender, *Telluride Story.*
13. Densil, "Social and Economic History of Southwestern Colorado."
14. O'Rourke, *Frontier in Transition.*
15. Rohe, "Environment and Mining in the Mountainous West."
16. O'Rourke, *Frontier in Transition.*
17. Lavender, *Telluride Story.*
18. Ibid.; O'Rourke, *Frontier in Transition.*
19. See Web site: http://www.cdphe.state co.us, Colorado Department of Public Health and Environment.
20. Denison and York, *Telluride: Tales of Two Early Pioneers*; O'Rourke, *Frontier in Transition.*
21. Willits, "San Miguel River Restoration Assessment, Vol. 1," 4.
22. Karen Tucker, Bureau of Land Management, Montrose, Colorado, pers. comm., July 20, 2000.
23. State of Colorado, Division of Minerals and Geology, "San Miguel Gold/ Dorie Placer Mine Bond Forfeiture Project."
24. San Miguel Watershed Coalition, "San Miguel Basin Watershed Plan Background."
25. O'Rourke, *Frontier in Transition.*
26. Ringholz, *Uranium Frenzy*; Athearn, "Last Great Mining Boom."
27. Athearn, "Last Great Mining Boom."
28. Gilleece, "Manhattan Project."
29. Ringholz, *Uranium Frenzy*; Athearn, "Cleaning up Uranium Country."
30. Athearn, "Last Great Mining Boom"; Athearn, "Cleaning up Uranium Country."
31. Athearn, "Last Great Mining Boom."
32. Dion, "Uranium Mining Resurfaces Near Naturita."

3. Anonymous, "Images of the Uravan, Colorado Area"; Athearn, "Cleaning up Uranium Country."
34. Ringholz, *Uranium Frenzy;* Athearn, "Cleaning up Uranium Country."
35. Ringholz, *Uranium Frenzy.*
36. Ibid.
37. Ibid., 245, quoting story from *Wall Street Journal,* October 6, 1967.
38. Athearn, "Cleaning up Uranium Country"; Morrison Knudsen Corporation, "Final Five-Year Review: Uravan Superfund Site."
39. Morrison Knudsen Corporation, "Final Five-Year Review: Uravan Superfund Site."
40. Colorado Department of Public Health and Environment, "Uravan Uranium Project, Environmental Concerns"; see Web site: http://www.cdphe.state.co.us/hm/rpuravan.asp, accessed May 10, 2006.
41. Morrison Knudsen Corporation, "Final Five-Year Review: Uravan Superfund Site."
42. Rockwell, *Uncompahgre Country.*
43. Lavender, *Telluride Story,* 29.
44. U.S. Forest Service, Lizard Head allotment file, Norwood, Colorado.
45. Ibid.
46. Ibid.
47. Ibid.
48. Ibid.
49. Leslie Stewart, October 3, 1989, note in Sheep Mountain allotment file, U.S. Forest Service, Dolores, Colorado.
50. Shupe and Brotherson, "Differential Effect of Cattle and Sheep Grazing"; Bowns and Bagley, "Vegetation Responses to Long-Term Sheep Grazing."
51. Klemmedson, "Interrelations of Vegetation, Soils and Range Conditions."
52. Ibid.; Paulsen, "Forage Value on a Mountain Grassland-Aspen Range."
53. Lizard Head allotment file no. 2210, U.S. Forest Service, Norwood, Colorado.
54. Basin S&G allotment file no. 2210, U.S. Forest Service, Norwood, Colorado.
55. Klemmedson, "Interrelations of Vegetation, Soils and Range Conditions."
56. Knight and Walter, *Guide to Plant Poisoning in North America.*
57. Ibid.
58. Ibid.
59. Zier and Baker, "A Century of Vegetation Change in the San Juan Mountains."
60. Andrews and Righter, *Colorado Birds.*
61. Baker, "Classification of Riparian Vegetation."
62. Basin S&G allotment file no. 2210, U.S. Forest Service, Norwood, Colorado.
63. Ibid.
64. Paulson and Baker, field observations, August 9, 2002.
65. E.g., Buechling and Baker, "Fire History from Tree Rings in a High Elevation Forest."
66. Ibid.
67. Baker, "Indians and Fire in the Rocky Mountains."
68. Kay, "Is Aspen Doomed?"
69. Baker and Veblen, "Spruce Beetles and Fires."

70. Vale, "Tree Invasion of Montane Meadows in Oregon"; Baker, "Livestock Grazing Alters Succession in a Colorado Subalpine Forest."
71. Kay, "Is Aspen Doomed?"
72. Buechling and Baker, "Fire History from Tree Rings in a High Elevation Forest."
73. Romme et al., "Aspen's Ecological Role in the West."
74. Mehl, "Old-Growth Descriptions for Major Forest Cover Types."
75. Ibid.
76. Fitzgerald, Meaney, and Armstrong, *Mammals of Colorado.*
77. Ruggiero et al., *Ecology and Conservation of Lynx.*
78. Kohler, "Six More Lynx Kittens Found in Colorado."
79. McKelvey, Aubry, and Ortega, "History and Distribution of Lynx."
80. Ibid.
81. Rodebaugh, "Keeping the Cats Coming."
82. See Colorado Division of Wildlife Web site: http://wildlife.state.co.us/species_cons/lynx.asp.
83. Buskirk et al., "Winter Resting Site Ecology of Marten."
84. Fitzgerald, Meaney, and Armstrong, *Mammals of Colorado.*
85. Ibid.; Buskirk et al., "Comparative Ecology of Lynx."
86. Colorado Division of Wildlife Lynx Update, November 20, 2003; see Web site: http://wildlife.state.co.us/species_cons/lynx.asp.
87. San Miguel Watershed Coalition, "San Miguel Basin Watershed Plan Background."
88. Linda Miller, Telluride resident, pers. comm., May 29, 2002; Telluride Consulting, *Profile: An Economic Study of Telluride.*
89. Art Goodtimes, San Miguel County commissioner, Norwood, Colorado, pers. comm., October 8, 2001.
90. Linda Miller, Telluride resident, pers. comm., May 29, 2002.
91. Art Goodtimes, San Miguel County commissioner, Norwood, Colorado, pers. comm., October 8, 2001.
92. Telluride Consulting, *Profile: An Economic Study of Telluride.*
93. Capps, "Real Estate Sales."
94. Art Goodtimes, San Miguel County commissioner, Norwood, Colorado, pers. comm., October 8, 2001.
95. Telluride Consulting, *Profile: An Economic Study of Telluride.*
96. Review of *Telluride Daily Planet* (Telluride, Colorado), 2000–2006.
97. Telluride Consulting, *Profile: An Economic Study of Telluride.*
98. Art Goodtimes, San Miguel County commissioner, Norwood, Colorado, pers. comm., October 8, 2001.
99. Rees Consulting, *San Miguel County Housing Needs;* Telluride Consulting, *Profile: An Economic Study of Telluride.*
100. San Miguel County Open Space Commission, *San Miguel County Land Conservation Options.*
101. Linda Luther, director, San Miguel County Open Space Commission, Telluride, pers. comm., August 9, 2002.
102. Wright, *Rocky Mountain Divide.*

103. Telluride Consulting, *Profile: An Economic Study of Telluride.*
104. Clifford, "Telluride Tackles Ski Town Sprawl."
105. Hickcox, "Time to Be Counted on Idarado Legacy Project."
106. Colorado Department of Public Health and Environment; see Web site: http://www.cdphe.state.co.us/hm/rpidarado.asp.
107. Camille Price, environmental protection specialist, Colorado Department of Public Health and Environment, Telluride, pers. comm., August 9, 2002; see Web site: http://www.cdphe.state.co.us/hm/rpidarado.asp, accessed May 9, 2006.
108. Murray, "Idarado Officials: Negotiations Are Over."
109. Clifford, "Telluride Tackles Ski Town Sprawl."
110. Ibid.
111. Review of *Telluride Daily Planet* (Telluride, Colorado), 2000–2001.
112. Anonymous, *Sheep Mountain Alliance News* (Telluride, Colorado), Spring 2002.
113. Ibid.
114. Barret, "Valley Floor Vote Leaves Hard Work Ahead."
115. Cagin, "New Council to Move Forward with Valley Floor Condemnation."
116. Capps and Beaudin, "Locals Split on Valley Floor Proposal"; *Telluride Daily Planet* staff, "Emotional Debate Ends in 'No' Vote."
117. Pat Willits, Trust for Land Restoration, Ridgway, Colorado, pers. comm., July 20, 2000; Carolyn Byrd, The Nature Conservancy, Telluride, Colorado, pers. comm., July 20, 2000; Mallory Dimmitt, The Nature Conservancy, Telluride, Colorado, pers. comm., August 8, 2002.
118. Pat Willits, Trust for Land Restoration, Ridgway, Colorado, pers. comm., July 20, 2000.
119. Ibid.
120. Baker, "Classification of Riparian Vegetation."
121. Baker, "Species Richness of Colorado Riparian Vegetation."
122. Mallory Dimmitt, The Nature Conservancy, Telluride, Colorado, pers. comm., August 8, 2002.
123. Willits, "San Miguel River Restoration Assessment, Vol. 1."
124. Ibid.
125. Ibid.
126. DiGiacomo, "Flash Flood Hits Upper River."
127. See Web site: http://www.co.blm.gov/ubra/coalition.
128. Karen Tucker, BLM recreation planner, Montrose, Colorado, pers. comm., July 20, 2000; Pat Willits, Trust for Land Restoration, Ridgway, Colorado, pers. comm., July 20, 2000.
129. Baker, "Classification of Riparian Vegetation."
130. Baker, "Regeneration of *Populus angustifolia.*"
131. Ibid.
132. Baker, "Recent Changes in Riparian Vegetation"; ibid.
133. Partners in Flight, *Land Bird Conservation Plan.*
134. San Miguel Watershed Coalition, "San Miguel Basin Watershed Plan Background."

135. Pam Zoline, Telluride Institute, Telluride, Colorado, pers. comm., November 12, 2002.
136. Ibid.
137. San Miguel Watershed Coalition, "San Miguel Basin Watershed Plan Background."
138. Ibid.
139. Karen Tucker, BLM recreation planner, Montrose, Colorado, pers. comm., July 20, 2000.
140. San Miguel Watershed Coalition, "San Miguel Basin Watershed Plan Background."
141. Delves, "Watershed Coalition Finds New Executive Director."
142. Mallory Dimmitt, The Nature Conservancy, Telluride, Colorado, pers. comm., June 4, 2003.
143. Ibid.
144. Templeton, *Visionaries*.
145. Dennis Murphy, BLM, Montrose, Colorado, pers. comm., May 12, 2003.
146. Linda Luther, San Miguel Watershed Coalition coordinator, 1998–2001, Placerville, Colorado, pers. comm., July 27, 2002.
147. Dennis Murphy, BLM, Montrose, Colorado, pers. comm., May 12, 2003, and June 1, 2004.
148. Rodebaugh, "Groups to Unveil Dolores River Plan."

I have chosen to be a choirboy in the desert chorus, and not to pretend that I am only an onlooker. I have joined the ranks of those who dance to the tune called *ecological restoration*. . . . It is as much an art as a science, for it allows us to improvise, to listen to the land, to intuit where the harmonics of a natural community are going, as well as where they have been. . . . We are learning of the need to restore not only the physical aspects of the habitats but also the cultural commitment to protect, to heal, to let the wildness of living communities continue to evolve.

—Gary Nabhan, *Cultures of Habitat*[1]

CHAPTER EIGHT

Perspectives

We write this during a serious drought, with the country gone brown, pinyon and sage dying, creeks dry, forests burning. It is as if nature were raising its voice, insisting on being heard. This is an era of ecological restoration because that voice was not carefully listened to in the past. The legacies of past overoptimism about the capacity of the land can be seen from almost any high hill in southwestern Colorado. The task now is to learn from these legacies, to increase ecological understanding of the nature of this place, so that landscapes might recover, regain productivity, and be restored to their natural diversity and resilience. What can be learned from legacies? How might time and effort in restoring the natural world best be spent? Can communities learn to listen more closely to nature, fostering a land ethic and a culture of habitat?

A MOSAIC OF LEGACIES ON THE LANDSCAPE

Not all human legacies were mistakes, of course. Where natural systems have been converted into productive farmlands and other uses, few would call for restoration if those lands are healthy places that include space for the natural community. But southwestern Colorado has a wide range of undesirable legacies, some impossible to undo, others less severe. Full restoration is probably impossible, for example, on the Animas River above Silverton, where toxic heavy-metal pollution from mining is deeply mixed into the streambed and the mountains are fractured by a century of hard-rock mining. Similarly daunting would be restoration of the natural communities of East Paradox Valley, where the native ecosystem has effectively been replaced by cheatgrass. In these cases human disturbance exceeded the ecosystem's natural capacity for recovery, and the legacy appears effectively permanent. On the other hand, the replacement of lower river valley riparian vegetation by saltcedar seemed irreversible a decade ago, but The Nature Conservancy has demonstrated success in controlling this weed in the San Miguel watershed, and there is interest in control elsewhere.

Only a little more hopeful than permanently damaged ecosystems are places that seem to be on the brink, significantly damaged and with little remaining resilience. Dry Creek Basin, with its degraded sagebrush communities and threatened Gunnison sage-grouse population, is a landscape on the brink, as is the Dolores bench grassland, its native bunchgrasses half dead and surrounded by cheatgrass. Both places seem headed toward an Animas River or East Paradox outcome. These places are on the brink because society has been slow to adjust land uses to match the ecology of these ecosystems, continuing to overestimate, for example, their capacity to recover from disturbance—particularly intense disturbances such as overgrazing and sagebrush removal. Areas where cattle have been removed (e.g., Goodman Point) or reduced often do show recovery of native plants, but recovery often requires decades.[2] These places are also on the brink because of invasive non-native plants that have the potential to replace natural vegetation.

Other places seem to have stabilized in a somewhat degraded state and have ongoing uses that are not yet sustainable or leading to recovery. A large portion of southwestern Colorado falls into this category. The Ponderosa Pine Partnership has demonstrated success in forest restoration, but restoration of native grasslands and forest understories awaits significant effort and reform of livestock grazing. Poor grazing practices continue to prevent restoration of healthy, native plant communities, even in the most ecologically significant places such as the old-growth ponderosa pine forest of Hermosa Creek. Sagebrush stands and pinyon-juniper woodlands cleared in the 1960s and 1970s to increase forage seldom received new approaches to livestock grazing and simply became degraded again. "Restoration" of sagebrush or pinyon-juniper woodlands still too often consists of cutting or burning trees or sagebrush to increase forage production without implementing needed changes in livestock management.

In some places natural communities have been passively recovering for some time from a legacy of past overuse or mistakes. Protected parks and natural areas are in this category. The southern portion of Black Canyon National Park, with its mixed mountain shrub ecosystem; the sagebrush communities of Goodman Point and Carpenter Park; and the pinyon-juniper woodlands of Sand Canyon and the Dominguez canyons are encouraging examples of ecosystems recovering from past overgrazing and other uses. Successful active restoration has emerged only in a few places—the Ponderosa Pine Partnership is an example.

Finally, a very few places were never strongly transformed or degraded or have nearly fully recovered from past overuse. Some subalpine landscapes, as in parts of the Weminuche and other wilderness areas, were never significantly altered by land uses. Remnants comparatively free of legacies are rare, however, at low elevations. The Animas River Canyon and preserves along the San Miguel River are rare examples on large, free-flowing western rivers. Efforts at restoration should not overshadow efforts to protect these remaining natural places and to prevent their degradation by newer forces. These remnants are important sources of information about how the natural world operates, and they provide inspiration and models for restoration.

The mosaic of legacies provides varying constraints and possibilities for protection and restoration of nature. Places on the brink, as well as threatened but valuable remnants, may warrant immediate attention, while degraded but stable places provide opportunity for more gradual restoration and adjustment in land use. But broad action to protect and restore the natural world and to create new land uses that do not leave undesirable legacies in part awaits broader cultural change, already under way in southwestern Colorado.

IN SEARCH OF NEW MODELS

What kind of society and economy would enable people to restore, maintain, protect, and coexist with nature in southwestern Colorado? We cannot propose a blueprint for such a society. We can, however, reflect on what can be learned from past cultures and societies and from the groups working today on protection and restoration of ecosystems in southwestern Colorado.

Clues from the Past

Past economies. What can be learned from the lifeways of Native Americans and early Euro-Americans in southwestern Colorado? There is a lesson in the crisis of the first agricultural peoples. The move of the Ancestral Puebloans south, after centuries of living in southwestern Colorado, may have been unavoidable because their populations had increased and society had become dependent on climatic conditions favorable to corn production. When the climate became much less favorable, stresses on their economic and social system forced them to leave their Colorado homes. Those who want to make southwestern Colorado home not just for themselves but also for their children and grandchildren might reflect on whether modern society's dependence on fossil fuels for long-distance trade and dispersed settlement may be just as vulnerable to collapse.

The hunting-and-gathering way of life practiced by Archaic peoples and the Utes never collapsed, so far as is known, until overrun by Euro-Americans and was the longest-lasting human economy in the region. While social units and cultures undoubtedly changed, their basic way of life persisted for several thousand years in southwestern Colorado, direct evidence of the sustainability of that way of life. Several traits may have been most significant. These groups had low populations, they were self-sufficient, and their economies were based on a diversity of resources. Together, these traits may have favored the maintenance of nature and their culture.

Compared with today, early Euro-Americans were also self-sufficient and small in number, but the Euro-American economy of the interior West from its beginning was built on trading raw natural resources and was highly dependent on distant markets. Pockets of more integrated local and regional economies did occur, as in the early linkage of the agriculturally rich Uncompahgre Valley and nearby mining towns, but these were the exception and have since disappeared. Euro-American settlers came with the goal of making southwestern Colorado their long-term home, and many succeeded, but early land use was strongly shaped by those in search of windfall profits—mining, speculative livestock enterprises, and early logging all liquidated natural capital and fueled the infamous boom-and-bust western economies that still occur today.

The Old West is giving way to the New West in some places, and the juxtaposition is as striking in southwestern Colorado as anywhere (see Plate 58). As different as these cultures appear, however, they share some shortcomings as foundations for healthy human and natural communities. In terms of the health of human communities, San Miguel County is doing as well as any New West economy to meet its citizens' needs. But while this county is taxing its booming real estate industry to purchase open space, the consumption of the space of nature by multimillion-dollar second and third homes continues, while a large percentage of Telluride's workers may never own a home or be part of the community. Towns with traditional economies seem to have, at least briefly, achieved a stronger sense of place and healthier human community than is the case in today's amenity towns. People lived where they worked, and their children likely experienced a richer relationship with place and knew the natural world far better than most children do today. But human health legacies from uranium mining in the Uravan area, property losses associated with oil and gas development in the San Juan Basin, and the instability of boom-and-bust cycles belie the social health of traditional economies.

Today, few aspire to a subsistence economy and lifestyle, but some aspects of them may provide important elements for a healthy contemporary economy. An economy that values greater local self-sufficiency and is based on economic activities integrated at the local and regional scale would probably be more stable and less inclined to deplete natural resources. A more diverse regional economy—one that recognizes the value of not only forage, wood, crops, and tourism but also other resources, such as the underappreciated pinyon nut (see Box—Ancient Pinyon-Juniper Woodlands, p. 166)—is also less likely to put excessive pressure on any one of these resources. Diversity is an emerging cornerstone of sustainability, as in agriculture where crop rotations have long been known to help conserve soil and water resources. Adding value to resources through local and regional processing allows each unit of raw material to support more people in the region at a higher standard of living. As the Ponderosa Pine Partnership discovered, ecologically sensitive logging may not be feasible if raw wood has to compete on the international market against unsustainably produced wood. With a more locally self-sufficient economy, global connections and trade could be engaged when they enrich the quality of life but do not deplete the resources of the local economy.

Past views of people and nature. It is important, if speculative, to consider the less material aspects of past societies' relationships to nature and place. Working with Native Americans in the Southwest today, Gary Nabhan notes a far less dualistic view of humans and nature than that of most Euro-Americans. The identities of the "larger, wilder world" and the people, culturally and individually, are intertwined.[3] Euro-American settlers, in contrast, brought a view of humans and nature as separate, even oppositional. Early settlers were struggling to survive in a new and, for them, difficult land. In early Euro-American stories, nature is often a threatening force, with dramatic tales of people surviving against great odds or with death at hand, often told with a remarkable sense of stoicism and humor. This view of nature was (and is) also highly utilitarian—nature exists to serve the needs of people. It must have been hard to imagine how powerful, often hostile nature could be harmed simply by trying to harness its forces.

In recent years it has been argued that this oppositional view of humans and nature is the root of western environmental problems and that people should recognize themselves as part of nature. According to William Cronon, a main proponent of this view, "Any way of looking at nature that encourages us to believe we are separate from nature—as wilderness tends to do—is likely to reinforce environmentally irresponsible behavior."[4] It is often said today that the boundaries societies draw around places in efforts to protect wild nature remove humans from their rightful place in nature. Yet distinguishing between domesticated and wild places is not entirely new; at least some Native Americans recognized places that had uses and meaning but that were the space of wild nature.[5]

Ironically and possibly inadvertently, the view of Cronon and others fits well with a strictly utilitarian approach to nature. If people are part of nature, then is it not natural for humans to be destructive of other parts of nature if doing so is in their presumed self-interest? Many of the legacies in this book occurred because some parts of nature did not evolve and will not persist with a strong human presence. When people attempt to be a major part of all natural communities, natural diversity is diminished.

In a world of potential long-term legacies, including extinctions, the paradox of the human relationship with nature may highlight an important ethical choice. Aldo Leopold's famous land ethic provides a powerful image that embraces the paradox. In perhaps his most famous passage from *A Sand County Almanac*,[6] people are clearly portrayed as part of nature: "In short, a land ethic changes the role of Homo sapiens from conqueror of the land-community to plain member and citizen of it. It implies respect for his fellow members, and also respect for the community as such." Yet Leopold clearly separates humans from the rest of nature in recognizing people's ability to alter the natural world: "A land ethic of course cannot prevent the alteration, management, and use of these 'resources,' but it does affirm their right to continued existence, and, at least in spots, their continued existence in a natural state."

People can choose to be a part of nature in a variety of ways. Leopold recognized the need for an explicit ethic of self-restraint, given increasing human numbers and technological prowess. Being a part of nature in a Leopoldian way means reshaping economies and interactions with nature so that nonhuman nature continues to exist, including some places "untrammeled by man, where man himself is a visitor." But a land ethic of restraint and coexistence with nature may best develop and be sustained where people have more intimate knowledge of, and connection with, nature. Nabhan suggests in the chapter's opening quote that a modern culture of habitat may arise where groups of people become engaged in restoration.

Toward a Modern Land Ethic and Culture of Habitat

Solving the tragedy of the commons through social restraint. Both traditional and amenity economies remain vexed with "tragedy of the commons"[7] situations that require solution if nature is to be protected from further loss. This tragedy occurs when access to a resource is so open that if one user forgoes exploitation in an effort to conserve a resource, another user will step in. Conservation behavior is illogical under such circumstances, and resources are degraded as all users compete in a free-for-all. It is easy to look back at the legacies of overexploitation as a part of history, a result of lawless frontier behavior. Yet the single-minded pursuit of fossil fuel energy today is enabled by national laws and policies that encourage maximum production over the near term, and the West's last wild places and even species, such as the Gunnison sage-grouse, are falling victim to a new energy boom. Around New West towns, sprawl is a twist on the tragedy of the commons, threatening the public value of undeveloped private lands (see Figure 8.1). When private land is subdivided, society loses common resources such as wildlife habitat, open space, and other environmental services from undeveloped land.

Tragedy-of-the-commons situations require social solutions. In the case of sprawl, the problem is largely cultural. U.S. society and ideology, particularly in the West, are among the most individualistic in the

Figure 8.1. *Landscape fragmentation from residential development and gas drilling along Highway 160 east of Durango, Colorado, 2003.*

world. The urge to "escape" society drives rural sprawl and is fed by a consumerist culture that blatantly sells views and elk meadows.[8] Coupled with consumerism is a reification of private property rights and a reluctance to empower local and state governments to establish or facilitate social institutions (laws, policies) that limit and direct growth. Local communities in southwestern Colorado are trying to deal with these difficult issues in creative ways—including transfer of development rights, planning, and incentives—but it will require even more creativity to solve today's tragedy-of-the-commons issues on private lands, where there are difficult competing values and equity issues.

Rapid and extensive development of private lands throws into sharp relief the wisdom of citizens and government leaders who fought for public lands 100 years ago. Protection of many other public commons and goods, including clean air and clean water, came about because of widespread concerns. The Endangered Species Act, perhaps the clearest statement of U.S. society's commitment to Leopold's land ethic, retains broad national support. Many of the community groups described in this book would not have convened without the impetus of the Endangered Species Act, Clean Water Act, or other national laws. There may be a very good reason for this reality. It is difficult for corporations or local citizens dependent upon a resource to speak up for restraint in its use, given the focused interests of stockholders and families. Institutions for common property protection develop in the broader society using a larger, longer-term lens. A community can create rules to protect an area, such as Carpenter Park, but the Gunnison sage-grouse and the Colorado River's water quality may require agreements at a higher level of society.

On the other hand, the current rush for energy resources in the West is driven not locally but by the national expectation of cheap gas and the national economy's general dependence on cheap fossil fuel energy. In this case, the gap in most Americans' knowledge about the impacts of their energy consumption hinders the development of laws and policies that would better protect nature and manage a transition to renewable sources of energy. Notably, some of the strongest opposition to aggressive gas development in the West today comes from local communities bearing the impacts of that development.

Reshaping economies while restoring and protecting nature. It would be utopian to dream of starting anew. Rather, we look to ongoing, positive hybridizations and transformations of the Old and the New West. The Ponderosa Pine Partnership is one of the best examples of an attempt to reshape a human livelihood and simultaneously restore the ecosystem, and it arose within an Old West industry. The San Miguel Watershed Coalition developed a strong vision for a restored watershed, with Old West and New West participants, and it has been able to use government policies and regulation, market mechanisms, and volunteer programs to incorporate traditional and amenity economies into the restoration project.

Some individuals and groups are charting new, more compatible courses for major industries in the region. Innovative ranchers are listening more closely to the land, searching for new enterprises and grazing practices that enable them not only to remain in ranching but also to provide space for all native species, including predators. The Heartland Cohousing Project is a mindful approach to residential development that recognizes the impacts of the footprint of new settlement and tries to minimize it while fostering a strong sense of community. The native seed project in the Uncompahgre Valley could contribute to both the restoration of natural communities and the viability of family farms in the region. The growth of farmer's markets throughout the region connects consumers to their food and is a movement toward greater regional self-sufficiency. These choices by individuals and communities may be only a side channel in the stream, but when streams shift course it is usually to a side channel.

Many individual projects also point the way toward coexistence with the natural world, arising in a variety of places. The proposed

Dominguez Canyon Wilderness and The Nature Conservancy's preserves along the San Miguel River indicate a willingness of the people
of southwestern Colorado and the nation to establish space for nature.
Reintroduction of bighorn sheep, lynx, and river otters indicates a desire and willingness to restore extirpated native animals. La Plata County's
weed program teaches landowners about noxious weeds and gives them
the tools to be good stewards of their land. The effort to eradicate saltcedar along the San Miguel River is a major societal commitment to
restore native ecosystems.

*A modern culture of habitat: Experiencing nature, collaborating, and watch-
ing outcomes.* Although social and economic systems are important, underlying these systems are the connections, or lack of connections, individuals have to nature and place. Nabhan looks to Native American
groups as model "cultures of habitat."[9] They lived, and many still live,
with more direct dependence on wild plants and animals, giving them
a richer knowledge of and a more intimate relationship with nature
than most Americans have today. Entomologist and philosopher Jeffrey Lockwood argues that being a native of a place gives our lives
much meaning, but being native is not about where a person was born;
it is coming to know a place through firsthand knowledge and experience.[10] It is not possible for everyone to live directly off the land today,
as Native Americans and early Euro-American settlers did. Our culture includes vegetarians as well as hunters and waitresses as well as
ranchers.

What kinds of connections and experiences are possible, given the
diversity of people today? The ability of people, including city dwell-
ers, to visit and discover nature is essential for a culture to have an
attachment to and awareness of nature. There is growing recognition
that recent generations have lost even minimal experiences of and connections with the natural world.[11] Access to natural places large enough
to accommodate a child's need for exploration and discovery (unlike
nature centers and parks that provide nature as packaged and known)
is more essential than ever. Canyons of the Ancients is the kind of place
that can fill that need, and we hope it will never succumb to the domes-
tication that nearby Mesa Verde has. Adults need the same opportunity
as children to discover the natural world, but their material interactions with nature may take on forms quite different than in the past.

Although collaborative groups are touted mainly as more democratic forums for natural resource management, we believe their greatest
potential, which has not yet been fully developed, is in connecting
citizens to nature. Collaboration brings together a broad spectrum of

people willing to learn about the ecology of a place of importance to them. These are not narrow groups of experts but include many ordinary people willing to commit to building a foundation of knowledge about natural communities. The Animas River Stakeholders Group and the San Miguel Watershed Coalition are examples of local people looking carefully at their damaged watersheds to understand what can be done to restore natural communities and processes. Not all participants may take shovel in hand, but they all visit the land and make decisions that shape society's future relationship with it. By providing this meaningful engagement with the natural world, such groups could facilitate a new culture of habitat, a culture where such interactions are the norm rather than the exception. But to achieve success requires the right conditions.

A recent study of collaborative natural resource management identified eight characteristics of groups that foster the type of group learning needed: (1) open communication, (2) diverse participation, (3) unrestrained thinking, (4) constructive conflict, (5) democratic structure, (6) multiple sources of knowledge, (7) extended engagement, and (8) facilitation.[12] These characteristics are not typical of our current culture, and growing pains are to be expected. None of the groups we studied or in which we participated has all these characteristics. The Ponderosa Pine Partnership, after great initial success, has not maintained extended engagement of diverse participants. None of the groups has succeeded in engaging nonlocal citizens who may know and care deeply about a place they visit but who cannot attend face-to-face meetings. Most groups, even with facilitation, are uncomfortable with constructive conflict and open communication. Groups may be set up and tilted toward particular interests intentionally or by chance, and few are studiously democratic. Neither public-land agencies nor private land managers have typically incorporated multiple sources of knowledge, perhaps because the uncertainty created by multiple views complicates management decisions and actions.

One tool that could be used to improve collaborative learning is extended firsthand observation and interaction with the place being protected, restored, or managed. People being in the field together can level social differences and the socially recognized hierarchy of expertise. It is much easier for a rancher, an agency resource manager, and a scientist to talk about something they are looking at together in the field than to talk about the same things in a meeting room. Frequent visits to the field might illuminate the connections between the ideological and the empirical; people are much more likely to modify their beliefs about the world through observation than through argument.

Careful observations of nature and the outcomes of human actions over time are also necessary if society is to understand and remain responsive to a changing nature. Collaborative groups typically espouse the use of adaptive management to accomplish this. Ludwig and colleagues described the principles of adaptive management: "We must consider a variety of plausible hypotheses about the world; favor actions that are robust to uncertainties; hedge; favor actions that are informative; probe and experiment; monitor results; update assessments and modify policy accordingly; and favor actions that are reversible."[13]

Unfortunately, adaptive management has rarely been well implemented.[14] There are many outstanding questions about what is being restored and the ways human actions influence other species and the workings of entire ecosystems. Yet mistakes and losses are often downplayed, and people move ahead boldly. For example, under Ludwig's guidelines, old-growth pinyon-juniper woodlands would not be cut or "decadent" sagebrush eradicated where there is uncertainty about how much old growth exists and how obligate species would be affected by its loss. Loss of old growth is not reversible within a meaningful time frame. Yet these remain practices on western public lands, now commonly under the guise of restoration.

The appropriate balance between action and observation is neither obvious nor easily agreed upon,[15] but collaborative groups in the region have dedicated relatively little time and money to observe the outcomes of their environmental manipulations to date. Field trips are too often used only to disseminate the knowledge of professionals and recognized experts. A promising exception is in San Miguel County, where a community-based monitoring system has been developed to understand the impacts of postfire salvage logging.[16]

Getting people into nature, then observing, experimenting, and monitoring outcomes, requires time and patience many groups feel they cannot afford. But the unwanted legacies of past human actions will take time and care to address. More people spending more time, together and alone, in the natural places they wish to restore would do much to overcome the shortcomings of collaborative groups and adaptive management as practiced today. The potential of these new forums to engage people in creating a land ethic and a new culture of habitat is tremendous.

For all their potential to connect people from all walks of life with the natural world, collaboration and adaptive management are unlikely to be the sources of inspiration for needed change. Collaborative groups are poor forums for major social or cultural change because fundamentally conflicting interests and values are, ideally, treated as equally valid.

We like to imagine what would have happened if Martin Luther King Jr. had given his famous "I Have a Dream" speech to a collaborative group in which several members were sympathetic to white supremacy. Very possibly the facilitator would have said, "Well, we appreciate Dr. King's heartfelt comments. Perhaps our representative from the Selma City Council would like to respond." Not all the powerful interests operating in southwestern Colorado today can prevail if the natural diversity and beauty that still exist here are to remain. Just as Telluride had to fight to protect its natural setting, a new relationship with nature requires not just collaborators but also inspirational voices and nonviolent resisters to the destruction of nature for short-term gain.

INSPIRATION AND HOPE IN SOUTHWESTERN COLORADO

Many polls have shown that citizens of the West, and of the United States as a whole, want to protect, restore, and coexist with the natural world. One barrier is a widespread lack of direct experience with nature, just discussed. Perhaps as important, however, is a sense of fatalism on the part of many citizens, who find legacies overwhelming and who feel that large, powerful forces determine the future, so individual action is ineffective. The current global economy and consumerist culture do present huge barriers to implementing a land ethic or developing a culture of habitat. However, the stories in this book attest to the power of individuals to bring about change—especially individuals working with others to shape the future in a particular place.

These inspirational people are not celebrities. Some are employees of highly constraining bureaucratic agencies, yet they manage to see and exploit opportunities to protect and restore particular places. Others are private landowners putting their land under conservation easements, restoring degraded land, or seeking improved ways of managing their land resources. Others are skilled in bringing divided communities together around a common vision of stewardship. Many are simply citizens who have worked to become knowledgeable about the natural world and dedicated their time to advocate for its restoration and protection.

Many positive changes come about slowly, after a lifetime or more of hard work by a few dedicated people or after years of discussion and collaboration. Such slow change can be discouraging. However, as Steve Glazer, a member of the Uncompahgre Selenium Task Force and the High Country Citizens Alliance, put it, "We have a moral responsibility to maintain hope."[17] Hope is not about settling into a comfortable certainty that everything will turn out all right. It is a willingness to go on trying, unsure of how things will turn out.

There is good reason for hope in southwestern Colorado. If a land ethic and a new culture of habitat are to arise anywhere, we have shown that this is a favorable place. Restoration is already under way, new initiatives are appearing, and there is much to be done that is interesting and creative. Understanding the legacies of past land uses may be discouraging at first, but restoring and protecting natural places can heal communities and help create a West that works for both people and nature.

NOTES

1. Nabhan, *Cultures of Habitat*, 318.
2. Anderson and Inouye, "Landscape-Scale Changes of a Sagebrush Steppe."
3. Nabhan, *Cultures of Habitat*, 11.
4. Cronon, "Trouble with Wilderness," 87.
5. Nabhan, *Cultures of Habitat*.
6. Leopold, *Sand County Almanac*, 240.
7. Hardin, "Tragedy of the Commons."
8. Hennen, "On Second Thought, Go Ahead and Fence Me In," 64.
9. Nabhan, *Cultures of Habitat*.
10. Lockwood, *Prairie Soul*.
11. Nabhan and Trimble, *Geography of Childhood*; Louv, *Last Child in the Woods*.
12. Schusler, Decker, and Pfeffer, "Social Learning for Collaborative Natural Resource Management."
13. Ludwig, Hilborn, and Walters, "Uncertainty, Resource Exploitation, and Conservation," 36.
14. Lee, "Appraising Adaptive Management."
15. Moir and Block, "Adaptive Management: Commitment or Rhetoric?"
16. Goodtimes, "Burn Canyon Monitoring Task Force."
17. Steve Glazer, High Country Citizens Alliance, Crested Butte, Colorado, pers. comm., July 25, 2002.

Adams, D. K., and A. C. Comrie. "The North American Monsoon." *Bulletin of the American Meteorological Society* 78 (1997): 2197–2213.

Adams, Karen R. "Anthropogenic Ecology of the North American Southwest." In *People and Plants in Ancient Western North America*, ed. Paul E. Minnis, 167–204. Washington, DC: Smithsonian Institution Press, 2004.

———. "Macrobotanical Remains." In *The Sand Canyon Archaeological Project: Site Testing*, ed. Mark D. Varien, http://www.crowcanyon.org/researchreports/sitetesting/start.htm, 1999 (accessed May 4, 2004).

Adams, Karen R., and Vandy Bowyer. "Sustainable Landscape: Thirteenth-Century Food and Fuel Use in the Sand Canyon Locality." In *Seeking the*

Center Place: Archaeology and Ancient Communities in the Mesa Verde Region, ed. Mark D. Varien and Richard H. Wilshusen, 123–142. Salt Lake City: University of Utah Press, 2002.

Adams, Karen R., and Kenneth Lee Petersen. "Environment." In *Colorado Prehistory: A Context for the Southern Colorado River Basin*, ed. William D. Lipe, Mark D. Varien, and Richard H. Wilshusen, 14–50. Denver: Colorado Council of Professional Archaeologists, 1999.

Agenbroad, Larry D., and India Hesse. "Megafauna, Paleoindians, Petroglyphs and Pictographs of the Colorado Plateau." In *The Settlement of the American Continents: A Multidisciplinary Approach to Human Biogeography*, ed. C. Michael Barton, Geoffrey A. Clark, David R. Yesner, and Georges A. Pearson, 189–195. Tucson: University of Arizona Press, 2004.

Allen, Craig D., Melissa Savage, Donald A. Falk, Kieran F. Suckling, Thomas W. Swetnam, Todd Schulke, Pater B. Stacey, Penelope Morgan, Martos Hoffman, and Jon T. Klingel. "Ecological Restoration of Southwestern Ponderosa Pine Ecosystems: A Broad Perspective." *Ecological Applications* 12 (2002): 1418–1433.

Alroy, John. "A Multispecies Overkill Simulation of the End-Pleistocene Megafaunal Mass Extinction." *Science* 292 (2001): 1893–1896.

American Farmland Trust. "Fact Sheet: Cost of Community Services Studies." Farmland Information Center, American Farmland Trust, http://www.farmlandinfo.org/documents/27757/FS_COCS_11-02.pdf, 2000 (accessed May 4, 2004).

———. "Tri-River Agricultural Land Protection Project, Planning Grant Application, Summary Form to Great Outdoors Colorado." Palisade, CO: American Farmland Trust, n.d.

Anderson, David G., and Michael K. Faught. "Paleoindian Artefact Distributions: Evidence and Implications." *Antiquity* 74 (2000): 507–513.

Anderson, Jay E., and Richard S. Inouye. "Landscape-Scale Changes in Plant Species Abundance and Biodiversity of a Sagebrush Steppe over 45 Years." *Ecological Monographs* 71 (2001): 531–556.

Andrews, Robert, and Robert Righter. *Colorado Birds: A Reference to Their Distribution and Habitat.* Denver: Denver Museum of Natural History, 1992.

Animas River Stakeholders Group. *Use Attainability Analysis for the Animas River Watershed.* Silverton, CO: Animas River Stakeholders Group, January 2001.

Anonymous. "Gunnison Sage Grouse Conservation Plan Dove Creek Colorado." Unpublished manuscript. Durango: Colorado Division of Wildlife, 1998.

———. "Gunnison Sage Grouse Conservation Plan San Miguel Basin Colorado." Unpublished manuscript. Montrose: Colorado Division of Wildlife, 1998.

———. "Images of the Uravan, Colorado Area, 1880–1890." Grand Junction, CO: Estalee Silver Collection, 1992.

———. "Land Use History—Range." Unpublished report on Boggy Analysis Area. Dolores, CO: U.S. Forest Service [ca. 1999].

Arnold, Joseph F., Donald A. Jameson, and Elbert H. Reid. *The Pinyon-Juniper Type of Arizona: Effects of Grazing, Fire, and Tree Control*. U.S. Department of Agriculture (USDA) Forest Service Production Research Report no. 84. Fort Collins, CO: Rocky Mountain Forest and Range Experiment Station, 1964.

Associated Press. "Wells Create Fears of Increased Pollution." *Cortez Journal* (Cortez, CO), December 27, 2003.

Athearn, Frederic J. "Cleaning up the Uranium Country: Remediation Versus Historic Preservation on the Colorado Plateau." *Southwestern Lore* 65, no. 3 (1999): 11–23.

———. "The Last Great Mining Boom: The Carnotite Industry in Western Colorado, 1890–1985." *Southwestern Lore* 61, no. 3 (1995): 17–25.

Baden, John, and Douglas S. Noonan, eds. *Managing the Commons*. Bloomington: Indiana University Press, 1998.

Baker, William L. "Alpine Vegetation of Wheeler Peak, New Mexico, U.S.A.: Gradient Analysis, Classification, and Biogeography." *Arctic and Alpine Research* 15 (1983): 223–240.

———. "Classification of the Riparian Vegetation of the Montane and Subalpine Zones in Western Colorado." *Great Basin Naturalist* 49 (1989): 214–228.

———. "Climatic and Hydrologic Effects on the Regeneration of *Populus angustifolia* James Along the Animas River, Colorado." *Journal of Biogeography* 17 (1990): 59–73.

———. "Indians and Fire in the Rocky Mountains: The Wilderness Hypothesis Renewed." In *Fire, Native Peoples, and the Natural Landscape*, ed. Thomas R. Vale, 41–76. Washington, DC: Island, 2002.

———. "Livestock Grazing Alters Succession After Fire in a Colorado Subalpine Forest." In *Fire and Environment: Ecological and Cultural Perspectives. Proceedings of an International Symposium*, ed. Stephen C. Nodvin and Thomas A. Waldrop, 84–90. USDA Forest Service General Technical Report SE-69. Asheville, NC: Southeastern Forest Experiment Station, 1991.

———. "Recent Changes in the Riparian Vegetation of the Montane and Subalpine Zones of Western Colorado, U.S.A." PhD diss. Madison: University of Wisconsin, 1987.

———. "Size-Structure Analysis of Contiguous Riparian Woodlands Along a Rocky Mountain River." *Physical Geography* 9 (1988): 1–14.

———. "Species Richness of Colorado Riparian Vegetation." *Journal of Vegetation Science* 1 (1990): 119–124.

Baker, William L., and Donna Ehle. "Uncertainty in Surface-Fire History: The Case of Ponderosa Pine Forests in the Western United States." *Canadian Journal of Forest Research* 31 (2001): 1205–1226.

Baker, William L., and Richard L. Knight. "Roads and Forest Fragmentation in the Southern Rocky Mountains." In *Forest Fragmentation in the Southern Rocky Mountains*, ed. Richard L. Knight, Frederick W. Smith, Stephen W. Buskirk, William H. Romme, and William L. Baker, 97–122. Boulder: University Press of Colorado, 2000.

Baker, William L., Jennifer A. Munroe, and Amy E. Hessl. "The Effects of Elk on Aspen in the Winter Range in Rocky Mountain National Park." *Ecography* 20 (1997): 155–165.

Baker, William L., and Deborah D. Paulson. "The Importance of Research on Natural Disturbance." UP-DATE, a publication of the Uncompahgre Plateau project, Montrose, Colorado, (Winter 2002): 1, 10–13.

Baker, William L., and Douglas J. Shinneman. "Fire and Restoration of Piñon-Juniper Woodlands in the Western United States: A Review." *Forest Ecology and Management* 189 (2004): 1–21.

Baker, William L., and Thomas T. Veblen. "Spruce Beetles and Fires in the Nineteenth-Century Subalpine Forests of Western Colorado, U.S.A." *Arctic and Alpine Research* 22 (1990): 65–80.

Baker, William L., and Gillian M. Walford. "Multiple Stable States and Models of Riparian Vegetation Succession on the Animas River, Colorado." *Annals of the Association of American Geographers* 85 (1995): 320–338.

Ballard, Warren B., Daryl Lutz, Thomas W. Keegan, Len J. Carpenter, and James C. deVos Jr. "Deer-Predator Relationships: A Review of Recent North American Studies with Emphasis on Mule and Black-Tailed Deer." *Wildlife Society Bulletin* 29 (2001): 99–115.

Banda, P. Solomon. "Seismic Drilling Will Be Used at Monument." *Durango Herald* (Durango, CO), September 24, 2002.

Barrett, Stephen. "Valley Floor Vote Leaves Hard Work Ahead." *Telluride Weekly Planet* (Telluride, CO), June 28, 2002.

Bartos, Dale L., "Landscape Dynamics of Aspen and Conifer Forests." In *Sustaining Aspen in Western Landscapes: Symposium Proceedings*, ed. W. D. Sheppard, D. Binkley, D. L. Bartos, T. J. Stohlgren, and L. G. Eskew, 5–14. Proceedings RMRS-P-18. Fort Collins, CO: USDA Forest Service, Rocky Mountain Research Station, 2001.

Bear, George D., and George W. Jones. *History and Distribution of Bighorn Sheep in Colorado.* Denver: Colorado Division of Wildlife, 1973.

Beck, Jeffrey, and Dean L. Mitchell. "Influences of Livestock Grazing on Sage Grouse Habitat." *Wildlife Society Bulletin* 28 (2000): 993–1002.

Beckwith, E. G., Lieut. *Reports of Explorations and Surveys to Ascertain the Most Practicable and Economical Route for a Railroad from the Mississippi River to the Pacific Ocean.* Washington, DC: Beverley Tucker, Printer, 1855.

Beidleman, Richard G. "Administrative History of the Black Canyon of the Gunnison National Monument." Unpublished manuscript. Colorado Springs: Colorado College, 1965.

Belnap, Jayne. "Magnificent Microbes: Biological Soil Crusts in Piñon-Juniper Communities." In *Ancient Piñon-Juniper Woodlands*, ed. M. Lisa Floyd, 75–88. Boulder: University Press of Colorado, 2003.

———. "Nitrogen Fixation in Biological Soil Crusts from Southeast Utah, USA." *Biology and Fertility of Soils* 35 (2002): 128–135.

Belnap, Jayne, and D. A. Gillette. "Vulnerability of Desert Biological Soil Crusts to Wind Erosion: The Influences of Crust Development, Soil Texture, and Disturbance." *Journal of Arid Environments* 39 (1998): 133–142.

Belnap, Jayne, J. H. Kaltenecker, R. Rosentreter, J. Williams, S. Leonard, and D. Eldridge. *Biological Soil Crusts: Ecology and Management.* Technical Reference 1730-2. Denver: U.S. Department of the Interior (USDI) Bureau of Land Management, 2001.

Belnap, Jayne, and O. L. Lange. *Biological Soil Crusts: Structure, Function, and Management.* New York: Springer-Verlag, 2001.

Belnap, Jayne, and S. L. Phillips. "Soil Biota in an Ungrazed Grassland: Response to Annual Grass (*Bromus tectorum*) Invasion." *Ecological Applications* 11 (2001): 1261–1275.

Bement, Robert E. "Colorado Rangelands: A Land Manager's Historical Perspective." *Rangelands* 15 (1993): 208–210.

Benham, Jack. *Silverton and Neighboring Ghost Towns.* Ouray, CO: Bear Creek, 1981.

Benkman, Craig W. "Adaptation to Single Resources and the Evolution of Crossbill (Loxia) Diversity." *Ecological Monographs* 63 (1993): 305–325.

———. "White-Winged Crossbill." In *The Birds of North America*, no. 27, ed. A. Poole, P. Stettenheim, and F. Gill. Philadelphia: Academy of Natural Sciences, and Washington, DC: American Ornithologists' Union, 1992.

Bennetts, Robert E., Gary C. White, Frank G. Hawksworth, and Scott E. Severs. "The Influence of Dwarf Mistletoe on Bird Communities in Colorado Ponderosa Pine Forests." *Ecological Applications* 6 (1996): 899–909.

Betancourt, Julio L. "Late Quaternary Biogeography of the Colorado Plateau." In *Packrat Middens: The Last 40,000 Years of Biotic Change*, ed. J. L. Betancourt, T. R. Van Devender, and P. S. Martin, 259–292. Tucson: University of Arizona Press, 1990.

Betancourt, Julio L., Elizabeth A. Pierson, Kate Aasen Rylander, James A. Fairchild-Parks, and Jeffrey S. Dean. "Influence of History and Climate on New Mexico Piñon-Juniper Woodlands." In *Managing Piñon-Juniper Ecosystems for Sustainability and Social Needs*, ed. Earl F. Aldon and Douglas W. Shaw, 42–62. USDA Forest Service General Technical Report RM-236. Fort Collins, CO: USDA Forest Service, Rocky Mountain Forest and Range Experiment Station, 1993.

Billings, W. D. "*Bromus tectorum*, a Biotic Cause of Ecosystem Impoverishment in the Great Basin." In *The Earth in Transition: Patterns and Processes of Biotic Impoverishment*, ed. G. M. Woodwell, 301–322. Cambridge: Cambridge University Press, 1990.

Binstock, Stuart, Esq. "Archaeopolitics." *SAA Archaeological Record* 2, no. 1 (2002): 6.

Bishop, Chad J., G. C. White, David J. Freddy, and Bruce E. Watkins. "Effect of Nutrition and Habitat Enhancements on Mule Deer Recruitment and Survival Rates." Fort Collins: Wildlife Research Report, Colorado Division of Wildlife, 2004.

Bissonette, John A. *Wildlife and Landscape Ecology: Effects of Pattern and Scale.* New York: Springer, 1997.

Black, Kevin D. "Archaic Continuity in the Colorado Rockies: The Mountain Tradition." *Plains Anthropologist* 36, no. 133 (1991): 1–29.

Black, Michael. "Historical Accounts of Water Quality in the Animas River Basin 1878–1991." Appendix 7B, Use Attainability Analysis for the Animas River Watershed. Silverton, CO: Animas River Stakeholders Group, 2001.

Blair, Rob. "Progress Report on Surficial Deposits and Geomorphology of Major Drainages of the Upper Animas River Watershed, Colorado." In *Science for Watershed Decisions on Abandoned Mine Lands: Review of Preliminary Results, Denver, Colorado, February 4–5, 1998,* ed. David A. Nimick and Paul von Guerard, 28. Open-File Report 98-297. Washington, DC: U.S. Geological Survey, 1998.

———. *The Western San Juan Mountains: Their Geology, Ecology, and Human History.* Boulder: University Press of Colorado, 1996.

Blaisdell, James P., and Walter F. Mueggler. "Effect of 2,4-D on Forbs and Shrubs Associated with Big Sagebrush." *Journal of Range Management* 9 (1956): 38–40.

Block, William M., and Deborah M. Finch. *Songbird Ecology in Southwestern Ponderosa Pine Forests: A Literature Review.* General Technical Report RM-GTR-292. Fort Collins, CO: USDA Forest Service, Rocky Mountain Forest and Range Experiment Station, 1997.

Bock, Carl E., and Jane H. Bock. *The View from Bald Hill: Thirty Years in an Arizona Grassland.* Berkeley: University of California Press, 2000.

Booth, Jack. "Demonstration Range Allotment Plan: Biggs C&H Allotment, San Juan National Forest." Dolores, CO: U.S. Forest Service, Biggs allotment file, 1965.

Bork, E. W., N. E. West, and J. W. Walker. "Cover Components on Long-Term Seasonal Sheep Grazing Treatments in Three-Tip Sagebrush Steppe." *Journal of Range Management* 51 (1998): 293–300.

Borrero, L. A. "The Prehistoric Exploration and Colonization of Fuego/Patagonia." *Journal of World History* 13 (1999): 321–355.

Boucher, B. J. *Walking in Wilderness: A Guide to the Weminuche Wilderness.* Durango, CO: Durango Herald, 1998.

Boudell, J. A., S. O. Link, and J. R. Johansen. "Effect of Soil Microtopography on Seed Bank Distribution in the Shrub-Steppe." *Western North American Naturalist* 62 (2002): 14–24.

Bowns, James E., and Calvin F. Bagley. "Vegetation Responses to Long-Term Sheep Grazing on Mountain Ranges." *Journal of Range Management* 39 (1986): 431–434.

Bowyer, Vandy E., and Karen R. Adams. "Sand Canyon Pueblo (5mt765) Archaeobotanical Report." Unpublished manuscript. Cortez, CO: Crow Canyon Archaeological Center, 2000.

Bradford, David, Floyd Reed, and Robbie Baird LeValley. *When the Grass Stood Stirrup-High: Facts, Photographs and Myths of West-Central Colorado.* Fort Collins: Colorado State University, Agricultural Extension, 2005.

Braun, Clait E. "Distribution and Status of Sage Grouse in Colorado." *Prairie Naturalist* 26 (1995): 1–9.

———. "Sage Grouse Declines in Western North America: What Are the Problems?" Jackson, WY: Proceedings of the Western Association of Fish and Wildlife Agencies, June 26–July 2, 1998.

Braun, Clait E., Maurice F. Baker, Robert L. Eng, Jay S. Gashwiler, and Max H. Schroeder. "Conservation Committee Report on Effects of Alteration of Sagebrush Communities on the Associated Avifauna." *Wilson Bulletin* 88 (1976): 165–171.

Braun, Clait E., Olin O. Oedekoven, and Cameron L. Aldridge. "Oil and Gas Development in Western North America: Effects on Sagebrush Steppe Avifauna with Particular Emphasis on Sage Grouse." *Proceedings of the North American Wildlife and Natural Resources Conference* 67 (2002): 337–349.

Briggs, Mark K. *Riparian Ecosystem Recovery in Arid Lands: Strategies and References.* Tucson: University of Arizona Press, 1996.

Brock, J. H. "Tamarix spp. (Salt Cedar), an Invasive Exotic Woody Plant in Arid and Semi-arid Habitats of Western USA." In *Ecology and Management of Invasive Riverside Plants*, ed. L. C. de Waal, L. E. Child, P. M. Wade, and J. H. Brock, 27–44. West Sussex, UK: John Wiley and Sons, 1994.

Bronaugh, W. M. "A Field Study of the Mountain Goat in the Needle Mountains." Unpublished report. Durango, CO: San Juan National Forest, 1977.

Brotherson, J. D., and D. Field. "Tamarix: Impacts of a Successful Weed." *Rangelands* 9 (1987): 110–112.

Brunson, Mark W. "Managing Naturalness as a Continuum: Setting Limits of Acceptable Change." In *Restoring Nature: Perspectives from the Social Sciences and Humanities*, ed. Paul H. Gobster and R. Bruce Hull, 229–244. Washington, DC: Island, 2000.

Bryner, Gary. "Coalbed Methane Development in the Intermountain West: Primer." Unpublished report. Boulder: Natural Resources Law Center, University of Colorado, 2002.

Buckles, William Gayl. "The Uncompahgre Complex: Historical Ute Archaeology and Prehistoric Archaeology of the Uncompahgre Plateau in West Central Colorado." PhD diss. Boulder: University of Colorado, 1971.

Buechling, Arne, and W. L. Baker. "A Fire History from Tree Rings in a High Elevation Forest of Rocky Mountain National Park." *Canadian Journal of Forest Research* 34 (2004): 1259–1273.

Busby, Frank E., John C. Buckhouse, Donald C. Clanton, George C. Coggins, Gary R. Evans, Kirk L. Gadzia, Charles M. Jarecki, Linda A. Joyce, Dick Loper, Daniel L. Merkel, George B. Ruyle, Jack Ward Thomas, Johanna H. Wald, and Stephen E. Williams. *Rangeland Health: New Methods to Classify, Inventory, and Monitor Rangelands.* Washington, DC: National Academy Press, 1994.

Buskirk, Steven W., Steven C. Forrest, Martin G. Raphael, and Henry J. Harlow. "Winter Resting Site Ecology of Marten in the Central Rocky Mountains." *Journal of Wildlife Management* 53 (1989): 191–196.

Buskirk, Steven W., Leonard F. Ruggiero, Keith B. Aubry, Dean E. Pearson, John R. Squires, and Keven S. McKelvey. "Comparative Ecology of Lynx in North America." In *Ecology and Conservation of Lynx in the United States*, ed. Leonard F. Ruggiero, Keith B. Aubry, Steven W. Buskirk, Gary M. Koehler, Charles J. Krebs, Kevin S. McKelvey, and John R. Squires, 397–417. General Technical Report RMRS-GTR-30WWW. Fort Collins, CO: USDA Forest Service, Rocky Mountain Research Station, 1999.

Butler, B. Robert. "Bison Hunting in the Desert West Before 1800: The Paleo-Ecological Potential and the Archaeological Reality." *Plains Anthropologist* 23 (1978): 106–112.

Butler, David L. *Effects of Piping Irrigation Laterals on Selenium and Salt Loads, Montrose Arroyo Basin, Western Colorado.* U.S. Geological Survey Water-Resources Investigations Report 01-4204, 14. Washington, DC: U.S. Government Printing Office, 2001.

Butler, David L., Richard P. Krueger, Barbara Campbell Osmundson, Andrew L. Thompson, and Steven K. McCall. *Reconnaissance Investigation of Water Quality, Bottom Sediment, and Biota Associated with Irrigation Drainage in the Gunnison and Uncompahgre River Basins and at Sweitzer Lake, West-Central Colorado, 1988–89.* U.S. Geological Survey Water-Resources Investigations Report 91-4103. Washington, DC: U.S. Government Printing Office, 1991.

Cagin, Seth. "New Council to Move Forward with Valley Floor Condemnation." *Telluride Watch* (Telluride, CO), December 16, 2003.

Callaway, Donald, Joel Janetski, and Omer C. Stewart. "Ute." In *Handbook of North American Indians, Vol. 11: Great Basin,* ed. Warren L. D'Azevedo, 336–367. Washington, DC: Smithsonian Institution Press, 1986.

Capps, Reilly. "Real Estate Sales Set New Record in 2005." *Telluride Daily Planet* (Telluride, CO), February 7, 2006.

Capps, Reilly, and Matthew Beaudin. "Locals Split on Valley Floor Proposal." *Telluride Daily Planet* (Telluride, CO), January 2, 2006.

Carson, Phil. *Across the Northern Frontier: Spanish Explorations in Colorado.* Boulder: Johnson Books, 1998.

Cassells, E. Steve. *The Archaeology of Colorado,* rev. ed. Boulder: Johnson Books, 1997.

Castello, John D., Donald J. Leopold, and Peter J. Smallidge. "Pathogens, Patterns, and Processes in Forest Ecosystems." *BioScience* 45 (1995): 16–24.

Chappell, Gordon S. *Logging Along the Denver & Rio Grande: Narrow Gauge Logging Railroads of Southwestern Colorado and Northern New Mexico.* Golden: Colorado Railroad Museum, 1971.

Chavez de Baca, Sonja. "Changing Land Use Effects on Selenium Loading." *Colorado NPS Connection,* Winter 2006, http://www.ourwater.org/econnection/connection20/seleniumlanduse.html (accessed May 7, 2006).

Chenoweth, William L. "The Uranium-Vanadium Deposits of the Uravan Mineral Belt and Adjacent Areas, Colorado and Utah." In *Guidebook, 32nd Field Conference, Western Slope Colorado,* ed. Rudy C. Epis and Jonathan F. Callender, 165–170. Socorro: New Mexico Geological Society, 1981.

Chittenden, George B. "Report of George B. Chittenden, Topographer of the San Juan Division, 1875." In *Ninth Annual Report of the United States Geological and Geographical Survey of the Territories, Embracing Colorado and Parts of Adjacent Territories: Being a Report of Progress of the Exploration for the Year 1875,* ed. F. V. Hayden, U.S. geologist, 351–368. Washington, DC: U.S. Government Printing Office, 1877.

Christiansen, E. M. "Naturalization of Russian Olive (*Elaeagnus angustifolia* L.) in Utah." *American Midland Naturalist* 70 (1963): 133–137.

Chronic, Halka, and Felicie Williams. *Roadside Geology of Colorado*, 2nd ed. Missoula, MT: Mountain Press, 2002.

Church, Stanley E., D. L. Fey, and Robert Blair. "Pre-Mining Bed Sediment Geochemical Baseline in the Animas River Watershed, Southwestern Colorado." U.S. Geological Survey, International Conference on Acid Rock Drainage, May 21–24, 2000, Denver, CO.

Church, Stanley E., B. A. Kimball, D. L. Fey, D. A. Ferderer, T. J. Yager, and R. B. Vaughn. *Source, Transport, and Partitioning of Metals Between Water, Colloids, and Bed Sediments of the Animas River, Colorado*. U.S. Geological Survey Open-File Report 97-151. Washington, DC: U.S. Government Printing Office, 1997.

City of Montrose. *Appendix. City of Montrose Comprehensive Plan*, March 10, 1998.

Clark, Amber. "Oil Wells on the Horizon for Canyons of the Ancients." *San Juan Citizens News* (Durango, CO), March 2005.

Clark, Arthur B. "Vegetation on Archaeological Sites Compared with Non-Site Locations at Walnut Canyon, Flagstaff, Arizona." *Plateau* 40 (1968): 77–90.

Clarren, Rebecca. "Colliding Forces: Has Colorado's Oil and Gas Industry Met Its Match?" *High Country News* (Paonia, CO), September 25, 2000.

Clary, Warren P. "Effects of Utah Juniper Removal on Herbage Yields from Springerville Soils." *Journal of Range Management* 24 (1971): 373–378.

Clary, Warren P., Sherel Goodrich, and Benton M. Smith. "Response to Tebuthiuron by Utah Juniper and Mountain Big Sagebrush Communities." *Journal of Range Management* 38 (1985): 56–60.

Clary, Warren P., and D. C. Morrison. "Large Alligator Junipers Benefit Early-Spring Forage." *Journal of Range Management* 26 (1973): 70–71.

Clements, William H., Daren M. Carlisle, James M. Lazorchak, and Philip C. Johnson. "Heavy Metals Structure Benthic Communities in Colorado Mountain Streams." *Ecological Applications* 10 (2000): 626–638.

Clifford, Hal. "Last Dance for the Sage Grouse?" *High Country News* (Paonia, CO), February 4, 2002.

———. "Telluride Tackles Ski Town Sprawl." *High Country News* (Paonia, CO), August 14, 2000.

Clinton, William J. "Establishment of the Canyons of the Ancients National Monument, Proclamation 7317." *Federal Register* 65: 37243, June 9, 2000.

Club 20. *Decline of the Aspen*. Grand Junction, CO: Club 20 Research Foundation, 1998.

Cohen, Jack D. "Preventing Disaster: Home Ignitability in the Wildland-Urban Interface." *Journal of Forestry* 98 (2000): 15–21.

Cole, D. N. "Trampling Disturbance and Recovery of Cryptogamic Soil Crusts in Grand Canyon National Park." *Great Basin Naturalist* 50 (1990): 321–325.

Cole, Kenneth L., Norman Henderson, and David S. Shafer. "Holocene Vegetation and Historic Grazing Impacts at Capitol Reef National Park Reconstructed Using Packrat Middens." *Great Basin Naturalist* 57 (1997): 315–326.

Coleman, John S., and Stanley A. Temple. "On the Prowl." *Wisconsin Natural Resources* 20, no. 6 (1996): 4–8.

Collier, Michael, Robert H. Webb, and John C. Schmidt. *Dams and Rivers: Primer on the Downstream Effects of Dams.* Circular no. 1126. Tucson, AZ: U.S. Geological Survey, 1996.

Colorado Division of Wildlife. *Wildlife in Danger: The Status of Colorado's Threatened or Endangered Fish, Amphibians, Birds and Mammals.* Denver: Colorado Division of Wildlife, n.d.

Colorado State University Cooperative Extension. *2000 Agricultural Fact Sheet. Tri River Area.* Fort Collins: Colorado State University, 2000.

Colorado Weed Management Association. *Troublesome Weeds of the Rocky Mountains.* Brighton: Colorado Weed Management Association, n.d.

Connelly, John W., Michael A. Schroeder, Alan R. Sands, and Clait E. Braun. "Guidelines to Manage Sage Grouse Populations and Their Habitats." *Wildlife Society Bulletin* 23 (2000): 967–985.

Conner, Carl E., Barbara J. Davenport, and Michael Piontkowski. "Archaeological Investigations at Site 5me5997 and 5me6144: Evaluative Test Excavations on Part of the Grand River Institute Griffith Land Exchange in Mesa County, Colorado." Grand Junction, CO: Bureau of Land Management, Grand Junction Resource Area, 1998.

Connolly, Marjorie R. "The Goodman Point Historic Land-Use Study." In *Sand Canyon Archaeological Project: A Progress Report*, ed. William D. Lipe, 33–44. Occasional Paper no. 2. Cortez, CO: Crow Canyon Archaeological Center, 1992.

Cook, C. Wayne, and Edward F. Redente. "Development of the Ranching Industry in Colorado." *Rangelands* 15 (1993): 204–207.

Cornelius, D. R., and C. A. Graham. "Sagebrush Control with 2,4-D." *Journal of Range Management* 11 (1958): 122–125.

Costello, David F., and H. E. Schwan. "Conditions and Trends on Ponderosa Pine Ranges in Colorado." Unpublished report. Fort Collins, CO: USDA Forest Service, Rocky Mountain Forest and Range Experiment Station, 1946.

Costello, David F., and George T. Turner. "Vegetation Changes Following Exclusion of Livestock from Grazed Ranges." *Journal of Forestry* 39 (1941): 310–315.

Cottam, Walter P., and George Stewart. "Plant Succession as a Result of Grazing and of Meadow Desiccation by Erosion Since Settlement in 1862." *Journal of Forestry* 38 (1940): 613–626.

Coupal, Roger, and Andy Seidl. "Rural Land Use and Your Taxes: The Fiscal Impact of Rural Residential Development in Colorado." Agricultural and Resource Policy Report APR-03-02. Fort Collins: Department of Agricultural and Resource Economics, Colorado State University, 2003.

Covington, W. W., and M. M. Moore. "Southwestern Ponderosa Forest Structure: Changes Since Euro-American Settlement." *Journal of Forestry* 92 (1994): 39–47.

Cox, George W. *Alien Species in North America and Hawaii: Impacts on Natural Ecosystems.* Washington, DC: Island, 1999.

Crane, Cathy J. "Cultural Adaptation Along the Tributaries of the San Miguel River, West Central Colorado." *Southwestern Lore* 44, no. 4 (1978): 1–10.

Crane, John R. "Planned Power Plant Causes Concern." *Durango Herald* (Durango, CO), May 3, 2005.

Cronon, William. "The Trouble with Wilderness; Or, Getting Back to the Wrong Nature." In *Uncommon Ground: Rethinking the Human Place in Nature*, ed. William Cronon, 69–90. New York: W. W. Norton, 1996.

Crooks, K. R., and M. E. Soulé. "Mesopredator Release and Avifaunal Extinctions in a Fragmented System." *Nature* 400 (1999): 563–566.

Cross, Whitman, Ernest Howe, J. D. Irving, and W. H. Emmons. "Description of the Needle Mountains Quadrangle." In *Geologic Atlas of the United States, Vol. 131: Needle Mountain Folio* (no pages). Washington, DC: USDI Geological Survey, 1905.

Crouch, Glenn L. *Aspen Regeneration in 6- to 10-Year-Old Clearcuts in Southwestern Colorado.* Research Note RM-467. Fort Collins, CO: USDA Forest Service, Rocky Mountain Forest and Range Experiment Station, 1986.

Crum, Sally. *People of the Red Earth: American Indians of Colorado.* Santa Fe, NM: Ancient City, 1996.

Curtis, James. *Riding Old Trails.* Grand Junction, CO: Country, 1976.

Dagget, D. *Beyond the Rangeland Conflict—Toward a West That Works.* Loveland, UT: Gibbs Smith, 1995.

Dailey, Thomas V., N. Thompson Hobbs, and T. N. Woodward. "Experimental Comparisons of Diet Selection by Mountain Goats and Mountain Sheep in Colorado." *Journal of Wildlife Management* 48 (1984): 799–806.

Daily, Gretchan C. *Nature's Services: Societal Dependence on Natural Ecosystems.* Washington, DC: Island, 1997.

D'Ambrosio, Dan. "Bill Proposed to Force Talks Before Drilling." *Durango Herald* (Durango, CO), January 5, 2005.

———. "County Compiles Criticism on HDs." *Durango Herald* (Durango, CO), November 23, 2004.

Daniels, Steven E., and Gregg B. Walker. *Working Through Environmental Conflict: The Collaborative Learning Approach.* Westport, CT: Praeger, 2001.

Darin, Thomas F., and Travis Stills. *Preserving Our Public Lands: A Citizen's Guide to Understanding and Participating in Oil and Gas Decisions Affecting Our Public Lands.* Lander: Wyoming Outdoor Council, and Durango, CO: Oil and Gas Accountability Project, 2002.

Daubenmire, R. F. "Plant Succession Due to Overgrazing in Agropyron Bunchgrass Prairie of Southeastern Washington." *Ecology* 21 (1940): 55–64.

Davis, J. B., P. T. Tueller, and A. D. Bruner. "Estimating Forage Production from Shrub Ring Widths in Hot Creek Valley, Nevada." *Journal of Range Management* 25 (1972): 398–402.

Dean, Jeffrey S., and Carla R. Van West. "Environment-Behavior Relationships in Southwestern Colorado." In *Seeking the Center Place: Archaeology and Ancient Communities in the Mesa Verde Region*, ed. Mark D. Varien and Richard H. Wilshusen, 81–99. Salt Lake City: University of Utah Press, 2002.

DeByle, Norbert V., and Robert P. Winokur. *Aspen: Ecology and Management in the Western United States*. General Technical Report RM-119. Fort Collins, CO: USDA Forest Service, Rocky Mountain Forest and Range Experiment Station, 1985.

Delaney, Robert W. *The Ute Mountain Utes*. Albuquerque: University of New Mexico Press, 1989.

Deloria, Vine, Jr. "American Indians and the Wilderness." In *Return of the Wild: The Future of Our National Lands*, ed. Ted Kerasote, 25–35. Washington, DC: Island, 2001.

Delves, Bob. "Watershed Coalition Finds New Executive Director." *San Miguel Watershed Coalition Watershed Connection* (Spring 2005) (no pages).

Denison, L. G., and L. A. York. *Telluride: Tales of Two Early Pioneers*. Odessa, TX: Indesign Studios, Loren S. Cruse, n.d.

Densil, Cummins. "Social and Economic History of Southwestern Colorado, 1860–1948." PhD diss. Austin: University of Texas, 1951.

Denver and Rio Grande Railroad. *Montrose County: The Land of Sunshine and Bountiful Harvests*. Denver: Republican, 1887.

Diamond, Jared. *Collapse: How Societies Choose to Fail or Succeed*. New York: Viking, 2005.

———. *The Third Chimpanzee*. New York: HarperCollins, 1992.

DiGiacomo, Ascenzo. "Flash Flood Hits Upper River." *San Miguel Watershed Coalition Watershed Connection* (Fall 2001) (no pages).

Dillard, Jeff. "Up from Texas." Unpublished diary. Delta, CO: Delta County Historical Society Museum, 1934.

Dillehay, Thomas D. *Monte Verde, a Late Pleistocene Settlement in Chile: The Archaeological Context and Interpretation, Vol. 2*. Washington, DC: Smithsonian Institution Press, 1997.

———. *The Settlement of the Americas: A New Prehistory*. New York: Basic Books, 2000.

Dion, D. "Uranium Mining Resurfaces Near Naturita." *Telluride Daily Planet* (Telluride, CO), October 1, 2004.

Di Tomaso, J. M. "Impact, Biology, and Ecology of Saltcedar (*Tamarisk* spp.) in the Southwestern United States." *Weed Technology* 12 (1998): 326–336.

Dixon, E. James. *Bones, Boats, and Bison: Archeology and the First Colonization of Western North America*. Albuquerque: University of New Mexico Press, 1999.

Donahue, Debra L. *The Western Range Revisited: Removing Livestock from Public Lands to Conserve Native Biodiversity*. Norman: University of Oklahoma Press, 1999.

Driver, Jonathan C. "Faunal Variation and Change in the Northern San Juan Region." In *Seeking the Center Place: Archaeology and Ancient Communities in the Mesa Verde Region*, ed. Mark D. Varien and Richard H. Wilshusen, 143–160. Salt Lake City: University of Utah Press, 2002.

Dubois, Coert. "Report on the Proposed San Juan Forest Reserve, Colorado." Unpublished report. Durango, CO: Supervisor's Office, San Juan National Forest, 1903.

Dudley, T. L., C. J. DeLoach, J. E. Lovich, and R. I. Carruthers. "Saltcedar Invasion of Western Riparian Areas: Impacts and New Prospects for Control." *Transactions of the North American Wildlife and Natural Resources Conference* 65 (2000): 345–381.

Duff, Andrew I., and Richard H. Wilshusen. "Prehistoric Population Dynamics in the Northern San Juan Region, A.D. 950–1300." *Kiva* 66 (2000): 167–190.

Dunmire, William W., and Gail D. Tierney. *Wild Plants and Native Peoples of the Four Corners.* Santa Fe: Museum of New Mexico Press, 1997.

Dyksterhuis, E. J. "Condition and Management of Range Land Based on Quantitative Ecology." *Journal of Range Management* 2 (1949): 104–115.

Ehle, Donna S., and William L. Baker. "Disturbance and Stand Dynamics in Ponderosa Pine Forests in Rocky Mountain National Park, USA." *Ecological Monographs* 73 (2003): 543–566.

Eisenhart, Karen S. "Historic Range of Variability and Stand Development in Piñon-Juniper Woodlands of Western Colorado." PhD diss. Boulder: University of Colorado, 2004.

———. "Historic Range of Variability of Piñon-Juniper Woodlands on the Uncompahgre Plateau, Western Colorado." Unpublished report. Montrose, CO: Bureau of Land Management, 2004.

Elias, Scott A. "Quaternary Paleobiology Update." *Quaternary Times* 29, no. 1, http://www4.nau.edu/amqua/v29n1/quaternary_paleobiology_update.htm, 1999 (accessed May 30, 2004).

Ellingson, Jack A. "Volcanic Rocks." In *The Western San Juan Mountains: Their Geology, Ecology, and Human History*, ed. Rob Blair, Tom Ann Casey, William H. Romme, and Richard N. Ellis, 68–79. Boulder: University Press of Colorado, 1996.

Ellison, Lincoln. "Influence of Grazing on Plant Succession of Rangelands." *Botanical Review* 26 (1960): 1–78.

Emmerich, W. E. "Tebuthiuron-Environmental Concerns." *Rangelands* 7 (1985): 14–16.

Engelmark, O., K. Sjöberg, B. Anderson, O. Rosvall, G. Agren, W. L. Baker, P. Barklund, C. Björkman, D. G. Despain, B. Elfving, R. Ennos, M. Karlman, M. F. Knecht, D. H. Knight, N. J. Ledgard, A. Lindelöw, C. Nilsson, G. F. Peterken, S. Sörlin, and M. T. Sykes. "Ecological Effects and Management Aspects of an Exotic Tree Species: The Case of Lodgepole Pine in Sweden." *Forest Ecology and Management* 141 (2001): 3–13.

English, N. E., Julio L. Betancourt, J. S. Dean, and J. Quade. "Strontium Isotopes Reveal Source of Architectural Timber at Chaco Canyon, New Mexico." *Proceedings of the National Academy of Sciences* 98 (2001): 11891–11896.

Erdman, J. A. "Pinyon-Juniper Succession After Natural Fires on Residual Soils of Mesa Verde, Colorado." *Brigham Young University Science Bulletin Biological Series* 11 (1970): 1–26.

Evans, R. D., and J. R. Johansen. "Microbiotic Crusts and Ecosystem Processes." *Critical Reviews in Plant Sciences* 18 (1999): 183–225.

Everitt, B. L. "Ecology of Saltcedar—a Plea for Research." *Environmental Geology* 3 (1980): 77–84.

FAUNMAP Working Group [Graham, Russell W., et al.]. "Spatial Response of Mammals to Late Quaternary Environmental Fluctuations." *Science* 272 (1996): 1601–1606.

Federal Register. "Notice of Designation of the Gunnison Sage Grouse as a Candidate Species." *Federal Register* 65, no. 250 (December 28, 2000): 82310–82312.

Fetter, Richard L., and Suzanne Fetter. *Telluride: "From Pick to Powder."* Caldwell, ID: Caxton, 1990.

Ffolliott, P. F. "Implications of Snag Policies on Management of Southwestern Ponderosa Pine Forests." In *Snag Habitat Management: Proceedings of the Symposium,* ed. Jerry W. Davis, Gregory A. Goodwin, and Richard A. Ockenfels, 28–32. General Technical Report RM-99. Fort Collins, CO: USDA Forest Service, Rocky Mountain Forest and Range Experiment Station, 1983.

Fiedel, Stuart. "The Peopling of the New World: Present Evidence, New Theories, and Future Directions." *Journal of Archaeological Research* 8 (2000): 39–103.

———. "Response to Dillehay," http://archaeology.about.com/library/excav/blmvfiedeli.htm (accessed May 30, 2004).

Fisher, Frederick S. "Uncompahgre River Basin Selenium Phytoremediation." Unpublished report, Section 319 Nonpoint Source Control Program. Montrose, CO: Shavano Conservation District, 2005.

Fitzgerald, James P., Carron A. Meaney, and David M. Armstrong. *Mammals of Colorado.* Denver: Denver Museum of Natural History, and Boulder: University Press of Colorado, 1994.

Flores, Dan. *The Natural West: Environmental History in the Great Plains and Rocky Mountains.* Norman: University of Oklahoma Press, 2001.

Floyd, M. Lisa, and Marilyn Colyer. "Beneath the Trees: Shrubs, Herbs, and Some Surprising Rarities." In *Ancient Piñon-Juniper Woodlands,* ed. M. Lisa Floyd, 31–60. Boulder: University Press of Colorado, 2003.

Floyd, M. Lisa, William H. Romme, and David D. Hanna. "Fire History and Vegetation Pattern in Mesa Verde National Park, Colorado, USA." *Ecological Applications* 10 (2000): 1666–1680.

Freeman, Ira S. *A History of Montezuma County, Colorado.* Boulder: Johnson, 1958.

Freyfogle, Eric T. "Community and the Market in Modern American Property Law." In *Land, Property, and the Environment,* ed. John F. Richards, 382–414. Oakland, CA: ICS, 2002.

Frodeman, Robert. "A Sense of the Whole: Toward an Understanding of Acid Mine Drainage in the West." In *Earth Matters: The Earth Sciences, Philosophy, and the Claims of Community,* ed. Robert Frodeman, 119–139. Upper Saddle River, NJ: Prentice-Hall, 2000.

Fryxell, F. M. "The Former Range of the Bison in the Rocky Mountains." *Journal of Mammalogy* 9 (1928): 129–139.

Gannett, Henry. "Report of Henry Gannett, M. E., Topographer of the Grand River Division, 1875." In *Ninth Annual Report of the United States Geological and Geographical Survey of the Territories, Embracing Colorado and Parts of Adjacent Territories: Being a Report of Progress of the Exploration for the Year 1875,* ed. F. V. Hayden, U.S. geologist, 335–350. Washington, DC: U.S. Government Printing Office, 1877.

———. "Report on the Arable and Pasture Lands of Colorado." In *Tenth Annual Report of the United States Geological and Geographical Survey of the Territories, Embracing Colorado and Parts of Adjacent Territories: Being a Report of Progress of the Exploration for the Year 1876,* ed. F. V. Hayden, U.S. geologist, 313–347. Washington, DC: U.S. Government Printing Office, 1878.

Garton, Edward O. "Gunnison Sage-grouse Population Trend Analysis." Final Report of Statistical Analysis Completed for U.S. Fish and Wildlife Service, Wyoming Ecological Services Field Office, Cheyenne, 2005.

Gelbard, Jonathan L., and Jayne Belnap. "Roads as Conduits for Exotic Plant Invasions in a Semiarid Landscape." *Conservation Biology* 17 (2003): 420–432.

Gill, R. Bruce. *Declining Mule Deer Populations in Colorado: Reasons and Responses.* Special Report no. 77, DOW-R-S-77-01. Denver: Colorado Division of Wildlife, 2001.

Gilleece, Beth M. Yoder. "The Manhattan Project on the Colorado Plateau." *Journal of the Western Slope* 5, no. 2 (1990): 20–29.

Gleichman, Carol L., and Peter J. Gleichman. "The Lower Sand Canyon Survey." In *The Sand Canyon Archaeological Project: A Project Report,* ed. William D. Lipe, 25–31. Occasional Paper no. 2. Cortez, CO: Crow Canyon Archaeological Center, 1992.

Glover, G. H. *Larkspur and Other Poisonous Plants.* Agricultural Experiment Station Bulletin no. 113. Fort Collins: Colorado State University, 1906.

Goldschmidt, Walter. *As You Sow: Three Studies in the Social Consequences of Agribusiness.* Montclair, NJ: Allanheld, Osmun, 1978.

Goodtimes, Art. "Burn Canyon Monitoring Task Force." *San Miguel Watershed Coalition Watershed Connection* (Spring 2004) (no page).

Gordon, Clarence. "Report on Cattle, Sheep, and Swine, Supplementary to Enumeration of Live Stock on Farms in 1880." In *Report on the Productions of Agriculture as Returned at the Tenth Census (June 1, 1880).* Washington, DC: U.S. Government Printing Office, 1883.

Graf, W. L. "Fluvial Adjustments to the Spread of Tamarisk in the Colorado Plateau Region." *Geological Society of America Bulletin* 89 (1978): 1491–1501.

Graham, Russell W. "Evolution of New Ecosystems at the End of the Pleistocene." In *Megafauna and Man: Discovery of America's Heartland,* ed. Larry D. Agenbroad, Jim I. Mead, and Lisa W. Nelson, 54–60. Scientific Papers, Vol. 1. Hot Springs: Mammoth Site of Hot Springs, South Dakota, Inc., 1990.

Grayson, Donald K. *The Desert's Past: A Natural Prehistory of the Great Basin.* Washington, DC: Smithsonian Institution Press, 1993.

Grayson, Donald K., and David J. Meltzer. "Clovis Hunting and Large Mammal Extinction: A Critical Review of the Evidence." *Journal of World Prehistory* 16 (2002): 313–359.

Grazier, Steve. "Panel's Plan Would Expand Canyon's Access." *Cortez Journal* (Cortez, CO), April 1, 2004.

Greager, Howard. *The Hell That Was Paradox.* Boulder: Johnson Books, 1992.

Greater Montrose Centennial, Inc. *Montrose, Colorado Centennial: 1882–1982.* Grand Junction, CO: Great Western, 1982.

Green, Barbara J.B. "Local Regulations Under the Areas and Activities of State Interest Act." Unpublished manuscript. Boulder: Sullivan Green Seavy, LLC, n.d.

Greene, Susan. "Drilling Tests Utes' Values." *Denver Post* (Denver, CO), September 9, 2001.

Greenhill, Jim. "Gas-Well Spacing May Fall to 80 Acres." *Durango Herald* (Durango, CO), November 7, 2002.

———. "Ranchers to Industry: Shape Up." *Durango Herald* (Durango, CO), November 15, 2002.

Greubel, Rand A. "A Closer Look at Eastern Ute Subsistence." *Southwestern Lore* 68, no. 3 (2002): 1–16.

Grilz, P. L., and J. T. Romo. "Water Relations and Growth of *Bromus inermis* Leyss (Smooth Brome) Following Spring or Autumn Burning in a Fescue Prairie." *American Midland Naturalist* 132 (1994): 340–348.

Grossman, D. H., D. Faber-Langendoen, A. S. Weakley, M. Anderson, P. Bourgeron, R. Crawford, K. Goodin, S. Landaal, K. Metzler, K. Patterson, M. Pyne, M. Reid, and L. Sneddon. *Terrestrial Vegetation of the United States, Vol. 1: The National Vegetation Classification System: Development, Status, and Applications.* Arlington, VA: The Nature Conservancy, 1998.

Guennel, G. K. *Guide to Colorado Wildflowers, Vol. 1: Plains and Foothills.* Englewood, CO: Westcliffe, 1995.

———. *Guide to Colorado Wildflowers, Vol. 2: Mountains.* Englewood, CO: Westcliffe, 1995.

Gunnison Basin Selenium Task Force. "Selenium in Western Colorado—Why Should You Care." Brochure. Gunnison, CO: Gunnison Basin and Grand Valley Selenium Task Force, n.d.

Gunnison Sage-grouse Rangewide Steering Committee. "Gunnison Sage-grouse Rangewide Conservation Plan." Denver: Colorado Division of Wildlife, n.d.

Guthrie, R. Dale. "Late Pleistocene Faunal Revolution—a New Perspective on the Extinction Debate." In *Megafauna and Man: Discovery of America's Heartland,* ed. Larry D. Agenbroad, Jim I. Mead, and Lisa W. Nelson, 42–53. Scientific Papers, Vol. 1. Hot Springs: Mammoth Site of Hot Springs, South Dakota, Inc., 1990.

Hafen, Leroy R. "Historical Summary of the Ute Indians and the San Juan Mining District." In *Ute Indians II, American Indian Ethnohistory: California and Basin-Plateau Indians*, ed. David Agee Horr, 267–324. New York: Garland, 1974.

Hafen, LeRoy R., and Ann W. Hafen. *Old Spanish Trail: Santa Fe to Los Angeles.* Glendale, CA: Arthur H. Clark, 1954.

Hall, Linnea S., Michael L. Morrison, and William M. Block. "Songbird Status and Roles." In *Songbird Ecology in Southwestern Ponderosa Pine Forests: A Literature Review*, ed. William M. Block and Deborah M. Finch, 69–88. General Technical Report RM-GTR-292. Fort Collins, CO: USDA Forest Service, Rocky Mountain Forest and Range Experiment Station, 1997.

Halweil, Brian. *Home Grown: The Case for Local Food in a Global Market.* Worldwatch Paper 163. Washington, DC: Worldwatch Institute, 2002.

Hamilton, Steven J. "Selenium Effects on Endangered Fish in the Colorado River Basin." In *Environmental Chemistry of Selenium*, ed. William T. Frankenberger Jr. and Richard A. Engberg, 297–313. New York: Marcel Dekker, 1998.

Hammerson, Geoffrey A. *Amphibians and Reptiles in Colorado: A Colorado Field Guide*, 2nd ed. Boulder: University Press of Colorado, and Denver: Colorado Division of Wildlife, 1999.

Hansen, Andrew J., Ray Rasker, Bruce Maxwell, Jay J. Rotella, Jerry D. Johnson, Andrea Wright Parmenter, Ute Langner, Warren B. Cohen, Rick L. Lawrence, and Matthew P.V. Kraska. "Ecological Causes and Consequences of Demographic Change in the New West." *BioScience* 52 (2002): 151–162.

Hanson, W. R., and L. A. Stoddart. "Effects of Grazing upon Bunch Wheat Grass." *American Society of Agronomy Journal* 32 (1940): 278–289.

Hardin, Garrett. "The Tragedy of the Commons." *Science* 162 (1968): 1243–1248.

Harper, Kimball T., and Jayne Belnap. "The Influence of Biological Soil Crusts on Mineral Uptake by Associated Vascular Plants." *Journal of Arid Environments* 47 (2001): 347–357.

Harrington, H. D., and L. W. Durrell. *How to Identify Plants.* Chicago: Swallow, 1997.

Harrison, R. D., B. L. Waldron, K. B. Jensen, R. Page, T. A. Manaco, W. H. Horton, and A. J. Palazzo. "Forage Kochia Helps Fight Range Fires." *Rangelands* 24 (2002): 3–7.

Hart, John H., and D. L. Hart. "Heartrot Fungi's Role in Creating Picid Nesting Sites in Living Aspen." In *Sustaining Aspen in Western Landscapes: Symposium Proceedings*, ed. W. D. Sheppard, D. Binkley, D. L. Bartos, T. J. Stohlgren, and L. G. Eskew, 207–213. Proceedings RMRS-P-18. Fort Collins, CO: USDA Forest Service, Rocky Mountain Research Station, 2001.

Hartley, Ralph J. *Rock Art on the Northern Colorado Plateau: Variability in Content and Context.* Brookfield, VT: Avebury, 1992.

Haynes, C. Vance. "Clovis-Folsom Geochronology and Climate Change." In *From Kostenki to Clovis: Upper Paleoindian Adaptations*, ed. Olga Soffer and N. D. Praslov, 219–236. New York: Plenum, 1993.

Hayward, C. Lynn, D. Elden Beck, and Wilmer W. Tanner. "Zoology of the Upper Colorado River Basin. I. The Biotic Communities." *Brigham Young University Science Bulletin, Biological Series* 1, no. 3 (1958): 1–74.

Heap, Gwinn Harris. *Central Route to the Pacific from the Valley of the Mississippi to California: Journal of the Expedition of E. F. Beale, Superintendent of Indian Affairs in California, and Gwinn Harris Heap from Missouri to California, in 1853.* Philadelphia: Lippincott, Grambo, 1854; reprinted by LeRoy R. Hafen and Ann W. Hafen, Glendale, CA: Arthur H. Clark, 1957.

Heidinga, L., and S. D. Wilson. "The Impact of an Invading Alien Grass (*Agropyron cristatum*) on Species Turnover in Native Prairie." *Diversity and Distributions* 8 (2002): 249–258.

Hemstrom, Miles A., Michael J. Wisdom, Wendel J. Hann, Mary M. Rowland, Barbara C. Wales, and Rebecca A. Gravenmier. "Sagebrush-Steppe Vegetation Dynamics and Restoration Potential in the Interior Columbia Basin, U.S.A." *Conservation Biology* 16 (2002): 1243–1255.

Hennen, Matthew A. "On Second Thought, Go Ahead and Fence Me In: The Privatization of Open Space in the West." Master's thesis. Laramie: University of Wyoming, 2000.

Hester, Dwight A. "The Pinyon-Juniper Fuel Type Can Really Burn." *USDA Forest Service, Fire Control Notes* 13 (1952): 26–29.

Hickcox, Gary. "Time to Be Counted on Idarado Legacy Project." *Telluride Daily Planet* (Telluride, CO), October 10, 2001.

Hinds, Thomas E. "Diseases." In *Aspen: Ecology and Management in the Western United States,* ed. Norman V. DeByle and Robert P. Winokur, 87–106. General Technical Report RM-119. Fort Collins, CO: USDA Forest Service, Rocky Mountain Forest and Range Experiment Station, 1985.

Hinshaw, Glen A. *Crusaders for Wildlife: A History of Wildlife Stewardship in Southwestern Colorado.* Ouray, CO: Western Reflections, 2000.

Hironaka, M., and E. W. Tisdale. "Secondary Succession in Annual Vegetation in Southern Idaho." *Ecology* 44 (1963): 810–812.

Hobbs, N. Thompson, Michael W. Miller, James A. Bailey, Dale F. Reed, and R. Bruce Gill. "Biological Criteria for Introductions of Large Mammals: Using Simulation Models to Predict Impacts of Competition." *Transactions of the North American Wildlife and Natural Resources Conference* 55 (1990): 620–632.

Holechek, J. L., H. Gomes, F. Molinar, D. Galt, and R. Valdez. "Short-Duration Grazing: The Facts in 1999." *Rangelands* 22 (2000): 18–22.

Holechek, J. L., and T. Stephenson. "Comparison of Big Sagebrush Vegetation in Northcentral New Mexico Under Moderately Grazed and Grazing Excluded Conditions." *Journal of Range Management* 36 (1983): 455–456.

Howard, V. W., Kathleen M. Cheap, Ross H. Hier, Thomas G. Thompson, and J. Andrew Dimas. "Effects of Cabling Pinyon-Juniper on Mule Deer and Lagomorph Use." In *Proceedings: Pinyon-Juniper Conference [Reno, Nevada, January 13–16, 1986],* ed. Richard L. Everett, 552–557. General Technical Report INT-215. Ogden, UT: USDA Forest Service, Intermountain Research Station, 1987.

Howell, Jim. "For Cool Season Grasses, Springtime Begins in the Fall." *The Savory Center, in Practice: Land and Livestock* 87 (2003): 10–13.

———. "Grazing in Nature's Image—Part 2." *The Savory Center, in Practice: Land and Livestock* 75 (2001): 10–13.

———. "Measuring the Desert." *The Savory Center, in Practice: Land and Livestock* 81 (2002): 12–14.

Hughes, L. E. "Tamarisk . . . Maybe Not Invincible." *Rangelands* 22 (2000): 11–14.

Hull, A. C., Jr. "Eradication of Big Sagebrush (*Artemisia tridentata*)." *Journal of Range Management* 2 (1949): 153.

Hull, A. C., Jr., and Mary K. Hull. "Presettlement Vegetation of Cache Valley, Utah and Idaho." *Journal of Range Management* 27 (1974): 27–29.

Hull, A. C., Jr., N. A. Kissinger Jr., and W. T. Vaughn. "Chemical Control of Big Sagebrush in Wyoming." *Journal of Range Management* 5 (1952): 398–402.

Hull, A. C., Jr., and G. J. Klomp. "Longevity of Crested Wheatgrass in the Sagebrush-Grass Type in Southern Idaho." *Journal of Range Management* 19 (1966): 5–11.

Hull, A. C., Jr., and J. F. Pechanec. "Cheatgrass—a Challenge to Range Research." *Journal of Forestry* 45 (1947): 555–564.

Ingelfinger, Franz M. "The Effects of Natural Gas Development on Sagebrush Steppe Passerines in Sublette County, Wyoming." Master's thesis. Laramie: University of Wyoming, 2001.

Ingersoll, Ernest. *The Crest of the Continent: A Record of a Summer's Ramble in the Rocky Mountains and Beyond.* Chicago: R. R. Donnelley and Sons, 1885.

Jackson, William H. "Report on the Ancient Ruins Examined in 1875 and 1877." In *Tenth Annual Report of the United States Geological and Geographical Survey of the Territories, Embracing Colorado and Parts of Adjacent Territories: Being a Report of Progress of the Exploration for the Year 1876,* ed. F. V. Hayden, U.S. geologist, 411–430. Washington, DC: U.S. Government Printing Office, 1878.

Jacobi, William R., and Wayne D. Shepperd. *Fungi Associated with Sprout Mortality in Aspen Clearcuts in Colorado and Arizona.* Research Note RM-513. Fort Collins, CO: USDA Forest Service, Rocky Mountain Forest and Range Experiment Station, 1991.

James, L. F., W. F. Hartley, K. E. Panter, B. L. Stegelmeier, D. Gould, and H. F. Mayland. "Selenium Poisoning in Cattle." In *Plant-Associated Toxins: Agricultural, Phytochemical, and Ecological Aspects,* ed. S. M. Colegate and P. R. Dorling, 416–420. Wallingford, UK: CAB International, 1994.

Jameson, Donald A., John A. Williams, and Eugene Wilton. "Vegetation and Soils of Fishtail Mesa, Arizona." *Ecology* 43 (1962): 403–410.

Jefferson, James, Robert W. Delaney, and Gregory C. Thompson. *The Southern Utes: A Tribal History.* Ignacio, CO: Southern Ute Tribe, and Salt Lake City: University of Utah Printing Service, 1972.

Jenkins, Amelia Fine. "Forest Health, a Crisis of Human Proportions." *Journal of Forestry* 95, no. 9 (1997): 11–14.

Jocknick, Sidney. *Early Days on the Western Slope of Colorado.* Denver: Carson-Harper, 1913.

Johnsen, Thomas N., Jr. "One-Seed Juniper Invasion of Northern Arizona Grasslands." *Ecological Monographs* 32 (1962): 187–207.

Johnson, Bruce K., John W. Kern, Michael J. Wisdom, Scott L. Findholt, and John G. Kie. "Resource Selection and Spatial Separation of Mule Deer and Elk During Spring." *Journal of Wildlife Management* 64 (2000): 685–697.

Johnson, K. L. *Rangeland Through Time: A Photographic Study of Vegetation Change in Wyoming, 1870–1986.* Miscellaneous publication no. 50. Laramie: Agricultural Experiment Station, University of Wyoming, 1987.

Johnston, Barry C. "Multiple Factors Affect Aspen Regeneration on the Uncompahgre Plateau, West-Central Colorado." In *Sustaining Aspen in Western Landscapes: Symposium Proceedings,* ed. W. D. Sheppard, D. Binkley, D. L. Bartos, T. J. Stohlgren, and L. G. Eskew, 395–414. Proceedings RMRS-P-18. Fort Collins, CO: USDA Forest Service, Rocky Mountain Research Station, 2001.

Jones, John R., Robert P. Winokur, and Wayne D. Shepperd. "Management Overview." In *Aspen: Ecology and Management in the Western United States,* ed. Norbert V. DeByle and Robert P. Winokur, 193–195. General Technical Report RM-119. USDA Forest Service, Rocky Mountain Forest and Range Experiment Station, 1985.

Jones, William R. "History of Mining and Milling Practices & Production in the Upper Animas River Drainage 1871–1991." Appendix 7C, Use Attainability Analysis for the Animas River Watershed. Silverton, CO: Animas River Stakeholder Group, 2001.

Kasper, Jan C. "Animal Resource Utilization at Colorado Paradox Valley Site." *Southwestern Lore* 43, no. 1 (1977): 1–17.

Kaufman, Kenn. *Focus Guide to the Birds of North America.* Boston: Houghton Mifflin, 2000.

Kaufmann, Merrill R., Russell T. Graham, Douglas A. Boyce Jr., William H. Moir, Lee Perry, Richard T. Reynolds, Richard L. Bassett, Patricia Mehlhop, Carleton B. Edminster, William M. Block, and Paul S. Corn. *An Ecological Basis for Ecosystem Management.* General Technical Report RM-246. Fort Collins, CO: USDA Forest Service, Rocky Mountain Forest and Range Experiment Station, 1994.

Kaufmann, Merrill R., William H. Moir, and Richard L. Bassett, eds. *Old-Growth Forests in the Southwest and Rocky Mountain Regions: Proceedings of a Workshop.* General Technical Report RM-213. Fort Collins, CO: USDA Forest Service, Rocky Mountain Forest and Range Experiment Station, 1992.

Kay, Charles E. "Aboriginal Overkill: The Role of Native Americans in Structuring Western Ecosystems." *Human Nature* 5, no. 4 (1994): 359–398.

———. "Are Ecosystems Structured from the Top-Down or Bottom-Up: A New Look at an Old Debate." *Wildlife Society Bulletin* 26 (1998): 484–498.

———. "Is Aspen Doomed?" *Journal of Forestry* 95, no. 8 (1997): 4–11.

Keen, Richard A. "Weather and Climate." In *The Western San Juan Mountains: Their Geology, Ecology, and Human History,* ed. Rob Blair, Tom Ann Casey, William H. Romme, and Richard N. Ellis, 113–126. Boulder: University Press of Colorado, 1996.

Kelly, Robert L. "Maybe We Do Know When People First Came to North America: And What Does It Mean If We Do?" *Quaternary International* 109–110 (2002): 133–145.

Kenney, Douglas S. *Arguing About Consensus*. Boulder: Natural Resources Law Center, University of Colorado School of Law, 2000.

Kerr, Andy. "Sage Grouse: The Spotted Owl of the Desert." *Wallowa County Chieftain* (Enterprise, OR), June 19, 1997.

Kingery, Hugh E., ed. *Colorado Breeding Bird Atlas*. Denver: Colorado Bird Atlas Partnership and Colorado Division of Wildlife, 1998.

Kleiner, Edgar F., and Kimball T. Harper. "Environment and Community Organization in Grasslands of Canyonlands National Park." *Ecology* 53 (1972): 299–309.

———. "Soil Properties in Relation to Cryptogamic Groundcover in Canyonlands National Park." *Journal of Range Management* 30 (1977): 202–205.

Klemmedson, James O. "Interrelations of Vegetation, Soils and Range Conditions Induced by Grazing." *Journal of Range Management* 9 (1956): 134–138.

Klemmedson, James O., and J. G. Smith. "Cheatgrass (*Bromus tectorum* L.)." *Botanical Review* 30 (1964): 226–262.

Kline, Jeff. "My Vision of the Piñon/Socioeconomic Potential of Piñon Woodlands." In *Managing Piñon-Juniper Ecosystems for Sustainability and Social Needs*, ed. Earl F. Aldon and Douglas W. Shaw, 3–8. General Technical Report RM-236. Fort Collins, CO: USDA Forest Service, Rocky Mountain Forest and Range Experiment Station, 1993.

Knight, Anthony P., and Richard G. Walter. *A Guide to Plant Poisoning in North America*. Jackson, WY: Teton NewMedia, 2001. See also the online database on plant poisoning: www.vth.colostate.edu/poisonous_plants.cfm.

Knight, Richard L., Wendell D. Gilgert, and Ed Marston, eds. *Ranching West of the 100th Meridian: Culture, Ecology and Economics*. Washington, DC: Island, 2002.

Knight, Richard L., George N. Wallace, and William E. Riebsame. "Ranching the View: Subdivisions Versus Agriculture." *Conservation Biology* 9 (1995): 459–461.

Kohler, Judith. "Six More Lynx Kittens Found in Colorado." *Durango Herald* (Durango, CO), December 31, 2004.

Kohler, Timothy A. "The Final 400 Years of Prehispanic Agricultural Society in the Mesa Verde Region." *Kiva* 66 (2000): 191–204.

Kohler, Timothy A., and Meredith H. Matthews. "Long-Term Anasazi Land Use and Forest Reduction: A Case Study from Southwest Colorado." *American Antiquity* 53 (1988): 537–564.

Komarek, Susan. *Flora of the San Juans: A Field Guide to the Mountain Plants of Southwestern Colorado*. Durango, CO: Kivaki, 1994.

Kostivkovsky, V., and J. A. Young. "Invasive Exotic Rangeland Weeds: A Glimpse at Some of Their Native Habitats." *Rangelands* 22, no. 6 (2000): 3–6.

Krech, Shepard, III. *The Ecological Indian: Myth and History*. New York: W. W. Norton, 1998.

Kuckelman, Kristin A. "Thirteenth-Century Warfare in the Central Mesa Verde Region." In *Seeking the Center Place: Archaeology and Ancient Communities in the Mesa Verde Region*, ed. Mark D. Varien and Richard H. Wilshusen, 233–253. Salt Lake City: University of Utah Press, 2002.

Kufeld, Roland. *History and Current Status of the Mule Deer Population on the East Side of the Uncompahgre Plateau.* Report no. 11. Denver: Colorado Division of Wildlife, 1979.

Landres, Peter B., Penelope Morgan, and Frederick J. Swanson. "Overview of the Use of Natural Variability Concepts in Managing Ecological Systems." *Ecological Applications* 9 (1999): 1179–1188.

Lanner, Ronald M. "The Eradication of Pinyon-Juniper Woodland: Has the Program a Legitimate Purpose?" *Western Wildlands* 3, no. 4 (1977): 12–17.

———. *The Piñon Pine: A Natural and Cultural History.* Reno: University of Nevada Press, 1981.

Larmer, Paul. "The 'Dobes Come Alive: Finding Beauty in a Trashed Land." *Denver Post* (Denver, CO), December 24, 2000.

Larsen, Esper S., Jr., and Whitman Cross. *Geology and Petrology of the San Juan Region, Southwestern Colorado.* Professional Paper no. 258, U.S. Geological Survey. Washington, DC: U.S. Government Printing Office, 1956.

Lavender, David. *One Man's West,* 3rd ed. Lincoln: University of Nebraska Press, 1964.

———. *The Telluride Story.* Ouray, CO: Wayfinder, 1987.

Laycock, William A. "Stable States and Thresholds of Range Condition on North American Rangelands: A Viewpoint." *Journal of Range Management* 44 (1991): 427–433.

Ledgard, Nick. "The Spread of Lodgepole Pine (*Pinus contorta*, Dougl.) in New Zealand." *Forest Ecology and Management* 141 (2001): 43–57.

Lee, Kai N. "Appraising Adaptive Management." In *Biological Diversity: Balancing Interests Through Adaptive Collaborative Management,* ed. L. E. Buck, C. C. Geisler, J. Schelhas, and E. Wollenberg, 3–26. Boca Raton, FL: CRC, 2001.

Leopold, Aldo. *A Sand County Almanac.* New York: Ballantine Books, 1949, reprinted in 1970.

Lesica, P., and T. H. DeLuca. "Long-Term Harmful Effects of Crested Wheatgrass on Great Plains Grassland Ecosystems." *Journal of Soil and Water Conservation* 51 (1996): 408–409.

Ligon, Franklin K., William E. Dietrich, and William J. Trush. "Downstream Ecological Effects of Dams: A Geomorphic Perspective." *BioScience* 45 (1995): 183–192.

Limerick, Patricia Nelson. *The Legacy of Conquest: The Unbroken Past of the American West.* New York: W. W. Norton, 1987.

Lipe, William D. "Basketmaker II (1000 B.C.–A.D. 500)." In *Colorado Prehistory: A Context for the Southern Colorado River Basin,* ed. William D. Lipe, Mark D. Varien, and Richard H. Wilshusen, 132–165. Denver: Colorado Council of Professional Archaeologists, 1999.

———. "Concluding Comments." In *Colorado Prehistory: A Context for the Southern Colorado River Basin,* ed. William D. Lipe, Mark D. Varien, and Richard H. Wilshusen, 405–435. Denver: Colorado Council of Professional Archaeologists, 1999.

———. "The Depopulation of the Northern San Juan: Conditions in the Turbulent 1200s." *Journal of Anthropological Archaeology* 14 (1995): 143–169.

Lipe, William D., and Bonnie L. Pitblado. "Paleoindian and Archaic Periods." In *Colorado Prehistory: A Context for the Southern Colorado River Basin*, ed. William D. Lipe, Mark D. Varien, and Richard H. Wilshusen, 95–131. Denver: Colorado Council of Professional Archaeologists, 1999.

Lipe, William D., and Mark D. Varien. "Pueblo III (A.D. 1150–1300)." In *Colorado Prehistory: A Context for the Southern Colorado River Basin*, ed. William D. Lipe, Mark D. Varien, and Richard H. Wilshusen, 290–352. Denver: Colorado Council of Professional Archaeologists, 1999.

Lipe, William D., Mark D. Varien, and Richard H. Wilshusen, eds. *Colorado Prehistory: A Context for the Southern Colorado River Basin*. Denver: Colorado Council of Professional Archaeologists, 1999.

Litzinger, William J., and Joseph C. Winter. "The Vegetation on Archaeological Sites of Cajon Mesa, Colorado-Utah." *Southwestern Lore* 60, no. 3 (1994): 4–33.

Lobao, Linda M. *Locality and Inequality: Farm and Industry Structure and Socioeconomic Conditions*. Albany: State University of New York Press, 1990.

Lockwood, Jeffrey A. *Prairie Soul: Finding Grace in the Earth Beneath My Feet*. Boston: Skinner House Books, 2004.

Lodge, David M., and Kristin Shrader-Frechette. "Nonindigenous Species: Ecological Explanation, Environmental Ethics, and Public Policy." *Conservation Biology* 17 (2003): 31–37.

Lorenz, R. J. "Introduction and Early Use of Crested Wheatgrass in the Northern Great Plains." In *Crested Wheatgrass: Its Values, Problems and Myths: Symposium Proceedings*, ed. K. L. Johnson, 9–20. Logan: Utah State University, 1986.

Louv, Richard. *The Last Child in the Woods*. Chapel Hill, NC: Algonquin Books, 2005.

Ludwig, D., R. Hilborn, and C. Walters. "Uncertainty, Resource Exploitation, and Conservation: Lessons from History." *Science* 260 (1993): 17, 36.

Lynch, Dennis L., William H. Romme, and M. Lisa Floyd. "Forest Restoration in Southwestern Ponderosa Pine." *Journal of Forestry* 98, no. 8 (2000): 17–24.

Lynch, Thomas F. "Commentary: On the Road Again . . . Reflections on Monte Verde." *Review of Archaeology* 22 (2001): 39–43.

Lyon, Alison G. "The Potential Effects of Natural Gas Development on Sage-Grouse (*Centrocercus urophasianus*) Near Pinedale, Wyoming." Master's thesis. Laramie: University of Wyoming, 2000.

Lyon, Alison G., and S. H. Anderson. "Potential Gas Development Impacts on Sage Grouse Nest Initiation and Movement." *Wildlife Society Bulletin* 31 (2003): 486–491.

Lyon, Peggy, and Michael Denslow. "Gunnison Gorge National Conservation Area Survey of Impacts on Rare Plants." Unpublished report. Fort Collins, CO: Colorado Natural Heritage Program to Bureau of Land Management, Montrose, CO, 2001.

Lyon, Peggy, Tom Stephens, Jeremy Siemers, Denise Culver, Phyllis Pineda, and Jennifer Zoerner. *The Uncompahgre River Basin: A Natural Heritage Assessment*. Fort Collins, CO: Colorado Natural Heritage Program, 1999.

Mack, R. N. "Invasion of *Bromus tectorum* L. into Western North America: An Ecological Chronicle." *Agro-Ecosystems* 7 (1981): 145–165.

Mack, R. N., and J. N. Thompson. "Evolution in Steppe with Few Large, Hooved Mammals." *American Naturalist* 119 (1982): 757–773.

Madany, Michael H., and Neil E. West. "Livestock Grazing–Fire Regime Interactions Within Montane Forests of Zion National Park, Utah." *Ecology* 66 (1983): 661–667.

Madsen, David B., and Steven R. Simms. "The Fremont Complex: A Behavioral Perspective." *Journal of World Prehistory* 12 (1998): 255–327.

Maestas, Jeremy D., Richard L. Knight, and Wendell C. Gilgert. "Biodiversity Across a Rural Land-Use Gradient." *Conservation Biology* 17 (2003): 1425–1434.

Magnan, Nick, and Andrew Seidl. "The Economic Base of Montezuma County, Colorado: Executive Summary." Economic Development Report EDR 04-03. Fort Collins: Colorado State University, 2004.

Mahoney, Nancy M., Michael A. Adler, and James W. Kendrick. "The Changing Scale and Configuration of Mesa Verde Communities." *Kiva* 66 (2000): 67–90.

Malouf, Carling I., and John M. Findlay. "Euro-American Impact Before 1870." In *Handbook of North American Indians, Vol. 11: Great Basin,* ed. W. L. D'Azevedo, 499–524. Washington, DC: Smithsonian Institution Press, 1986.

Manier, Daniel J., N. Thompson Hobbs, David M. Theobald, Robin M. Reich, Mohammed A. Kalkhan, and Mark R. Campbell. "Canopy Dynamics and Human Caused Disturbance on a Semi-Arid Landscape in the Rocky Mountains, USA." *Landscape Ecology* 20 (2005): 1–17.

Manier, Daniel J., and Richard D. Laven. "Changes in Landscape Patterns Associated with the Persistence of Aspen (*Populus tremuloides* Michx.) on the Western Slope of the Rocky Mountains, Colorado." *Forest Ecology and Management* 167 (2002): 263–284.

Marshall, Muriel. *The Awesome 'Dobie Badlands.* Montrose, CO: Western Reflections, 1999.

———. *Red Hole in Time.* College Station: Texas A&M University Press, 1988.

———. *Where Rivers Meet: Lore from the Colorado Frontier.* College Station: Texas A&M University Press, 1996.

Martin, Paul S. "Pleistocene Overkill." *Natural History* 76 (1967): 32–38.

Martin, Paul S., and David A. Burney. "Bring Back the Elephants!" *Wild Earth* 9, no. 1 (1999): 57–64.

Martin, Paul S., and Richard G. Klein. *Quaternary Extinctions: A Prehistoric Revolution.* Tucson: University of Arizona Press, 1984.

Martin, Tunyalee. "Tamarisk Control in Southern California." Unpublished report, The Nature Conservancy: http://tncweeds.ucdavis.edu/success/ca003.html, 2001 (accessed May 30, 2004).

Martorano, Marilyn A. "Culturally Peeled Trees and Ute Indians in Colorado." In *Archaeology of the Eastern Ute: A Symposium,* ed. P. R. Nickens, 5–21. Occasional papers no. 1. Denver: Colorado Council of Professional Archaeologists, 1988.

Masnick, George. "America's Shifting Population: Understanding Migration Patterns in the West." *Changing Landscape* (Winter–Spring 2001): 8–15.

Mason, Lamar R., Horace M. Andrews, James A. Carley, and E. Dwain Maacke. "Vegetation and Soils of No Man's Land Mesa Relict Area, Utah." *Journal of Range Management* 20 (1967): 45–59.

Matthews, Meridith H. "Agricultural Intensification and Multiple Cropping Practices: Testing Change in Exploration of Pioneer Plant Resources." Master's thesis. Boulder: University of Colorado, 1985.

———. "The Dolores Archaeological Program Macrobotanical Data Base: Resource Availability and Mix." In *Dolores Archaeological Program: Final Synthetic Report*, ed. David A. Breternitz, Christine K. Robinson, and G. Timothy Gross, 151–184. Denver: USDI Bureau of Reclamation, 1986.

McArthur, E. Durant. "Sagebrush Systematics and Evolution." In *The Sagebrush Ecosystem: A Symposium*, 14–22. Logan: Utah State University, College of Natural Resources, 1979.

McCullough, Dale R., ed. *Metapopulations and Wildlife Conservation*. Washington, DC: Island, 1996.

McCutchen, Henry E. "Desert Bighorn Sheep." In *Our Living Resource: A Report to the Nation on the Distribution, Abundance and Health of U.S. Plants, Animals and Ecosystems*. U.S. Geological Survey, Biological Resources Division: http://biology.usgs.gov/s+t/SNT/index.htm (accessed May 30, 2004).

McDaniel, Kirk C., and Timothy T. Ross. "Snakeweed: Poisonous Properties, Livestock Losses, and Management Considerations." *Journal of Range Management* 55 (2002): 277–284.

McDonald, Jerry N. *North American Bison: Their Classification and Evolution*. Berkeley: University of California Press, 1981.

McKelvey, Kevin S., Keith B. Aubry, and Yvette K. Ortega. "History and Distribution of Lynx in the Contiguous United States." In *Ecology and Conservation of Lynx in the United States*, ed. Leonard F. Ruggiero, Keith B. Aubry, Steven W. Buskirk, Gary M. Koehler, Charles J. Krebs, Kevin S. McKelvey, and John R. Squires, 207–264. General Technical Report RMRS-GTR-30WWW. Fort Collins, CO: USDA Forest Service, Rocky Mountain Research Station, 1999.

McMahon, Todd C. "Paradox Valley, Colorado: Cultural Interactions and Considerations for Reinterpretation." *Southwestern Lore* 66, no. 3 (2000): 1–29.

McPherson, Robert S. "Canyons, Cows, and Conflict: A Native American History of Montezuma Canyon, 1874–1933." *Utah Historical Quarterly* 60 (1992): 238–258.

Meaney, Carron A., and Dirk Van Vuren. "Recent Distribution of Bison in Colorado West of the Great Plains." *Proceedings of the Denver Museum of Natural History*, Series 3, no. 4 (December 1993): 1–10.

Mehl, Mel S. "Old-Growth Descriptions for the Major Forest Cover Types in the Rocky Mountain Region." In *Old-Growth Forests in the Southwest and Rocky Mountain Regions: Proceedings of a Workshop*, ed. Merrill R. Kaufmann, William H. Moir, and Richard L. Bassett, 106–120. General Technical Report

RM-213. Fort Collins, CO: USDA Forest Service, Rocky Mountain Forest and Range Experiment Station, 1992.

Meltzer, David J., Donald K. Grayson, Gerardo Ardila, Alex W. Barker, Dena F. Dincauze, C. Vance Haynes, Francisco Mena, Lautaro Nunez, and Dennis J. Stanford. "On the Pleistocene Antiquity of Monte Verde, Southern Chile." *American Antiquity* 62 (1997): 659–663.

Memmott, K. L., V. J. Anderson, and S. B. Monsen. "Seasonal Grazing Impact on Cryptogamic Crusts in a Cold Desert Ecosystem." *Journal of Range Management* 51 (1998): 547–550.

Miller, James R., Jennifer M. Fraterrigo, N. Thompson Hobbs, David Theobald, and John Wiens. "Urbanization, Avian Communities, and Landscape Ecology." In *Avian Ecology and Conservation in an Urbanizing World*, ed. John M. Marzluff II, Reed Bowman III, and Roarke Donnelly, 117–137. Norwell, MA: Kluwer Academic, 2001.

Miller, Patricia. "Panel Urges River Trails Annexation." *Durango Herald* (Durango, CO), June 18, 2003.

Miller, Richard F., and Jeffrey A. Rose. "Fire History and Western Juniper Encroachment in Sagebrush Steppe." *Journal of Range Management* 52 (1999): 550–559.

———. "Historic Expansion of *Juniperus occidentalis* (Western Juniper) in Southeastern Oregon." *Great Basin Naturalist* 55 (1995): 37–45.

Miller, Richard F., T. J. Svejcar, and N. E. West. "Implications of Livestock Grazing in the Intermountain Sagebrush Region: Plant Composition." In *Ecological Implications of Livestock Herbivory in the West*, ed. M. Vavra, W. A. Laycock, and R. D. Pieper, 101–146. Denver: Society for Range Management, 1994.

Mitchell, John E., Richard L. Knight, and Richard J. Camp. "Landscape Attributes of Subdivided Ranches." *Rangelands* 24, no. 1 (2002): 3–9.

Moir, W. H., and W. M. Block. "Adaptive Management on Public Lands in the United States: Commitment or Rhetoric?" *Environmental Management* 28 (2001): 141–148.

Moore, Gregory. "Animas Trout Making a Comeback." *Durango Herald* (Durango, CO), April 23, 2004.

Morrison, Brad. "Prescribed Burn Plan for the Hermosa Drainage." Unpublished report. Durango, CO: U.S. Forest Service, San Juan National Forest, 1989.

Morrison Knudsen Corporation. "Final Five-Year Review: Umetco Minerals Corporation Uravan Superfund Site, Uravan, Colorado." Unpublished report to the U.S. Environmental Protection Agency, Region VIII, by Morrison Knudsen Corporation, Littleton, CO, 2000.

Muller, Brian, Cameron Bertron, and Li Yin. "Tri-River Growth Futures Project: Final Report." Unpublished report to the Colorado Department of Local Affairs, the Great Outdoors Colorado Trust Fund, American Farmland Trust, and the Hewlett Foundation. Denver: University of Colorado, 2001.

Murray, Ben. "Idarado Officials: Negotiations Are Over." *Telluride Daily Planet* (Telluride, CO), January 22, 2004.

Nabhan, Gary Paul. *Cultures of Habitat: On Nature, Culture and Story.* Washington, DC: Counterpoint, 1997.

Nabhan, Gary Paul, and Stephen Trimble. *The Geography of Childhood: Why Children Need Wild Places.* Boston: Beacon, 1994.

National Geographic Society. *Field Guide to the Birds of North America,* 3rd ed. Washington, DC: National Geographic Society, 1999.

Nelson, Ruth Ashton. *Handbook of Rocky Mountain Plants,* 4th ed., rev. Roger L. Williams. Niwot, CO: Roberts Rinehart, 1992.

Newberry, J. S. *Report of the Exploring Expedition from Santa Fe, New Mexico, to the Junction of the Grand and Green Rivers of the Great Colorado of the West in 1859, Under the Command of Capt. J. N. Macomb.* U.S. Army, Engineer Department. Washington, DC: U.S. Government Printing Office, 1876.

Nossaman, Allen. *Many More Mountains, Vol. 1: Silverton's Roots.* Denver: Sundance, 1989.

———. *Many More Mountains, Vol. 2: Ruts into Silverton.* Denver: Sundance, 1993.

Novak, S. J., and R. N. Mack. "Tracing Plant Introduction and Spread: Genetic Evidence from *Bromus tectorum* (Cheatgrass)." *BioScience* 51 (2001): 114–122.

Nowak, C. L., R. S. Nowak, R. J. Tausch, and P. E. Wigand. "A 30,000 Year Record of Vegetation Dynamics at a Semi-Arid Locale in the Great Basin." *Journal of Vegetation Science* 5 (1994): 579–590.

Odell, Eric A., and Richard Knight. "Songbird and Medium-Sized Mammal Communities Associated with Exurban Development in Pitkin County, Colorado." *Conservation Biology* 15 (2001): 1143–1150.

Operation Healthy Communities. *Pathways to Healthier Communities: Archuleta, Dolores, La Plata, Montezuma and San Juan Counties,* 4th ed. Durango, CO: Operation Healthy Communities, 2001.

Opler, Marvin K. "The Southern Ute of Colorado." In *Acculturation in Seven American Indian Tribes,* ed. Ralph Linton, 119–203. New York: D. Appleton-Century, 1940.

O'Rourke, Paul M. *Frontier in Transition: A History of Southwestern Colorado.* USDI Cultural Resource Series no. 10. Denver: Bureau of Land Management, Colorado State Office, 1992.

Owen, J. Robert. "Water Quality and Sources of Metal Loading to the Upper Animas River Basin." Unpublished report. Denver: Colorado Department of Public Health and Environment, Water Quality Division, 1997.

Oyler-McCance, Sara. "Genetic and Habitat Factors Underlying Conservation Strategies for Gunnison Sage-Grouse." PhD diss. Fort Collins: Colorado State University, 1999.

Oyler-McCance, Sara, Kenneth P. Burnham, and Clait E. Braun. "Influence of Changes in Sagebrush on Gunnison Sage Grouse in Southwestern Colorado." *Southwestern Naturalist* 46 (2001): 323–331.

Panos, Nicholas P. "H.B. 1041 as a Tool for Municipal Attorneys." *Colorado Lawyer* 23 (1994): 1309–1311.

Partners in Flight. *Land Bird Conservation Plan, CO,* 2000: http://www.rmbo.org/pif/copif.html (accessed May 30, 2004).

Passey, H. B., V. K. Hugie, and E. W. Williams. "Herbage Production and Composition Fluctuations of Natural Plant Communities as Related to Climate and Soil Taxonomic Units." *American Society of Agronomy Special Publication* 5 (1964): 206–221.

Patou, K. A., and P. T. Tueller. "Evolutionary Implications for Grazing Management Systems." *Rangelands* 7 (1985): 57–61.

Paulin, Kathleen, Jeffrey J. Cook, and Sarah R. Dewey. "Pinyon-Juniper Woodlands as Sources of Avian Diversity." In *Proceedings: Ecology and Management of Pinyon-Juniper Communities Within the Interior West*, ed. Stephen B. Monsen and Richard Stevens, 240–243. Proceedings RMRS-P-9. Ogden, UT: USDA Forest Service, Rocky Mountain Research Station, 1999.

Paulsen, Harold A., Jr. "Forage Value on a Mountain Grassland-Aspen Range in Western Colorado." *Journal of Range Management* 22 (1969): 102–107.

Pavlacky, David C., and Stanley H. Anderson. "Habitat Preferences of Pinyon-Juniper Specialists Near the Limit of Their Geographic Range." *Condor* 103 (2001): 322–331.

Peale, A. C. "Report of A. C. Peale, M.D., Geologist of the Grand River Division, 1875." In *Ninth Annual Report of the United States Geological and Geographical Survey of the Territories, Embracing Colorado and Parts of Adjacent Territories: Being a Report of Progress of the Exploration for the Year 1875*, ed. F. V. Hayden, U.S. geologist, 31–101. Washington, DC: U.S. Government Printing Office, 1877.

Pearson, G. A. "Herbaceous Vegetation a Factor in Natural Regeneration of Ponderosa Pine in the Southwest." *Ecological Monographs* 12 (1942): 315–338.

Pearson, Mark. "Public Comments: Don't Drill the HDs." *San Juan Citizen News* (Durango, CO), March 2005.

Perera, Ajith H., Lisa J. Buse, and Michael G. Weber. *Emulating Natural Forest Landscape Disturbances: Concepts and Applications*. New York: Columbia University Press, 2004.

Peters, Robert L., Evan Frost, and Felice Pace. *Managing for Forest Ecosystem Health: A Reassessment of the "Forest Health Crisis."* Washington, DC: Defenders of Wildlife, 1996.

Petersen, Kenneth Lee. "Tabehuache and Elk Mountain Utes: A Historical Test of an Ecological Model." *Southwestern Lore* 43, no. 4 (1977): 5–21.

————. "A Warm and Wet Little Climatic Optimum and a Cold and Dry Little Ice Age in the Southern Rocky Mountains, USA." *Climatic Change* 26 (1994): 243–269.

Petersen, Kenneth Lee, and Meredith H. Matthews. "Man's Impact on the Landscape: A Prehistoric Example from the Dolores River Anasazi, Southwestern Colorado." *Journal of the West* 26, no. 3 (1987): 4–16.

Pieper, Rex D. "Overstory-Understory Relations in Pinyon-Juniper Woodlands in New Mexico." *Journal of Range Management* 43 (1990): 413–415.

Pieper, Rex D., and R. K. Heitschmidt. "Is Short-Duration Grazing the Answer?" *Journal of Soil and Water Conservation* 43 (1988): 133–137.

Pimentel, David, Lori Lach, Rodolfo Zuniga, and Doug Morrison. "Environmental and Economic Costs of Nonindigenous Species in the United States." *BioScience* 50 (2000): 53–65.

Pitblado, Bonnie. L. "Late Paleoindian Occupation of the Southern Rocky Mountains: Projectile Points and Land Use in the High Country." PhD diss. Tucson: University of Arizona, 1999.

———. "Paleoindian Presence in Southwest Colorado." *Southwestern Lore* 60, no. 4 (1994): 1–20.

———. "Peak to Peak in Paleoindian Time: Occupation of Southwest Colorado." *Plains Anthropologist* 43, no. 166 (1998): 333–348.

Planty-Tabacchi, Anne-Marie, Eric Tabacchi, Robert J. Naiman, Collette Deferrari, and Henri Décamps. "Invasibility of Species-Rich Communities in Riparian Zones." *Conservation Biology* 10 (1996): 598–607.

Poff, N. LeRoy, J. David Allan, Mark B. Bain, James R. Karr, Karen L. Prestegaard, Brian D. Richter, Richard E. Sparks, and Julie C. Stromberg. "The Natural Flow Regime: A Paradigm for River Conservation and Restoration." *BioScience* 47 (1997): 769–784.

Pojar, Tom. "Progress in Understanding Recruitment in Mule Deer Herds." Unpublished report. Montrose, CO: Colorado Division of Wildlife, 2001.

Popp, John B., Patrick D. Jackson, and Richard L. Bassett. "Old-Growth Concepts from Habitat Type Data in the Southwest." In *Old-Growth Forests in the Southwest and Rocky Mountain Regions: Proceedings of a Workshop,* ed. Merrill R. Kaufmann, William H. Moir, and Richard L. Bassett, 100–105. General Technical Report RM-213. Fort Collins, CO: USDA Forest Service, Rocky Mountain Forest and Range Experiment Station, 1992.

Potter, Loren D., and John C. Krenetsky. "Plant Succession with Released Grazing on New Mexico Range Lands." *Journal of Range Management* 20 (1967): 145–151.

Preston, Mike, and Carla Garrison. *The Ponderosa Pine Forest Partnership: Community Stewardship in Southwestern Colorado.* Cortez, CO: Ponderosa Pine Forest Partnership, 1999.

Pyke, David A. "Comparative Demography of Co-occurring Introduced and Native Tussock Grasses: Persistence and Potential Expansion." *Oecologia* 82 (1990): 537–543.

Pyke, David A., Jeffrey E. Herrick, Patrick Shaver, and Mike Pellant. "Rangeland Health Attributes and Indicators for Qualitative Assessment." *Journal of Range Management* 55 (2002): 584–597.

Pyne, Stephen J. *Fire in America: A Cultural History of Wildland and Rural Fire.* Princeton: Princeton University Press, 1982.

Quinn, Ronald D., and Lin Wu. "Quaking Aspen Reproduce from Seed After Wildfire in the Mountains of Southeastern Arizona." In *Sustaining Aspen in Western Landscapes: Symposium Proceedings,* ed. W. D. Sheppard, D. Binkley, D. L. Bartos, T. J. Stohlgren, and L. G. Eskew, 369–376. Proceedings RMRS-P-18. Fort Collins, CO: USDA Forest Service, Rocky Mountain Research Station, 2001.

Rahel, Frank J. "Homogenization of Fish Faunas Across the United States." *Science* 288 (2000): 854–856.

Rasmussen, Lars L., and Jack D. Brotherson. "Response of Winterfat (*Ceratoides lanata*) Communities to Release from Grazing Pressure." *Great Basin Naturalist* 46 (1986): 148–156.

Reader, Tim. "A Survey of Montezuma County Forest Products Related Businesses and Mill Residue Assessment." Unpublished report. Fort Collins: Colorado State Forest Service, 1998.

Reed, Alan D. "The Gateway Tradition: A Formative Stage Culture Unit for East-Central Utah and West-Central Colorado." *Southwestern Lore* 63, no. 2 (1997): 19–26.

———. "The Numic Occupation of Western Colorado and Eastern Utah During the Late Prehistoric and Protohistoric Periods." In *Across the West: Human Population Movement and the Expansion of the Numa*, ed. D. Madsen and D. Rohde, 188–199. Salt Lake City: University of Utah Press, 1994.

———. "The TransColorado Natural Gas Pipeline Archaeological Data Recovery Project, Western Colorado and Northern New Mexico." Unpublished report. Montrose, CO: Alpine Archaeological Consultants, 2001.

Reed, Alan D., and Michael D. Metcalf. *Colorado Prehistory: A Context for the Northern Colorado River Basin.* Denver: Colorado Council of Professional Archaeologists, 1999.

Reed, Verner Z. *The Southern Ute Indians of Early Colorado.* Golden, CO: Outbooks, 1893, reprinted in 1980.

Rees Consulting, Inc. *San Miguel County Housing Needs and Trends Analysis.* Unpublished report. Telluride, CO, 2000.

Reichard, Susan H., and Peter White. "Horticulture as a Pathway of Invasive Plant Introductions in the United States." *BioScience* 51 (2001): 103–113.

Reidhead, Darlene A. *Tour the San Juans, EZ-GUIDE, Silverton to Animas Forks.* Cortez, CO: Southwest Printing, 1994.

Reynolds, T. D., and C. H. Trost. "The Response of Native Vertebrate Populations to Crested Wheatgrass Planting and Grazing by Sheep." *Journal of Range Management* 33 (1980): 122–125.

Rhode, David, and David B. Madsen. "Where Are We?" In *Across the West: Human Population Movement and the Expansion of the Numa*, ed. D. Madsen and D. Rohde, 213–221. Salt Lake City: University of Utah Press, 1994.

Richter, Brian D., and Holly E. Richter. "Prescribing Flood Regimes to Sustain Riparian Ecosystems Along Meandering Rivers." *Conservation Biology* 14 (2000): 1467–1478.

Riebsame, William E., Hannah Gosnell, and David M. Theobald. "Land Use and Landscape Change in the Colorado Mountains I: Theory, Scale, and Pattern." *Mountain Research and Development* 16 (1996): 395–405.

Righter, Robert, Rich Levad, Coen Dexter, and Kim Potter. *Birds of Western Colorado Plateau and Mesa Country.* Grand Junction, CO: Grand Valley Audubon Society, 2004.

Ring, Ray. "Write-off on the Range." *High Country News* (Paonia, CO), May 30, 2005.

Ringholz, Raye C. *Uranium Frenzy: Boom and Bust on the Colorado Plateau*. New York: W. W. Norton, 1989.

Ripple, William J., and Eric J. Larsen. "Historic Aspen Recruitment, Elk, and Wolves in Northern Yellowstone National Park, USA." *Biological Conservation* 95 (2000): 361–370.

Roberts, Richard G., Timothy F. Flannery, Linda K. Ayliffe, Hiroyuki Yoshida, Jon M. Olley, Gavin J. Prideaux, Geoff M. Laslett, Alexander Baynes, M. A. Smith, Rhys Jones, and Barton L. Smith. "New Ages for the Last Australian Megafauna: Continent-Wide Extinction About 46,000 Years Ago." *Science* 292 (2001): 1888.

Robinson, T. W. *Introduction, Spread, and Areal Extent of Saltcedar (Tamarix) in the Western States*. Professional paper 491-A, U.S. Geological Survey. Washington, DC: U.S. Government Printing Office, 1965.

Rockwell, Wilson. *Uncompahgre Country*. Denver: Sage Books, 1965.

Rodebaugh, Dale. "Aspen Agreement." *Durango Herald* (Durango, CO), December 9, 2004.

———. "Four Corners Power Plant Emissions Among Worst in U.S." *Durango Herald* (Durango, CO), June 5, 2005.

———. "Groups to Unveil Dolores River Plan." *Durango Herald* (Durango, CO), May 27, 2003.

———. "Keeping the Cats Coming: 37 Lynx Await April Release into Colorado Wilds." *Durango Herald* (Durango, CO), March 18, 2004.

———. "Mine, River Cleanup—with a Twist." *Durango Herald* (Durango, CO), April 12, 2006.

———. "Need Cited for Protection of Canyons." *Durango Herald* (Durango, CO), April 8, 2004.

Rodebaugh, Dale, and Josh Blumenfeld. "Ranchers Watch Grazing Dwindle in National Forest." *Durango Herald* (Durango, CO), June 12, 2003.

Roe, Frank Gilbert. *The North American Buffalo: A Critical Study of the Species in Its Wild State*, 2nd ed. Toronto: University of Toronto Press, 1970.

Rogers, G. E. *Sage Grouse Investigations in Colorado*. Technical Publication no. 16. Denver: Colorado Game, Fish, and Parks Department, 1964.

Rogler, G. A., and R. J. Lorenz. "Crested Wheatgrass—Early History in the United States." *Journal of Range Management* 36 (1983): 91–93.

Rohe, Randall. "Environment and Mining in the Mountainous West." In *The Mountainous West: Explorations in Historical Geography*, ed. William Wyckoff and Larry M. Dilsaver, 169–193. Lincoln: University of Nebraska Press, 1995.

Rolf, James M. "Aspen Fencing in Northern Arizona: A 15-Year Perspective." In *Sustaining Aspen in Western Landscapes: Symposium Proceedings*, ed. W. D. Sheppard, D. Binkley, D. L. Bartos, T. J. Stohlgren, and L. G. Eskew, 193–196. Proceedings RMRS-P-18. Fort Collins, CO: USDA Forest Service, Rocky Mountain Research Station, 2001.

Rolston III, Holmes. "The Wilderness Idea Reaffirmed." *Environmental Professional* 13 (1991): 370–377.

Romme, William H. "Creating Pseudo-Rural Landscapes in the Mountain West." In *Placing Nature: Culture and Landscape Ecology*, ed. Joan Nassauer, 139–161. Washington, DC: Island, 1997.

Romme, William H., and Robert Bunting. "A History of the San Juan National Forest." Unpublished report. Durango, CO: USDA Forest Service, San Juan National Forest, 2001.

Romme, William H., M. Lisa Floyd, David Hanna, Henri D. Grissino-Mayer, Dan Green, and Jeffrey S. Redders. "Ponderosa Pine Forests of Southwestern Colorado: Ecology and History." Unpublished report. Durango, CO: USDA Forest Service, San Juan National Forest, 1998.

Romme, William H., Lisa Floyd-Hanna, David D. Hanna, and Elisabeth Bartlett. "Aspen's Ecological Role in the West." In *Sustaining Aspen in Western Landscapes: Symposium Proceedings*, ed. Wayne D. Shepperd, Dan Binkley, Dale L. Bartos, Thomas J. Stohlgren, and Lane G. Eskew, 243–259. Proceedings RMRS-P-18. Fort Collins, CO: USDA Forest Service, Rocky Mountain Research Station, 2001.

Romme, William H., D. W. Jamieson, D. Kendall, A. W. Spencer, S. Allerton, J. Follett, D. Grant, K. Kanigel, D. Kinnibrugh, M. March, Y. Potemkin, S. Sage, and T. Tichy. "Biological Diversity in the Hermosa Unit, San Juan National Forest, Colorado: Baseline Description and Recommendations for Ecosystem Management." Unpublished report. Durango, CO: USDA Forest Service, San Juan National Forest, 1996.

Romme, William H., David W. Jamieson, Jeffery S. Redders, Ginger Bigsby, J. Page Lindsey, Deborah Kendall, Robert Cowen, Thomas Kreykes, Albert W. Spencer, and Joseph C. Ortega. "Old-Growth Forests of the San Juan National Forest in Southwestern Colorado." In *Old Growth Forests in the Southwest and Rocky Mountain Regions: Proceedings of a Workshop*, ed. Merrill R. Kaufmann, W. H. Moir, and Richard L. Bassett, 154–165. General Technical Report RM-213. Fort Collins, CO: USDA Forest Service, Rocky Mountain Forest and Range Experiment Station, 1992.

Romme, William H., Mike Preston, Dennis L. Lynch, Phil Kemp, M. Lisa Floyd, David D. Hanna, and Sam Burns. "The Ponderosa Pine Partnership: Ecology, Economics, and Community Involvement in Forest Restoration." In *Ecological Restoration of Southwestern Ponderosa Pine Forests*, ed. Peter Friederici, 99–125. Washington, DC: Island, 2003.

Romo, J. T., P. L. Grilz, and E. A. Driver. "Invasion of the Canadian Prairies by an Exotic Perennial." *Blue Jay* 48 (1990): 130–135.

Roosevelt, Anna Curtenius. "Who's on First?" *Natural History* 109, no. 6 (2000): 76–79.

Rosentreter, R., D. J. Eldridge, and J. H. Kaltenecker. "Monitoring and Management of Biological Soil Crusts." In *Biological Soil Crusts: Structure, Function, and Management*, ed. Jayne Belnap and Otto L. Lange, 457–468. Berlin: Springer-Verlag, 2001.

Ruffner, E. H. *Annual Report upon Explorations and Surveys in the Department of the Missouri, Being Appendix SS of the Annual Report of the Chief of Engineers for 1878*. Washington, DC: U.S. Government Printing Office, 1878.

Ruggiero, Leonard F., Keith B. Aubry, Steven W. Buskirk, Gary M. Koehler, Charles J. Krebs, Kevin S. McKelvey, and John R. Squires. *Ecology and Conservation of Lynx in the United States*. General Technical Report RMRS-GTR-30WWW. Fort Collins, CO: USDA Forest Service, Rocky Mountain Research Station, 1999.

Rummell, Robert S. "Some Effects of Livestock Grazing on Ponderosa Pine Forest and Range in Central Washington." *Ecology* 32 (1951): 594–607.

Ryerson, Daniel E., Thomas W. Swetnam, and Ann M. Lynch. "A Tree-Ring Reconstruction of Western Spruce Budworm Outbreaks in the San Juan Mountains, Colorado." *Canadian Journal of Forest Research* 33 (2003): 1010–1028.

Saab, Victoria A., Carl E. Bock, Terrell D. Rich, and David S. Dobkin. "Livestock Grazing Effects in Western North America." In *Ecology and Management of Neotropical Migratory Birds: A Synthesis and Review of Critical Issues,* ed. Thomas E. Martin and Deborah M. Finch, 311–353. New York: Oxford University Press, 1995.

San Juan Mountains Association. *Noxious Weed Gang Taking Over the West*. Durango, CO: San Juan Mountain Association, n.d.

San Miguel County Open Space Commission. *San Miguel County Land Conservation Options: A Landowner's Guide*. Telluride, CO: San Miguel County Open Space Commission, n.d.

San Miguel Watershed Coalition. "San Miguel Basin Watershed Plan Background. 1998." Unpublished report. Placerville, CO: San Miguel Watershed Coalition, 1998.

San Miguel, George L., and Marilyn Colyer. "Mesa Verde Country's Woodland Avian Community." In *Ancient Piñon-Juniper Woodlands*, ed. M. Lisa Floyd, 89–110. Boulder: University Press of Colorado, 2003.

Sánchez, Joseph P. *Explorers, Traders, and Slavers: Forging the Old Spanish Trail, 1678–1850*. Salt Lake City: University of Utah Press, 1997.

Savage, M., Peter M. Brown, and J. Feddema. "The Role of Climate in a Pine Forest Regeneration Pulse in the Southwestern United States." *Ecoscience* 3 (1996): 310–318.

Savage, M., and T. W. Swetnam. "Early 19th-Century Fire Decline Following Sheep Pasturing in a Navajo Ponderosa Pine Forest." *Ecology* 71 (1990): 2374–2378.

Savory, A. *Holistic Management: A New Framework for Decision Making,* 2nd ed. Washington, DC: Island, 1999.

Sayre, N. F. *The New Ranch Handbook: A Guide to Restoring Western Rangelands*. Santa Fe, NM: Quivira Coalition, 2001.

Scharpf, R. F., and J. R. Parmenter Jr., eds. *Symposium on Dwarf Mistletoe Control Through Forest Management*. General Technical Report PSW-31. Berkeley: USDA Forest Service, Pacific Southwest Forest and Range Experiment Station, 1978.

Schlanger, Sarah H. "Patterns of Population Movement and Long-Term Population Growth in Southwestern Colorado." *American Antiquity* 53 (1988): 773–793.

Schmid, J. M., and S. A. Mata. *Natural Variability of Specific Forest Insect Populations and Their Associated Effects in Colorado.* General Technical Report RM-GTR-275. Fort Collins, CO: USDA Forest Service, Rocky Mountain Forest and Range Experiment Station, 1996.

Schmitt, L. J., and W. H. Raymond. *Geology and Mineral Deposits of the Needle Mountains District, Southwestern Colorado.* Geological Survey Bulletin 1434. Washington, DC: U.S. Government Printing Office, 1977.

Schober, Bob. "Conservation Easements Contain Pitfalls, Agent Says." *Durango Herald* (Durango, CO), November 19, 2001.

———. "County Gas Well Permits Equal to Last Year." *Durango Herald* (Durango, CO), March 15, 2002.

Schott, M. R., and R. D. Pieper. "Influence of Canopy Characteristics of One-Seed Juniper on Understory Grasses." *Journal of Range Management* 38 (1985): 328–331.

Schusler, Tania M., Daniel J. Decker, and Max J. Pfeffer. "Social Learning for Collaborative Natural Resource Management." *Society and Natural Resources* 15 (2003): 309–326.

Sedgwick, James A., and Ronald A. Ryder. "Effects of Chaining Pinyon-Juniper on Nongame Wildlife." In *Proceedings: Pinyon-Juniper Conference [Reno, Nevada, January 13–16, 1986],* ed. Richard L. Everett, 541–551. General Technical Report INT-215. Ogden, UT: USDA Forest Service, Intermountain Research Station, 1987.

Sexton, J. P., J. K. McKay, and A. Sala. "Plasticity and Genetic Diversity May Allow Saltcedar to Invade Cold Climates in North America." *Ecological Applications* 12 (2002): 1652–1660.

Sheep Mountain Alliance. "SMA News." Telluride, CO: Sheep Mountain Alliance, Spring 2002.

Sheley, Roger L., and Janet K. Petroff, eds. *Biology and Management of Noxious Rangeland Weeds.* Corvallis: Oregon State University Press, 1999.

Shepperd, Wayne D. *Initial Growth, Development, and Clonal Dynamics of Regenerated Aspen in the Rocky Mountains.* Research Paper RM-312. Fort Collins, CO: USDA Forest Service, Rocky Mountain Forest and Range Experiment Station, 1993.

Shinneman, Douglas J. "Determining Restoration Needs for Piñon-Juniper Woodlands and Adjacent Semi-Arid Ecosystems on the Uncompahgre Plateau, Western Colorado." PhD diss. Laramie: University of Wyoming, 2006.

Shupe, J. B., and Jack D. Brotherson. "Differential Effects of Cattle and Sheep Grazing on High Mountain Meadows in the Strawberry Valley of Central Utah." *Great Basin Naturalist* 45 (1985): 141–149.

Sibley, David Allen. *The Sibley Guide to Birds.* New York: Alfred Knopf, 2000.

Sieg, Carolyn Hull, Barbara G. Phillips, and Laura P. Moser. "Exotic Invasive Plants." In *Ecological Restoration of Southwestern Ponderosa Pine Forests,* ed. Peter Friederici, 251–267. Washington, DC: Island, 2003.

Simmons, Virginia McConnell. *The Ute Indians of Utah, Colorado and New Mexico.* Boulder: University Press of Colorado, 2000.

Simon, William, Barb Horn, and David Wegner. "Current and Historical Review of the Animas Watershed Fisheries." Appendix 6A, Use Attainability Analysis for the Animas River Watershed. Silverton, CO: Animas River Stakeholders Group, 2001.

Singer, Francis. "Bighorn Sheep in the Rocky Mountain National Parks." In *Our Living Resource: A Report to the Nation on the Distribution, Abundance and Health of U.S. Plants, Animals and Ecosystems.* U.S. Geological Survey, Biological Resources Division, http://biology.usgs.gov/s+t/SNT/index.htm (accessed May 30, 2004).

Singleton, S. "Collaborative Environmental Planning in the American West: The Good, the Bad and the Ugly." *Environmental Politics* 11, no. 3 (2002): 54–75.

Sluis, Tom. "Bighorn Sheep Released in San Juans." *Durango Herald* (Durango, CO), February 14, 2003.

Smith, Anne M. "Cultural Differences and Similarities Between Uintah and White River." In *Ute Indians II, American Indian Ethnohistory: California and Basin-Plateau Indians,* ed. David Agee Horr, 325–338. New York: Garland, 1974.

———. *Ethnography of the Northern Utes.* Papers in Anthropology no. 17. Albuquerque: Museum of New Mexico Press, 1974.

Smith, Duane A. " 'A Country of Tremendous Mountains': Opening the Colorado San Juans, 1870–1910." In *The Mountainous West: Explorations in Historical Geography,* ed. William Wyckoff and Larry M. Dilsaver, 92–113. Lincoln: University of Nebraska Press, 1995.

Smith, Dwight R. *Effects of Cattle Grazing on a Ponderosa Pine–Bunchgrass Range in Colorado.* USDA Forest Service Technical Bulletin no. 1371. Washington, DC: U.S. Government Printing Office, 1967.

Spencer, Albert W., and William H. Romme. "Ecological Patterns." In *The Western San Juan Mountains: Their Geology, Ecology, and Human History,* ed. Rob Blair, Tom Ann Casey, William H. Romme, and Richard N. Ellis, 129–142. Boulder: University Press of Colorado, 1996.

Stahelin, R. "Factors Influencing the Natural Restocking of High Altitude Burns by Coniferous Trees in the Central Rocky Mountains." *Ecology* 24 (1943): 19–30.

State of Colorado, Division of Minerals and Geology. "San Miguel Gold/Dorie Placer Mine Bond Forfeiture Project (Permit #M87-124)." Unpublished report. Grand Junction, CO: Division of Minerals and Geology, 1995.

State of Colorado, Water Quality Control Division. *Total Maximum Daily Load Assessment: A Watershed Approach for the Upper Animas River Basin.* Denver: Colorado Department of Public Health and Environment, 2002.

Steadman, David W. "Prehistoric Extinctions of Pacific Island Birds: Biodiversity Meets Zooarchaeology." *Science* 267 (1995): 1123–1131.

Stein, Theo. "Otter's Comeback a Splashing Success: Species May Soon Be Removed from State's Endangered List, Officials Say." *Denver Post* (Denver, CO), March 26, 2003.

Stevens, S. H., J. M. Pearce, and A.A.J. Rigg, eds. *Natural Analogs for Geologic Storage of Co$_2$: An Integrated Global Research Program. Proceedings of the First*

Conference on Carbon Sequestration [Washington, DC, May 15–17, 2001]. U.S. Department of Energy, National Energy Testing Laboratory, http://www.netl.doe.gov/publications/proceedings/01/carbon_seq/6a1.pdf (accessed May 30, 2004).

Stewart, Julian H. *Ute Indians I. Aboriginal and Historical Groups of the Ute Indians of Utah.* New York: Garland, 1974.

Stewart, K. C., J. G. Crock, and R. C. Severson. *Chemical Results and Variability Assessment of Selected Water-Extractable Constituents from Soils of the Uncompahgre Area, West-Central Colorado.* U.S. Geological Survery Open-File Report 93-507. Washington, DC: U.S. Government Printing Office, 1993.

Stewart, Omer C. *Culture Element Distributions: Xvii. Ute–Southern Paiute.* Anthropological Records 6, no. 4. Berkeley: University of California Press, 1942.

———. "Escalante and the Ute." *Southwestern Lore* 18 (1952): 47–51.

Stinner, D. H., B. R. Stinner, and E. Martsolf. "Biodiversity as an Organizing Principle in Agroecosystem Management: Case Studies of Holistic Resource Management Practitioners in the USA." *Agriculture, Ecosystems and Environment* 62 (1997): 199–213.

Stromberg, Juliet C., and Matthew K. Chew. "Herbaceous Exotics in Arizona's Riparian Ecosystems." *Desert Plants* 13, no. 1 (1997): 11–17.

Svejcar, T., and R. Tausch. "Anaho Island, Nevada: A Relict Area Dominated by Annual Invader Species." *Rangelands* 13 (1991): 233–236.

Szaro, R. C., and R. P. Balda. *Selection and Monitoring of Avian Indicator Species: An Example from a Ponderosa Pine Forest in the Southwest.* General Technical Report RM-89. Fort Collins, CO: USDA Forest Service, Rocky Mountain Forest and Range Experiment Station, 1982.

Taylor, J. P., and K. C. McDaniel. "Restoration of Saltcedar (*Tamarix* sp.)–Infested Floodplains on the Bosque del Apache National Wildlife Refuge." *Weed Technology* 12 (1998): 345–352.

Telluride Consulting. *Profile 2001. An Economic Study of Telluride, Mountain Village, and San Miguel County from January 1985 to January 2001.* Telluride, CO: Telluride Consulting, 2001.

Telluride Daily Planet staff. "Emotional Debate Ends in 'No' Vote." *Telluride Daily Planet* (Telluride, CO), February 15, 2006.

Templeton, Marie. *The Visionaries: First and Second Generation of the Piñon, Ute and Nucla Areas.* Ridgway, CO: Rimrocker Historical Society and Country Graphics, 1998.

Tenenbaum, David. "Land Trusts: A Restoration Frontier?" *Ecological Restoration* 18 (2000): 167–172.

Terrel, Ted L., and J. Juan Spillett. "Pinyon-Juniper Conversion: Its Impact on Mule Deer and Other Wildlife." In *The Pinyon-Juniper Ecosystem: A Symposium,* 105–118. Logan: Utah State University, College of Natural Resources, 1975.

Theobald, David M. "Fragmentation by Inholdings and Exurban Development." In *Forest Fragmentation in the Southern Rocky Mountains,* ed. R. L. Knight, F. W. Smith, S. W. Buskirk, W. H. Romme, and W. L. Baker, 155–174. Boulder: University Press of Colorado, 2000.

Theobald, David M., H. Gosnell, and W. E. Riebsame. "Land Use and Land-scape Change in the Colorado Mountains II: A Case Study of the East River Valley." *Mountain Research and Development* 16 (1996): 407–418.

Theobald, David M., James R. Miller, and N. Thompson Hobbs. "Estimating Cumulative Effects of Development on Wildlife Habitat." *Landscape and Urban Planning* 39 (1997): 25–37.

Thornton, Russell. *American Indian Holocaust and Survival: A Population History Since 1492.* Norman: University of Oklahoma Press, 1987.

Thurow, Thomas L., and C. A. Taylor. "Viewpoint: The Role of Drought in Range Management." *Journal of Range Management* 52 (1999): 413–419.

Tisdale, E. W., and M. Hironaka. *The Sagebrush-Grass Region: A Review of the Ecological Literature.* College of Forestry, Wildlife and Range Sciences Bulletin no. 33. Moscow: University of Idaho, 1981.

Travis, William R., David M. Theobald, and Daniel B. Fagre. "Transforming the Rockies: Human Forces, Settlement Patterns, and Ecosystem Effects." In *Rocky Mountain Futures: An Ecological Perspective*, ed. Jill S. Baron, 1–26. Washington, DC: Island, 2002.

Truett, Joe. "Bison and Elk in the American Southwest: In Search of the Pristine." *Environmental Management* 20 (1996): 195–206.

Tuan, Yi Fu. *Escapism.* Baltimore: Johns Hopkins University Press, 1998.

Turchi, Gail M., Patricia L. Kennedy, Dean Urban, and Dale Hein. "Bird Species Richness in Relation to Isolation of Aspen Habitats." *Wilson Bulletin* 107 (1995): 463–474.

Uncompahgre Valley Water Users Association. *Information Handout.* Montrose, CO: Uncompahgre Valley Water Users Association, n.d.

U.S. Congress, Office of Technology Assessment. *Harmful Non-Indigenous Species in the United States.* Washington, DC: U.S. Government Printing Office, 1993.

U.S. Department of Agriculture, Forest Service. "Grand Mesa–Uncompahgre National Forest History." Unpublished report. Delta, CO: Grand Mesa, Uncompahgre, and Gunnison National Forest, 1975.

———. "Information Packet: Includes News Clippings and a Summary of the Uncompahgre Case from Uncompahgre Regional Forester, Donald E. Clark." Unpublished report. Delta, CO: Uncompahgre National Forest, 1952.

———. *Wilderness Management Direction. Decision Notice, Finding of No Significant Impact, and Final Environmental Assessment.* Durango, CO: San Juan–Rio Grande National Forest, 1998.

U.S. Department of Agriculture, Forest Service, and U.S. Department of the Interior. *A Report to the President in Response to the Wildfires of 2000: Managing the Impacts of Wildfires on Communities and the Environment.* Washington, DC: U.S. Forest Service, 2000. http://www.fireplan.gov (accessed May 30, 2004).

U.S. Department of Agriculture, Statistical Service. *1997 Census of Agriculture, Vol. 1, Part 6, Chapter 2—Colorado County-Level Data.* Washington, DC: U.S. Government Printing Office, 1999.

U.S. Department of Commerce, Bureau of the Census. *1978 Census of Agriculture, Vol. 1—State and County Data, Part 6—Colorado.* Washington, DC: U.S. Government Printing Office, 1981.

———. *1982 Census of Agriculture, Vol. 1—Geographic Area Series, Part 6—Colorado, State and County Data.* Washington, DC: U.S. Government Printing Office, 1984.

———. *1987 Census of Agriculture, Vol. 1—Geographic Area Series, Part 6—Colorado, State and County Data.* Washington, DC: U.S. Government Printing Office, 1988.

———. *1992 Census of Agriculture, Vol. 1—Geographic Area Series, Part 6—Colorado, State and County Data.* Washington, DC: U.S. Government Printing Office, 1994.

———. *Agriculture, Vol. II, Part 3—The Western States. Fifteenth Census of the United States: 1930.* Washington, DC: U.S. Government Printing Office, 1932.

———. *U.S. Census of Agriculture: 1959, Final Report—Vol. 1—Part 4—Counties, Colorado.* Washington, DC: U.S. Government Printing Office, 1961.

U.S. Department of the Interior, Bureau of Land Management. *Draft Environmental Impact Statement and Draft Planning Amendment for the Powder River Basin Oil and Gas Project.* WY-070-02-065. Cheyenne: Bureau of Land Management, Wyoming State Office, 2002.

———. "Dry Creek Basin Coordinated Resource Management Plan." Unpublished report. Dolores, CO: Bureau of Land Management, 1994.

———. *Dry Creek Basin Oil and Gas Environmental Assessment (No. CO-SJPLC-03-030EA).* Durango, CO: Bureau of Land Management, San Juan Field Office, 2003.

———. *Environmental Assessment Record for the Gibbler Roller Chopping.* Grand Junction, CO: Bureau of Land Management, 2001.

———. "Finch Seeding, Project Completion Report." Unpublished report. Dolores, CO: Bureau of Land Management, 1961.

———. "Grand Junction Resource Area Final Wilderness Environmental Impact Statement." Grand Junction, CO: Bureau of Land Management, 1989.

———. *The Great Basin: Healing the Land.* Reno, NV: Bureau of Land Management State Office, 2000.

———. "Range Management Plan, Escalante Unit." Mimeo. Ouray, CO: Bureau of Land Management, n.d.

U.S. Department of the Interior, Bureau of Land Management, and U.S. Department of Agriculture, Forest Service. *Coal Bed Methane Development in the Northern San Juan Basin of Colorado.* Durango, CO: Bureau of Land Management, San Juan Field Office, and San Juan National Forest, 2000.

U.S. Department of the Interior, Bureau of Reclamation. *Colorado Bureau of Reclamation Projects.* 1978-667.405. Washington, DC: U.S. Government Printing Office, 1978.

———. *Lining Ponds to Reduce Salt and Selenium Loading to the Gunnison River.* Washington, DC: U.S. Bureau of Reclamation, 2004.

U.S. Department of the Interior, National Park Service. *Visitor Guide for Curecanti National Recreation Area and Black Canyon of the Gunnison National Park.* N.p.: Currents, Summer 2000.

Ute Mountain Ute Tribe. *Early Days of the Ute Mountain Ute.* Salt Lake City: University of Utah Printing Service, and Towaoc, CO: Ute Mountain Ute Tribe, 1985.

Vale, Thomas R. "Presettlement Vegetation in the Sagebrush-Grass Area of the Intermountain West." *Journal of Range Management* 28 (1975): 32–36.

———. "Sagebrush Conversion Projects: An Element of Contemporary Environmental Change in the Western United States." *Biological Conservation* 6 (1974): 274–284.

———. "Tree Invasion of Montane Meadows in Oregon." *American Midland Naturalist* 105 (1981): 61–69.

———, ed. *Fire, Native Peoples, and the Natural Landscape.* Washington, DC: Island, 2002.

Van Vuren, Dirk. "Bison West of the Rocky Mountains: An Alternative Explanation." *Northwest Science* 61 (1987): 65–69.

Van West, Carla R., and Jeffrey S. Dean. "Environmental Characteristics of the A.D. 900–1300 Period of the Central Mesa Verde Region." *Kiva* 66 (2000): 19–44.

Vance, Joel. "Sapsucker." *Wyoming Wildlife* 65, no. 11 (2001): 6–13.

Varien, Mark D., William D. Lipe, Michael A. Adler, Ian M. Thompson, and Bruce A. Bradley. "Southwestern Colorado and Southeastern Utah Settlement Patterns: A.D. 1100–1300." In *The Prehistoric Pueblo World, A.D. 1150–1350,* ed. Michael A. Adler, 86–113. Tucson: University of Arizona Press, 1996.

Varien, Mark D., Tito Naranjo, Marjorie R. Connolly, and William D. Lipe. "Native American Issues and Perspectives." In *Colorado Prehistory: A Context for the Southern Colorado River Basin,* ed. William D. Lipe, Mark D. Varien, and Richard H. Wilshusen, 370–404. Denver: Colorado Council of Professional Archaeologists, 1999.

Varien, Mark D., Carla R. Van West, and G. Stuart Patterson. "Competition, Cooperation, and Conflict: Agricultural Production and Community Catchments in the Central Mesa Verde Region." *Kiva* 66 (2000): 45–65.

Varien, Mark D., and Richard H. Wilshusen. *Seeking the Center Place: Archaeology and Ancient Communities in the Mesa Verde Region.* Salt Lake City: University of Utah Press, 2002.

Vavra, M., and M. L. McInnis. "Grazing in the Great Basin: An Evolutionary Perspective and Applications for Today." In *Oregon's High Desert: The Last 100 Years,* 20–31. Special Report no. 841. Corvallis: Agricultural Experiment Station, Oregon State University, 1989.

Veblen, Thomas T. "Disturbance Patterns in Southern Rocky Mountain Forests." In *Forest Fragmentation in the Southern Rocky Mountains,* ed. Richard L. Knight, Frederick W. Smith, Steven W. Buskirk, William H. Romme, and William L. Baker, 31–54. Boulder: University Press of Colorado, 2000.

Vincent, K. R., S. E. Church, and D. L. Fey. "Geomorphological Context of Metal-Laden Sediments in the Animas River Floodplain, Colorado." In *Toxic*

Substances Hydrology Program—Proceedings of the Technical Meeting [Charleston, South Carolina, March 8–12, 1999], ed. D. W. Morganwalp and H. T. Buxton, 99–105. U.S. Geological Survey Water Resources Investigations Report 99-4018A. Washington, DC: U.S. Government Printing Office, 1999.

Voigt, William, Jr. *Public Lands Grazing: Use and Misuse by Industry and Government*. New Brunswick, NJ: Rutgers University Press, 1976.

Walker, Peter A., and Patrick T. Hurley. "Collaboration Derailed: The Politics of 'Community-Based' Resource Management in Nevada County." *Society and Natural Resources* 17 (2004): 737–751.

Wallace, Henry. *The Western Range. Letter from the Secretary of Agriculture Transmitting in Response to Senate Resolution No. 289. A Report on the Western Range—a Great but Neglected Natural Resource*. 74th Congress, 2nd sess., Senate Document no. 199. Washington, DC: U.S. Government Printing Office, 1936.

Warner, Ted J. *The Dominguez-Escalante Journal: Their Expedition Through Colorado, Utah, Arizona, and New Mexico in 1776*. Provo, UT: Brigham Young University Press, 1976.

Warren, S. D., and D. J. Eldridge. "Biological Soil Crusts and Livestock in Arid Ecosystems: Are They Compatible?" In *Biological Soil Crusts: Structure, Function, and Management*, ed. Jayne Belnap and Otto L. Lange, 401–415. Berlin: Springer-Verlag, 2001.

Watkins, Bruce. "Mule Deer." *UP-Date, Uncompahgre Plateau Project Newsletter* (Fall 2001) (no page).

Watkins, Bruce, James H. Olterman, and Thomas M. Pojar. "Mule Deer Studies on the Uncompahgre Plateau, Colorado 1997–2001." Unpublished report. Montrose: Colorado Division of Wildlife, 2001.

Webb, Merrill. "Importance of Pinyon-Juniper Habitat to Birds." In *Proceedings: Ecology and Management of Pinyon-Juniper Communities Within the Interior West*, ed. Stephen B. Monsen and Richard Stevens, 244–248. Proceedings RMRS-P-9. Fort Collins, CO: USDA Forest Service, Rocky Mountain Research Station, 1999.

Weber, William A., and Ronald C. Wittmann. *Colorado Flora: Western Slope*, 3rd ed. Boulder: University Press of Colorado, 2001.

Weir, Glendon Hoge. "Palynology, Flora and Vegetation of Hovenweep National Monument: Implications for Aboriginal Plant Use on Cajon Mesa, Colorado and Utah." PhD diss. College Station: Texas A&M University, 1976.

Welch, Bruce L., and Craig Criddle. *Countering Misinformation Concerning Big Sagebrush*. Research Paper RMRS-RP-40. Fort Collins, CO: USDA Forest Service, Rocky Mountain Research Station, 2003.

Weller, Chris, Janice Thomson, Pete Morton, and Greg Aplet. *Fragmenting Our Lands: The Ecological Footprint from Oil and Gas Development*. Denver: The Wilderness Society, 2002.

Wenger, Stephen R., Michael R. Grode, and Anthony D. Apa. "Inventory of Sagebrush Defoliation and Mortality in Gunnison and Dry Creek Basins 2003." Unpublished report. Grand Junction, CO: Colorado Division of Wildlife, 2003.

West, Elliott. *The Contested Plains: Indians, Goldseekers, and the Rush to Colorado.* Lawrence: University Press of Kansas, 1998.

West, George E. "The Oldest Range Man." In *Pioneers of the San Juan Country, Vol. II,* ed. the Sarah Platt Decker Chapter, D.A.R., Durango, Colorado, 112–123. Colorado Springs: Old West, 1946 (written in 1945).

West, Neil E. "Distribution, Composition, and Classification of Current Juniper-Pinyon Woodlands and Savannas Across Western North America." In *Proceedings: Ecology and Management of Pinyon-Juniper Communities Within the Interior West,* ed. S. B. Monsen and R. Stevens, 20–23. Proceedings RMRS-P-9. Fort Collins, CO: USDA Forest Service, Rocky Mountain Research Station, 1999.

———. "Intermountain Salt-Desert Shrubland." In *Ecosystems of the World 5: Temperate Deserts and Semi-Deserts,* ed. Neil E. West, 375–397. Amsterdam: Elsevier Scientific Publishing, 1983.

———. "Successional Patterns and Productivity Potentials of Pinyon-Juniper Ecosystems." In *Developing Strategies for Rangeland Management,* ed. B. D. Gardner, 1301–1332. National Research Council/National Academy of Sciences. Boulder: Westview, 1984.

West, Neil E., and James A. Young. "Intermountain Valleys and Lower Mountain Slopes." In *North American Terrestrial Vegetation,* 2nd ed., ed. Michael G. Barber and W. D. Billings, 255–284. Cambridge, UK: Cambridge University Press, 2000.

Western Governors Association. *Coal Bed Methane Best Management Practices: A Handbook.* Denver: Western Governors Association, 2004.

Whisenant, S. G. "Changing Fire Frequencies on Idaho's Snake River Plains: Ecological and Management Implications." In *Proceedings—Symposium on Cheatgrass Invasion, Shrub Die-off, and Other Aspects of Shrub Biology and Management,* ed. E. D. McArthur, E. M. Romney, S. D. Smith, and P. T. Tueller, 4–10. General Technical Report INT-276. Ogden, UT: USDA Forest Service, Intermountain Research Station, 1990.

White, Clifford A., Charles E. Olmsted, and Charles E. Kay. "Aspen, Elk, and Fire in the Rocky Mountain National Parks of North America." *Wildlife Society Bulletin* 26 (1998): 449–462.

Whitson, Thomas D., Larry C. Burrill, Steven A. Dewey, David W. Cudney, B. E. Nelson, Richard D. Lee, and Robert Parker. *Weeds of the West,* 5th ed. Jackson, WY: Pioneer of Jackson Hole, 1999.

Whitson, Thomas D., Mark A. Farrell, and Harold P. Alley. "Changes in Rangeland Canopy Cover Seven Years After Tebuthiuron Application." *Weed Technology* 2 (1988): 486–489.

Wickham, J. D., T. G. Wade, K. B. Jones, K. H. Riiters, and R. V. O'Neill. "Diversity of Ecological Communities of the United States." *Vegetatio* 119 (1995): 91–100.

Wilcove, D. S., D. Rothstein, J. Dubow, A. Phillips, and E. Losos. "Quantifying Threats to Imperiled Species in the United States." *BioScience* 48 (1998): 607–615.

Willits, Patrick. "San Miguel River Restoration Assessment," 2 vols. Unpublished report. Ridgway, CO: Trust for Land Restoration, 2001.

Wilshusen, Richard H. "Basketmaker III (A.D. 500–750)." In *Colorado Prehistory: A Context for the Southern Colorado River Basin*, ed. William D. Lipe, Mark D. Varien, and Richard H. Wilshusen, 166–195. Denver: Colorado Council of Professional Archaeologists, 1999.

———. "Estimating Population in the Central Mesa Verde Region." In *Seeking the Center Place: Archaeology and Ancient Communities in the Mesa Verde Region*, ed. Mark D. Varien and Richard H. Wilshusen, 101–120. Salt Lake City: University of Utah Press, 2002.

Wilshusen, Richard H., and Ronald H. Towner. "Post-Puebloan Occupation (A.D. 1300–1840)." In *Colorado Prehistory: A Context for the Southern Colorado River Basin*, ed. William D. Lipe, Mark D. Varien, and Richard H. Wilshusen, 353–369. Denver: Colorado Council of Professional Archaeologists, 1999.

Wilson, S. D., and J. W. Belcher. "Plant and Bird Communities of Native Prairie and Introduced Eurasian Vegetation in Manitoba, Canada." *Conservation Biology* 3 (1989): 39–44.

Winter, J. C., and W. J. Litzinger. "Floral Indicators of Farm Fields." In *Hovenweep 1975*, ed. J. C. Winter, 123–168. Archaeological Report no. 2. San Jose: San Jose State University, 1976.

Wondolleck, Julia M., and Steven L. Yaffee. *Making Collaboration Work: Lessons from Innovation in Natural Resource Management*. Washington, DC: Island, 2000.

Wright, John B. "Reflections on Patterns and Prospects of Conservation Easement Use." In *Protecting Land: Conservation Easements Past, Present, and Future*, ed. Julie Ann Gustanski and Roderick H. Squires, 498–504. Washington, DC: Island, 2000.

———. *Rocky Mountain Divide: Selling and Saving the West*. Austin: University of Texas Press, 1993.

Wyckoff, Don G. "Secondary Forest Succession Following Abandonment of Mesa Verde." *Kiva* 42 (1977): 215–231.

Wyckoff, William. *Creating Colorado: The Making of a Western American Landscape, 1860–1940*. New Haven: Yale University Press, 1999.

Yarnell, Richard A. "Implications of Distinctive Flora on Pueblo Ruins." *American Anthropologist* 67 (1965): 662–674.

York, R. "Forest History, Vol. I: San Juan & Montezuma National Forests, Colorado. An Update to: Scott, M. R. 1932. History of the San Juan National Forest." Durango, CO: San Juan National Forest, Supervisor's Office, 1984.

Young, James A. "Changes in Plant Communities in the Great Basin Induced by Domestic Livestock Grazing." In *Natural History of the Colorado Plateau and Great Basin*, ed. K. T. Harper, 113–123. Boulder: University Press of Colorado, 1994.

Young, James A., and F. L. Allen. "Cheatgrass and Range Science: 1930–1950." *Journal of Range Management* 50 (1997): 530–535.

Young, James A., and R. E. Eckert Jr. "Historical Perspectives Regarding the Sagebrush Ecosystem." In *The Sagebrush Ecosystem: A Symposium*, 1–13. Logan: Utah State University, College of Natural Resources, 1979.

Young, James A., Raymond A. Evans, and Paul T. Tueller. "Great Basin Plant Communities—Pristine and Grazed." In *Holocene Environmental Change in the Great Basin*, ed. R. Elston, 187–215. Research Paper no. 6. Reno: Nevada Archaeological Survey, 1976.

Young, James A., and B. A. Sparks. *Cattle in the Cold Desert*. Logan: Utah State University Press, 1985.

Young, Jessica R., Clait E. Braun, Sara Oyler-McCance, Jerry W. Hupp, and Tom W. Quinn. "A New Species of Sage-Grouse (*Phasianidae: Centrocercus*) from Southwestern Colorado." *Wilson Bulletin* 112 (2000): 445–453.

Zier, James L., and William L. Baker. "A Century of Vegetation Change in the San Juan Mountains, Colorado: An Analysis Using Repeat Photography." *Forest Ecology and Management* 228 (2006): 251–262.

page numbers in italics indicate illustrations

Index